PARIS *to the* PAST

ALSO BY *Ina Caro*

THE ROAD FROM THE PAST
Traveling Through History in France
(1994)

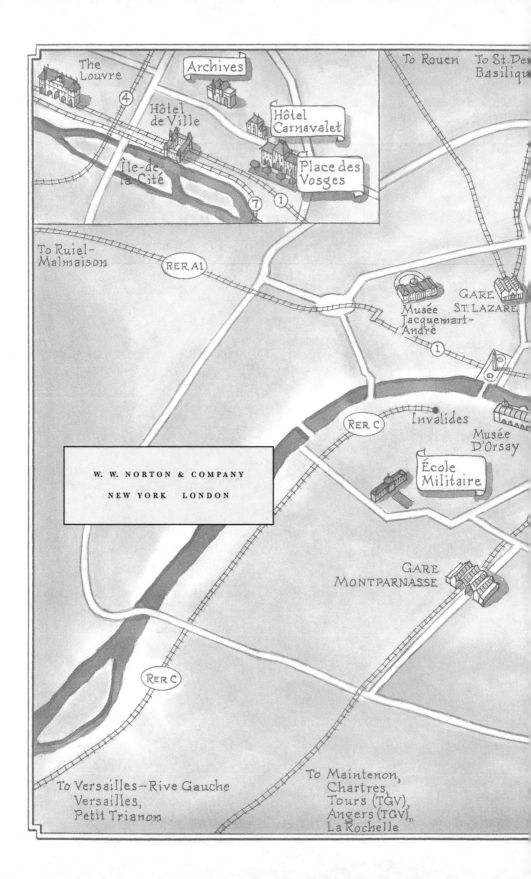

W. W. NORTON & COMPANY

NEW YORK   LONDON

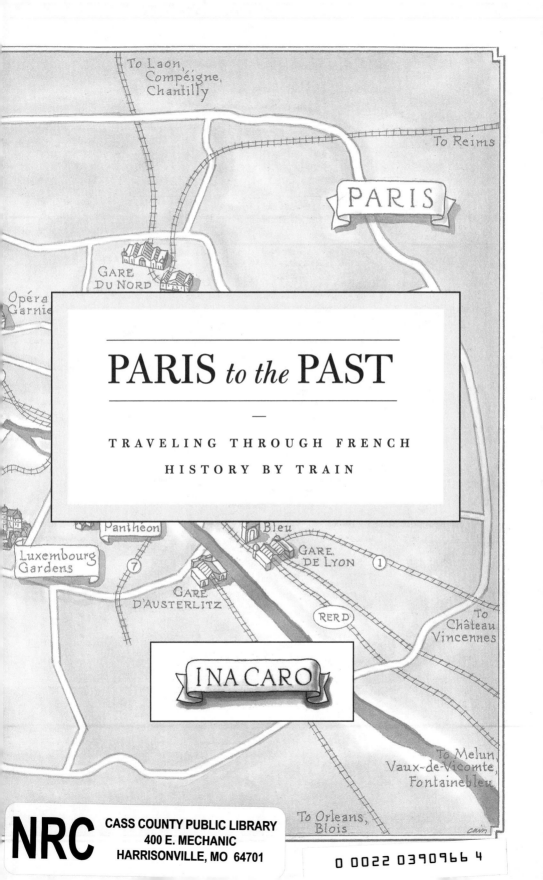

To Laon,
Compéigne,
Chantilly

To Reims

PARIS

GARE
DU NORD

Opéra
Garnier

PARIS *to the* PAST

—

TRAVELING THROUGH FRENCH

HISTORY BY TRAIN

Panthéon

Bleu

GARE
DE LYON ①

Luxembourg
Gardens

⑦

GARE
D'AUSTERLITZ

RER D

To
Château
Vincennes

INA CARO

To Melun,
Vaux-de-Vicomte,
Fontainebleu

To Orleans,
Blois

cain

For information about permission to reproduce selections from this
book, write to Permissions, W. W. Norton & Company, Inc.,
500 Fifth Avenue, New York, NY 10110

For information about special discounts for bulk purchases, please
contact W. W. Norton Special Sales at
specialsales@wwnorton.com or 800-233-4830

Manufacturing by RRD Harrisonburg
Book design by Barbara M. Bachman
Production manager: Julia Druskin

LIBRARY OF CONGRESS CATALOGING-IN-PUBLICATION DATA

Caro, Ina.
Paris to the past : traveling through French history by train / Ina Caro. —1st ed.
p. cm.
Includes bibliographical references and index.
ISBN 978-0-393-07894-7 (hardcover)
1. France—Description and travel. 2. Paris Region (France)—Description and
travel. 3. Caro, Ina—Travel—France. 4. Railroad travel—France.
5. France—History, Local. 6. Historic sites—France. I. Title.
DC29.3.C373 2011
944—dc22
2011003060

W. W. Norton & Company, Inc.
500 Fifth Avenue, New York, N.Y. 10110
www.wwnorton.com

W. W. Norton & Company Ltd.
Castle House, 75/76 Wells Street, London W1T 3QT

1 2 3 4 5 6 7 8 9 0

For Bob

This is not an age when prince charmings, idealistic knights, and true love at first sight are taken seriously. When I was still in my teens, I fell in love with Bob, and he has been my Prince Charming ever since. And I want to thank him for never once changing into a frog, and for visiting with me the castle of Sleeping Beauty, which lies in an enchanted valley filled with a thousand castles and food so magical that fish and asparagus taste better than cake.

Contents

PART ONE

The Middle Ages:
CATHEDRALS AND FORTRESSES

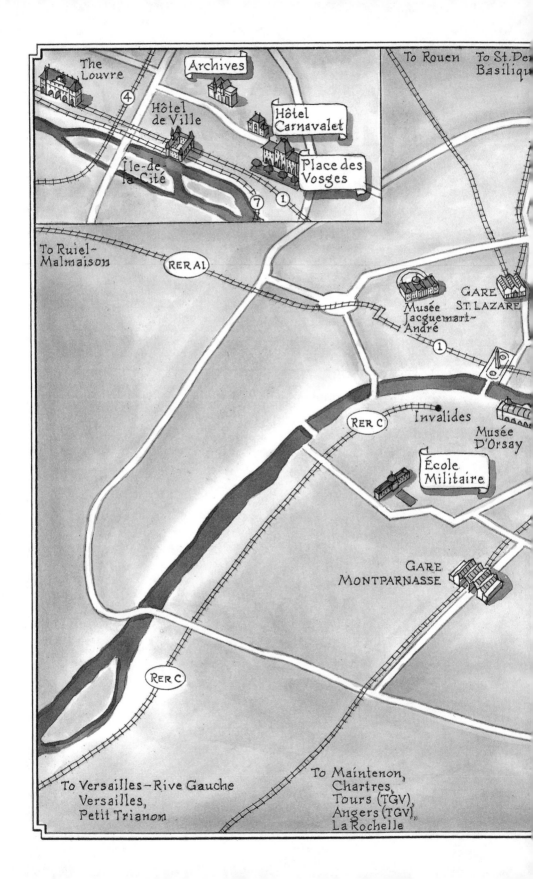

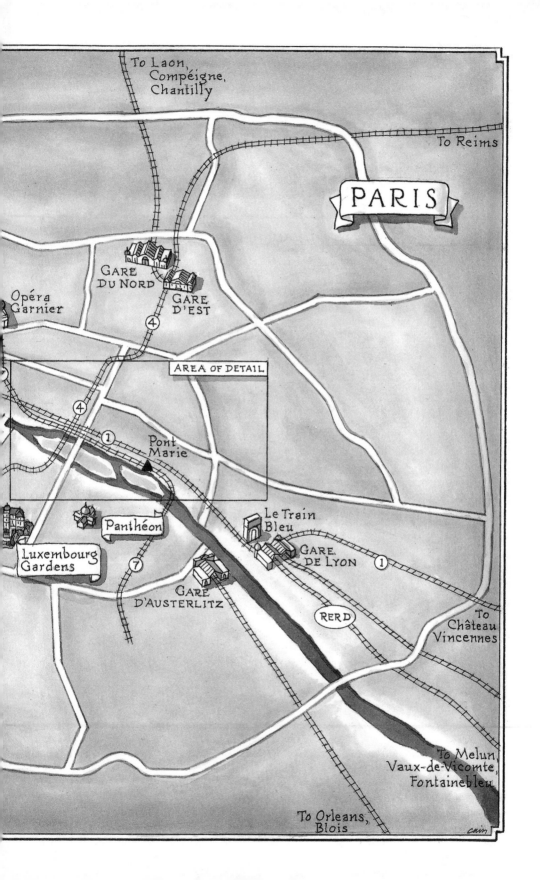

List of Maps

—

PARIS *to the* PAST

Two Love Affairs

———

BOB AND I FELL IN LOVE, FIRST WITH EACH OTHER, AND THEN
with France. In both cases it was love at first sight—but there was quite
a long time between the sightings.

I cannot recall precisely when I fell in love with history, but I do
know exactly when I fell in love with Bob. I was, in fact, sixteen when
I saw him for the first time. I was at a mixer at Princeton with my best
friend from Trenton High when I saw him across the room. Even with
his crew cut, I thought he was the handsomest boy I had ever seen. The
moment I saw him, I turned to my friend standing next to me and said,
"That's the boy I'm going to marry." You can ask Marcia Kaminker, or
whatever her name is now, if that isn't true.

On our honeymoon, three years later, we drove all across America.
Since Bob did not do quite as well at blackjack in Las Vegas as he was
sure he would, my father had to come and bail us out at the Pennsylva-
nia Turnpike tollbooth when we returned from our two-month journey.
Our trip across country had been so much fun that we planned to take
the same type of trip in France, as soon as we had saved enough money.

It would be, however, many years later before our love affair with
France began. First, there was a baby and then there was a book, a book
that Bob had quit his job as a reporter at *Newsday* to write. The book
would turn out to be *The Power Broker*, and many things were to happen with it of which we have always been proud, but at the time he was
working on it, no one seemed particularly interested in it, and Bob was
writing it for what we called "the world's smallest advance." We said
that with a laugh for a while, but as time passed, it wasn't so funny.

Bob had thought it would take him nine months to finish. He simply couldn't imagine anything taking him more than nine months to write. But it actually took seven years, and we were broke for most of those years—totally broke. After the first year, we had to sell our little house on Long Island and move to an apartment in the Bronx, leaving our piano and beloved pool table behind.

It had been a long time since I had been able to look either my butcher or my dry cleaner in the eye when *The New Yorker*, much to Bob's amazement, bought an excerpt from the book for enough money for me to pay my bills and for Bob and me to finally take our trip to France.

We took the check, paid the butcher and dry cleaner, and left for France the next day. We didn't even stop to make a hotel reservation—Bob asked the flight attendant where to stay in Paris and she suggested a little hotel on the Rue Saint-Hyacinthe. It was 1974, and you could do that then, not make reservations in France. The hotel was in a great location, but old and small. I remember that the concierge couldn't get the air-conditioning to work, nor could she grasp the concept of the "collect call" on the telephone. She also scrubbed everything with Clorox—including the sidewalk in front of the hotel. We thought it was just the grandest place in the world. When we returned several years later, we felt surely the rooms must have shrunk.

After a week in Paris, we rented a car and began driving through countrysides more glorious than anything we had ever imagined. So glorious, in fact, was that maiden trip that year after year we returned to France, stayed a few nights in a hotel in Paris, and then spent a month or two driving around a different section of the country. What I quickly realized was that each section seemed to have its own history. One year we drove around the Dordogne Valley in central France and the Hundred Years War came alive. The next year, we explored Languedoc in the south, with its walled medieval city and Romanesque churches. On each trip, I felt as if I were escaping from the present into the past, into ages I had loved reading about in school. Although history had been my major in college—my thesis in graduate school had dealt with Dagobert I, who was a seventh-century French king—it wasn't until our first trip to France that it dawned on me that visiting sites where major historic events occurred, places built a hundred, a thousand, years ago, could still evoke the period in which they were built.

This is because the French preserve their history, restoring their fortresses and castles so that you can see them as they were, while in America we too often demolish ours. This difference struck me one day as I was leaving—as quickly as possible, I might add—a bullfight at the amphitheater in the ancient Roman city of Nîmes. Nauseated by the sight of a gored and insufficiently padded horse, I couldn't help thinking, as I was rushing from my seat, that the amphitheater must have looked exactly the same when gladiators were fighting there nearly two thousand years before. And I wondered if, had I been in that arena two thousand years ago, the sight of a gladiator's blood would have sickened me then as the horse's blood had now.

It wasn't until years later, when we were traveling in northern Italy, that I realized how unique the French were in preserving their past. I remember picking up a brochure at a hotel we were staying at in Florence. It urged tourists to visit the Piazza dell'Anfiteatro in Lucca, which had once been the site of a Roman coliseum, and which, the brochure said, had "preserved its characteristics since Roman times." Well, we went to Lucca in search of this ancient Roman coliseum, hoping to be transported back to the time when gladiators fought there. After an hour or so of looking, we found ourselves standing in the center of a large oval piazza, with laundry hanging on lines from the windows of apartments built into the surrounding oval walls. In frustration, I asked a woman selling flowers, in my best Italian accent: "*Dov'é Colosseo?*" She laughed and responded in English (everyone always answers me in English no matter what language I try to speak): "You are standing in the middle of it."

While I did discover a memorable cracked-wheat soup made from a centuries-old recipe in Lucca, I did not find the evocation of the ancient Roman world. But I would in France—whether at Orange, Arles, or Nîmes—cities the Emperor Augustus built as miniature Romes for his legionnaires when southern France was a Roman province (that's why it's called "Provence"). Because the French, being the French, preserve their past with such pride and with such meticulous attention to detail, we actually had the sense of stepping back into the past. One restorer, at the Castle of Beynac, actually spent twenty years petrifying wood in a solution so that the staircase he was restoring would be exactly like the one that had fallen into dishabille. A countess who was restoring her château at Villesavin came close to tears when she told me she didn't have the money to replace the gilded lead roof that had been removed by Napoleon, who had used the lead to make bullets for his soldiers. Because restoration is so scrupulously executed, French fortresses, castles, and cathedrals seem to be frozen in the period in which they were built, making it possible to turn a French vacation into a magical tour through time.

At first there was a problem with our French trips. It arose from the fact that while American history is relatively short, French history is not. This fact has serious consequences for the American traveler. On our French vacations, we visited hundreds of places built over a span of more than two thousand years. We heard of so many dates, so many names of kings—eighteen Louis's who were kings and many others who were dukes and counts. Seeing so many styles of architecture created a veritable jigsaw puzzle with all the pieces still unassembled.

Then one year we visited the Loire Valley, sometimes called the Valley of the Kings, where a succession of kings built a succession of castles. While vacationing there, I discovered a way to put all those pieces and kings in place, so that our trips would be fun and not a jumble of dates and architectural styles.

The solution was quite simple. At the time, we were staying at a hotel near many of the châteaux built by the Kings of France. One morning, before Bob got up, I placed an overlay of time on the map of the Loire Valley in the Green Michelin. I simply mapped out visits to the châteaux *in the order they were built*. In other words, I arranged our tour chronologically, rather than geographically. I started with the château built earliest in time, a period when feudal lords, more powerful than the king, were constantly battling to increase their lands. It was a time when the king was merely first among many feudal lords. I started at twelfth-century Chinon, a massive, defensive fortress, a man-made cliff of walls and martial keeps, rising out of a natural escarpment. We traveled chronologically through the Middle Ages to Loches, Amboise, and Langeais, traveling through years during which the King of France became increasingly more powerful, imposing order and security over an ever-greater area of France.

As the king increased his power by marriage and by war, and as his domain expanded and peace came, I saw the defensive aspects of the châteaux melt away. By the time we reached the early Renaissance, we saw moats transformed into reflecting pools and huge defensive towers turned into tiny decorative turrets. When we reached sixteenth-century Chambord, the last royal château built in the Valley of the Kings, the château we saw was no longer that of a feudal lord, but an opulent palace of a supreme monarch, a monumental manifestation of royal power realized in stone. As we traveled castle by castle, century by century, we could see France's increasing security and stability in the architecture as the king expanded the borders of his kingdom to include all of what we now call France. I saw, as I visited these castles in the order they were built, not only the transformation of fortresses into palaces but the evolution of the monarch from an elected-first-among-equals into an absolute monarch ruling all of France. By this simple rearrangement of our vacation, we could feel the flow of years as we traveled, rather than a blurred succession of kings and a confusion of ages.

TRAVELING CHRONOLOGICALLY WORKED not only historically but architecturally, since architecture not only reflects both the spirit and needs of its age, but also evolves over the years, one style developing from another. Each age or style incorporates certain aspects of its predecessor and eliminates those that have become obsolescent or undesirable. For example, arches change. The soaring rounded Roman arch found at Orange, Arles, and Nîmes, built to overwhelm with its magnificence, crumbles. Its stones litter the years of the Dark Ages before it begins to rise again. When it rises, it is first the squat, rounded arch of the early Christian Church. Over the centuries, it rises higher and higher, and is transformed from austerity and simplicity into the elaborate storytelling arch of the eleventh-century Romanesque arch. And then, when at the very pinnacle of this beauty, for example, at Vézelay, in Burgundy, it is transformed again into the simple pointed Gothic arch at Saint-Denis. Over the next period of three hundred years, the Gothic arch evolves from simplicity to flamboyance and then, when simplicity is once again desired, it becomes the simple basket arch of the early Renaissance.

Secular architecture changes as well. For example, as France over the centuries became internally secure and castles were no longer constantly besieged by enemy knights, medieval moats were no longer needed for defense. But the French found moats aesthetically appealing, so they transformed them into reflecting pools when they built their early-Renaissance castles. Archères, windows too narrow to be pierced by the arrows of besieging knights—and the only openings in the somber fortress walls—were, as the need for safety was superseded by the growing desire for luxury, replaced with large casement windows. The cleared expanse of ground between the castle and the outer wall—once called no-man's-land—where attacking knights were caught in a crossfire of defenders' arrows, was at first visible from the new casement windows, quickly became a garden, designed to appear like the luxurious tapestries that hung on castle walls. These visible, concrete changes, and so many more, can be seen throughout *Paris to the Past* as we travel through French history. On our journey, we will encounter a succession of kings, over a span of more than eight centuries. And during those years, we will watch loosely linked feudal baronies and counties being welded into a nation, into modern France.

Traveling to places chronologically also creates a subconscious blueprint of history, an outline or chart in the mind. As you visit first a medieval castle, then one from the early Renaissance, and then yet another from the Age of Louis XIV, you sense France evolving. Traveling this way is like watching a nation growing up, like traveling through its biography. You watch French culture develop and flower until it became the cultural center of Western civilization in the nineteenth century.

As our vacations piled up over the years, I found that traveling chronologically worked quite well. It would be a simple leap of imagination to take my overlay of time, which I had placed upon the Loire Valley, and then place it on the entire map of France. When, as we were planning our next vacation in France, I first suggested to Bob that we think of our car as a time machine and travel chronologically and geographically through almost two thousand years of French history—he was skeptical but game.

I charted a route you could follow. To experience the earliest period in the history of France, we would start in the south, in Provence, an area that had been a province of Rome even before Caesar divided the rest of Gaul into three parts in 58 B.C. Next, we drove west, emerging from the Roman era, across the Rhône River, into Languedoc, where we encountered the next era, the Dark Ages. In Languedoc we visited the ruins of a fifth-century hilltop abbey, built into a limestone cave, where monks had fled during the first barbarian invasions that followed Rome's fall and where I could almost envision the waves of violence that laid waste to the Rhône Valley below. We drove west yet again to the marbled city of Narbonne, once the wealthy capital of Roman France. The Romans had once miraculously connected Narbonne by canal to the Mediterranean, transforming this inland settlement into a prosperous seaport. By the sixth century, it was a small inland city once again, since the illiterate barbarian rulers did not know how to collect taxes and therefore had no money to maintain the canal or schools.

Then we drove southwest to the early Middle Ages in Languedoc, to an isolated Romanesque monastery, hidden from the world; then west again to the late Middle Ages, to the fabulous walled medieval city of Carcassonne. Our travels thus far had all been in the south. Now we turned north to thirteenth-century Albi, where a sect protesting the corruption of the Church had been massacred in the hideously brutal Albigensian Crusade.

Traveling deeper and deeper into the Middle Ages, we continued northwest to the fourteenth century and the Hundred Years War in the Dordogne Valley, where French and English knights built castles facing each other across the river; then north to the Age of Cathedrals and the rise of the emergent middle class at Bourges in the late Middle Ages; and north again to the fifteenth and sixteenth centuries of the early

Renaissance in the Loire Valley, where we saw a veritable trail of castles built by a succession of kings. As I visited these castles in the order they were built, I saw not only the transformation of fortresses into palaces, as the need for military defensive features disappeared, but I also saw something more: for the very purpose of the fortress changed as well. For as the king evolved politically from a feudal lord elected by his peers into an absolute monarch, the evolution was reflected, century by century, in the growing magnificence of the royal castles.

Our voyage through time eventually ended on the Île-de-France, in the seventeenth century, when absolutism was at its height: at Versailles, the magnificent Baroque palace that encapsulates the majesty and power of the Sun King. This simple idea, to travel through French history chronologically—to visit places in the order they were built—had made our vacations in France memorable, experiences we would treasure forever.

Our car, I saw, could indeed be a time machine that could transport us through the history of France. After reading H. G. Wells's *Time Machine* when I was nine, I had early on become fascinated with the idea of traveling back in time. Of course, everything is possible when you are nine and have a strong foundation in fairy tales. But so many years had passed between then and the time Bob and I took our first French journey through time that I think I was surprised when this Wellsian notion actually worked—when, once I had mapped out a chronological map, our time machine carried us through France in a way that made its history resonate more three-dimensionally than I had thought possible. It worked so well that I wrote my first book about France and called it *The Road from the Past* since it invited readers to travel the same roads Bob and I had taken through the history of France.

WE CONTINUED, YEAR AFTER YEAR, to take these wonderful vacations in France. Each year we would fly to Paris, spend a week or so in a hotel there, and then rent a car and spend a couple of months driving around the country. And then one year a problem arose. Instead of booking a hotel in Paris, we rented an apartment on the Left Bank overlooking the Seine. And we didn't want to leave. Not ever. Once we began walking along the Seine in the moonlight every evening, there was no other place in the world we wanted to be. I wanted always to be able to see the reflected lights shimmering in the river, to watch the magic that occurs when a *bateau-mouche*, gliding down the river, illuminating the Baroque buildings that line the shore, finally arrives at Notre-Dame and shines its light on the cathedral. And of course I had always loved going to concerts in churches, watching a ballet or opera at the ornate Opéra Garnier, looking at nineteenth-century paintings and statues at the Musée d'Orsay, seeing festivals of old American movies in the Latin Quarter, where the movies are in English and the subtitles are in French. I had always loved sitting on the Pont des Arts, watching a painter or listening to a musician or looking at Cardinal Mazarin's Palace at one end of the bridge and the Louvre at the other, or looking east along the Seine and seeing the Île-de-la-Cité, where Paris was born, and then looking west and seeing the dream that Paris has become. And after that year of living by the river, I had fallen so totally in love with Paris that I wanted to stay, creating a dilemma of how to visit all the places outside of Paris I had not seen, while not leaving it.

I needed to find a new time machine.

THEN I HAD AN IDEA—the idea this new book is about: how to travel through French history chronologically while staying in Paris.

I still remember how the idea came to me. Bob and I had taken the Line 1 Métro in Paris to the Château de Vincennes station. Only the week before, having had so much fun at the races at Longchamps and wanting to go again, we had read in the newspaper that the races had moved to Vincennes. We were taking the Métro to the Château de Vincennes station because we mistakenly thought the Vincennes racetrack—Hippodrome de Vincennes—was there. But, it was not. The racetrack was on the other side of the Bois de Vincennes, over three kilometers away. But something else was at the Vincennes stop. As soon as we ascended from the Métro, I saw what looked suspiciously like an enceinte, the immense outer wall of a medieval castle. Still not realizing our mistake, we crossed a drawbridge, expecting to see the racetrack on the other side of the high wall; instead, to my absolute astonishment, we discovered a perfect fourteenth-century fortress complete with not only the enceinte but also an inner wall, a moat, a drawbridge, an iron portcullis, four huge turreted towers, arrow-slit windows and machicolations—those stone parapets, supported by arches, that protrude over the face of the wall.

I was amazed to realize that Vincennes—this perfect example of fourteenth-century fortification—is a mere fifteen minutes by Métro from central Paris. In fact, to see a better example, you would have to drive eight hundred kilometers to Carcassonne.

And then, riding the Métro back to our apartment, I had an idea. I happened to look up at the list of station stops. The French list all the stations along a Métro line above the windows in each car—in print large enough to see from any seat, even at my age. Although I had seen this list of stations many times before, I had merely been grateful in the past to learn that I was going in the right direction as I noted the train's progress along the line. This time, however, when I looked at the list and saw that Château de Vincennes was the first station—the eastern terminus—and that La Défense, a modern skyscraper-filled area of Paris, was the western terminus of the Line 1 Métro, my reaction was quite different. I realized that one end of the line was Château de Vincennes, Charles V's fourteenth-century medieval fortress, and the other was La Défense, the neighborhood that defines the twenty-first century vision of Paris. In a moment of revelation, in which I felt like a cartoon character in a comic strip with a lightbulb flashing above my head, I realized that if you looked at a Métro map from a historical perspective, the Line 1 Métro was traveling from the fourteenth century to the twenty-first, from medieval Paris to the present.

When I looked at the names of other stops on Line 1, I saw other places where the past was marvelously evoked. I realized that the Line 1 Métro had stops not only at Charles V's fourteenth-century Château de Vincennes, but also at the Hôtel de Ville, designed by Francis I in the sixteenth century; at the Place de la Concorde, created by Louis XV in the mid-eighteenth century; and at the Palais-Royal, remodeled by Philip Égalité in the late eighteenth century.

I also noticed that there were stops on other Métro lines that would make it possible to visit other ages of French history on the Métro. For example, Line 4 could take us to the Île-de-la-Cité, where Paris had begun over two thousand years before. By descending the steps to the Gallo-Roman rooms and walls at the crypt beneath the plaza in front of Notre-Dame, one can see remnants left by a tribe called the Parisi, who settled Paris centuries before Caesar conquered Gaul in 58 B.C. That same line also takes one to the third-century Roman baths at Cluny. The possibilities on that Métro ride, I realized all in a moment, were just about endless. If I wanted, I could then skip a few centuries and take Line 13 to the twelfth-century Basilique de Saint-Denis—the first Gothic church ever built, where the Abbot Suger used stained glass in church windows for the first time, and where the mausoleums of almost all the Kings of France can be found; or Line 6 to the nineteenth-century Opéra Garnier. Before that Métro ride ended, I had realized I could stay—in an apartment or hotel—in Paris and visit quite of bit of France's past by merely taking the subway.

But I also realized that it was not only the Métro I could take from central Paris to French history. There was another train, the RER (Réseau Express Régional) as well. An express regional train to the sub-urbs with connections at Métro stations throughout the city, it connects Paris not only to suburbia, but to castles that were once in the coun-tryside. The castle at the Saint-Germain-en-Laye station, for example, is only twenty minutes from central Paris by the RER Line B. I had spent an enjoyable day at Saint-Germain both lunching at the Pavillion Henri IV, where the Sun King was born, and visiting the nearby castle, which is now a Gallo-Roman museum. And Saint-Germain was only one castle reachable by the RER. I could take the commuter train to the Versailles of Louis XIV; or to Rambouillet, with its ancient castle and restored gardens; or to Le Nôtre's gardens at Sceaux; or to Chan-tilly, a fabulous château built by one of the oldest aristocratic families in France; or to Malmaison, where Napoleon and Josephine lived when they were young and he was first consul of France; or to Fontainebleau, which both Francis I and Napoleon loved.

One day, looking at my Paris Métro map, I noticed something else. The Métro stopped at all the grand railroad stations that Napoleon III had built in Paris in the nineteenth century—the Gare de l'Est (a station from which trains depart to the east), the Gare du Nord (with trains to the north), Gare Saint-Lazare (with trains to the northwest), Gare de Lyon (with trains to the south). I realized I could keep my apartment in Paris and travel not only by Métro and RER, but by the French railroad trains. And some of these trains—the high-speed TGVs (Train à Grande Vitesse)—remain marvels to an American traveler at speeds far greater than any Acela. They were introduced in 1981, and the French have been expanding the TGV lines throughout their country ever since. I realized I could take either a regular train or the TGV to many of the historic places I wanted to see in France. Since the TGV travels at speeds over 200 miles per hour, I could reach all but one of the places I wanted to see in France in ninety minutes and most places in less than an hour, and be able to return to Paris the very same night. I could, much as readers of *Paris to the Past* will be able to do, stay at my hotel or apartment in Paris and never have to pack or unpack. I could take a train from Paris, travel century by century, chronologically through time, and be back in Paris each night, usually in time for dinner. Unlike the time traveler in Michael Crichton's book *Timeline*, I didn't need to be faxed to the Middle Ages, I could take the TGV from Paris.

This was all made possible by Napoleon. Not Napoleon I, the conqueror of much of Europe, but his nephew, Napoleon III (1852 to 1870), called, disparagingly, the Bourgeois Emperor, "a sphinx without a secret," "a great unfathomed incapacity," "a melancholy parrot," a "hat without a man." Nonetheless, he, not his uncle, is my hero, because his dreams were of being Augustus, the emperor who turned Rome into a city of marble. As readers will see, Napoleon III wanted to make Paris a city of marble like Augustus's Rome. He wanted to make Paris the center of the world, the center of Europe, really, as Rome once had been. While all roads led to Rome under Augustus, all rail lines under Napoleon III would begin leading to and from Paris. Hiring the Baron von Haussmann to clear the slums of Paris, he replaced them with wide boulevards that led to the circle of railroad stations that would connect Paris with the rest of France and Europe. Under his plan, the Gare de l'Est, completed in 1847, was the first of the many fabulous stations with their marbled walls, frescoed dining rooms, and hotel suites that circle the city of Paris. Following the Gare de l'Est, the Gare du Nord was built in 1862, the Gare Saint-Lazare in 1885, the Gare de Lyon in 1889, and, finally, the Gare d'Orsay in 1900. These stations were built not for the weary, harassed commuters of our time who gulp their food from paper plates and wipe their hands with paper napkins while standing at chest-high metal tables at the Gare Montparnasse, the only modern railroad station in Paris, but as marble palaces for the travelers of the nineteenth century. Since the Gare d'Orsay has actually been converted into a museum, you don't have to imagine but can experience for yourself the luxury in which travelers once dined while they waited for their trains. Or you can visit the nearby marble-walled Gare d'Orsay waiting room preserved as it once was for nineteenth-century travelers, a place still filled with statues and paintings of a quality that would have once adorned the palaces of the nobility. It's a reminder of how glorious an experience traveling once was—and how mean it has now become. Or, better still, dine at Le Train Bleu at the Gare de Lyon, whose lavish turn-of-the-century decorations are simply overwhelming (we try to eat there on Sundays when most restaurants in Paris are closed.) These stations were built for the middle-class traveler—not what we call the middle class in America, but the upper middle class, the nouveau riche of the late nineteenth century, whose main desire was to live and be treated as the aristocracy once had been, an aspiring, bourgeois French middle class who built their new mansions along the boulevards that replaced the slums of Paris.

These stations, whose arteries of tracks fan out from the heart of the city, connect the north, south, east, and west of Paris to the north, south, east, and west of France and Europe. And there is another benefit. These trains connect modern Paris to ancient France in a very special way, since they drop travelers in the hearts of ancient cities that have been so miraculously preserved. Trying to get to the inner core of cities like Poitiers, Nantes, Tours, Rouen, or Laon, which have remained unchanged for centuries, is difficult if you try to arrive by car because all around the ancient city sprawling, faceless suburbs have grown up and spread out as the cities expanded, like the tangle of forests that grew up around the castle of Sleeping Beauty to keep her suitors out. While the core remained unchanged as the modern city expanded outward, these suburbs created a traffic-clogged twenty-first-century barrier for cars. *But not for trains.* French railroads, whose nineteenth-century stations were built in the old cities before the suburbs grew, whisk you through this maze of faceless suburbs and deposit you sans traffic jams in the city's ancient past. While staying in the Loire Valley, I once spent hours driving through a maze of streets with heavy traffic trying to find medieval Tours and, regrettably, never did, but by train Tours is only an hour from Paris. You simply step off in the heart of medieval Tours and don't have to find a place to park.

As a result of the TGV, distance becomes less relevant than time, making the medieval city of Tours and the cathedral city of Chartres equidistant in time—both cities are one hour from Paris—even though Tours, connected by TGV, is 237 kilometers from Paris, and Chartres, connected by a regular train, is 89 kilometers away. There is, in fact, another advantage to traveling by train. Places such as Eleanor of Aquitaine's troubadour court at Poitiers and Blanche of Castile's fortress at Angers—places I had always wanted to see but which were especially hard to reach by car—suddenly became easy to reach.

WHEN MY MÉTRO RIDE back from Vincennes—and my travel epiphany—ended, I raced back to my apartment; I couldn't keep from running. I took out a big map of France and a batch of railroad timetables, and began charting journeys out of Paris by train—journeys that would enable Bob and me to travel through French history and still be able to return to our apartment in Paris each night. As I planned these journeys, I selected not only those places that I felt were the most aesthetically pleasing embodiments of each age, but also found historical personages from the past to be my guides. I spent day after day in libraries to find their memoirs to inform me why they built their churches and castles the way they did. It was, for example, on a guided tour at the château at Dampierre that I had taken on one of our first trips to France that I realized that I needed an actual historical person to make my trip come alive, to enable me to understand the special features of the age. This simple realization occurred as my twentieth-century guide was droning on and on about seventeenth-century period furniture, and I was stifling one yawn after another. Then I noticed a portrait of Marie de Rohan, the woman who had actually built this château. Marie de Rohan had fascinated me from the time I learned that this deliciously wicked woman, who was, in fact, a character in *The Three Musketeers*, really did exist and really did try to arrange an affair between the Queen of France and the Duke of Buckingham. The château had seemed rather dull when I knew only that it was rebuilt at the time of Louis XIV, but came to life when it was the home of the duchess who had tried to arrange an affair for her friend the Queen of France. And that it was upon the very chairs in this château that Marie sat with the Queen of France and poisoned her mind against the queen's friend Nicolas Fouquet, Louis XIV's financial minister. After I realized whose château I was visiting, the Louis XIV wainscoting was no longer a bore but part of an exquisite setting where exciting historical events had taken place, and it is these kinds of detail that I have added to this book.

It dawned on me that all the places I really loved visiting had been built by memorable characters whose fascinating lives helped explain the age in which they lived: a fascinating genius of an abbot at Saint-Denis to tell us how he was inspired to create the first Gothic cathedral; a wicked bishop at Reims; a widowed queen at Angers fighting off rebellious nobles to save the kingdom for her son; Joan of Arc defeating the English at Orléans; a mistress and a queen fighting for the affection of a king at Blois; Fouquet, Louis XIV's brilliant finance minister at magical Vaux-le-Vicomte; Madame de Pompadour, the daughter of a shunned courtesan, who became the mistress of a king at the Petit Trianon. While I wasn't able to interview any of the people who built the places, I was able to find their memoirs and letters, which not only told me about why and how they built their castle, but also about their lives. While these gossipy recollections are sometimes slanted and sometimes not altogether true, they are endlessly fun to read and certainly enliven every place I visited.

Also—and for me this is just as important—there are not only cathedrals and palaces evoking a particular period and great stories at every place I have chosen, but terrific restaurants at almost every site as well. It is a terrible thing for a historian to have to admit, but the quality of my lunch really does influence how I feel about the places I visit. I realize most academic historians would not be willing to make the same confession, but for me it's true. While the city of Bourges, with its radiant cathedral and eclectic merchant palace of Jacques Coeur (whose Errol Flynn life encapsulated the rise of the middle class in France), may have been an apt site for embodying an age, I have to admit Bourges was one of my least favorite excursions, simply because it was at a restaurant there that I first learned that you could really have a lousy meal in France. In contrast, the city of Reims, where all the Kings of France were once crowned, is perhaps one of my favorite train trips because of Les Crayères, a Champagne vintner's château that Gerard Boyer converted into the most heavenly three-star restaurant and hotel in France, which I was lucky enough to visit twice before he retired. I hope you don't think that all the places selected in this book have three-star restaurants; for Bob and I very much pride ourselves on discovering bistros and dives. In fact, one of my most pleasurable eating experiences wasn't at a starred restaurant at all. It was just by accident, for example, that I happened to visit Tours on July 26 when the Festival of Sainte-Anne, also called the Festival of Garlic and Basil, filled the entire medieval part of the city with tables serving local wines and delicious provincial food. That day I thanked the patron saint of appetites, whoever he is, for the enormous appetite that I'm always able to summon.* Ordinarily this can be a problem, since I am always hungry, but at that day at Tours, I was

---

* Although I don't think I could win the Coney Island hot-dog-eating contest, I did once outeat Bob's roommates at Princeton in a spaghetti-eating contest—although they were all over 6 feet tall and members of the Princeton basketball team—and my appetite hasn't changed a bit.

grateful for once for my ability to taste and consume just about every delicious morsel that the gracious people of that town were offering.

This journey through time, as reflected in *Paris to the Past*, is possible since I believe that we are the product of our past and all the generations that have come before us. We are unknowingly touched by ages long ago, sifted through a filter of time, by a mother's words, books we read, movies seen, our minds becoming the treasure chest or garbage pail of the preceding ages. We need only a remnant of the past, a castle or cathedral seen through contemporary eyes, to make these past ages come alive.

PART ONE

—

The Middle Ages

CATHEDRALS AND FORTRESSES

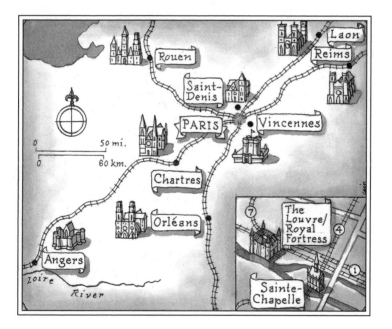

CHAPTER 1

SAINT-DENIS
The Monarchy and the
Gothic Cathedral

—

Line 13 Métro to Basilique de Saint-Denis

I HAD MY IDEA—TO TRAVEL BY TRAIN THROUGH THE HISTORY OF France, taking day trips from central Paris by train or Métro, traveling in chronological order to a different century each day, and returning to Paris each evening. And I woke up the next morning knowing exactly how I wanted to begin: by taking the Métro to the twelfth-century Basilica of Saint-Denis.

My first experiences with the basilica were not what I'd call love at first sight.

A lot had happened to the royal abbey at Saint-Denis in the eight hundred years between the time the basilica was built and the time, in the 1970s, when I saw it for the first time—and not much of what had happened was good. Saint-Denis is the necropolis (burial place) of the kings and queens of France—almost all of the country's rulers going back to the seventh century have their tombs there—and during the French Revolution it wasn't only Marie-Antoinette and Louis XVI who had lost their heads, but also the statues of kings that decorated Saint-Denis's western façade as well. Revolutionaries also opened all the royal tombs of the kings and queens of France and dumped their remains into a lime pit. The basilica was used by the revolutionaries to store grain. Shortly after Napoleon declared himself emperor, he had it restored, but the restoration was somewhat of a disaster. Not only was the grain and dirt removed but one of Saint-Denis's twin steeples was accidently removed as well, leaving an empty space in the sky where it should have been.

Saint-Denis is located in a suburb about ten kilometers from central Paris that was euphemistically called a working-class *banlieue* in the 1970s. I had been nervous as I walked the few blocks from the Métro station to the basilica on my first visit there. Graffiti always makes me nervous, and the buildings along the way were covered with graffiti then. The lovely open plaza in front of the church was then a parking lot for cars that had seen better days. And the carefully laid-out parks surrounding the basilica that are there today had not yet been developed. I don't remember if there was graffiti on the basilica itself, but its façade was so grimy that it looked like it hadn't been scrubbed since the twelfth century when it was built.

Although I hadn't been impressed the first time I saw Saint-Denis, something kept drawing me back. Over the years, whenever I had a free morning, I found myself taking the twenty-minute Métro ride there. When I learned that a chubby little figure, whose image is carved on the façade, was that of the Abbot Suger, the man responsible for building Saint-Denis, I was intrigued. I began reading everything I could find about this lopsided church and the man who built it. I learned that this was the first Gothic cathedral ever built and that it was here that stained glass was used for large windows for the very first time.

Then one year I found Saint-Denis—and its subway station—transformed. The Métro station had been cleaned up and was as welcoming as those depositing me at the Musée d'Orsay or at the Louvre. And the neighborhood had been cleaned up as well. The graffiti was gone. Not only that—the church had been marvelously restored—although it was still missing one of its steeples. As I was about to enter the church, or cathedral, as it was now called, I wasn't told by the woman collecting my entrance fee that the English guide was out to lunch, or couldn't be found—as I had been told on previous trips—but was given an audio guide in English that had just been recorded and a chart showing the location of all seventy-two tombs of the kings and queens of France that had made it through the Revolution.

But sometimes love grows slowly.

When I entered the now glittering interior of the basilica, I knew what had been slowly dawning on me for over twenty years. The restorers had waved their magic wand, and I could see Saint-Denis, like Cinderella, with all the soot and grime removed. And then I realized why I kept coming back. Saint-Denis is the birthplace of the beautiful France I've come to cherish.

The Romanesque cathedrals built during the previous three hundred years are interesting, but I had always found the low ceilings and dark interiors depressing. And I understood why the spartan castles of feudal lords—fortresses really—built during that same period were reason enough for knights to leave France and set out on crusades in sunnier places. It wasn't until the Abbot Suger built Saint-Denis in 1144, until he erected the first Gothic cathedral, that France began to change into the France I love. I had read that he was called the Father of the Gothic Cathedral and the Father of the French Monarchy, and as I looked at the transformed basilica of Saint-Denis, I thought he might even be the father of the beautiful France I love as well. It was Suger, after all, who first pierced the solid stone walls of the dark ages to create the world's first rose window so that jeweled light would shine on and glorify the king he wished to raise above all men. And it was the Gothic cathedrals and palaces of kings—not gloomy fortresses of feudal lords—that lifted my spirits and seemed to restore my soul on every visit to France.

When the basilica was first built, however, it was attacked because of its beauty. The powerful Bernard of Clairvaux, the spokesman and personification of the rigid asceticism that predominated in the eleventh- and twelfth-century ecclesiastical world, called it a "synagogue of Satan." Bernard detested decorations of any sort, and asked, "What has gold to do in the sanctuary?"

Suger, on the other hand, was a flamboyant character who, like me, could not resist beautiful things. He had "an insatiable passion for gold, enamel, crystal and mosaics, for pearls and precious stones" at a time when austerity was the rule. And he believed—or said he believed; it is difficult to know which with this artificer, who could bend any argument to his ends—that "the contemplation of earthly brilliance, in the form of precious metals, jeweled objects, enamelware and colored glass, was an important means of leading the Christian believer to divine enlightenment." After installing gilded bronze doors in his basilica, he expressed the hope that the "physical 'brightness' of the work of art will 'brighten' the minds of the beholders by a spiritual illumination." While it would have been imprudent for Suger to confront Bernard de Clairvaux directly with his novel ideas, and he didn't dare to do so, he would later write in his autobiography of his "delight" in "the beauty of the house of God" he had created, where "the loveliness of the many-colored gems has called me away from external cares."

Those words seemed to resonate with me. They touched something in me as I remembered how I would come to France each year feeling somewhat overwhelmed by the minutiae of life, and then two months later leave totally refreshed. Suger's words, in fact, augured the dawn of a new and glittering age.

I STILL REMEMBER the moment Bob and I stepped inside this rather ordinary-looking church in a rather seedy part of Paris. We had been totally unprepared for what we saw. Inside Saint-Denis are the tombs of practically every French king from Clovis, the first Merovingian King of the Franks, who converted to Christianity in the fifth century, to Louis XVIII, the last French king, who ruled in the nineteenth century. While most of their regal bones were predictably removed during the king-hating French Revolution, their tombs remain: fourteen centuries of funeral sculpture—sculptures of the highest artistic accomplishments of each age, since kings could—and did—hire the best artists to design their mausoleums. Bob and I had once driven hours to the palace of the Dukes of Burgundy at Dijon to see just one tomb—the grandiose sarcophagus of Duke Philip the Bold, whose effigy lies on a stone canopy atop a carved procession of mourners each of whom expresses their individual reactions to death. But here, right in Paris, twenty minutes by Métro, were the tombs of seventy-two French kings and queens. And the sarcophagi of the Renaissance kings here equal or surpass the tomb of Philip the Bold, which we had thought so magnificent.

Visiting the Tombs

As you enter the now visitor-friendly basilica, you are handed a chart showing the location of each of the tombs. When I first saw this chart, I was tempted to start with the tomb of Clovis (d. 511), to visit the tombs sequentially, and to end with the sarcophagus of Louis XVI and Marie-Antoinette (1793). I don't advise you to do that unless you are wearing a heavy sweater. The early tombs are found mostly in the crypt below, and it's cold down there! If you start there, notice that the effigies of the deceased are depicted as corpses lying on their stone slabs ready to be taken to heaven. Since the individual wasn't deemed significant in the early Middle Ages, most of the effigies look pretty much the same. You can barely tell one king from another. Their gisants (recumbent effigies) and death masks are carved in stylized, stereotypical forms, more ornamental than lifelike, statues with dangling feet, and bodies barely leaving the stone from which they were carved. Seeing one or two is quite enough.

Although our first trip had been in April, it was freezing in the crypt. I was actually shivering, so we decided to give short shrift to the Merovingian and Carolingian kings located there. We began with the tomb of King Dagobert in the crypt. Dagobert was the powerful Merovingian king who, in 630, ordered that this royal abbey be built on the spot to which St. Denis had walked—head in hand—to be buried, and ordered all subsequent kings to be buried there as well. St. Denis, I might add, is not only the patron saint—or protector—of the French monarchy, but the Catholic Church also named him the patron saint of headaches—because of the way he died. He was decapitated.

Dagobert now has two tombs. While this Merovingian king still retains his seventh-century tomb in the freezing crypt below, he acquired a rather impressive monument located in the transept crossing of the basilica above when Louis IX, in the thirteenth century, decided that the French king thought responsible for all the Kings of France being buried here should have a more significant memorial.

Dagobert's recumbent body now rests at the base of a large, solid, flamboyant thirteenth-century memorial in the shape of a Gothic arch. Above his body, carved into the arch, are a series of sculptures that tell the Dagobert legend: how demons tried to steal Dagobert's crown and soul after he died, but how St. Denis came to his rescue. The patron saint of the monarchy would not permit the king, who founded the basilica in his honor, to be treated in that way.

Not far from Dagobert's improved monument, on the far left wall of the basilica, is the tomb of Louis XII (1498–1515) and his queen, Anne of Brittany, the first of several early Renaissance sarcophagi. It is designed by the Giusti brothers, Florentine sculptors whom Louis XII had summoned to France during his reign. Giovanni Giusti had been influenced by the work of Michelangelo before coming to France, and this tomb is thought to "echo" an early version of the tomb that Michelangelo designed for Pope Julius II.

Walking through the basilica, we could almost see how the Italian Renaissance was brought to France. After Louis XII died, Francis I (1515–1547), who succeeded him, commissioned the brothers to design this tomb. Look at the lifelike gisants of Louis XII and Anne that lie beneath an arched canopy. Each of the arches is filled with a small, exquisitely carved statue of an apostle identified by his emblem. St. Peter, for example, is sitting in one of the arches holding his emblem—the keys to heaven—in his hand. Statues of the four virtues are at the four corners. On top of the canopy, Anne of Brittany and Louis have risen up from the dead to pray. Even if you see nothing else, this early-Renaissance tomb of Louis XII, a mausoleum of incredible elegance, individuality, emotional and spiritual beauty, is worth the twenty-minute Métro ride to Saint-Denis.

Louis XII and Francis I are the French kings most responsible for bringing the Italian Renaissance to France. Francis I, who, along with the rest of his family, can be found praying nearby in the nave, had his accomplishments carved in low relief around the base of his tomb. Both kings fell in love with Renaissance Italy, tried to conquer it, but instead were conquered by the Italian artists they brought back to France. Francis I would bring the finest Italian artists, Leonardo da Vinci, Benvenuto Cellini, and Francesco Primaticcio, to his castle in the Loire and to Fontainebleau.

Nearby, also in the nave, is the elegant Renaissance tomb of Henry II (1547–1559) and Catherine de Médicis. Seeing herself depicted as a corpse, in a mausoleum designed by Primaticcio, Catherine de Médicis was so horrified at her appearance that she commissioned her favorite Renaissance sculptor, Germain Pilon, to carve her so that she appeared peacefully sleeping, and frankly far more beautiful—and a great deal thinner—than I would have thought from reading descriptions of her. However, Henry's statue on top is so lifelike and appealing that every time I had visited one of the castles in the Loire Valley in which he lived, I would come back here, to his statue at Saint-Denis, to visit him.

Seeing these tombs in chronological order is like taking an incredible walk through not only the history of France, but of French art as well. As you do so, you can see how the death masks, gisants, statues, and mausoleums of the Kings of France evolve artistically from the sixth to the nineteenth century. However, you don't have to see them all, or see them all at once. Over the years, I came back periodically to visit each of my favorite kings as I traveled through the history of France. Visiting them at Saint-Denis after seeing the castles that they built all over France helped to bring the past alive.

WHILE LEGEND HAS IT that Dagobert was responsible for the Necropolis being here at Saint-Denis, that is not exactly true. He may have ordered that a royal abbey be built at Saint-Denis and that all subsequent kings be buried there, but after his death in 639, the mini-empire he created began to fall apart, and kings began choosing different sites for their internment. It was really the Abbot Suger who is responsible for the Necropolis being here. He used and embroidered the Dagobert and St. Denis legends until it was accepted as true that all kings had to be buried here. The Abbot Suger, in fact, did everything that needed to be done so he could build the Basilica of Saint-Denis the way he wanted it built and thereby ally his church closely with the monarchy in France in the process. The more I read about this chubby little abbot, the more I came to admire him, and I believed that Bob would be fascinated as well. Suger may have been shorter and, at times, jollier than Robert Moses or Lyndon Johnson—the two men Bob has written about—but he was just as gifted in accumulating power. Bob had never heard of Suger, which is not surprising since his name is virtually unknown in America. However, Suger is quite well known in France, where he had been given two very impressive titles: Father of the Gothic Cathedral and Father of the Monarchy. He is called the Father of the Gothic Cathedral because the abbey church he built at Saint-Denis is the parent of all Gothic cathedrals. And he is called the Father of the Monarchy because in order to create the basilica he wanted, he realized he would have to create a powerful monarch. If he desired the one—his Gothic basilica, with walls of stained-glass, he had to create the other—a strong king who could both endow and protect it.

I COULDN'T WAIT to tell Bob about Suger, and on our Métro trip to Saint-Denis, I began pouring out the details of his extraordinary life. I felt Bob couldn't appreciate Saint-Denis without knowing how it came to be built, and he couldn't know how it came to be built without knowing about the Abbot Suger.

I began with Suger's rise to power. Suger was born a peasant, and in the twelfth century a person born a peasant was supposed to die a peasant. He certainly wasn't supposed to become an abbot. Prior to the twelfth century, social mobility did not exist in feudal France. Remaining in the class in which you were born was thought to be God's will. Suger's rise to power therefore reveals quite a bit about both his brilliance and his deviousness and the changes that began to take place in the twelfth century.

In 1091, as the story goes, his parents gave their ten-year-old son as an oblate, or lay servant, to the Benedictine monks at the Royal Abbey of Saint-Denis. Suger tells us he was grateful all his life to the monks for taking him in and considered them his adopted parents. He was not only a very short boy—much smaller than the other boys at school—but a very poor one among the sons of the aristocracy. In addition, he had learned to read, while the aristocracy at this time was mostly illiterate and proud of it.

My heart went out to him thinking how lonely he must have been when he first arrived at the abbey. He spent most of his time alone in the archives. While a young monk, he began searching for deeds that could expand the domains of Saint-Denis. When he didn't find what he was looking for, he created or forged them. This obviously endeared him to his abbot, whose wealth and power were thereby greatly increased, and, oddly, to me as well. Although I don't usually approve of forgery, the age in which he lived provided mitigating circumstances. I could over-look his creativity in this regard since actual deeds and documents had been destroyed in abbeys and monasteries throughout France during the barbarian invasions of the Dark, or early Middle, Ages. He needed the considerable wealth these forgeries provided to finance this church. His literary creativity was not confined to forging deeds. He also wrote a chanson de geste, or epic poem, entitled "How Charlemagne Brought the Cross and the Crown of the Lord from Constantinople to Aachen and How Charles the Bald Brought them to Saint Denis." He may, how-ever, have gone too far after he became abbot, for while he held that position, documents began to appear that granted the Basilica of Saint-Denis total control over all the churches in France. These forgeries were prolific during his lifetime and ceased immediately upon his death.

It was not long after his arrival that he displayed other qualities that I have always admired, qualities that were to be characteristic of him all his life: a brilliant mind and memory that amazed his teachers, one that moved the monks to allow the lowborn boy to be educated with the sons of the aristocracy; and a gregariousness, charm, and wit that delighted his schoolmates and his teachers. He was fond of quoting the Latin poet Horace and of telling stories—he could tell about the esca-pades of any king of France—and would do so, entertaining his class-mates and, later, the monks with his tales late into the night. Suger, in fact, seemed to have charmed his way to power, charming not only the Abbot of Saint-Denis, the pope, and the Duke of Normandy, but also most significant, a fellow student his own age named Louis Capet, who happened to be the son of King Philip, and who would later become King Louis the Fat. (His tomb is located on the left side of the nave as you enter the basilica.)

When the Abbot of Saint-Denis died in 1122, the monks there named Suger to replace him—without waiting for the king's nomination (*licentia eligendi*), as was required. They did so because Suger had for years been telling his fellow monks how close his friendship was with the king, how they had become childhood friends when they had attended school together. The monks had assumed the king would be pleased by their actions, but Louis the Fat was not. He was furious. Abbots in the twelfth century were chosen from the nobility, the second or landless sons, whose powerful families thereby became indebted to the king for the appointment. The right of appointment—but not the investiture—of church officials was an important right that the French king had only recently won from the Church, and friendship did not enter into the political equation. When the monks came to tell the king what they had done, Louis imprisoned them in his castle at Orléans.

Suger, who was in Rome at the time, tells us in his autobiography that he asked the advice of Pope Calixtus II, in whose service he had been for the past year. After conferring with the pope, Suger sent messengers from Rome to the king. Suger does not tell us what he wrote that persuaded the king to confirm his appointment and to release his fellow monks. Unlike Bob, whose subjects lived in the twentieth century, I couldn't interview anyone from the twelfth century to find out exactly what happened. However, after this episode, the relationship between the King of France and the pope, which had been strained during the reign of Louis the Fat's father, was strengthened. Suger, with his insight into political power, had grasped the need for stronger ties between the monarchy and the Church while he was still a young man. His abbot, impressed by Suger's talents, sent the twenty-six-year-old monk to the Normandy coast to fix the finances of the Berneville monastery there. Suger had observed how the alliance between the Duke of Normandy and the Church resulted in a stable feudal government. (Before the alliance, monasteries' treasures had been constantly looted. After the duke gave them his protection, looters were punished by having their hands lopped off).

Suger also noticed how wealthy the monasteries of Normandy were when compared to those located, like his basilica, on the Île-de-France. And he saw that the monasteries were wealthy because of the protection of the Duke of Normandy. In a flash of political genius, he had a revolutionary idea: if he could strengthen the power of the King of France, and at the same time make him the Church's protector, the basilica would no longer have to be a fortress as well as a place of worship. He could build Saint-Denis the way he wanted. With the protection of a strong king, he could replace thick walls with huge windows and display the jewel-encrusted reliquaries and Bibles that he loved. With the king's protection, the roving bands of robbers that plagued the Île-de-France, smashing windows as they pillaged, would disappear. And the local lords, who held his pilgrims and their purses ransom, would no longer be a problem.

To increase the king's power, Suger developed a novel stratagem. He proposed that the king ally himself with tradesmen and merchants in towns throughout France. The evolution of this policy shows how Suger's mind worked. While a young monk, he had noticed that Louis the Fat's father had protected the Jews in the city of Tours from the local barons in exchange for payments to the crown. Suger saw that this minor act of royal blackmail could be a means to create the rich and powerful monarch he needed to protect his beloved royal abbey, while at the same time reducing the power of the 150 barons who were the king's unruly vassals in his realm, which at the time included only the area around Paris, known as the Île-de-France. In a truly original and brilliant policy, he advised Louis to protect merchants and towns—and not only in the Île-de-France, but throughout all of France—an ingenious move that spread the influence of the king far beyond the borders of his realm, binding the merchants and their communes to the king while at the same time weakening the power of local lords. Louis took his advice, granting eight charters that gave basic rights to communes that required taxes to be paid to the king, in exchange for independence. In the future, communes would make only a single annual payment to local barons instead. Before, they had to make payments whenever the barons needed money. In many ways, the feudal system hadn't been terribly good for business. The new charters allowed the merchants to have a militia of their own, which prevented local lords from hijacking their mule trains or charging tolls at river crossings as they had done in the past.

When Louis the Fat died, his son, Louis the Young, became king. Not understanding the wisdom of his father's policy, he reacted in typical medieval fashion to a request by the merchants of Poitiers for more independence by hacking off the hands of some and exiling others. But Suger, who had retired to the Royal Abbey to build his basilica, was so horrified by the new king's bloody actions, that he rushed to Poitiers to reverse them and make sure the merchants and townspeople were allowed to return. Suger explained to the king the economic advantages of taxes as well as the political advantages of a weakened aristocracy. Over time, this policy did in fact result in gradually reducing the power of the aristocracy and increasing the power and finances of the monarchy.* I should mention that most of what we know about Suger comes from his autobiography. While today everyone is writing their autobiography, twelfth-century abbots did not usually write theirs. Nothing like an autobiography had been written since St. Augustine wrote his *Confessions* at the end of the fourth century, because the individual and his accomplishments weren't considered important in medieval society. And, I should emphasize that, like most autobiographies, Suger's should not be totally believed.

---

* Suger believed that "those who plundered" should be punished by "the ripping out of the eyes." His position, however, was more favorable to merchants and, consequently, the growth of cities.

———

I HAD BARELY BEGUN telling Bob about the Abbot Suger when our Métro train arrived at the Basilique de Saint-Denis station, abbreviating my historical tale and bringing us back into the present. You can of course get to the basilica from central Paris on foot, following a popular twelfth-century pilgrimage path promoted by Suger. It was supposedly first taken by St. Denis, France's patron saint, who, after being decapitated at Montmartre, picked up his head and walked five miles to the site where his basilica now stands. I, however, prefer taking the Line 13 Métro. It's not that I'm afraid of losing my head, I'm more afraid of losing my pocketbook. The walk is no longer through beautiful countryside or even through pleasant neighborhoods, while the Métro is so very easy and so quick. However, you should pay attention. Be aware that Line 13 now forks at the La Fourche station, with trains going in two directions. You want the train going to Saint-Denis Université, not the one destined for Gabriel Péri—Asnières-Gennevilliers. (If your train stops at the Brochant station, you have taken the wrong train, as I obviously have, so get off, go back one stop to the La Fourche station, and wait for a train labeled Saint-Denis Université. This will add about ten minutes to your trip.) Also, be sure to get off at the Basilique de Saint-Denis station and not Saint-Denis–Porte de Paris or Saint-Denis–Université.

Arriving at Saint-Denis

The escalator from the Métro leaves you in a modern shopping mall two minutes or less from the basilica. When Bob and I turned a corner and saw this strange-looking church with its missing steeple and crenellated crown, Bob gave me a rather quizzical look, and I could tell he was wondering why I had brought him to see this very ordinary-looking church. At the same time, a thrill went through me. I knew that this desecrated and pillaged place, dedicated to a somewhat fabricated saint, was the inspiration for the miracles that are Notre-Dame, Chartres, Reims, and Sainte-Chapelle—the umbilical cord tying the new architecture to the old. Every inch of decoration on its walls once had a symbolic meaning for the medieval worshipers who entered, firmly believing that St. Denis, whose relics were displayed inside in jewel-encrusted reliquaries, would intercede for them with God once their prayers were heard.

Saint-Denis is not as Suger left it. Not only is one steeple gone, so are the mosaic floors, the golden altar, the sardonyx chalice, the gilded carved bronze doors, and the statue columns of the Kings of France that guarded them. When Saint-Denis was completed in 1144, it was the most glorious church in France, and Suger had expected it to be an everlasting monument to himself. Even in its present state of dishabille, however, seeing Saint-Denis is a fascinating experience—but only if you know what you are seeing.

Look at the façade from across the plaza and let your eyes start at the crenellated crown, topped with embrasures and merlons, for, as Suger's autobiography reminds us, churches in the twelfth century were not immune from attack, but, as Suger states, the embrasures and merlons might also be used for defense "should circumstances require it." Echoing the walls of the king's fortified medieval castles, the crenellated crown also symbolizes the union of Church and State, the dual royal and spiritual authority possessed by the royal abbey. This abbey of St. Denis, France's patron saint, was the abbey that guarded and kept both the royal crown and the Oriflamme—the red and gold battle standard that Suger claimed Charlemagne carried into battle when he fought the Saracens—which may or may not be true. However, Louis the Fat certainly carried the Oriflamme into battle when he fought the combined forces of the Holy Roman Emperor and the English king in 1124. And every French king carried this standard into battle for the next three hundred years. A replica can be seen inside.

At Saint-Denis you will see four columns topped with crowns on the front of the church. These are actually buttresses built to hold up the façade, with its three arched doorways. Before the use of buttresses— before Saint-Denis, in other words—cathedrals, the cathedrals of the Romanesque era that preceded the Gothic, could have only one doorway. The façades of Romanesque churches may have three arches, as there are at Saint-Denis, but only the center arch contains a door. Massive solid-stone walls filling the two side arches were still necessary to keep the Romanesque churches upright. But here we see technological progress, medieval-style. With the addition of buttresses to relieve the outward pressure created by the arches, all three arches could contain doors at Saint-Denis.

The arches of the façade are rounded, but inside Saint-Denis the arches are pointed. This was not the first time buttresses and pointed arches had been used in France. Suger had seen both elements of design while on a mission in Normandy in 1107.

During his time in Normandy, Suger had the two inspirations—about the nature of cathedrals and about the nature of the monarchy—that were to transform them both. In Normandy, Suger saw a different style of church construction and a different style of government than he had seen in the Île-de-France. When the young monk arrived in Caen, at William the Conqueror's Abbey of Saint-Étienne, he would have seen the pointed arch and the H design of twin steeples that was characteristic of the new churches then being built in Caen and throughout Normandy and which would be characteristic of all the Gothic cathedrals built over the next three centuries. The Normans had started using the pointed arch shortly after their invasion of Sicily in 1061, where they found the Saracens, whom they had conquered, using it in their construction. Whether the Norman conquerors just brought back to Normandy the idea of the pointed arch or brought back the Saracen builders, I do not know, but pointed arches began appearing in Normandy shortly after Sicily was conquered. The pointed arch differed from the rounded arch used in Romanesque churches by greatly reducing lateral or outward pressure on walls, so that massive solid-stone walls were no longer necessary to keep the building upright. Unlike the Romanesque arch, it directs the weight of vaults downward. But the Normans hadn't taken the next steps: to raise the ceilings and replace massive stone walls with large windows of glass. It took Suger to do that.

The western façade of Saint-Denis, like those of the Gothic cathedrals that followed, not only provides an entrance but also a compass for tourists lost in French cities. Since I have no sense of direction, learning that the entrance is always at the western end of the cathedral has been quite helpful on my travels through France. Most cathedrals built between the twelfth and fifteenth centuries are laid out west to east, from the setting sun to the rising sun. This is because the setting sun was symbolic of the end of man's day on earth, while the rising sun is symbolic of the coming of Christ. The dark north side of cathedrals always has scenes from the Old Testament, while the sunny south side depicts stories from the New Testament. It was only after I learned this fact that I was able, using Notre-Dame as my compass, to determine that the apartment Bob and I were renting was in the southeast of Paris.

The theme of Suger's west façade is the Last Judgment. In fact, if you visit enough cathedrals, the theme on the western façade is almost invariably the Last Judgment because the sun setting in the west was symbolic of the end of man's day on earth. "Medieval theologians and artists confused the meaning of the word *occidens* (the western side) with the verb *occidere*, meaning 'to kill,' so it seemed natural to them to represent the end of the world on the western facade." The Last Judgment scene on the tympanum over the right doorway is Christ administering the Eucharist to St. Denis, who is with his faithful companions Rusticus and Eleutherius.

In this Last Judgment scene, Suger had his chubby little figure carved at the foot of Christ, asking for salvation, a carving that made it to the twenty-first century. This carving—and, in fact, all Suger's creative endeavors, including his autobiography, were Suger's attempts to be remembered as the creator of Saint-Denis: for example, an inscription in a mosaic over the door, and one on the bronze doors that once read FOR THE SPLENDOR OF THE CHURCH THAT HAS FOSTERED AND EXALTED HIM, SUGER HAS LABORED FOR THE SPLENDOR OF THE CHURCH. I mention this only because it was so unusual in the Middle Ages—a period when neither individualism nor individual accomplishment were considered important—for Suger to want succeeding ages to know he was the creator of Saint-Denis.

While still standing across the plaza, you can see a round window, a so-called rose window. You are looking at the world's first rose window—a circular or wheel-shaped stained-glass window in which divisions of stone tracery radiate out from the center in a petal-like pattern. This rose window is regarded as "one of the great innovations of architectural history." It would become a hallmark of all the great Gothic cathedrals. The stone tracery, which is very simple here, would become increasingly more intricate over the next three hundred years. It was Suger's intention when he created the first rose window at Saint-Denis that jeweled light would shine on the figure of his king, whose throne was placed directly in front of the window on the upper level of the basilica.*

This may also be the first time that stained glass was used for a window in a church. While it is not totally clear what inspired Suger to use stained glass, it is quite clear he already loved stained glass during the year (1121–1122) he spent in the service of the pope in Rome. At that time, Suger visited the workshops of Byzantine jewelers who used stained glass as jewels to decorate reliquaries and Bibles. While in Rome he learned who the best artisans were. Again, in 1137, when Louis the Fat sent him to Poitiers to ensure that the marriage of his pious son Louis to Eleanor of Aquitaine took place, he visited the workshops of the Byzantine jewelers there. It wasn't by chance or luck that when Suger was ready to create the first rose window and the windows of the chevet that the finest workmen were called to Saint-Denis. He writes that his windows were made by the "exquisite hands of many masters from different regions." These same Byzantine jewelers that Suger had assembled to create the windows at Saint-Denis would, when they completed their work, travel, as a group, to each new cathedral as it was being built—Laon in 1160, Notre-Dame de Paris in 1163, Chartres in 1194, and Reims in 1211.

Suger appears to have been the first person to think of using stained glass for large windows. He may have seen church windows that told stories during his time in Normandy, but the glass in those windows was merely painted glass. Glass into which metallic oxides—cobalt

---

* Architectural historian Vincent Scully writes that the intent here was to display the king "as the man of perfect proportions in the circle and the square, thus in touch with the cosmic order of the universe."

oxide for azure blue, copper oxide for green, manganese oxide for purple, manganese dioxide for yellow—were added when the glass was still molten to produce the colored effect had been used as jewels to decorate small precious objects that could be quickly carried away in times of danger, not for large windows, which would be easily broken. When Suger began work on his basilica, he thanked the Lord for providing the "makers of the marvelous windows, a rich supply of sapphire glass, and ready funds" to complete the work. Suger appears to have been cheated by the more sophisticated Byzantine artists he hired. He purchased actual sapphires at their request. They then told him that they ground the jewels up to make the dazzling blues seen in the Tree of Jesse window. The artists, who had been summoned from a far more civilized culture, and who considered the Franks, and their abbot, gullible barbarians, appear to have pocketed the sapphires and then used cobalt to produce the blues.

THERE WAS ANOTHER, philosophical, inspiration for Suger's use of stained-glass windows, one dating back to the time when he was just a young boy. When he first arrived at the Royal Abbey of Saint-Denis, he filled his long hours alone in the archives reading everything from deeds to the writings of St. Denis. The deeds he found—or forged— increased both the wealth of Saint-Denis and Abbot Adam's affection for the peasant boy. However, it was the writings of St. Denis that made him want to bring light into his basilica. He truly loved the St. Denis he came to know in those archives. However, the St. Denis Suger learned to love as a boy was not, as Suger and the monks of the Royal Abbey thought, one man or one saint but the combined biography of three men: two saints and a philosopher. The first was the Athenian Dionysius the Areopagite, who had witnessed the eclipse in the first century that had taken place when Christ died. The second St. Denis was a Parisian bishop by the same name who was decapitated at Montmartre in 250 and supposedly walked five miles to be buried where the abbey was built. The third was a sixth-century Syrian Platonic philosopher, who, while not a saint, also had the same name, Dionysius the Areopagite. This third Denis, an artificer like Suger himself, added a few lines here and there in his writings implying that he not only was a disciple of St. Paul but also had witnessed the eclipse of the sun that had accompanied the death of Christ. Because of these additions, this philosopher's writings were assumed to be the first-century writings of the Athenian St. Denis. In the ninth century, the Byzantine emperor Michael the Stammerer gave these writings to Charlemagne's son, who, thinking they were those of the first-century St. Denis, deposited them in the archives of the abbey where he believed the saint's relics were, and where, in the eleventh century, a precocious young boy found them, and most likely thought that they were the writings of his beloved first century St. Denis.

These writings attribute a mystical meaning to light. It was probably the Syrian philosopher who inspired Suger as an adult to bring light into the Basilica of Saint-Denis. For Suger, the rose window symbolized the eye of God letting in the light, a theme that would be consistent throughout the Age of Cathedrals. That these writings profoundly affected Suger is undeniable because the same phrases that appear in Suger's poetry and other writings—"God, the father of Light" and "the superessential Light" and "emanations of the Light Divine"—are very similar to the phrases used by the Syrian Denis. The philosopher's writings are certainly expressed architecturally here in a way that resulted in the luminous cathedrals that would rise up in France.

I do feel that Suger, much as I have grown to admire him, had to have known the truth about the three Denises by the time he became abbot. It didn't take Peter Abelard long to find out the truth. Abelard, the most famous philosopher and teacher of his age, had sought refuge at the Royal Abbey in 1119, after the terrible denouement of his love affair with his pupil Eloise. He began spending his time in the abbey's archives, where he quickly discovered that the St. Denis who was buried on the spot where the abbey had been built could not have been the same St. Denis who lived at the time of Christ and who was ordered by St. Paul to convert the heathens of France. He announced that the relics being revered at the Royal Abbey as the patron saint of France were those of another, insignificant St. Denis. This saint was a mere bishop of Paris born three centuries too late to have known either Christ or the Apostle Paul. The bones and relics that were attracting a multitude of paying pilgrims, the relics that pilgrims not only traveled to but gave their wealth and land to, the relics that would pay for the building of Suger's new church, were not the bones and relics of the saint who provided the link between Christ, the royal abbey, and the French crown. This revelation struck at the very foundation of a Church in the process of expansion. When Abelard announced his discovery, he was nearly killed by the monks at Saint-Denis, who imprisoned him and called him a "traitor to the whole country."

Thinking about all of this brought me back to current time. If Bob had lived in the twelfth century, he too would probably have been lynched by the monks of Saint-Denis for an observation he made about the patron saint of France. He pointed out that Denis is the French for Dionysus, the name of the Greek god of wine. And that the Basilica of Saint-Denis, long before Paris had expanded into the countryside, had been located in a grape-growing—or wine-producing—region. I had to admit that the god of wine would have made an excellent patron saint of France.

THE DAY BEFORE MY LAST visit to Saint-Denis, I had taken the TGV to Poitiers. While it is the only city reachable by train that has three Romanesque churches, I can't really recommend the trip. I wanted to experience what it would have been like in the twelfth century to visit Saint-Denis, after seeing only Romanesque churches—what it would have been like if I had never been in a Gothic cathedral before. That is precisely the experience I had. In Poitiers the ceilings of the churches I visited were low, the walls were solid, and the naves ended in a solid wall of stone. The churches there were untouched by the Gothic revolution. The next day, when I entered Saint-Denis, it was a startling experience. Instead of entering a low, dark tunnel created by a Romanesque barrel vault, I entered into a high and open nave, filled with light filtered through stained-glass, creating the illusion of sparkling jewels on stone floors. The Romanesque churches had been solid and static. But there was nothing solid or static about Saint-Denis. As the clouds moved across the sun, the basilica was filled with moving shadows and ghostly shapes, giving it a mystical quality. The height of the nave seemed to lift my spirits.

The interior is high because Suger wanted to raise the "ceiling" of his squat Romanesque basilica higher than anyone thought possible. I will never forget reading his simple narrative telling how he carried out his wish. I was struck by both his absolute determination to raise the ceiling and his practical genius in doing so. He needed twelve very tall trees to support the construction he envisioned. He summoned the keepers of the abbey's forests and asked them, as he recalls in his auto-biography, "whether we could find there, no matter how much trouble, any timbers" of the height he wanted. They smiled, he wrote, "or rather would have laughed if they had dared," as though he had asked a silly question, and told him there were no trees that tall. That night the little abbot couldn't sleep and very early the next morning, his measurements in his pocket, he gathered together a hunting party not of the officials who administered the forests but of the woodsmen and carpenters who worked in them. Although he was fifty-seven and no longer a young man, he remained indefatigable. He would not let anything stand in his way—neither the height of trees nor centuries of custom. He searched all day through his forests until he found twelve trees tall enough to support the construction he envisioned.

It was at that precise moment that the Gothic cathedral began to soar. When Suger had traveled to Normandy in 1107, he saw the pointed arch on churches built in Caen. The Normans had used the pointed arch but not structurally in the way Suger would. Realizing that the pointed arch directs the weight of vaults downward, Suger used it struc-turally, creating ribbed vaulting or arches that are constructed separately from and stand out from the vault's main surface, so that the building no longer had to rely on solid walls for support. This was done for the first time in 1144, when Suger created his choir; not only did he cross arches to create vaults, but his ingenious mind conceived of trapezoids and pentagons so that the eastern end of the building seemed to rely on no stone at all for support. The windows of the choir were unobstructed because of the use of this new device—the rib vaults—which would become a common denominator in all Gothic cathedrals that followed. Suger described this choir as "a circular string of chapels, by virtue of which the whole [church] would shine with the wonderful and uninterrupted light of [sixteen] most luminous windows, pervading the interior beauty."

I HAD READ that one of the original stained-glass windows from the twelfth century remained at Saint-Denis—that all the others were destroyed as they were being taken by oxcart to an exhibition—and on my first trip to the dingy little church in the squalid square, there it was before me. It is called the Tree of Jesse window and is still visible to any visitor. The story told in this window is based on lines from the Old Testament: "A shoot shall spring forth from the stem of Jesse, and a flower shall blossom at the summit of that shoot, and on it shall repose the spirit of the Lord." Carvings on Romanesque façades had visually interpreted these lines with a shoot growing out of Jesse's head that blossoms into a horn of oil with which Samuel anoints David—the youngest of Jesse's seven sons. The emphasis in the prior centuries was on telling the Old Testament story of Samuel anointing David.

Suger, however, wanted a different emphasis, for he was promoting the idea of a hereditary king of France. When the Tree of Jesse story appears in the window at Saint-Denis, a dramatic change in the composition has taken place. The emphasis is not on the Old Testament story of Jesse and the anointing of his son David, but on Christ's royal ancestors, the kings of Judah. It was created at a time when the feudal nobility of France felt the king should be elected by them. In the Saint-Denis Jesse window, Jesse is pictured with an actual tree rising out of his navel. On each of the branches is seated one of the kings of Judah, emphasizing their descent from Jesse. The emphasis is on the hereditary nature of the kings of Judah. In addition, each of the kings is sheltered by a large fleur-de-lis, the heraldic symbol of the French monarchy, expressing symbolically a political idea that coincides with the rise of the monarchy. In fact, it is in the late twelfth century that the election of kings begins to fade from memory and the hereditary monarchy, which would dominate French history for the next seven centuries begins to evolve. The populace reading this window, while illiterate, was familiar with biblical stories, and the story they are now reading has a message: monarchy is not an elected office; it is hereditary. Like so much else that Suger did, this device lasted. The window telling the Tree of Jesse story would appear in all of the cathedrals built over the next three hundred years. The image caught on because it was the right image at the right time. The chaos of the feudal world prepared the country for a hereditary king. Of course, it didn't hurt that Capetian kings, for over three hundred years—from 987, when Hugh Capet was elected king, to 1328—always produced an heir. Some historians say it wasn't Suger's policies but the Capetian kings' ability to produce an heir that was the Capetian dynasty's greatest contribution to the strengthening of the monarchy and the stability of France.

AS BOB AND I stood looking at the world's first stained-glass window, I found myself trying to visualize how astounding the dedication ceremony of the Basilica of Saint-Denis must have been on that June day in 1144. King Louis VII and his queen, Eleanor of Aquitaine, and a procession of archbishops and bishops had assembled outside. What must it have been like when Suger's gilded bronze doors were opened for the first time and they walked inside? What must have been their feelings? They didn't find a dark, narrow candlelit nave ending in a wall of stone. Instead they stepped into a nave flooded with the mystical light that came from stained-glass windows, like windows they had never seen. As the procession of bishops made their way to a golden altar encrusted with "hyacinths, rubies, sapphires, emeralds and topazes, and large pearls," upon which sat enameled reliquaries and a matchless chalice, made from a solid piece of agate [sardonyx], they walked on sparkling floors of brightly colored glass mosaic tiles [tesserae]. The jewels, the gold, the mosaic tiles, all would have caught the morning light from the sun as it streamed through sixteen of the largest stained-glass windows ever made and filled the "circular string of chapels" beyond the golden altar. It was for the radiating chapels, Suger's choir, each filled with walls of glass, that Suger had searched his forests for trees tall enough to raise his ceiling to heaven. Suger, who thought of everything, for whom every detail had to be perfect, had timed the ceremony so that as the members of the procession walked toward the altar, they were walking toward the sunlight that was rising in the east.

Saint-Denis's influence was immediate and profound. Archbishops and bishops, awed by the height and beauty of his basilica, went back and rebuilt their cathedrals higher and in more beautiful ways. (Many bishops had an "accidental" fire that destroyed their old Romanesque cathedrals, thus requiring immediate reconstruction.)

During the course of the Age of Cathedrals, for three hundred years, from 1144 to the early fifteenth century, society, which for so long had been static, began to change. If you retrace the route taken by the Byzantine jewelers as they proceeded to each new cathedral as it was being built, you can see the changes taking place in society mirrored in the art of the Gothic cathedrals you visit. You will see the religious symbolism of art gradually decrease and artistic virtuosity become increasingly more important as the accomplishments of the individual become more important. You will see the change in the medieval world in the growth of cities such as Laon, Chartres, Reims, Rouen, Tours, and Paris as the people of France began moving from rural areas to urban areas. You will see the beginning of guilds and the middle class in the windows of these cathedrals that guilds endowed at Laon, Chartres, and Rouen. Then, finally, as you walk along wonderfully restored, ancient streets in Tours, you can see where, after centuries of traveling, the descendants of the Byzantine jewelers finally settled down in the fifteenth century.

It was in the fifteenth century, after the Italian Renaissance was brought to France, that the name Gothic was contemptuously applied to this wondrous art of the cathedrals to imply that it was a style worthy only of the Goths—the Germanic barbarians who despoiled the ancient world of Greece and Rome. During the reign of Louis XIV, Suger's symbolic rose window, with its "Eye of God," became, at the Cathedral of Orléans, the Sun King's face, framed with the symbol of the sun. Written below his face was the Sun King's motto: NEC PLURIBUS IMPAR

(ABOVE ALL MEN). But by this time, Suger's concept of the king, that "the King should do no wrong," a concept that endeared Suger to me and the king to the people of France, had spread beyond the border of his years, and had become by the time of Louis XIV a not-so-lovable concept that "the King *can* do no wrong."

SITTING ON THE TRAIN returning to our apartment after our first visit to Saint-Denis, Bob told me that even if he had known nothing of its history, or the man responsible for its construction, seeing the Renaissance tombs of the Kings of France would alone have been worth the twenty-minute Métro trip. For me, however, seeing the carving of the chubby little abbot on the façade of Saint-Denis made the trip quite poignant. I knew Suger had had himself carved on the façade so that I, ten centuries later, would know that he was the creator of Saint-Denis, would know he had brought all the elements of the Gothic cathedral together for the first time. He had wanted me, a visitor from the future, to know how, with this church, he had transformed cathedrals from something centuries old into something new. I was sorry his basilica was not as he had left it: that all the jewels and enamels he had finagled from princes were gone; that his fabulous chalice was in a museum across the ocean, in Washington, D.C.; that his original stained-glass windows were at Cluny; that his statue columns were dispersed; and that his neighborhood was such a mess. He wanted so much to be remembered for the glorious church he had created. But he got his wish as far as I was concerned. I knew, having seen Saint-Denis, that I would always remember him that way.

CHAPTER 2

LAON
Early Gothic

—

Train from Gare du Nord to Laon

*H*ISTORICALLY, THE TRIP TO THE WALLED MEDIEVAL CITY OF
Laon fits naturally and beautifully into any chronological tour of France.
In fact, at Laon, a time traveler can stop in at practically any century. It
was the city the Celts, sometime before the first century B.C., named
after Loucetios, their god of light. The Romans later fortified it with
walls to check the invasions of the Franks, Burgundians, Vandals, and
Huns between 400 and 600 A.D., and Loucetios became their god of
lightning and of war. It was the city the Carolingians made their capital
in 888. It was then the city Hugh Capet, the first Capetian king, chose
to be the center of his kingdom in the tenth century, when, with the help
of the Catholic Church, he replaced the descendants of Charlemagne
as the ruler of the Franks. And more important for the tourist, it is here,
on a dramatic site over 600 feet above the surrounding chalky plains of
Picardy, that an early Gothic cathedral was built in 1230 that became
one of the great intellectual centers of France and is today the perfect
cathedral to visit to see the transition from the Romanesque style to the
Gothic. Because so much of the Basilica of Saint-Denis has not survived, Laon is a much better place for the traveler through time to see
that transition.

The first time I took the train to Laon, it was raining and I came alone. Bob would not be arriving in France for another week, and having read so much about spectacular Laon, I couldn't wait even another day to see it. Like Hugh Capet in 991, who at first had made Laon his capital city and then shortly thereafter packed up and took his archives to Paris, I too, after a few soggy hours of walking around the town, wanted to return to Paris. Perhaps my expectations were too high. I had read that its early Gothic cathedral rose dramatically from a mountaintop, where it sat like an acropolis. That it was "a mountain with its crown of towers silhouetted against the sky." I envisioned a town that was a combination of Carcassonne, Loches, and Angers. In the pouring rain, it was none of those.

My train from the Paris Nord station had taken an hour and thirty-five minutes to travel the eighty-four miles from Paris. There are direct trains practically every hour from Paris to Laon, taking about one hour and thirty-five minutes, but there are also trains requiring a change of trains, so it is best to check the schedule at sncf.com. When I arrived at Laon, the rain was so heavy I could barely make out a misty apparition of a cathedral sitting upon its mountain acropolis. I could see no towers, no donjons, no crenellated walls, no machicolations, from below. I have to admit the ride on the Poma, a six-seat cable car that went straight up the mountain, 656 feet, from lower Laon to upper (or older) Laon, was fun. All the way up, the cathedral dominated my view, but when I left the tram, it had disappeared and I couldn't find it or the tourist office on the plaza facing it. As I wandered about in the rain, I came to a medieval gateway called the Porte des Chenizelles, which once commanded one of the four main routes leading out of the town. Two other gateways, the Porte d'Ardon, which once led to a Carolingian royal palace, and the Porte de Soissons, which is guarded on each side by two somber, twelfth-century towers, are more impressive fortifications. The attraction of this gateway, a panoramic view of the valley below, was nonexistent in the rain. I followed the sign but saw no panorama, only an ocean of gray through the rain. As for the medieval Porte itself, I was not very impressed.

I asked someone for directions to the cathedral and felt rather foolish when I was told it was around the corner from where I was standing. Entering a very gloomy cathedral, I sat down and read my Green Michelin and the brochures I had picked up at the tourist office.

Two weeks later, I returned to Laon, this time on a sunny day and with Bob. I have a new axiom. Before saying you hate a town that you have seen alone and in the rain, "Return on a sunny day with someone you love." Or, at the very least, come to Laon only on a sunny day.

When I returned to Laon with Bob, I was prepared to hate the place. But the sun was shining when we arrived. This time we could see all five cathedral towers from the station below. Bob, standing at the foot of the mountain and looking up at the cathedral, thought the view was spectacular. I wanted to hit him when he quoted the same book I had read that had described Laon as "a mountain with its crown of towers silhouetted in the sky." The ride up on the Poma, which is right outside the train station and seems to leave every five minutes, was as much fun as a roller coaster, but I still wasn't prepared to love Laon.

We entered the cathedral together. It is one of the oldest Gothic cathedrals in France, built in 1230, after a fire destroyed the earlier Romanesque cathedral. This fire was not like those that destroyed most other Romanesque cathedrals; in this case the citizens of Laon, a hundred years before, had set fire to the bishop's palace, and the fire had spread, destroying the entire town in the process. The spark that provoked this fire was part of a larger trend in France, one that might interest a traveler through history. Agricultural advances in the eleventh century had allowed large numbers of peasants to settle in cities that had for so long been only places of refuge or centers for religious celebrations. By the twelfth century a new merchant class had slowly begun to develop, and the cloth merchants of Laon had begun to trade with the outside world—with Scandinavian and Italian merchants in particular. It was the new merchant class of Laon that set this fire. Guilbert de Nogent, a citizen of Laon who witnessed the events that took place that day, related what had happened. During the absence of their bishop in 1115, the people of Laon arranged with King Louis the Fat to set up a commune. (The creation of communes throughout France, you will recall, had been Suger's idea to extend the power of the king.) The

King granted the citizens the right to "pay their usual due of servitude to their lords once only in the year, and to make good any breach of the laws they have committed by payment fixed by law." At Laon the feudal lord was also the bishop. When the bishop returned and learned how his power had been diminished, he bribed Louis the Fat to annul the rights recently granted to the commune. When the people learned that the compact with the king had been broken, they attacked, according to Guilbert de Nogent; and the "bishop" fled "to the vault of the church and hid himself in a cask." The citizens seized one of the bishop's pages and "learned from the traitor's nod where to look for him. . . . Entering the vaults therefore, and searching everywhere, at last they found him. And as he piteously implored them, ready to take oath that he would henceforth cease to be their Bishop, that he would give them unlimited riches, that he would leave the country, and they with hardened hearts jeered at him, one named Bernard lifting his battle-axe brutally dashed out the brains of that sacred, though sinner's head."

Since the merchants, in particular the wealthy cloth merchants, won back their rights, there were no hard feelings toward the new bishop or toward the cathedral for whose construction they liberally contributed. While the merchants of Laon helped build the church, as did merchants and guild members in each city where the new cathedrals were being built, their problems were not over. King Philip VI, in 1331, a century after the cathedral was completed, rescinded the rights of the commune.

On my first visit to Laon, I had not been very impressed with its cathedral. I had hardly noticed the changes that had taken place in church design since Suger had built Saint-Denis, but on our second trip, Bob did. I had failed to see why it was historically illuminating, but as I sat there with Bob, he pointed out the square lantern dome— the symbol of heaven—over the crossing in the center of the cathedral, which I hadn't noticed on my first trip. With the light shining on the rounded Romanesque arches in the gallery, we were both taken with their beauty. Bob's reaction to the beauty of the nave was so spontaneous and visceral, as it always is to things of beauty, that it proved infectious. As we sat together in the nave, I also noticed that there was far more light coming into the cathedral than at Saint-Denis and that light was pouring into the nave through stained-glass windows not only from aisle windows but in through windows in the clerestory level as well—a fourth story had been added to the nave, which added not only light, but also height. At Saint-Denis there had only been three stories. Romanesque churches had a single barrel vault. I had to admit that Laon's cathedral was the perfect place to visit to see the transition between the Romanesque and Gothic cathedrals. On a rainy day, Notre-Dame de Laon had been rather gloomy and the cathedral had left me flat, but now, seeing it in the sunlight, I could feel the upward pull of its soaring height as I was filled with strong aesthetic and religious emotions. The cathedral at Laon needed the sun to really be appreciated, to illuminate how light was used to revolutionize French architecture. In the sun, the cathedral at Laon was radiant.

Before returning to Paris, we had lunch at a brasserie across from the cathedral so we could look at the façade as we ate. As we sat there, I noticed for the first time that the two baronial towers above the façade had a peculiar herd of carved oxen, twisting out of openings and peeking out here and there. Remembering that cathedrals were books for the illiterate populace, I searched for and found a legend that explained why these oxen were carved on the tower. When the cathedral was being built, the oxen carrying the stones up the mountainside to the plateau understandably dropped from exhaustion, and fresh oxen miraculously appeared to replace them. Now from their perch on two of the five towers of the cathedral, they appear, like the bulls of pagan myths that were endowed with magical powers, to be watching over the city.

It is a good idea to contact the tourist office in Laon before you go and arrange to take one of their guided tours of the town. I recommend the one that will take you to the cathedral and then along cobbled streets to the twelfth-century Hôtel-Dieu, the oldest Gothic hospital in France. It also includes a visit to the early-twelfth-century Chapel of the Knights Templar—an intriguing octagonal structure, designed to echo the Church of the Holy Sepulchre in Jerusalem, as do most chapels built by the Knights Templar. On our train back to Paris, I compared my two trips to Laon and concluded that this city named after the Celtic god of light should only be visited on a sunny day. On a sunny day you are aware that medieval Laon perfectly evokes that transitional time in history when the twelfth century becomes the thirteenth and Romanesque architecture becomes Gothic. Looking at Laon from below, it appears to be typical of the walled cities built by the Romans on escarpments overlooking a river. Its many towers evoke today a time when a city was still a fortress, an administrative and religious center. Because of its location on the top of a mountain, when you first see the cathedral from below, you feel today an evocation of the time when Laon was a medieval fortress of God, a place to which people came in search of refuge or a celebration of religious rights. Laon both evokes the unchanging world of the isolated abbeys and churches that existed during the Romanesque period and anticipates the coming of the Gothic cathedral, a time when change would be accepted. The Gothic cathedral was the creation of the emerging merchant class. The cultural advances made by civilizations in the south had only just begun to reach the shores of southern France in the twelfth century. By the thirteenth century, Laon's merchants had begun to trade with those distant countries and feel the impact of the changes taking place. Freed from the yoke of their feudal lords for two centuries, they used their profits to build a glorious cathedral here. But not as glorious as the cathedral that would be built at Chartres, where we go next.

CHAPTER 3

CHARTRES
The High Gothic Cathedral at Chartres

—

Train from Gare Montparnasse to Chartres

THE TRIP TO CHARTRES IS UNMITIGATED PLEASURE FROM THE moment you arrive and see the gleaming white cathedral in its perfect setting, with its two towers—one somber and Romanesque, the other graceful and flamboyant—architecturally spanning the Age of Cathedrals from 1134 to 1513. Aesthetic pleasure increases as you enter the cathedral, which is dappled with the filtered, jeweled light from 27,000 square feet of stained-glass windows. You feel your spirit pulled heavenward in the soaring nave of France's first High Gothic cathedral, a pull so strong that as I stood there I longed to believe in Chartre's saints and miracles, to be a part of the spiritual beauty all around me, rather than inspecting it with my binoculars. And, finally, there is the sensual pleasure of having a heavenly provincial lunch in any one of the many gracious restaurants that welcome tourists no matter how badly they pronounce the items on the menu.

The train trip to Chartres takes less than an hour from the Gare Montparnasse, and once you arrive, it is a short, pleasant walk to the cathedral. If you are lucky, as I was on my last trip, Malcolm Miller, a tall, thin scholar who has been giving tours of Chartres in English for over forty years, will still be there to guide you through the cathedral, telling you its history (with snide but hilarious comments about various kings and bishops), explaining the stories depicted in the stained-glass windows, and interpreting the symbolism of the statues and friezes. If he is not there, you can buy one of his books and tour the cathedral while reading his comments—purged, unfortunately, of his humor and bitter sarcasm.

Whereas at Saint-Denis artists and craftsmen were experimenting with new materials, new methods of construction, and new ideas, at Chartres they got everything just right. And over the centuries, unlike other cathedrals, it remained just right despite wars, revolution, and restoration. The result, today, for me, or, I guess for any visitor who has ever been there on a sunny day, is simply the most perfect place to visit the Age of Cathedrals. There remains, of course, the temptation to seek some undiscovered place, unspoiled by vast numbers of tourists; however, after visiting the great cathedrals of France, both Bob and I agree that if you have time to travel to only one Gothic cathedral, it should be the High Gothic Cathedral of Notre-Dame de Chartres.

Even the large number of tourists at Chartres is an advantage. Like Versailles, which also is burdened by masses of tourists, Chartres has a large number of excellent restaurants that the tourists help support. I can heartily recommend two, La Vieille Maison and Le Buisson Ardent. While *La Belle France* preferred La Vieille Maison, which, they noted, "Chartres residents had singled out as the best restaurant in town," I was charmed by the old beamed ceilings and the head waiter at Le Buisson Ardent, who ignored my abominable French accent and steered me to a delicious leek-and-frogs-leg soup that, I am ashamed to admit, I will remember as long as I will remember the cathedral's stained-glass windows. But in contrast to Versailles, where the masses of tourists create serpentine lines outside the palace and dense masses of people inside, the crowds at Chartres are never overwhelming.

While Suger had to use every devious device at his disposal to convince his monks at Saint-Denis that their ancient, dilapidated, but sacred basilica should be torn down and rebuilt, the bishop of Chartres had no such problems. A convenient fire in 1194—the last of several—destroyed those parts of the old cathedral the bishop no longer wanted. He must have had good taste. The twelfth-century royal, or western façade, a masterpiece of artistic and intellectual design, and the Carolingian crypt below, with its ninth-century murals, remained untouched.

The history that follows that fire is fascinating, and knowing the details helps us to understand the unquestioning religious beliefs of the people who built this cathedral. During the first few days after the fire, the people of Chartres were reluctant to heed their bishop's pleas to contribute to the building of a new cathedral. They were inconsolable in their grief, believing that the Sancta Camisia—the sacred tunic thought to have been worn by Mary when she gave birth to Christ— had been destroyed in the fire. Long thought by its citizens to have protected their city from harm, the Camisia had been given to Chartres by the Carolingian Emperor Charles the Bald in 876. Thirty-five years later, in 911, when the Viking raider Rollo (from whom William the Conqueror was descended) was making his way toward Chartres, raping, pillaging, and devastating France as he went, the bishop placed the tunic on the city ramparts. When Rollo, instead of leveling their city, turned north before reaching it, converted to Christianity, and settled in Normandy, never to raid again, the citizens of Chartres believed their city had been protected by their Camisia. (Actually it is more likely that Rollo's about-face was influenced instead by the timely intervention of the Carolingian emperor.) Charles the Simple gave Rollo the duchy of Normandy in exchange for his allegiance to the emperor and a promise to cease his annual raid through France. From then until the time of the fire, the city, the cult of Mary, and the cult of the tunic prospered, as Chartres became a popular stop for pilgrims who attended one of the four annual fairs held in the cloister, or visited the shrine of the Queen of Heaven on their way south to the three great pilgrimage destinations Santiago de Compostela, Rome, and Jerusalem.

FOR THREE DAYS after the fire of 1194, the citizens of Chartres believed Mary's tunic had burned in the fire and that their city had lost her protection. Many, in fact, were preparing to leave and settle elsewhere. Then a procession of priests, led by the bishop, marched through the town. They were miraculously carrying the tunic. It had, they said, survived the fire because it was untouched in the Carolingian crypt beneath the choir. This was, of course, interpreted as a sign from Mary that better accommodations were needed to house her tunic.

The result, less than thirty years later, was the new cathedral that was the true miracle of Chartres. There are times when a new style of architecture so fits the changing culture and economics of the day that it creates a veritable explosion that spreads out from a core, just as Gothic architecture emerged from Saint-Denis. But while the elements of the new architecture were first seen at Saint-Denis, the inspiration that ignited the explosion can no longer be seen or felt by a visitor going there.

Chartres is different and becomes a milestone event in this book's tour of French history. Its construction began in the twelfth century just as Saint-Denis was being completed, and possessed even then, as it does today, a total harmony of composition. It was built so perfectly that today its walls are still without a crack. It is quite remarkable, but you can still see and feel the religious energy that made that explosion take place. It is as though it were built at the very moment in time when the deep religious spirit of the Age of Faith was most profound.

The timing of its construction was crucial. The architectural problems in the building of huge cathedrals had just been solved, and cathedral ceilings and towers, for the most part, had stopped collapsing—although at Beauvais, a town just north of Paris, the architects never stopped their cathedral's ceiling from collapsing—and the sculptures and stained-glass windows were the artistic manifestations of ideas and deep religious beliefs that were still dominant in the hearts of men. These symbolic motifs were fresh at Chartres and expressed the religious consciousness of the day. They had not become stale with repetition as they would when applied to façade after façade, in cathedral after cathedral, over the next three hundred years, by artists and craftsmen who eventually were unaware of the symbolism and concepts that originally inspired their creation. In fact, motifs rich in religious symbolism in the twelfth century would become merely decorative by the fifteenth.

A trip to Chartres illuminates for us so much of what was taking place at this time. Monasteries, which had ushered in the twelfth-century renaissance with their agricultural revolution, declined in importance, both politically and as centers of learning. During the Age of Cathedrals, they were replaced by cathedral schools in the cities. It is significant that the cathedral at Chartres was built not only at a time when cathedral schools were replacing monasteries as centers of learning, but also at that very moment in time when the university at Chartres was the intellectual center of France—before it was overshadowed by the university at Paris. When its west façade was conceived in 1145, Chartres was the center of the classical revival in the twelfth century; and those influencing the sculptural design at Chartres were the best minds of the day. Most people, including the aristocracy, were illiterate in the twelfth and thirteenth centuries, and books were expensive and rare. Victor Hugo, who knew his French history, would write in *Notre-Dame de Paris*: "In the Middle Ages men had no great thought that they did not write down in stone." If you stop to consider the implications of that statement as well as another that Hugo wrote—"The Gothic sun set behind the colossal press at Mainz"—you realize that the cathedral was, for three hundred years, until books were printed, a book to its people. It was the cathedral's stained-glass windows and sculptures that told the stories of the Bible, that related the lives of saints. The windows expressed the ideas that concerned contemporary society, and appealed to people on so many different levels. Once you look at the cathedral as a book written in stone, it becomes obvious how very important it was that the best minds of the day were expressing their thoughts in the stones at Chartres. At Saint-Denis the statue columns of the kings and many of the carvings—which once had symbolic meaning for the twelfth-century worshiper—were destroyed during the Revolution. We can no longer see many of the ideas expressed there in stone, but we can at Chartres.

Chartres is historically significant in other ways. The classical revival there was part of a larger movement in Europe called Scholasticism, which sought to use human reason, the philosophy of Aristotle and Plato, to understand the Christian revelations. In part, this classical revival took place at Chartres because of the city's incredible wealth. Fulbert, who was the first great teacher to found a cathedral school, would later become bishop of Chartres. This meant that Fulbert suddenly became an incredibly wealthy man, since the bishop's annual income in the tenth century from grain harvests and silver mines alone was $7,600,714 (in 2007 dollars). He used this wealth to create a library at Chartres containing classical Latin writers and those few—very few—Greek writers who had been translated into French.* Bernard, a neo-Platonist philosopher who was Abelard's teacher, and Bernard's younger brother Thierry, were leading intellectuals in the early twelfth century. The brothers were both chancellors at Fulbert's cathedral school of Chartres when the design for the right portal of the western façade was being conceived. It is their thoughts we can read today, "written in stone," on the right portal of the western façade.† Unlike previous Catholic theologians, they were classical scholars who found the pagan classical heritage compatible with the teachings of the Church. Bernard's belief was that the Christian "dwarf" had to first digest and assimilate the teachings of the ancient world in order to go beyond those teachings and understand Divine Wisdom. He would write: "We are like dwarfs seated on the shoulders of giants, thus we see more things than the ancients." Thierry compiled a book entitled the *Heptateuchon*, which was basically an encyclopedia of the seven liberal arts.

It is no coincidence that these arts, which Thierry and Bernard believed were essential to learn before man could come to understand Divine Wisdom, are depicted in the archivolt (decorative moldings) framing Divine Wisdom in the tympanum of the right portal of the cathedral's west façade. Here at Chartres, since the façade was being built in the twelfth century, pagan philosophers—the great men of antiquity—are given a monument in stone. By the thirteenth century, you can see if you look at a window in the transept at Chartres that the scholastic attempt to reconcile classical learning with religion had already been crushed by the Church. Here the ancient scholars representing rea-

* In France at this time, no one was able to translate Greek—perhaps resulting in the expression, "It's all Greek to me."

† This façade of 1145, which still exists, replaced Fulbert's façade of 1030, which was destroyed by fire. The façade built in 1145 remains, but another fire in 1194 destroyed the rest of the cathedral, which was rebuilt in 1195 and employed the same artists assembled by Suger.

son have been replaced by four prophets—Isaiah, Ezekiel, Daniel, and Jeremiah—who now carry four evangelists on their shoulders— SS. Matthew, John, Mark, and Luke—the implication being that the evangelists can go beyond the teachings of the prophets. The meaning of Bernard's original phrase is recaptured by Sir Isaac Newton, in 1675,* at the beginning of the Age of Enlightenment when he says: "If I have seen further than others, it was only by standing upon the shoulders of giants." (By our century, this was no longer a concept expressing the search for religious or scientific truth but a catchy phrase inserted by Hillary Clinton's speechwriters for a commencement address; she told a Harvard medical school graduating class that "they would 'stand on the shoulders' of their illustrious forerunners.")

Just as the concept underlying Bernard's phrase ("we are like dwarfs . . .") was altered by the beliefs of succeeding ages, the culture in which we live circumscribes what we see when we try to read the twelfth-century thoughts Bernard and Thierry expressed on the west façade of Chartres—but it is not impossible to read their thoughts.

As we looked at the tympanum over the right entrance on the west façade, Christ is sitting enthroned on the lap of the Virgin. In the context of the architectural composition of the right door, Christ is Divine Wisdom incarnate, the source of human wisdom. The Virgin and Christ are surrounded by the seven liberal arts (each personified by a "giant") that Bernard and Thierry considered indispensable for human wisdom and whose works "serve the purpose of understanding Christ, the Wisdom of the Lord." Bob and I stood there and tried to puzzle out who the men were that Bernard and Thierry considered "giants" and whose images are carved here. Frankly, only a few of the carvings were immediately discernible without the guidebook or a guide: Cicero (Rhetoric), Aristotle (Dialectic), Euclid (Geometry), Boethius (Arithmetic), Ptolemy (Astronomy), and Priscanus (Grammar).

It is not only medieval philosophy but medieval political ideas that can be read in the sculptures of the west façade at Chartres. As you stand looking at the west façade, you will see statues of kings

---

* Letter from Sir Isaac Newton to Robert Hooke, 1675.

and queens. When I first saw them, I was rather puzzled. Since it was called the royal portal, I assumed they were the Kings of France. Not so. They are the kings and queens of Judah. But I was not the first to make such a mistake. The kings that surrounded the portals at Saint-Denis were mistaken for the Kings of France during the Revolution and decapitated. The same fate befell the kings in the gallery of Notre-Dame in Paris. For some reason, the statues of the kings at Chartres were spared. The kings of Judah were sculpted in the royal portal because each statue column is the personification of a quality medieval society wanted their kings to have. In 1108, at the coronation ceremony of Louis the Fat, for example, the priest asked God that he be "strengthened by the faith of Abraham, equipped with the clemency of Moses, fortified with the strength of Joshua, exalted by the humility of David and adorned with the wisdom of Solomon." The statue column of Solomon at Chartres is the personification of the wisdom medieval society wanted Louis VI to have.

Not all Chartres's column statues are kings. There are prophets and priests as well to indicate the desirability of harmony between Church and State or, as Suger wrote, the "unity of the kingship and priesthood . . . because he who provides for the other helps himself."

Before the twelfth century, the Catholic Church was the unifying power of Europe, with the pope at the head of a vast network of monasteries and bishoprics. Now, as Chartres was being built, nationalism in France was just beginning to evolve: a national king was an idea in the making. The monarchy was aided in its expansion by French bishops who preferred to ally themselves with a weak king rather than a strong pope. This is precisely what you see reflected in the sculptures of the royal portal: a shift in the balance of power from Catholic Church to monarchy from the twelfth to the thirteenth century.

When the statue columns of the door jambs were completed in the twelfth century, Chartres was outside the royal realm: the statue columns are balanced between Judean kings, queens, and prophets, indicating a desire for harmony between Church and State. Harmony between Church and State was uppermost in the mind of Ivo, the twelfth-century bishop of Chartres, who devised a compromise with the pope that allowed the King of France to bestow temporal, but not spiritual, power on newly elected church officials, to give them "the worldly possession of the church but not the insignia" of their office. This compromise, which gave the king the power to invest a bishop with temporal position but not with religious authority, saved France from the useless struggles over investiture that plagued the Holy Roman Emperor (who wanted the right to invest Church officials with both sacred and temporal powers). It was Bishop Ivo's compromise that formed the basis of the Concordat of Worms, in 1122, which finally ended the conflict between the emperor and the pope.

The statue columns on the door jambs on the west façade were carved over many years and still echo the changes taking place in society during the twelfth century. The earliest statue columns—at the right portal—are the most elongated, and the most idealized, showing the least human emotion. They barely emerge from the stone. They are squeezed into stone columns, with arms straitjacketed at their sides and with faces that stare out at you seemingly in surprise. The statue columns of the center—the last to be sculpted—are the most humanized. And if you walk around the cathedral, and examine statue columns created in the thirteenth century, you will see that unlike the frontality of the twelfth-century statues, the statues here have more freedom of movement in their friezes and more freedom from their columns: heads are turning and tilted and show emotion; arms break the circumference of the column—in fact, you are no longer aware that the statues are part of the column. At first the emotion of statues has both a confessional and spiritual quality, then the statues become more and more sensual. (If you really get caught up in the changes taking place in Gothic sculpture, as I did, you might want to take a trip to Reims and see the laughing angels, the most sensual of all the medieval statues, and, for me, the most enigmatic.)

As the monarchy becomes more powerful, the statues become more sensual and the number of statues of kings increases, until, with the signing of the Concordat of Bologna in 1516, the King of France has complete control over the Church of France and Suger's concept of the king as a vassal and protector of the Church is completely reversed, the clergy becoming a "docile instrument of the monarchy."

When this happens, as you'll see in later chapters, it is time to stop visiting cathedrals and visit instead the palaces and châteaux of the Kings of France, since it is no longer Church architecture that expresses the soul of France but the palaces of the kings. Atop the royal château at Chambord, for example, Francis I placed a fleur-de-lis above the lantern dome that was the church's symbol of heaven to announce in stone what the pope had just conceded in the Concordat of Bologna: that the king controlled the church in France.

CHARTRES'S WINDOWS AND sculptures not only inform us of contemporary ideas, but also of daily life at the time it was built. We can see the beginning of the middle class depicted in these windows.

Because of the impact of the agricultural revolution of the eleventh century, not as many peasants were needed on farms and some had moved to Chartres. Over the years, some had been transformed into wealthy burghers. By the thirteenth century, they were filled with gratitude and deep religious devotion to Mary, whom they believed had protected their city and made them wealthy. The medieval tradesmen and merchants expressed this gratitude by paying for forty-four stained-glass windows, each of which has a medallion showing which guild or trade gave the window. We can see in each medallion a man, frozen in time, carrying out his trade: a vintner pruning his vine, a baker (baker's shovel) carrying a basket of bread, a fishmonger holding up a fish for a customer, a money changer bent over a bench piled with coins and scales, a wheelwright constructing a wooden wheel, a blacksmith shoeing a horse, a carpenter shaping wood, a butcher selling meat while a pig's carcass hangs from a nail, a furrier showing a fur-lined cape to a woman of the aristocracy.

France was still a feudal society in the thirteenth century, as these windows clearly depict. Showing the other side of feudalism, there are forty-four windows given by the nobility that show the position and power they held in France at the time. If you go from window to window with your binoculars—which I highly recommend you bring to Chartres—you will see not only their gratitude to Mary, but an entire picture of medieval life in Chartres in the twelfth and thirteenth centuries. In addition to the windows, sculptures also provide us with a picture of daily life in the thirteenth century. As you continue, take your binoculars and examine the zodiac on the northern entrance, where you will find medieval life described in stone. Each month has a single figure carrying out the task that would take place. For example, in March, when the wind is still cold, a peasant wears his winter cloak and hood; in April the peasant is carrying an ear of corn to symbolize the crop growing at this season; in May a knight has a falcon on his wrist because this is the month the nobility held their tournaments before going off to war (fighting stopped during the winter months); in July the peasant is cutting the corn with his sickle; in August the harvest continues. These tableaux are extraordinary in that they show the effects of the seasons in medieval life: the cyclical nature of time during the Middle Ages.

What you cannot see is how integral a part of the daily life the cathedral was for these medieval townspeople. The cathedral was where communions, marriages, and funerals were held; where passion plays were presented; where craftsmen and workmen waited to be hired. Outside the cathedral's southern portal, in its cloister, merchants erected stands during the four annual fairs celebrating the life of Mary, which attracted pilgrims from all over Europe and made the people of Chartres wealthy. During these fairs, food and wine were permitted to be sold inside the cathedral so that the merchants could avoid the taxes levied by the Count of Chartres on goods sold outside.

Chartres is considered one of the great wonders of the world for a reason. There are 176 windows containing no fewer than 27,000 square feet of stained glass here. And they are all original. Each of them tells a story from either the Bible or the life of a saint. While you won't be in Chartres long enough to examine all the windows, you might take a look at the Tree of Jesse window and compare it with the one we saw at Saint-Denis. It is one of the three twelfth-century lancet (narrow, pointed) windows of the royal façade and is considered to be the finest stained-glass window in France. It was made by the same Byzantine craftsmen who created the Tree of Jesse window at Saint-Denis, but unlike the window there, it has never needed restoration. It is today like the jewels that these expert craftsmen, jewelers really, placed on the reliquaries they had been making before Suger summoned them to Paris. The first thing you notice are the luminous colors—colors intensified by the sapphire-blue background, the same sapphire blue that was used in the original windows at Saint-Denis. Looking at the color here, you can understand why Suger believed the jewelers when they told him the blue was made from crushed sapphires. Even without understanding the political symbolism of the window—the idea that the office of king is hereditary—it is utterly breathtaking to behold. It was color and harmony of colors that were the primary concerns of the twelfth-century artist—not the linear design or naturalism of the artists in later centuries.

However, it was not only the colors in the Tree of Jesse window that caught my interest, but its composition. As at Saint-Denis, Jesse is asleep, with a tree rising out of his navel. On each of the branches are the crowned kings of Judah, sheltered on each side by the leaves of the tree, which have taken on the heraldic form of the fleur-de-lis, the French royal symbol in the twelfth century.[*] At Chartres you can see the window as Suger originally described it so many centuries before.

Malcolm Miller, who has been enriching the lives of tourists who follow him about the cathedral, has also written an excellent guidebook on the windows of Chartres. With it and a pair of binoculars, you will be able to enjoy the stories being told in each of the windows. However, on my last trip to Chartres, my beloved tour guide failed me. When our little tour group arrived at the nave, we found, instead of rows of chairs for us to sit in, a large number of white-robed people who looked as though they had dropped out of the sky, drugged, from the 1960s. They appeared to be in some sort of trance as they moved, on their knees, along the meandering path of a labyrinth inlaid on the floor of the nave. The circular labyrinth, divided into four quadrants, is com-

* Legend has it that Clovis, the first Frankish king to convert to Christianity, either put a fleur-de-lis in his helmet when he went to battle or that the Virgin Mary presented him with a fleur-de-lis at his baptism.

posed of twelve rings, which loop twenty-eight times in a meandering path, eventually leading to a central rosette. Since it occupied almost the entire width of the nave, it was difficult to get around them or ignore them. I confess I had been to Chartres any number of times without having noticed the existence of the labyrinth before, and wouldn't have noticed it this time if they hadn't taken up so much of the center of the cathedral. I naturally asked Mr. Miller the meaning of the labyrinth and what these people were doing. He dismissed both my questions with a crotchety "It's the summer solstice," perhaps because it was an afternoon tour and he was tired, or perhaps because they were occupying the space where we usually sat and listened to his pronouncements on Chartres. In any case, he couldn't be bothered with an additional explanation. The questions of what the labyrinth was doing on the floor in the center of the nave, and why on June 21—the longest day of the year, when the sun appears to stand still—the white-robed figures were wearing out the menisci of their knees, continued to puzzle me.

As I became more and more involved with the Gothic temperament and Gothic cathedrals, I wanted to know the connection between the summer solstice and the labyrinth. The answer was found not in any of my books on architecture or history but on the Web. There I learned that these people were taking a symbolic pilgrimage, an ancient ritual walk, to the sites in the Holy Land to meet Jesus. Walking the meandering course of the labyrinth symbolizes for the adult his pilgrimage on earth with all its false turnings—there are no dead ends in the labyrinth at Chartres—as the adult symbolically takes the wrong paths of life but eventually reaches the center. By walking the labyrinth with others, we are reminded that we are all on the path together. The labyrinth was placed at the western entrance of the cathedral so it could symbolize our first steps on our spiritual journey.

On our way back to Paris, remembering our lovely day and lunch, Bob and I agreed that if you have time to travel to only one Gothic cathedral, it should be Chartres. Chartres was a book for the illiterate medieval worshipers who prayed there that can be read and enjoyed today, relating what medieval society was like in the twelfth and thirteenth centuries. To make it a perfect day, the trip to Chartres should perhaps be followed in the evening by a concert back in Paris at the Rayonnant chapel of Sainte-Chapelle. At Sainte-Chapelle the evening will be as magical as the day, as you listen to medieval music, entirely surrounded by walls of stained glass.

If, however, you want to follow the development of the Gothic cathedral, your next stop should be the cathedral at Reims, where the Kings of France were crowned.

CHAPTER 4

The CORONATION CEREMONY
at the
CATHEDRAL of REIMS

—

Train from Gare de l'Est to Reims

T HE GARE DE L'EST, WHERE ONE CATCHES THE TGV TO REIMS, is startlingly grand at seven-thirty on a Sunday morning.* The marble-walled waiting room is elegant enough to serve as an entrance to a palace. In 1868, after two of these stations had been opened in Paris, the author Théophile Gautier wrote that they were "the new cathedrals of humanity, the centres where all ways converge." Neither image—palace or cathedral—is inappropriate. When you walk into the Gare de l'Est, the architectural eclecticism, common at the time, could evoke either feeling, depending on where your eye happens to settle. One wall is a palatial arcade of Renaissance-style arches separating the waiting room from the quays. This arcade appears to bisect a large Gothic-style rose window.

As we walked through one of the arches, I realized, however, that the window was just a half-circle, composed of a web of slender iron filaments in the form of eight triangles made to look like a rose window. Each of the triangles was filled with a rose petal formed by intricate ironwork. The space outside of each petal was filled with ornamental filigree similar to the tracery of a rose window in a Gothic cathedral but

---

* The trip to Reims—pronounced "Rance," which almost rhymes with France, and is spelled Rheims in English and Reims in French—takes only forty-five minutes by TGV.

with modern ironwork instead of delicate mullioned stonework and, more significant, in its use of clear glass instead of stained. In both periods, artists and artisans were fascinated with the effects of light on color. The light coming through the clear glass, filling the nineteenth-century station with natural light, was satisfying in an era fascinated with science and its creations, while the light filtering through the reds and blues of stained glass, filling medieval cathedrals with a supernatural light, where spirits seemed to move across the nave as clouds passed across the sky, was satisfying in an era obsessed with the mysteries of religion.

After leaving the waiting room, we entered an area where an immense iron-and-glass Art Nouveau ceiling covered both tracks and trains. We were struck by the beauty of the ironwork just as, over a century before, the Impressionist painters had been, when the materials of the Industrial Age were used architecturally for the first time and they had come, easels in hand, to paint them. The secular, nineteenth-century rose-style window made this train station the perfect place for me to launch my trip to the thirteenth-century medieval cathedral at Reims, since it was there that bar tracery windows first appeared in a Gothic cathedral. However, my reason for wanting to visit Reims was not architectural, but historical and cultural, since it was in the cathedral in Reims where, from the tenth century to the nineteenth, thirty-two Kings of France were crowned, and I had hoped that my visit to the site of royal coronations would provide a deeper understanding of the symbiotic relationship between the French monarchy and the Catholic Church.

It was no coincidence that cathedral spires were rising in towns throughout France at the same time the Capetian dynasty was rising to power. The bishops of France had preferred to ally themselves with a weak king rather than a strong pope: agreed that "the king should not invest bishops with the ring and staff, symbols of their spiritual office, but they owed the temporalities of their sees to the king and should pay homage for them."[*] With this simple compromise, France avoided the struggles over investiture (appointments) that would delay the unification of Germany for centuries. In France, the king could appoint bish-

* Bishop Ivo of Chartres (1040–1115).

ops, whereas the German emperor continually fought the pope for this right, during which time German bishops, really feudal lords—became more and more independent of him and of a central authority.

During the more than three hundred years of the Capetian dynasty (987–1328), while the cathedral spires were rising throughout France, the French monarchy was becoming the richest and most powerful in Europe, extending its control and unifying all of what is now France. Reims Cathedral was one of eighty cathedrals and five hundred abbeys, built during the reigns of Philip Augustus (1180–1223) and his grandson St. Louis (1226–1270). As at Chartres, a fire, this one on May 6, 1210, destroyed the Romanesque cathedral at Reims, but unlike the people of Chartres, the people of Reims did not give lovingly of their money or of themselves to construct a new cathedral. The poor relationship between the bishop and the people of Reims was longstanding and so fraught with strife that the bishops had to fortify not only their palace next to the cathedral, but also their château located near the Porte de Mars, which they used until the end of the Hundred Years War. It was necessary for the archbishop to use his personal income—rental collections from housing and fees from mills owned by the cathedral chapter—rather than donations from the townspeople, to pay for the first stages of construction. You will, therefore, find no windows donated by local merchants or guilds at Reims as you did at Chartres. Even papal bulls granting indulgences for contributions and others requesting donations failed to wrest funds from the reluctant populace.

Until the twelfth century, when Louis the Fat granted a charter to those burghers living inside the walls of the old city of Reims, the archbishops of Reims ruled as feudal lords over the city's citizens, never hesitating "to employ dungeon and rack" in his quarrels with the populace. This charter replaced the feudal fees and duties that the citizens had paid to the archbishop with a simple annual tax or tithe.

In 1233, the archbishop, who was short of funds to complete the cathedral, was enraged to discover that the city's burghers had so much money that they were lending it to the towns of Troyes and Auxerre. He demanded 10 percent. Infuriated by the request, the townspeople refused. The archbishop retaliated by prohibiting them from leaving their parishes. The situation escalated. The people erected a barricade, using stones the archbishop had ordered cut for the construction of the new cathedral, and then attacked the archbishop's palace, killing one of his marshals, before the king finally intervened and forced a compromise.

It was not only construction costs of the new cathedral to which the burghers of Reims objected, but the costs of the coronation ceremony as well. Whereas having the coronation ceremony in Reims made its archbishop the most important ecclesiastical authority in France, it imposed a considerable financial drain on the burghers, who paid for the catering costs. Every time a king died and a new king was crowned, 2,000 guests were invited to a banquet held in the archbishop's palace (called the "Tau Palace" because the Salle de Tau, where the banquet was held, formed a T (Greek tau) with the cathedral, to which the room is attached). For example, following the coronation of Philip VI in 1328, guests were served, among other things, 243 salmons, 4,000 shrimps, 2,000 cheeses, 40,350 eggs, 82 sides of beef, 884 rabbits, 10,700 chickens, 801 capons, 1,600 patés du porc, and 60,000 liters of wine. No wonder the people of Reims shouted "Long live the king."

THE TRAIN ARRIVED in Reims right on schedule, forty-five minutes later. I have, in fact, found the trains in France to be so punctual that I could set my watch by them.

Bob and I had expected a very modern rebuilt city, since Reims had suffered terribly during the two world wars. But even before we left the railway station, a whimsical nineteenth-century creation, we were captivated by the town. On our way to the cathedral, we walked past a pretty little park and then down a broad pedestrian boulevard bordered by charming nineteenth-century houses of two and three stories. Waiters at restaurants all along the way were setting up sidewalk tables with colorful umbrellas in preparation for Sunday brunch.

When we arrived at the cathedral, I first looked at the western façade from a distance, taking notice of the three rose windows filling the archivolts over the three portals. They were very different from the rose window cut into the solid stone of the western façade at Chartres. Here I saw a new—new in the thirteenth century—type of tracery, a bar tracery, which consists "of intersecting rib-work made up of slender shafts." Whereas at Chartres, openings for glass seemed to be cut out of the even surface of the façade, here the intricate stonework looked three-dimensional and, to me, like lacy icing on an ornate wedding cake.

As I walked closer to the cathedral, I took out my binoculars with great gravitas to examine the façade in a scholarly fashion. I had come totally prepared for a thoughtful and learned examination, having spent the previous week with very esoteric books dealing at length with this façade's iconographic symbolism. The theme carved here, unlike all the other cathedrals I had visited, is not the somber Last Judgment, but the joyful theme of coronation. When my eyes landed on the gallery of kings, however, I burst out laughing. There, in the center of the gallery of kings, was Clovis, the first Frankish king to convert to Christianity and, consequently, the iconographical symbol of the union of the French Church and the monarchy. What I saw, however, was not the serious iconographical symbol that I expected, but a comically sculpted nude Clovis dressed only in what looked like a barrel. Of course, it wasn't supposed to be just an ordinary barrel, but a baptismal font. But I wouldn't have known that if I hadn't traveled to Poitiers and actually seen a fourth-century baptismal font at the Baptistère St. Jean de Poitiers. When I thought of how hard Clovis's wife, Queen Clotilda, a devout Christian when he married her, had tried to get her pagan husband into that barrel to be baptized, I started laughing again, perhaps too loudly, because I noticed Bob had started moving away from me. But I couldn't stop. I just kept conjuring up an image of this savage pagan warrior, chief of the Franks, worshiped by his fellow tribesmen as a descendant of Germanic gods, regarded for centuries by Frenchmen as the symbol of the union of Church and Monarchy, an alliance that was supposed to mark "the beginning of a new society," depicted as a ridiculous-looking comic-strip character who had just lost his clothes at strip poker.

Clovis had, in fact, found Clotilda in a nunnery, where she was hiding from her uncle, who had just murdered her father, a Burgundian king. As soon as they were married, she began begging her husband to abandon his pagan gods and convert to Christianity. Clovis became adamant in his refusal when their first son died shortly after being baptized. He blamed it on being placed in water—baths were not being considered beneficial to the health in the fifth century. When I visited Poitiers, my guide explained to me that the early bishops of Poitiers had been careful to heat the baptismal fonts, so that the rite of baptism would not be blamed for subsequent deaths from pneumonia. If you visit the lower level of the bishop's palace in Reims, you will see the remains of Roman baths built when this was an important Roman provincial city. While the caption by the bath informed me that it was used for the baptism of Clovis, there is no evidence that the bishop who baptized Clovis or his son thought to heat the water in this baptismal barrel in Reims, a city much farther north and much, much colder than Poitiers.

Clovis continued to refuse to convert until he found himself about to be defeated in a battle by the Alemanni in 496. According to Gregory of Tours, who wrote about the event one hundred years later but nonetheless claimed to be able to quote him exactly: " 'Jesus Christ . . . I vow that if thou wilt grant me victory over these enemies, . . . I will believe in thee and be baptized in thy name.' And when he said thus, the Alemanni turned their back, and began to disperse in flight."

Queen Clotilda thereupon asked St. Remi, Bishop of Reims, to baptize Clovis. When St. Remi arrived, he told Clovis the story of Jesus' martyrdom, to which the barbarian king exclaimed, "If only I'd been there at the head of my valiant Franks, I would have avenged his wrongs." Then St. Remi baptized him and 3,000 of his men with appropriate pomp on December 25, 498, in the squares of Reims, where "the aroma of incense" from "candles of fragrant odor burned brightly, and the whole shrine of the baptistery was filled with a divine fragrance."

His baptism was an important event in the history of France. With his conversion, the kingdom of the Franks—Francia or Frankland—became the first Christian kingdom in the West, and the Roman Catholic Church put its authority behind him and succeeding Frankish kings. However, as time travelers, we shouldn't let our twenty-first-century terminology prevent us from understanding fifth-century events. Although called a king, Clovis should be thought of more today as a tribal chieftain. His conversion meant that, prior to baptism, Clovis and his army pillaged churches, taking away any and all things of value. After the baptism, when a soldier of his smashed a church vase, Clovis applied royal justice by taking his ax and smashing the soldier's head; and the Church reciprocated by supporting Clovis in his power struggles against the Arian kingdoms of the Visigoths and Burgundians south of the Loire.

There was another significant event that was supposed to have taken place at this baptism in 498, which explains why Clovis is the central figure in a façade whose symbolic theme is the coronation, and which also provides the fundamental argument for Reims being the city where the Kings of France must be crowned. At some point during the years that passed between 498 and the thirteenth century, the legend was altered by medieval spinmasters so that St. Remi not only baptized Clovis, but anointed him king as well. This new, embellished baptism ceremony no longer took place in the squares of Reims. According to the new legend, it was moved inside the cathedral, where all coronation ceremonies were held from then on: "So great was the crowd at the church that the priest whose duty it was to hand St. Remi the oil to anoint Clovis was unable to do so. The saint addressed a silent prayer to God, and miraculously, there appeared from heaven a white dove [symbolizing the Holy Spirit] carrying in its beak a small crystal ampulla filled with holy oil; with this St. Remi proceeded to anoint the King."

This event, as a visitor will see, is exquisitely carved in gold on the Reliquaire de la Sainte Ampoule on display at the Tau Palace. Although it was said to have been used to anoint Clovis in the fifth century, new methods of dating artifacts hypothesize that it was probably created in the thirteenth century for St. Louis.

ALSO ON DISPLAY at the Tau Palace are unforgettable sixteenth-century Flemish tapestries, which, in depicting Clovis defeating the pagan tribe of the Alemanni and his subsequent coronation, clarified for us how the French monarchy traced its descent from the kings of Judah, a logical progression we had previously found difficult to comprehend. Before the baptism, Clovis traced his descent from pagan German gods, but afterwards he traced his descent from Christ, via the kings of Judah. He did this in order to maintain the divinity he lost by converting to Christianity. Since I rather doubt this fifth-century head-smashing barbarian warrior ever made the somewhat convoluted intellectual leap himself (depicted in the tapestries), I assume it was done for him by the same twelfth- or thirteenth-century royal spin doctors that added the coronation ceremony to Clovis's baptism.

The theme of the central portal of the west façade is the coronation. The designers wanted to make clear to the medieval French worshiper that the Kings of France, like the kings of Judah, derived their right to rule directly from God—but now, only if they were crowned at Reims. Therefore, Clovis is centrally located in the kings' gallery, above two anointed kings of Judah—King David and King Solomon. Also on the façade is Mary, being crowned by Christ. If you were living in medieval France, you would have known that Clovis was anointed in 498 with oil brought down from heaven by a dove, and therefore, derived his right to rule directly from God. When Charlemagne's son Louis the Pious was crowned in Reims in 814, the archbishop of Reims was said to have dipped a needle into that same phial to scrape a tiny dot of holy oil with which to anoint him king. Hugh Capet, the first king of the Capetian dynasty, had seen the ceremonial value of being crowned at Reims and was crowned there in 987. Since that time, all but two kings of France had been crowned at Reims. When St. Louis was crowned in 1237, it was recorded that the archbishop anointed him with another drop of Clovis's holy oil before placing the crown of gold fleurs-de-lis on his head and handing him Charlemagne's scepter and the sword, symbols of the belief that he, like Charlemagne, was God's defender on earth.

The coronation ceremony at Reims deliberately replicated the practice of the ancient kings of Israel, from whom Christ was thought to be descended. In particular, it replicated the incident in the Old Testament's Book of Prophets in which the Lord instructed Samuel to anoint David "and the spirit of the Lord gripped David from that day on," which is one reason David is on the cathedral's façade.

A sculptural scene of what I thought was David slaying Goliath was directly under the barrel-clad Clovis on the cathedral's façade. I assumed that I didn't need anyone to explain the familiar David and Goliath story I had learned in Sunday school. I remember thinking that David, who was not much older than me at the time, was lucky because, living in the very distant past, he was able to have a much closer relationship to God—God would even talk back to him—than I could in my century, which was so much farther from Creation. I learned how the young shepherd faced the giant Philistine armed only with five stones and his slingshot, and saved Israelites from slavery with just one of those stones. However, I had only read the Old Testament version of the event, and if that was all I knew, I was as ignorant and blind as the statue here at the Tau Museum symbolizing the Jewish Synagogue. She is standing beside a statute of Christianity and has her crown askew and is blindfolded, symbolizing that Jews like me couldn't see the true meaning of the Lord. In preparation for my trip to Reims, I came across a little book of Latin verses in the Columbia University library that explained what these figures were really doing. The verses were written in 1205 by Petrus of Riga, a canon of Reims, who had put into verse explanations of symbols found in biblical glossaries. These glossaries, which were based on the writing of St. Augustine, became popular in the thirteenth century, when the iconography was becoming so arcane and layered with symbolic interpretations that people were having as much trouble in the thirteenth century as I am today in understanding what they were seeing carved on their cathedrals' walls and depicted in the stained-glass windows.

According to the glossaries, David isn't really David but is the symbol of Christ, and Goliath is not really Goliath but the symbol of evil or the Devil. (The originals of these cathedral statues, like the blindfolded synagogue statue, are in the Tau Museum next to the cathedral, where you can get so close to them that binoculars are definitely not needed; on the façade, Goliath is over the rose window, where I would never have been able to see him even though his huge statue weighs six tons.) The five stones that David picks up from the river to fight Goliath represent the five books of the Law of Moses. According to Petrus of Riga, this meant that although the Jewish people had received the law of God, the law remained as stones in the river, covered by streaming water. The water is not water, but is symbolic of the violent passions that blinded the Jews. It remained for David (Christ), to take the stones out of the water so that the laws of God, concealed by human passions, could be revealed. In case I didn't get the message from this sculptural composition, the juxtaposition of two statues in the museum, one representing the Jewish synagogue, blindfolded with her crown askew, and the other, representing the Catholic Church, her eyes wide open and her crown neatly placed upon her head, made this part of the message quite clear to me with or without a glossary.

BY THE TIME of Joan of Arc in the fifteenth century, Reims was deemed the only place a coronation could take place. While I've suggested this book will let you travel through the history of France, some train trips will do even better: you can retrace a piece of history right along the route the train takes, reliving it from your train window. When I looked out the window at the Marne River on the way to Reims, the view seemed untouched by time, or by the many wars that had been fought along these seemingly tranquil river banks. Not only was I crossing the battlegrounds of the Hundred Years War, but the train was following practically the same route that Joan of Arc had taken when she led her unwilling dauphin to Reims to be crowned. It was, in fact, on Saturday, July 16, 1429, almost to the day of my trip to Reims (Sunday, July 17, 2005), that she made that trip on horseback. (Although my train trip was far more comfortable and far shorter than the Maid of Orléans's journey, retracing her route—seeing the same riverbanks where her horse must have stopped for water, ancient trees that might have shaded her centuries ago—made me feel closer to the events of the past and her tragic but courageous life.)

Joan of Arc, believing as did David, that God was with her in her battle, planned to end the Hundred Years War by first defeating the English in battle at Orléans and then crowning Charles VII at Reims. She had rallied the people of France together, aided by a legend said to date back to the time of Merlin, that France would be devastated by one woman and saved by another, a virgin dressed in white from the Bois-

Chenu. After her miraculous victory at Orléans, Joan, who dressed in white and who was called the Maid of Orléans to emphasize her virginity, was increasingly identified with the virgin of this legend. The legend of Joan of Arc became more important than the actual events of her life. Joan, sensing that her time on earth was growing short after Orléans, sought to quickly put an end to the war by crowning Charles VII. However, Charles was afraid to have his coronation at Reims. Believing, with good reason, that he was a bastard, and therefore not the legitimate heir to the French throne, he had retreated to the Loire Valley, where he spent the seven years before Joan of Arc's arrival cowering either in the safety of his fortress at Chinon or behind the double walls of his nearby castle at Loches. In fact, everyone believed Charles VII to be a bastard, including his mother, the scandalous Queen Isabella, who had been conducting a flagrant affair with the king's younger brother, the dashing Louis of Orléans, regent of France, at the time of Charles's conception. The queen, however, did not name Louis as the father of the dauphin, but merely said he was the "bastard by one of my lovers." But, even if he was a bastard, he was still of royal blood—as Joan would tell him—it was just not his father's royal blood. His father, King Charles VI, was insane at the time, and was said to be found running through his palace corridors howling like a wolf.

Joan of Arc was insistent that the dauphin be crowned at Reims and the following conversation allegedly took place:

"Where shall we go?" asked Charles VII at Chinon, secretly counting on flight to the Dauphiné in the south of France.

"To Reims, Sire," replied Joan of Arc. "There lies the salvation of France."

"But I was crowned at Poitiers!"

"Poitiers can only crown the Kings of Bourges," replied the Maid. "Kings of France are made at Reims."

Only when he was crowned and anointed with the holy oil left in the ampule since the time of Clovis would he be accepted as the Vicar of Christ, with his right to rule France directly derived from God. It was not until Joan of Arc led him unwillingly through enemy lines and he was properly crowned at Reims that he was accepted by the people of France as their king.

The coronation of kings at Reims took place, in fact, until the French Revolution. Neither the coronation ceremony nor the ancillary concept of the divine right of kings was considered democratic or appropriate for the new secular republic, and coronation ceremonies were discontinued. However, with the passing of only a few years and the passing of secular democracy, Napoleon I saw the political advantage in having his legitimacy as emperor sanctioned by the pope and was anointed at Notre-Dame in Paris, as Henry IV had been. When the monarchy returned to France with the Restoration, the coronation ceremony returned to Reims. The last coronation ceremony was in 1825, when Charles X was anointed King of France.*

Inside the Cathedral at Reims

I entered the cathedral moments before Mass was about to begin. At first, I sat in a portion of the apse near a locked door leading to the museum located in the Palace of Tau. I had not read the sign on the door outside the cathedral, which Bob had read, informing tourists that the entrance to the bishop's palace and museum was through the courtyard when services were being held. I sat there, initially disgruntled at wasting my time sitting through a Mass, and then, fascinated, first by the canopied throne, decorated with fleurs-de-lis, in the center of the nave, which looked very much like the canopy and throne I had seen in an etching of Joan of Arc watching her dauphin being crowned at Reims.

---

* However, the practice may not come to an end with the last French king. The biographer of John Ashcroft, attorney general of the United States under Ronald Reagan, and two-term governor of Missouri, says that Ashcroft had his staff anoint him before each of his two terms as governor. Since no white dove appeared in his Missouri office with a phial of holy oil to sanction the event, he had to settle for using a bowl of Crisco. Ashcroft felt, as did the Capetian kings, that he was replicating the practice of "the ancient kings of Israel, David and Saul," who, as Ashcroft wrote, "were anointed as they undertook their administrative duties." *New York Times*, January 7, 2001.

I realized it must have been under this very canopy that all the Kings of France had once been crowned. Then my eyes were drawn upward to the rose window of the north transept, with its story of Creation. I was looking at one of the few thirteenth-century stained-glass windows that had made it through two world wars. Your eyes are always drawn upward when you enter a Gothic cathedral because the windows letting in the jeweled light are above the aisles or galleries on each side of the nave. I was suddenly glad I had come and that the door to the museum was locked. I had seen a picture of the cathedral taken shortly after the First World War, and while the photograph of the roofless cathedral enabled me to understand for the first time how Gothic arches of different widths could all be the same height, I reasoned that so much of the cathedral had been destroyed that the sense of time and place evoking the thirteenth century had been destroyed in the twentieth-century bombing.

As I sat listening to the centuries-old Mass, however, I realized that I was overcome with a sense of peace. Being Jewish, I am not sure precisely why. Perhaps it was because the cathedral here at Reims seemed more French than Catholic, or perhaps because I couldn't understand what they were chanting, or perhaps it was the pageantry of the procession of ornately dressed priests and choir I was witnessing, made more dramatic by the reddish glow in which the participants were bathed, as they moved across a floor that was a kaleidoscope of reds, ambers, and blues, acting out an ancient ritual; or perhaps it was the very perfection of the cathedral itself, with the extraordinary balance of all its parts to the whole that filled me with a sense of peace. I had been sitting alone, but as the ceremony of the Mass continued, I felt a need to be a part of the congregation and changed my seat. As I was walking toward my new seat, I found myself facing the western portal, and saw from the center of the cathedral the double row of elegant columns, each clad with four slender columnettes, all crowned together, and all the columns alike, as they marched regally down the nave. There had been no such uniformity of columns and capitals at Chartres, and the uniformity here produces an unimaginable harmony. The harmony had such a soothing effect. When I was seated, the bases of the columns were higher than my head, and the nave, while only 6 feet higher than the nave at Chartres, seemed much higher because it was narrower, this narrowness producing the illusion of much greater height, an accentuated height created to echo the celestial heaven. Perhaps my mood was affected by the way the delicate mullioned stonework tracery in the windows seemed to make the walls beyond the columns disappear and suspend reality. Or perhaps it was just being part of the religious ritual in a cathedral where every element was created for that ritual.

After the service, the magic of the experience ended abruptly as tourists poured into the nave of the cathedral. Once again, I walked around with my binoculars, examining the stained-glass windows rather than experiencing their effect as part of the religious ceremony.

Tau Palace

Bob was waiting for me in the Palace of Tau, the archbishop's palace, which is connected to the cathedral. Although destroyed during the First World War, it has been totally restored to the way it was in the thirteenth century. This palace now contains the most exciting collection of Gothic art I have ever seen. There is something utterly thrilling about being inside a museum looking at sculptures, and then being able to look out the window at one of the greatest Gothic cathedrals in the world, where the sculptures had once been. The museum's collection of tapestries includes not only those depicting Clovis's victory over the Alemanni and his baptism or coronation, which now hang in the Tau Room, but also seventeen tapestries, completed in 1530, that narrate the life of the Virgin.

The Treasury of the Palace, where the cathedral's sacred art is kept, contains a sapphire talisman that Charlemagne is said to have had sorcerers make for his wife to keep their love constant. Not only are two sapphires, one oval and one square, set in gold, encrusted with emeralds, garnets, amethysts, and pearls, but if you look through the oval sapphire, you actually see a cross said to have been made from a piece of the True Cross and a small piece of the Virgin's hair. Charlemagne gave the amulet to his wife, and Napoleon, perhaps trying to create a connection with the legendary emperor, removed it from Charlemagne's tomb at Aix-la-Chapelle so that Josephine could wear it at her coronation. Napoleon III's wife, the Empress Eugénie, later gave both the amulet and a twelfth-century jeweled chalice that had once been used in coronation ceremonies to her uncle, the archbishop of Reims. Someone at Reims, as at Saint-Denis, realizing the value of legend in promoting the eminence of the cathedral, let it be known that this twelfth-century chalice had been used by St. Remi when he baptized Clovis in 498. Another reliquary, with an angel on top holding a crown, was supposed to have contained a thorn from the Crown of Thorns. You will also see the scepter, crown, sword, and coronation robes worn by King Charles X, as well as the costumes that the courtiers wore.

The most exciting part of the collection is the group of original cathedral sculptures, saved from destruction during the two world wars by the citizens of Reims in caves usually reserved for the safekeeping of champagne: it's worth mentioning that Reims, once an important Roman provincial city, has a classical legacy that far exceeds the physical remnants of Rome's presence. You can still see structures the Romans built in Reims, such as the Porte de Mars (four arches marking the entry of four Roman roads that once connected this city with the rest of the Roman world), or the underground cryptoporticus (where wines, textiles, and other goods were stored while they waited to be traded in the second century). However, for me, Rome's true legacy in Reims are the beautiful cathedral statues, with classical torsos and drapery, but with faces radiating a spiritual hope. Sculpted in the thirteenth century, they nonetheless exude the spirit of Rome. It is as though time skipped over the period between the fall of Rome and the thirteenth century, and the thirteenth-century sculptors of Reims were somehow trained in first- and second-century classical studios, though filled with the religious fervor of thirteenth-century medieval Catholic seminaries.

Once, years before, I had gone to an exhibit of medieval art at Paris's Grand Palais and was particularly drawn to a statue referred to as the *Laughing Angel of Reims*. The exhibit's brochure merely classified it in a time period in which sculptors were creating statues with increased sensuality. Not satisfied with that explanation, I asked the curator for more information and was told, incorrectly, that the angel was carrying an instrument of the Crucifixion. I then asked why the angel was smiling rather than expressing a more solemn emotion. The reply was that the angel was smiling only because the artist wanted to express emotion. Art history books on the period contend that the smile I saw on this beautiful angel was part of a trend by French sculptors in the thirteenth century whereby they created a stylized facial expression to indicate beauty and blessedness. This smile has come to be called the "Gothic smile."

On my return to the United States, not satisfied with these answers to my question, I asked a medieval-art professor from a noted university why the *Angel of Reims* was, in fact, smiling rather than crying. I was told that the angel I saw was not an angel of God but of the Devil. As soon as I walked into the Tau Palace and saw the angel—with its identifying legend—I realized it was my question that was stupid, not the answer that I had been given. The angel with whom I had fallen in love was the angel Gabriel. The instrument he had in his hand was not an instrument of the Passion but rather a trumpet, with which he is joyously announcing to Mary the imminent arrival of Christ. I suddenly realized why all the angels at Reims are laughing. They are announcing the coming of Christ, the Savior and Redeemer. The theme is not the Last Judgment, but the Annunciation. This is Mary's church, Notre-Dame once again, and the annunciation is a joyous occasion for these angels. As Christ crowns Mary, all these wonderful angels are smiling, or would have been if they all still had faces—some of the original statues have not worn so well.

Looking at the sculptures at Reims, we can see great changes in those of the thirteenth century. By that time, artists were creating statues with increased sensuality. In addition, statues had left the columns to which they had been confined in the twelfth century to become freestanding. There is also a change in the intended effect of the thematic designs. The dominant theme is not the Last Judgment, in which Christ is depicted as an Old Testament judge damning and sending to Hell, or saving and sending to Heaven. The Christ we see in the thirteenth-century cathedral at Reims is the Savior, who died for our sins, and the theme is salvation and hope. Perhaps that is why I felt such peace at Reims. I was never comfortable with damnation.

Les Crayères

Subsequent trips to Reims were greatly improved by our visits to Les Crayères, formerly the château of the Madame Pommery, then the most sublime three-star restaurant and hotel in France, which was run by Gerard Boyer and his wife. It was with true horror that I read that the restaurant and hotel had been sold, for it was at my first lunch at Les Crayères that, after years of sipping banal cocktail-party champagne, I had the most exquisite awakening as we tasted a delightfully different champagne with every heavenly course. In all honesty, it was one of the most memorable dining experiences of my life. My first glass of champagne was sipped as Bob and I sat on comfortable wicker chairs on a glassed-in sunporch overlooking English-style gardens, while amuses-bouches were served to whet our appetites. As we moved inside, we passed portraits of Rubenesque nineteenth-century women whose ample curves attested to their obvious enjoyment of meals. The country elegance of the dining room, filled with fresh flowers in large copper pots, was the perfect setting for the hedonistic experience that we were about to have. I can still taste the ravioli de homard et ris de veau and I am desolate that I will never have it again. We worked up our appetites for dessert by moving from the comfort of the dining room to the comfort of a delightful garden terrace, where we were served chocolate soup with gingerbread and gingerbread ice cream, and sipped yet another delightfully different champagne.

On the way back to Paris, the train stopped at Épernay, where the wine used in coronation ceremonies had been made since before the time of Louis XIV. From my window, I could see a medieval church steeple and clock tower on the champagne brewery. Although this town was in the direct path of invaders from the time of Attila the Hun, and was itself the site of so many battles that it had been leveled twenty-five times, it seemed from my train window untouched by time. The clock tower on the champagne brewery stood as a monument to the only battle that was happily lost at Épernay—the seventeenth-century battle waged against exploding champagne bottles by the blind Benedictine monk Dom Pérignon, who tried and failed to rid champagne of its bubbles. In his unconditional surrender to the bubbles, which, curiously, the king and court adored, Dom Pérignon developed a stronger glass and wire to hold the popping cork in place.

As the train moved on, I thought, as much as I was able to think in my present condition, about the academic controversy over why the angels on the cathedral of Reims were laughing. Before lunch I had concluded they were rejoicing at the coming of Christ; after lunch, with an inane smile on my face, I began to develop another theory about these statues carved in the heart of the champagne country.

CHAPTER 5

THE LOUVRE
A Late-Twelfth-Century Fortress

Line 1 Métro to Louvre

*T*HOSE WHO DISMISS THE GREAT-MAN THEORY OF HISTORY have obviously not considered the consequences of Louis the Fat's obesity on the city of Paris, or for that matter on me. Before his reign (1108–1137), the Frankish king was little more than an itinerant feudal lord, traveling from his castle on the Île-de-la-Cité to his castles and hunting lodges at Orléans, Compiègne, Fontainebleau, Saint-Germain-en-Laye, and others within his realm, where he collected feudal dues, administered royal justice, or perhaps just escaped the stench rising from moats into which his castle latrines had emptied during his stay. These travels, called *chevauchées*, were caravans in which his feudal lords, his men-at-arms, and his servants were entertained as lavishly as his vassals were able. Oaths of homage and loyalty as well as produce were collected or eaten on these rounds. However, Louis VI became known as Louis the Fat after his stepmother tried—unsuccessfully—to poison him. Although he didn't die, he became too obese to travel. And so the custom developed for the king's vassals and subjects to come to Paris for the administration of justice, and, by default, Paris began to be the administrative center of the royal realm.

During the reign of his grandson Philip Augustus (1180–1223), Paris became the political, economic, and intellectual center of a greatly expanded royal realm, and the king's official archives were permanently transferred there. Philip Augustus also appointed royal officials known as *sénéchaux*, which like the granting of city charters also curtailed the independence of the feudal lords. He conquered all the lands his father had lost to the Plantagenets when he divorced Eleanor of Aquitaine, and added even more.

However, most important for me, Philip was the first king to love Paris—Henry IV, four hundred years later, would be the second. As soon as he was crowned king, he began to beautify the city and make it more secure. He had all the streets leading to the city gates paved with sandstone and the roads entering the city widened to seven meters.

Philip's palace on the Île-de-la-Cité is gone, as is the rampart which encircled the Île-de-la-Cité—except for a few stones, which you can see if you descend into the smelly museum located in the plaza of Notre-Dame.

When Philip endowed the university, the intellectual center of France in effect moved from Chartres to Paris. Latin-speaking students replaced grapevines on the Left Bank in the area around Mont-Sainte Geneviève and the Panthéon. While today there are university buildings clustered all over this area, they were all built later. Search as I did, the only remnant from the university of the thirteenth century is the name given to it—the Latin Quarter—since the students spoke Latin there until the French Revolution.

The homes of fifty Jewish merchants who once lived along a narrow road leading from the Petit Pont on the Left Bank, across the Île-de-la-Cité to the Right Bank, which divided the lands of the Church from the lands of the State, are gone. These merchants had enjoyed the protection of Capetian kings since the reign of Philip I (1060–1108) in exchange for ample fees, a policy that had had a positive effect on commerce in Paris. Philip Augustus altered this policy of tolerance. Fresh from his coronation in Reims on February 16, 1180, the young king arrested all the Jews in Paris and confiscated their property. According to one contemporary source, he did so because he believed the allegation that Jews used Christian blood to make matzoh. After tasting French bread, I can understand that Christians would find anyone peculiar who preferred matzoh to French baked bread, but even so, no matter how bad matzoh tastes, even if you *are* French, I don't think it was grounds for religious persecution. Another contemporary chronicler wrote that Christians at this time harbored ill will toward the Jews living in their midst because they taught their children to read and write. At first, this might not seem like grounds for anger. But consider that twelfth and thirteenth-century society was basically illiterate. Since no one knew how to read or write, there was no written record of debts. When a person died, the debt owed to him went to the grave with him. However, when the Jewish parent died, the children had a written record of the debt, and it was not forgotten. The punishment meted out by Philip Augustus seems to indicate money rather than matzoh motivated the young king. When he confiscated the Jews' property, he demanded a payment of 15,000 silver marks for its return and declared all but a fifth of the debts Christians owed to Jews null and void. That fifth he claimed for the royal treasury. The debts incurred by Bishop Maurice de Sully for Notre-Dame's construction costs were among those declared null and void.

Two years later, in April 1182, Philip Augustus decided to expel the Jews from his realm, giving "them leave to sell each of his movable goods before the time fixed, that is, the Feast of St. John the Baptist. But their real estate, that is houses, fields, vineyards, barns, winepresses, and such like, he reserved for himself and his successors, the kings of the French." My real surprise at this edict was learning that Jews actually owned vineyards in France. A few saved themselves and their possessions by converting to Christianity, and continued living on the Île-de-la-Cité. Most, however, left the kingdom and moved north to Champagne, whose countess offered them protection. The Jews, and the towns in Champagne to which they moved, prospered during the years Philip was off on the Third Crusade.

After his return from the Crusade, the king was again in need of money. He found that not only had commerce declined in Paris since he had expelled the Jews, but also that his income had been greater when he taxed the Jews and maintained a steady income. He therefore commanded the "Royal Jews" to return to the royal realm and, ironically, forbade them to leave again. When they returned, he, not the Jews, established the rate of interest moneylenders were allowed to charge. I do not know whether he set the rate out of ignorance or personal greed, but the Jews were no longer allowed to lend money without the king's stamp, and the king received a fifth of the earned income. The rate the king set was a penny per pound per day, or 43 percent per year, which certainly did not protect borrowers from undue usury, as he proclaimed.

When the Jews returned, however, they found their homes were gone. The narrow road on the Île-de-la-Cité on which they once lived had been widened during their absence. To the west of the road was the Capetian Palace—later to be replaced by the Palace of Justice.

To the east was the rising Cathedral of Notre-Dame, which, being so close to the royal palace of the Capetians, was supervised daily by the successive kings and queens who lived there while it was being constructed. Also to the east, at this time, was the episcopal palace, complete with donjon and crenellations, where lived Bishop Maurice de Sully, who had torn down a dingy Carolingian fortress and replaced it with a twelfth-century palace that would be destroyed during the Revolution of 1830. There is now a park where it once had been.

Also gone is Les Halles, which Philip Augustus built for the merchants of Paris. It was then a huge two-story stonework enclosure supported on pillars, where the merchants were protected by the king's police. Unfortunately, Les Halles was torn down in the 1960s, years before my first trip to Paris.

Despite all his accomplishments, I had planned to skip over the forty-three years of Philip Augustus's reign. I have always felt that to travel back in time I needed some remnant of the past, some architectural reminder that could bring the past alive, that could evoke in my mind an age or a person, and for many years I was unaware of the existence of any such structure.

I would not have written one word about Philip Augustus if Bob and I had not, on a very hot and rainy day in Paris, taken the Line 1 Métro to the delightfully air-conditioned Louvre.* The Louvre, whose name comes from an Anglo-Saxon word meaning fortified château or camp, had been the palace of the Kings of France before it became a museum for the world. When I descended the escalator beneath I. M. Pei's glass pyramid to the lower or "Entresol" level, in the Sully Wing beneath the Cour Carreé, I had no idea of the enormity of what had been discovered beneath the palace when the pyramid was being built. The Michelin I was using at the time was ten years out of date or I would have been a little prepared for what I was about to see. I knew Philip had built a wall around Paris and a fortress where the Louvre now is; however, I had no idea that any of it still existed. I thought the entire medieval structure had been torn down and replaced in the early Renaissance by Francis I, who had gone around France replacing medieval castles with Renaissance châteaux.

The first thing we saw was a model of a medieval castle whose construction was begun by Philip Augustus in 1190. The model looks like a typical medieval structure, with a crenellated curtain wall consisting of embrasures (indentations enabling defending archers to shoot) and merlons (raised portions behind which the defending archer could stand for protection). There were ten towers placed at intervals just far enough apart so that every spot around the wall was within range of the defending archers. As is customary, two of the ten towers guard the entrance to the castle, the weakest point of the fortress. The wall surrounded a courtyard with a donjon (tower) in the center. According to one historian, Philip Augustus was following the example of William the Conqueror, who had built a similar donjon, surrounded by a wall, within the city of London after having conquered it in the eleventh century.

The model one can see is the size of a child's medieval castle and was reconstructed on the basis of romanticized pictures found in a medieval manuscript, the *Très Riches Heures* by the Duc de Berry. When I

---

* Air-conditioning was not common in Paris at that time. In fact, Bob and I, thinking we might buy one for our rented apartment, went to a department store where the salesman was explaining to a group of prospective French customers what an air conditioner was.

turned around, I was startled to see the actual base of the fortress. Perhaps because I was underground—inside an elegant palace-museum—the size of the fortress took on unexpected proportions. It was built by Philip Augustus at the weakest part of Paris, the western edge, which had not yet been settled, as a defense against an expected attack during his absence by the Plantagenets. Henry II of England had garrisoned his troops only forty miles outside the city when construction was begun. By the time the castle and wall were completed, they were viewed as a defense against Richard the Lionheart. Philip, you will remember from your reading of *Ivanhoe*, was the French king who conspired with King John to kidnap Richard. When Richard the Lionheart escaped from his prison at Dürnstein Castle and learned that his lands had been lost by his brother (known as Bad King John to readers of *Ivanhoe*, but as John Lackland to his subjects in England, for losing Normandy and Brittany), he attacked and recaptured the castle at Loches in the Loire Valley by scaling a wall that today appears impossible to scale. And if you have seen that wall, it would be evident that the wall around Paris would never have stopped Richard. But, as history reveals, he never reached Paris during Philip Augustus's time. Consequently, the Louvre was used only for storing arms and men. The Kings of France had not yet moved from their palace on the Île-de-la-Cité.

Only the sloping bottom of Philip's wall remains, where it once rose from a moat. This sloping wall, which is a triangle of stone added to the original wall to prevent attackers from tunneling into the castle, was the most indestructible part of the medieval castle and is probably the reason it is still here. As you walk around, you can see the twin towers guarding what was once the drawbridge. You can also see the marks on the stone of medieval stonecutters.

However, while walking around this base gave me the sense of just how enormous the wall was, I am not sure how much I was seeing and experiencing at the moment and how much my mind was adding to the picture from what I had seen on my visits to the huge medieval castles of Angers, Amboise, Beynac, Castlenaud, and Chinon. I mention this only because as Bob and I were overawed by the base of Philip Augustus's fortress, two American girls walked past us and we overheard one of them say with real boredom in her voice: "Once you've seen one stone, you've seen them all." Perhaps what was so very exciting was seeing this medieval defensive structure, and then emerging from the underground and seeing the elegant Louvre above: seeing what had been, and then what would be.

The fortress Philip Augustus built was connected to more than three miles of walls that would, after twenty-one years of construction, circle the city of Paris, enclosing an area of 620 acres. The wall was 10 feet wide and 30 feet high. It had been designed to meet the military needs of the day. Massive, round crenellated towers, each over 36 feet high, were placed at intervals along the wall, and each of these towers was self-contained. If a garrison of knights in any one tower was under siege and cut off, it could rely on its own cistern for collecting rainwater and stores of salted pork. Each had three floors, and on each floor was a fireplace. Towers built toward the end of the thirteenth century contained latrines, which emptied into the moat that surrounded the wall. At each level the towers were pierced by long slits so narrow that it was almost impossible for an attacking archer to shoot inside. From the inside, though, these slits look quite different, fanning out into pie-shaped wedges, with each arrow-slit window making the point of a triangle from which the archer inside was able to defend a wide arc outside; the slits were positioned around the tower so that no area was out of view and range of at least one archer. By the thirteenth century, when these towers were built, the range of the crossbow allowed the towers to be placed 150 feet apart. The wall made Paris seem a secure place in a very insecure time and therefore attracted people from the country-side to settle there. In fact, Philip Augustus wanted people to come and build their houses right up to the wall, which they did.

Today, you can take the Line 4 Métro to the Étienne Marcel stop and visit one such "house"—the Tour Jean Sans Peur, at 20 Étienne Marcel, in the 2nd Arrondissement—where the northernmost part of Philip's wall would have been. It is now a delightful little museum that opened on October 9, 1999. You learn here that Robert d'Artois, brother of St. Louis, purchased it in 1270. It was built right up against the ramparts and allowed its occupants to cross Paris without descending into the streets. There was also a secret door or passageway leading to the ramparts that would allow its occupants to escape from Paris if necessary.

One day after our visit to the Louvre, Bob and I were walking from our apartment on the Left Bank to the Place des Vosges. We had crossed the Seine and were walking along the Rue des Jardins Saint-Paul, where you will not find a garden but a large cemented area used as a soccer field. As we passed the soccer field, we noticed a portion of Philip Augustus's wall that we had passed many times before. Now, knowing what it was, we stopped to look at it. Children were playing soccer in the cemented field at the foot of the wall, and Bob, assuming that the children knew what the wall once had been, remarked how wonderful it was that the past was so much a daily part of a French child's life. Although we had passed this wall each time we made our way from our apartment on the Left Bank to the Place des Vosges, it had never breached our consciousness until we saw the fortress to which it was once attached. In fact, we hadn't even noticed the two huge towers 150 feet apart—the range covered by the crossbow in the thirteenth century—bookending the wall. After seeing the base of the fortress in the Louvre, I was able to visualize how this part of the rampart connected with the rest. You can see another section of the wall, the southernmost section, if you walk along the Rue Clovis to the Rue du Cardinal-Lemoine near the Panthéon.

The castle and the ramparts attached to it would, after twenty years of construction, have encircled Paris and provided the ultimate in thirteenth-century defensive construction, which was needed, since Philip Augustus was engaged in wars and crusades most of the time he ruled. With his victory at the Battle of Bouvines in 1214, he added Flanders, Normandy, Maine, Bretagne, Anjou, and Aquitaine to the royal realm, doubling the area under his direct control. (Perhaps the most lasting result of this battle was not for France but for England and America. The defeat of King John at Bouvines placed him in such a weakened position that he was forced to sign the Magna Carta.)

The Albigensian Crusade, which began during Philip's reign, resulted in the addition of Languedoc to the royal realm. This was a "crusade"against a sect in southwest France that rejected the idea of papal indulgences, simplified religious ritual, and had stopped contributing to papal coffers. The crusade appears to have been the result of a combination of the pope's desire to restore income diminished by a heresy in a once-profitable area of Languedoc and Philip's desire to expand his realm. Both Philip and the pope used the religious fanaticism of their people to achieve their ends. While at first Philip Augustus rejected the idea of a crusade, contending that such heresies existed in most countries, he agreed when the pope promised that his impoverished, landless knights from the Île-de-France could have the rich fiefs of any heretical lord they killed in Languedoc. Consequently, the knights from the Île-de-France who owed their allegiance to the King of France replaced newly deceased lords in Languedoc, and Languedoc was added to the royal realm.

It was during this "crusade" in the town of Beziers, in the province of Languedoc, that perhaps as many as 60,000 persons were killed in the name of God. Chronicles quoted in *The Troubadours* by Robert S. Briffault relate, "They slaughtered clerks, women and children so thoroughly that not one escaped. Seven thousand persons who had sought sanctuary in the church of Sainte Madeleine were butchered there; six thousand were burnt alive in the Church of Saint Nazaire."

When the crusaders asked how to distinguish heretics from faithful believers, Abbot Arnaud Amaury replied in a rhetoric familiar to twenty-first-century terrorists "that the distinction was unimportant. Kill everyone, he said. As the Cistercian monk Césaire d'Heisterbach was to record, Arnaud said: "Kill, kill, God will know his own."

That was only the first of many slaughters that ravaged the once rich and prosperous province of Languedoc, where Jews, Christians, and Moslems had lived in peace and prosperity since the time of Charlemagne.

The Spanish-style inquisition that followed the Albigensian Crusade was shaped by the Spanish-born queen of France, Blanche of Castile, while she was regent for her son, Louis IX. She was also the builder of the unforgettable castle at Angers, where we will go next.

CHAPTER 6

ANGERS
Blanche of Castile's
Early-Thirteenth-Century Fortress

—

TGV from Gare Montparnasse to Angers

T HE TGV TO ANGERS TOOK BOB AND ME BACK IN TIME TO THE Middle Ages during the reign of St. Louis, to an early-thirteenth-century fortress in the Valley of the Kings—the Loire Valley. Not only did this trip take us back in time, but it was also one of those magical days in the French provinces, like the trip to Chartres, that linger in your mind for years thereafter like your first taste of the Loire Valley's white asparagus in the spring. And, given the number of centuries we were crossing by train, it was a relatively short trip. For example, if we had made our way from Paris to Angers in the thirteenth century, as had Blanche of Castile and her son Louis IX, it would have taken us, at the "forty miles a day" they averaged then, almost five days to travel the nearly two hundred miles, while today, by TGV, we were there in ninety minutes or less. Traveling by car takes longer, three hours or more just to reach the city's outskirts, but with the train, you arrive at an old nineteenth-century station right in the heart of the medieval city. Although Bob and I, over the course of twenty years, had visited by car most of the castles of the French kings located in the Loire Valley (and all the French kings, until the time of Louis XIV, had built a castle there), we had never visited Angers. It was simply too far—more than 168 kilometers along a crowded two-lane highway—to drive from a hotel, Domaine des Hauts de Loire, between Blois and Amboise, where we have stayed since it first opened. But taking the TGV makes the trip sheer delight.

The logistics of getting there by train from Paris are easy: you make a reservation, which you can now do online, and take a TGV from the Montparnasse station.

Since we had our first-class reservations and tickets, we knew the precise car and seat we had on the train. When we entered our car, we found the seats arranged with one seat facing another seat on one side of the aisle, and two seats facing two seats on the other side. I had purchased seats side by side, but seeing the little table between the single seats—and being thirty minutes early—I sent Bob off to the ticket window to exchange our *côte à côte* seats for the single seats *en face* so we could play backgammon.

Ninety minutes later, we were in Angers. The trip was so fast, we hardly had time to finish our game of backgammon and read the Michelin description of the city before we arrived. The pleasant ten-minute walk from the station is hardly worth mentioning. Don't bother asking where the castle is, there are signs pointing to the château everywhere.

Angers

Then suddenly, as we turned the last corner, we were upon the feudal fortress of Angers, a thirteenth-century military dinosaur built on a rocky promontory overlooking the Maine River. No matter how often I come, each time I turn the corner and see the immense round towers of Angers, I am stunned. In the whole United States there is not a sight like this. The fortress's seventeen towers of alternating lustrous black schist and white stone always loom larger than I've remembered. It is not just the height of the towers—they lost their tops and conical caps during the Wars of Religion but still remain

164 feet high—but their volume. Each one of them could have maintained an entire garrison—its arms, its food, its water—during a siege. At first the towers seem windowless, but then you notice the narrow arrow-slit windows.

When you then visit the inside of one of the towers, the Tour de Moulin, you can see that the windows were designed to protect the archers inside.

Although there is only a narrow slit on the outside, making it virtually impossible for those attacking the castle to hit anyone within, the archer inside has a wide triangular area in which to move about, standing or kneeling with his crossbow (the longbow was not yet in use in France), so that the narrow slit provides a wide target range. The towers are connected by curtain walls, along which you can walk. The bottom of the curtain wall is much thicker than the rest of the wall since a "plinth," or solid slope of masonry, had been added to prevent "mining," or tunneling, through the wall at the bottom. As we stood at the end of the curtain wall of the fortress, we were overlooking the Maine River, five miles north of its junction with the Loire at the very spot where the thirteenth-century knights of Blanche of Castile watched and waited for the attacking forces of the Counts of Aquitaine and Brittany. For added protection, the walls and towers were encircled by a deep moat. During the Renaissance, when there was no longer a need for defense, the moat was turned into a waterless garden where exotic and dangerous animals meandered through green mazes to amuse the aristocrats inside the castle, whereas we tourists are provided with grazing deer today. While Blanche of Castile served as Regent of France (1226–1234), ruling for her son until he came of age, she had the feudal right to determine the depth of all moats in the French kingdom, since the deeper the moat, the more protection it afforded the defender. Correspondence shows her allowing one count to dig a moat 10 meters deep while another was permitted 12 meters. Her moat at Angers was especially deep at 20 meters. As tourists, we can now use a drawbridge, except from twelve to two, when the castle is closed for lunch. Angers is perhaps the best example—even with the tops of its towers lopped off—of thirteenth-century defensive feudal military architecture easily accessible from Paris.*

Although you might read in some books that the fortress at Angers was built by Louis IX, it was actually constructed by his mother, Blanche of Castile. She is a fascinating, if somewhat detestable, character, one of those intriguing figures of the Middle Ages that make you pull your hair out because you really want to know all about her personal life but those details were not considered important in the Middle Ages and weren't recorded. You can learn how much she spent on clothes, that she built the castle at Angers and the Cistercian abbey at Royaumont outside of Paris, selected the architect who designed Sainte-Chapelle in Paris, sent troops to Languedoc to slaughter the Albigensians, and rescinded Philip Augustus's lenient treatment of students at the Paris university. (While King Philip Augustus, her father-in-law, had forbidden his royal sergeants-at-arms to ever lay hands on students, Blanche sent armed men after a minor disturbance, "who rushed upon such of them as they chanced to find, the same being innocent and unarmed, and did kill some, wound others, and thrash still others without mercy.") She was intolerant and committed brutal acts in the name of God. These acts and similar ones committed by her son, who was later sainted, are, however, dismissed by her biographers and other historians of this period with statements like "tolerance for heretics, Moslems, Jews, or even usurers was regarded as a sign of weakness . . . dangerous to the state." Keenly aware of the dynamics of power, she arranged political alliances through marriages that increased the royal realm and reduced the threat of revolt. But most significant of all, she saved the monarchy for her son Louis IX and helped create the legend (which will be dealt with in the next chapter) that resulted in his being canonized.

Her background is of interest. Blanche, or Blanca, was the daughter of King Alfonso VIII of Spain and the granddaughter of Eleanor of Aquitaine. Born in 1188, she was thirteen when she was married to the

---

* The walled city of Carcassonne, with its walls, ramparts, and castle, parts of which were built during the reign of St. Louis, is better, but is not a day trip from Paris. It is three hours via TGV to Toulouse, and then ninety-two kilometers by car to Carcassonne, a city described in my last book, *The Road from the Past*. I would certainly advise staying at least one night.

eldest son of King Philip Augustus. She was chosen instead of her older sister—Urraca—because it was thought Blanche would be easier for the French to pronounce.

The marriage took place in Aquitaine, which was then part of the English realm, because Philip Augustus had been excommunicated. Having found his second wife, Ingeborg, repulsive, he declared their marriage annulled. He then married a third time without the pope's consent. The pope excommunicated him and placed all his lands under papal interdiction. I only mention this little piece of medieval gossip, which would have been more intriguing if you were living in the thirteenth century, because the events that transpired at this wedding ceremony here in the English realm in 1200 would, twenty-six years later, play a decisive role in forcing Blanche to build the fortress at Angers.

While the facts seem a bit complicated, royal life was full of intrigues. King John of England, Blanche's uncle, attended the ceremony, as did his young vassal Hugh of Lusignan, the future Count of La Marche. Hugh, however, made the mistake of introducing his beautiful fourteen-year-old fiancée, Isabella of Angoulême, to the English king. Isabella was not only beautiful, but seems to have possessed a quality that begged men to devour her "like water to a man dying of thirst." King John was so smitten by Isabella that he kidnapped her, married her, and brought her back to England, where he crowned her queen. Her father, the Count of Angoulême, was happy to see his daughter married to a king rather than to a count.

The abduction, however, gave Philip Augustus grounds for confiscating John's possessions in France—Normandy and Aquitaine—which he did first by decree and then by force. Despite her appeal to the king, Queen Isabella was widely disliked by the courtiers of England, some of whom referred to her as "Jezebel" (the evil power behind the throne), and others as a modern (medieval) Helen. She is described disparagingly as "dancing late into the night and sleeping until noon." When, sixteen years later, King John died, she was so hated that she was asked to leave England and return to France "with all possible haste."*

* Pernoud, p. 99.

Indeed, when she returned to Angoulême, Hugh, to whom she had been engaged sixteen years before, was now engaged to her daughter Joan. Isabella, at thirty, apparently still looked, in the words of a contemporary troubadour, like "a ripe peach hanging on a sun-kissed wall in Provence." She turned her charms on her old beau, who jilted the daughter and married the mother. It is Isabella who, ten years later, forced Blanche to build Angers.

THE CIRCUMSTANCES UNDER which she built Angers gives rise to admiration. At the time it was built, Blanche was Regent of France. Louis VIII had died suddenly of dysentery in 1226 after a reign of only three years (1223–1226). As Louis lay dying, he summoned the knights who had accompanied him on his last campaign and had them swear fealty to his queen, whom he appointed to be regent during the minority of his eleven-year-old son. In a previous century, Suger had acted as regent when his king left on a crusade, and there had been no problems, but naming a woman regent was previously unheard of in France. Blanche built the fortress of Angers during the tempestuous years that followed as a means of saving the monarchy for her young son.

Even before Louis's death, there had been a growing discontent among the nobility over their gradual loss of power as a succession of strong Capetian kings centralized the administration of the realm. While four hundred years later, by the time of Louis XIV, kingship in France would have evolved from an elected first among equals to a hereditary and absolute monarch, the elective nature of French kingship in the thirteenth century was still fresh in the minds of the French aristocracy. The first reaction of the nobility to having a woman as regent for an uncrowned, unknighted child, was to demand that the office of king once again be elective, as it had been in 987, when Hugh Capet had been elected by the lords of France. Over the years, because of the support of the church and because of the Capetian king's ability to produce heirs, the hereditary nature of the monarchy had become grudgingly accepted as custom. Even so, many Capetian kings had taken the expediency of crowning their sons before they died. Louis VIII's untimely death had prevented him from doing that.

Blanche's hold on her regency, at first, was as secure as a bubble of air in a freshly baked soufflé. Not only was she a woman—"Queen Blanche ought not to govern so great a thing as the kingdom of France, and it did not pertain to a woman to do such a thing," said one vassal—but she was a Spanish woman and her son, the heir to the throne, was but a defense-less eleven-year-old boy. When her husband died, there was no time to mourn if she was to save the monarchy for her son. Within days of the king's death, Blanche arranged for little Louis to be knighted. Accord-ing to medieval law and custom, no one could be crowned king if he had not already been dubbed a knight, a ceremony that marked the coming of age. To save time, Blanche arranged for the dubbing ceremony to take place at Soissons, on the way to Reims, where custom decreed the coronation should take place. As Louis knelt and was dubbed a knight, the words "Bless this sword . . . so that it may be a defense for churches, widows and orphans, for all servants of God against the fury of the hea-then" were spoken. These words, which both marked his coming of age and his symbolic endowment with arms, were quite similar to those that he would hear days later at his coronation.

As soon as Louis was knighted, Blanche was able to send out couri-ers summoning the king's vassals throughout France to Reims for the coronation ceremony. The king had died on November 8, 1226. The coronation took place twenty-one days later. Blanche's biographer Régine Pernoud emphasizes how quickly Blanche accomplished this feat, in a time when the "best speed was some forty miles a day," and when I think of all the preparations that were necessary for a corona-tion, it is impossible not to be in awe of her. She managed, during this twenty-one-day period, not only to send messengers on horseback with invitations to the coronation and arrange accommodations for her own entourage, but to find time for every detail. For example, she traveled to Saint-Denis to have her son try on the crown (finding it too large, which would have emphasized her son's youth, she made sure the abbot of Saint-Denis altered it to fit Louis's blond head, and had it transported from the abbey to Reims in time for the coronation). She made sure that the Oriflamme (a banner carried into battle by all French kings), the royal scepter, and the sword of Charlemagne—all of which were kept at the Abbey of Saint-Denis—were brought to Reims as well.

To save her young son's strength for the coronation, Blanche had him ride in a carriage for the last fifty-seven kilometers to Reims. However, when they reached the outer walls of the city, knowing the significance of the proper royal image as a fearless warrior, she had him leave the carriage and mount a powerful white charger, draped with the symbol of the fleur-de-lis, before entering the city. As he rode to the entrance to the cathedral, Louis is described as being "a handsome child, blond, delicate, fragile-looking," and "tall for his age," while a thirteenth-century chronicler wrote that the people of Reims "felt 'both weal and woe' on that occasion' " (weal because of the beauty of their new king and woe probably at the cost of the coronation that they had to bear).

At the ceremony, Louis was dressed in a royal-blue satin robe, a cloak of violet on his shoulder, and golden spurs on his feet, and the Archbishop of Reims anointed him from the same ampule of holy oil that had supposedly anointed Clovis. He trembled as he took the solemn oath, and asked God for "courage, light, and strength to use his authority well, to uphold the divine honor, defend the Church and serve the good of his people." As a golden crown of fleurs-de-lis was placed on Louis's head, the young king held up the royal scepter, and while he was holding it, his uncle, the Count of Boulogne, handed him Joyeuse, the famous sword of Charlemagne, with its hilt of heavily sculpted gold pommel and long golden grip decorated with fleurs-de-lis inside a diamond pattern. It was said "the lad of twelve held up firmly the sword of the Emperor Charlemagne, whose blood ran in his veins." Suger had realized the symbolic significance of having the King of France recognized as the rightful heir of Charlemagne (the pope's defender of Christianity against the infidel). To emphasize the connection, Suger brought the emperor's sword and banner to Saint-Denis for the king's use in ceremonies and in battle. However, it was not until the reign of Louis

IX, who by the time of his death was thought to be the living embodiment of Christianity, that the French king would be so considered.

While many nobles had responded to the summons to the coronation, not all attended. Some were missing because they hadn't received the invitation in time. In the case of others, including the Count of La Marche (Hugh of Lusignan) and his troublesome wife, Isabella, the reasons were more ominous.

As soon as Isabella had married the Count of La Marche, she had begun urging her husband to petition Louis VIII to reclaim lands in England that had been given to her as a dowry by King John as well as her lands in Aquitaine. When, ten years later, the king died suddenly, Isabella immediately saw the possibility of not only regaining Aquitaine but of having her husband become king of France. She urged her husband to rebel against Blanche. Hugh, whom all his vassals knew was ruled by his wife, joined forces with the Count of Brittany and the Count of Champagne.

Blanche, who was compared to the "she-wolf" in the then popular story of Reynard and the Fox (*Le Roman de Renart*), was able to outwit the rebellious nobles by a surprise attack at Bellême in February. In the Middle Ages, no one ever fought during the winter, but always waited for the spring. A chronicler wrote:

> It was so cold . . . Queen Blanche . . . sent word throughout the army to all those who would fain win the day, that they go forth and hew down trees, walnut and apple, and all firewood they might find, to bring it to the army. . . . And those in the army made great bonfire without the tents and pavilions, so well that the cold could not harm man nor horse.[*]

The reason the aristocracy fought in the spring becomes clear from the complaints that continued for over twenty years, from the townspeople

[*] *Grandes Chroniques de France*, Vol. VIII, pp. 43–44.

living in the areas where forests and wooden houses had been cut down to supply the wood necessary to keep Blanche's troops warm.

While the fall of Bellême Castle did not result in a decisive victory, Blanche was able to secure the defection of Theobold, Count of Champagne, who now came over to her side. Blanche was also able to extend, for three years, a truce between England and France, which gave her enough time to build the castle at Angers.

Hugh and his allies plotted to kidnap the twelve-year-old king and then take over the regency by force. The plan was to kidnap Louis while he was returning to Paris from his castle at Orléans on a road that is today paved and named unglamourously "N20." Louis was about twenty-six kilometers outside of Paris when he learned of their plans. He hurried to the safety of a nearby fortress at Montlhéry (still there today), where he was joined by his mother. The fortress had absolute control of the route between Paris and Orléans and presented a safe haven for the young king and his mother.

What happened next was quite dramatic. Blanche appealed for help to the towns and villages in and around Paris. These free towns had grown wealthy during their years of alliance with the Capetian monarchy, an alliance that resulted in security and safety for the townspeople, freeing them from laws and taxes based on the whims of local nobility. They were only too happy to supply militias to protect their young king. When they heard that he was unable to return safely to Paris, the townspeople and their militias came out to rescue him, lining the entire twenty-six-kilometer route between Montlhéry and Paris. According to what Louis later told his biographer Jean de Joinville, "all the countryside poured out to bless him." As he made his way from the fortress of Montlhéry to Paris, "the road was thronged with people . . . armed and unarmed, all loudly praying to Christ to give him health and long life, and to defend and keep him from his enemies."[*] In relating this incident, he told his biographer, "it was from that hour he dedicated himself to the welfare of his people."[†]

---

[*]   Joinville, p. 27.

[†]   O'Reilly, p. 152.

While Louis's escape was thought at the time to be the result of "divine providence" that had protected the king from his rebellious counts and dukes, who saw "that the hand of God was with him," Blanche, although pious, felt that "divine providence" needed assistance in the future, especially on France's southwest border, where royal troops quartered in Angers were constantly being attacked by the rebellious knights from Aquitaine and Brittany. Royal troops had been using a donjon built along the banks of the Maine River centuries before by Foulques Nerra, Count of Anjou. Foulques Nerra had built some twenty-three of these donjons in the Loire Valley during the tenth century when he was trying to carve out an empire for himself. Each of them was a tall, square tower with stone walls 9 feet thick, one of which can be seen at Montrichard today. Blanche decided that this was inadequate both defensively and psychologically for her needs. She razed the donjon, replacing the single tower with the awe-inspiring seventeen towers connected with curtain walls that you see today at Angers. To make room for the towers and connecting ramparts—which, when completed, would cover over half a mile—she had to clear a whole section of land along the banks of the Maine, where, in addition to Foulques Nerra's tower, there were churches, cemeteries, and vineyards. The bishop and canons of Angers, who owned this land, complained that royal agents had not only taken their land, but the stone and plaster they had procured for the cathedral.

The Apocalypse Tapestries

Also within the castle walls are the famous Apocalypse Tapestries, which alone are worth the trip to see. When the tapestries were first made, between 1375 and 1380, they were 436 feet long and 20 feet high and contained 105 scenes. For one hundred years, from the late fourteenth century when they were commissioned, to the end of the fifteenth century, they had decorated the stone walls of the castle of Angers. In 1480 the Count of Angers gave them to the Cathedral of St. Maurice, where they hung until the Revolution. In the nineteenth century, when a priest found these tapestries stored in a church attic, the top border depicting a heaven filled with angels, and a bottom border filled with flowers, four feet in all, had disappeared, and only seventy-eight of the original scenes remained.

A huge vaulted room at the castle, supported by Gothic arches and columns, was specially designed to display them safely and protect their colors. It takes a few moments for your eyes to adjust after entering the room, since the lighting is designed to simulate that in a Gothic cathedral. Once you can see, you are looking at not only the oldest tapestries in existence but, according to the respected French historian of medieval art Émile Mâle, "one of the finest works of art inspired by the Apocalypse in the Middle Ages."

The Apocalypse Tapestries were created a century after the castle was built by Blanche. The tapestries that decorated the Angers walls during the time Blanche and her son dwelt there were embroidered in a style similar to the tapestry seen at Bayeux. It was not until after the First Crusade in 1095 that the art of weaving a tapestry had been brought to France from the Middle East. There, pictures were painted on the back of a fabric, and craftsmen then created the pictures by winding the weft, or horizontal threads, around the warp, or vertical threads. They pressed the stitches tightly against one another so that the colored weft yarns entirely covered the undyed warp yarns, always facing the back of the fabric on which the cartoon had been drawn, so that the tapestry was a mirror image of the cartoon. When the castle of Angers was built, the only tapestries of this type being made in France were small ones with emblematic designs or decorative motifs. There were no dramatic, monumental tapestries such as these.

To create the Apocalypse Tapestries, Hennequin of Bruges, the court painter of King Charles V, painted the cartoon on the back of the fabric to be woven. Then, under the direction of Nicholas Bataille, craftsmen wove the design onto the fabric.

Before he began, Hennequin of Bruges asked the King of France for an "illustrated manuscript of the Apocalypse from his library to use as a model." He was given what is now referred to as Manuscript No. 403 in the Bibliothèque Nationale, pictures of which you can easily find on the

Internet. It is interesting to compare two scenes—one from this manuscript and one from the tapestry—both depicting St. John's words in
Chapter 12, verses 1 through 5, in the Revelation of John, the last book
in the New Testament. There are similarities and significant differences.
The differences are what make the tapestry a profoundly moving work
of art. The illustrations from the early Middle Ages are two-dimensional
and express a total disregard for proportions of the human body, portraying the individual only as part of medieval society. By the time the
tapestries were created, individualism had become more important in
society, so not only are the tapestries three-dimensional, but the individual is anatomically correct and his emotions are considered worthy
of artistic depiction. The manuscript says that "a great sign appeared in
heaven: A woman clothed with the sun, and the moon under her feet,
and on her head a crown of twelve stars"; but while in both the illustra-
tion and tapestry scene a mother is floating in the sky holding a child, in
the tapestry the calm spiritual serenity of the mother in the manuscript
is gone. Instead there is the solid earth. The medieval device found in
the manuscript, in which consecutive events occur simultaneously—the
woman holding the child, the angel taking the child—is replaced in the
tapestry by a series of scenes in which the angel is in the process of
taking the child from the frightened mother. Her fear is evident in the
way the sun is depicted. In the manuscript, she is encircled by the sun;
in the tapestry the sun has become her hair, giving her a frenzied look.
While in the manuscript St. John is not part of the scene, in the tapestry
he stands, eyes downcast, looking at a seven-headed serpent from the
archway of a structure symbolic of a Gothic church.

The child in the illustrated manuscript—"And she brought forth a
man child, who was to rule all nation with an iron rod"—is depicted
without regard to human proportion, as an adult male reduced in size,
while the child in the tapestry has the proportions of a baby.

But most of all the manuscript is static and unexpressive of any
human feeling, while the tapestry is alive, full of movement and emotion. According to one historian, Léopold Delisle, "Hennequin of
Bruges invented nothing," but that historian saw only the similarities
between the picture in the manuscript and the scene in the tapestry, not

the differences, and it is the differences that make these tapestries such a great work of art.

What also makes these tapestries such a great work of art is the circumstances that existed at the time they were created, the late four-teenth century, during the Hundred Years War. It was a time of violence, plague, and famine. It was a time when it surely seemed the Apocalypse was at hand. Sculptures depicting the Apocalypse during the reign of St. Louis were far more optimistic in spirit than the overriding despair found in these tapestry scenes. At Reims, the angels of the Apocalypse are smiling and sensuous and the emphasis is not on the end of time but on salvation. Émile Mâle writes that the smiling angels of Reims are bad art while the Apocalypse Tapestries are great art. I would disagree. One is not bad and the other good, but they are two different interpretations of the Apocalypse of St. John, each expressing the spirit of the artist's age. When these tapestries were created, the optimism of an earlier time had vanished. The artist lived in a century when there was intermit-tent famine and when the bubonic plague had destroyed one-quarter of the population of Europe. The Hundred Years War was already into its thirty-eighth year before he started work, and would last seventy-three years after he finished, while the laughing angels of Reims were carved during a period of peace and prosperity, when the king, St. Louis, the beloved and charismatic embodiment of the religious ideals of his age, had welded his kingdom together into what was thought to be the cen-ter of the world. Different times and different artists produce different art and images.

We should also look at these tapestries from the point of view of the people who lived at the time they were made. They were deeply reli-gious. They knew well the words that Christ had uttered with refer-ence to the time of the Last Judgment—"ye shall know neither the day nor the hour." They lived with the expectation that at any moment they would hear the trumpets of the angels signaling that the end of time was at hand, the end that would be heralded by a period of crime, war, and pestilence. What a profoundly moving experience these dramatic tapes-tries must have been to the people who first saw them.

When Bob and I reached the castle, we crossed the moat and were inside the castle walls. We then climbed the stairs and walked along the ramparts, where, when we turned one way we had a lovely view of the church and the logis (quarters) of the kings inside the walls, and when we looked the other way we saw the Maine River, whose waters were transformed that spring day by the warm sun and the white sand into an illusion of a silver mirror reflecting the lush green trees along its edge.

When the castle closed at noon, we walked across the street and ate at Le Toussaint, which had three crossed forks in Michelin that year but has since closed.* The woman who seated us was charming and friendly. The high-backed wooden chairs, a style created in the Middle Ages when back-stabbings were common, prevented our possible assassination but also made us quite comfortable. We had one of the five tables by the window, so we ate our lunch while looking at the castle towers, with their layers of black and white stone.

As the waiter brought us our meal, I tried to think of Blanche and how her troubles with Isabella and Hugh had resulted in the castle we were looking at. But my lunch was evoking more serious concerns than distant medieval battles. It was spring, and my meal began with white asparagus—so delicious. There is nothing like the first white asparagus of the season in the Loire. I had had white asparagus the day before in Paris, but they were just not the same. I savored my first taste, somewhat as Bob savors a painting he really likes, staring at it, hoping to engrave it in his mind. However, my pleasure was mixed with fear. On our last trip to Normandy, a farmer had told us to enjoy the blossoms of the apple orchards because they might soon be replaced—the farmers there were being told by bureaucrats in the European Union to plant asparagus in Normandy instead of apples because economists in Brussels had determined there were too many apples and not enough asparagus grown in France. As I tasted my second asparagus, a horror came over me when I thought that I might never again taste white asparagus from the Loire Valley, that they might be grown in Normandy instead, where they might not taste the same. I remembered with distaste the hard English

* The one-star Le Favre d'Anne at 18 Quai Carmes is worth the ten-minute walk across the river. While it also has high-backed chairs and delicious food, I felt the aspargus were lost in their presentation.

cider I had sipped when on a trip in England, which tasted nothing like the sweet Normandy cider I enjoyed with my seafood platter at restaurants along the docks of Trouville, and wondered if white asparagus from Normandy would have an altered taste or, worse still, be like the tasteless, refrigerated white asparagus of America. As I tasted my third white asparagus, I remembered the perfectly round, easily packable, but tasteless tomato I had purchased the day before in Paris at a market near our apartment, a tomato indistinguishable from the tasteless refrigerated tomatoes from farm conglomerates in America, and realized that a French salade de tomate, such a delight in the past, might never be as good again. I remembered my trip to the Eisenhower Library in Abilene, in the middle of Kansas farm country, and the restaurant there with its buffet table devoid of any fresh vegetables except the aptly named iceberg lettuce. As I ate my last white asparagus, I prayed that today's barbarian economists would leave French agriculture and the lone, persnickety French farmer alone.

CHAPTER 7

SAINTE-CHAPELLE
in PARIS

—

Line 4 Métro to Île-de-la-Cité

*A*FTER VISITING THE FORTRESS IN ANGERS BUILT BY BLANCHE of Castile during the regency for her son, I wanted to visit Sainte-Chapelle, the royal chapel her son built next to his palace on the Île-de-la-Cité when he finally came of age in 1234. Although I had visited it many times before, I wanted to visit it again, this time with my binoculars, so that I could read the story related in one of the chapel's stained-glass windows, which told the legend of how the son—Louis IX—brought the most sacred of all relics—the Crown of Thorns and a segment of the True Cross—to France, relics that the chapel was built to display.

Shortly before I left for France one spring, a friend of mine mentioned that she had recently visited Sainte-Chapelle while she had been in Paris. When I asked her, "Isn't it the most exquisite church you've ever seen?" she looked at me with astonishment, as if marveling how two people with such different tastes could be friends. She replied that she didn't think it was particularly special; in fact, she had found the chapel rather dark, its decorations garish.

"Dark! Was it raining when you were there?" I asked.

"No."

When I asked: "Didn't you feel that the stained-glass windows gave the church a radiant, jewel-like quality?" she replied that she hadn't noticed any stained glass. She felt that the ceiling was low and claustrophobic and covered with so many golden fleurs-de-lis that the over-all effect was tasteless. Realizing what she had done, I asked if she had gone upstairs to the king's chapel or if she had only visited the chapel on the ground floor (built for servants and lesser nobility).

"Upstairs? Is there an upstairs?"

There is, indeed, an upstairs, one not to be missed. A perfect way to end a day visiting the Age of Cathedrals is to take the Line 4 Métro to the Cité stop and attend a concert there, in the royal chapel at Sainte-Chapelle.* Sitting in the upper portion of this thirteenth-century Ray-onnant chapel, a place once reserved for St. Louis and the royal family is like sitting inside a giant inverted jewel box. The walls seem made entirely of stained glass, and what stone does remain is so delicately sculpted into radiating tracery or gilded that it doesn't seem like stone at all. The vaulted ceiling is studded with stars, while the ceiling of the lower chamber is covered with fleurs-de-lis. If you don't want to attend a concert of medieval music, you might want to take a guided tour given in English three days a week by an official Sainte-Chapelle guide or one of the English walking tours listed on the Internet. Like the French, I love taking guided tours of monuments. I have taken two tours of Sainte-Chapelle, an official one and the English Walking Tour, and while some historical accuracy was sacrificed in order to amuse tour groups, it was nothing I couldn't live with. Taking these tours is the most entertaining way to learn about Sainte-Chapelle. You won't miss the upstairs chapel and, without a guide to point it out, there is no way you could find the hole in the wall through which St. Louis secretly watched members of his court pray. The guides are very good at explaining such things as how buttresses were masterfully used at Sainte-Chapelle to make them appear to be part of the interior decoration.

In any case, you should visit Sainte-Chapelle while you are in Paris. It is the most perfect embodiment of the Gothic Rayonnant style, or court style. It evolved from the high Gothic of Chartres, Reims, and Amiens, but adds far more elaborate, radiating window tracery. Once

---

* These concerts are given several times a week, and tickets can be purchased at any FNAC (a Paris retail chain which sells everything from television sets to tickets to cultural and sporting events).

completed in 1248, it overawed and delighted everyone who saw it, and those who could afford to do so—like Henry III of England, who, according to jingles popular at the time, wanted to take it home with him—copied it immediately.*

Although I have said that attending a concert at Sainte-Chapelle is like sitting inside a jewel box, that is not exactly true. It is actually like sitting inside an opulent inverted reliquary (a jewel-encrusted chest containing holy relics), in which stone has replaced precious metals and stained glass has replaced enamels and gems. Like a reliquary crafted by a goldsmith, every inch of the interior of Sainte-Chapelle is covered with elaborate decoration; even the twelve statues of the apostles, each of which stands on a platform between two windows, and which are carved so that they look like they are the pillars holding up Sainte-Chapelle, are similar to the embossed figures that decorate reliquaries. They were meant to be symbolic of the fact that the twelve apostles are the true pillars of the church.

Sainte-Chapelle was deliberately constructed as an inverted reliquary because it was built to house the most sacred of all Christian relics: the Crown of Thorns and a large segment of the True Cross. (On the chapel's steeple, you can see a Crown of Thorns carved in stone just under what is now called the Cross of Lorraine and just above carved fleurs-de-lis.)

Louis IX was able to acquire these relics and bring them to Paris because his cousin Baldwin [Baudouin] II, the emperor in Constantinople, being in financial difficulty, had pawned them to a Venetian pawnbroker by the name of Nicolò Quirino. However, pawning the Crown of Thorns did not solve Baldwin's financial problems, so in 1237 he traveled to Paris, where he hoped to borrow money from his cousin. During the course of their conversations, he admitted, to King Louis's shock, that he had pawned the Crown of Thorns. I confess I was at first

---

* Until I visited the cathedral at Strasbourg, which was built shortly after Sainte-Chapelle, where I found the stained-glass windows small and the nave dark after seeing the cathedrals at Chartres, Reims, and Rouen, I hadn't realized how architecturally advanced the area controlled by Capetian kings had become. The train trip to the ancient city of Strasbourg, with its marvelous food and delightful little islands divided by branches of the River Ill, is now only two hours from Paris via TGV.

a bit dubious about the nature of Louis IX's shock as well as his piety, even though I had read countless times how this slender young king would be discovered dressed as an unshod monk, giving alms to the poor in the early morning hours or washing the feet of lepers. However, after reading the following conversation, related by his friend and biographer Joinville, I concede that Louis was a man who would have been deeply shocked to hear that anyone could have pawned the Crown of Thorns.

> "Which would you prefer [Louis IX asked Joinville]: to be a leper or to have committed some mortal sin?" And I, who had never lied to him, replied that I would rather have committed thirty mortal sins than become a leper. The next day . . . he called me to him, and making me sit at his feet said to me: "Why did you say that yesterday?" I told him I would still say it. "You spoke without thinking, and like a fool," he said. "You ought to know there is no leprosy so foul as being in a state of mortal sin."

Although I was convinced of his piety, I continued to wonder whether or not piety is a pejorative or a positive quality. In St. Louis's case there seems to have been somewhat of a correlation between his piety and confiscation.

For example, Louis IX "solicited Pope Alexander IV to persuade him to entrust him with the responsibility for the Inquisition." This was done, according to Joinville, to "make confiscation to the benefit of the sovereign." And when Joinville states that the local lords "now acquiesced," Joinville was referring to Louis's knights from the Île-de-France, to whom Louis had given the confiscated property of Albigensian lords.

Also, before leaving on a crusade to Jerusalem in 1254, he ordered the expulsion of all Jews, and, of course, the confiscation of all their possessions. Being a true believer, he also expelled and confiscated the property of Christian usurers in Normandy who, by the way, were charging higher rates than the Jews.

Whether because of piety, or because he realized the relics were the key to medieval power—that by bringing the relics to Paris, he would bring to the French monarchy the prestige and symbolic value of the relics—Louis agreed to pay the money pledged to the Venetian merchant to get the Crown of Thorns out of hock.* It cost him 135,000 livres, an enormous sum at that time; in fact, it was more than half the revenues of the royal domains.

Before allowing her son to purchase the relics, Blanche of Castile spent two years taking every precaution to ensure they were authentic: that is to say, that her son bought the same relics found in Jerusalem by St. Helena, mother of the Emperor Constantine, around 280. These relics had been kept in reliquaries at the Church of the Holy Sepulchre in Jerusalem until 628. When the Emperor Heraclius felt he was no longer able to protect the Holy City, he transferred both the Crown of Thorns and the True Cross from Jerusalem to Constantinople. The relics had remained in the possession of the emperors at Constantinople until Baldwin II had pawned them. While at the time there was no way these relics could actually be authenticated as the Crown of Thorns worn by Christ and the True Cross, they could be authenticated as the relics in the possession of the emperors in Constantinople for nearly a thousand years.

As you enter the nave of Sainte-Chapelle, facing the apse and the angels over the altar, look toward your right. It is the last window on the right that I had come to see. It tells the legend of the relics from the time St. Helena found them to the time when St. Louis brought them to Paris, depicted in sixty-seven scenes. Twenty-six panes are original. Reading from left to right and bottom to top, the story depicts the Emperor Constantine sending his mother, St. Helena, to Jerusalem to find the holy relics. In the next pane, St. Helena enters Jerusalem. She discovers the True Cross and the nails. Skipping to level nine, Louis IX is depicted with a crown on his blond head, wearing a blue outer robe over a pink undergarment, while his brother Robert is dressed in a lavender robe. They are carrying the Crown of Thorns. Both the king and his brother

---

* It would only cost 40,000 livres to build Sainte-Chapelle.

are barefoot. In one of the panes is a town with blue buildings, which is probably Sens, where Baldwin's messengers traveled with the relics but where there are no blue buildings. Blue was used in stained-glass windows to create harmonious rather than muddy color schemes. The thirteenth-century artist, more interested in color than realism, needed the blue for his composition, so he colored the buildings accordingly. By the twelfth level, the Crown of Thorns has arrived in Paris and is being displayed by a bishop dressed in purple. The Crown of Thorns is green on a yellow cushion. The king and queen are in the background. (Note that the queen is Blanche of Castile and not King Louis's wife.)

What is so unusual about this window is its depiction of events that took place during St. Louis's lifetime. All the windows in the cathedrals we have visited so far were pictorial narrations of biblical stories; but this window, unlike the previous fourteen windows in this chapel—1. Genesis; 2. Exodus; 3. The Ten Commandments; 4. Deuteronomy; 5. Judges; 6. Isaiah and the Tree of Jesse; 7. St. John the Evangelist; 8. Christ's Passion; 9. John the Baptist; 10. Ezekiel; 11. Jeremiah; 12. Judith; 13. Esther; 14. Kings (Samuel, David, and Solomon)—is not a scene from either the Old or the New Testament. Also, the window depicting the story of Louis IX is deliberately placed next to the window of the kings, to imply Louis IX's descent from the kings of Judah.

After Blanche was satisfied with their authenticity, she, her son, the king, and Robert, his younger brother, traveled to the town of Ville-neuve-l'Archevêque, where they met the two Dominican friars who had been entrusted with carrying the chest containing the Crown of Thorns from Venice. Blanche ordered the chest opened at once. Inside it was a silver box with the seals of the doge of Venice and the barons of the Byzantine Empire. Comparing these seals to ones attached to the letter of patent previously sent her to authenticate the relics that had been given to the two friars, Blanche found them identical. After breaking open the seals, Blanche found a gold box inside the silver one. And inside of that was the Crown of Thorns, or what was thought to be the crown worn by Christ at his Passion—actually a circle of straw to which a few fragments were attached. Portions of the Crown of Thorns had been dispersed throughout Europe by a succession of emperors over the centuries. Charlemagne had, according to a stained-glass window at Chartres, been given pieces of the Crown of Thorns and the True Cross as a reward for his successful crusade against the Saracens. He had brought these relics back to Aix-la-Chapelle (now Aachen), where he built a chapel attached to his palace to display them. Charlemagne modeled his Palatine Chapel after the Church of the Holy Sepulchre in Jerusalem, where the relics had once been kept. This established in the mind of a pilgrim the symbolic transfer from Jerusalem to Aachen. Now, in the thirteenth century, there was to be a symbolic transfer to Paris.

After the relics had been deemed authentic, the reliquary was placed back on the litter and carried by two men dressed as penitents. King Louis walked in front of the litter singing hymns, while his brother Robert walked behind. For seven days the procession made its way to Paris, on an ancient highway built by the Romans. During those seven days, the common people lined the road, trying to get a glimpse of the sacred relics and their king, who had brought them to France. On the seventh day, the procession arrived outside Paris, at the walls built by Philip Augustus near the abbey of Saint-Antoine. (You can still see a portion of this wall if you take the Line 1 Métro to the Saint-Paul station and walk behind the Cathedral of Saint-Paul to what is called the Jardin de Saint-Paul. One side of the field is a portion of the wall, the largest remaining part of the wall built by Philip Augustus, that guarded Paris during the time of Louis IX.

Blanche, as we learn, had set up a platform outside the wall to display the relic so that the people of Paris could come and venerate the Crown of Thorns. Then clerks, monks, prelates, and knights formed another procession, also singing hymns, as they carried the Crown of Thorns to the new Cathedral of Notre-Dame where Mass was sung before the precious relic was taken to the palace.

A few years later, in 1241, the ever indigent Baldwin II, still in need of money, pawned what was left of the True Cross to the Knights Templar, and again Louis IX paid the pledge. He eventually acquired other relics, including those of more dubious authenticity, from his impecunious cousin, relics supposedly in the possession of the emperor: the Iron Lance, the Sponge, and Nail of the Passion. The arrival of each of these relics was accompanied by elaborate ceremonies that the people of Paris loved, followed by a solemn procession in which the new acquisition was brought to the palace on the Île-de-la-Cité, which had over the years been the palace of provincial Roman prefects, then Carolingian counts, and then Clovis and his descendants. Paris had become the administrative center of France during the reigns of the Capetian kings. With the building of Saint-Denis and Notre-Dame, and the growth of its university, Paris had become a cultural and intellectual center as well. Now, during the reign of St. Louis, with the creation of Sainte-Chapelle, Paris became more—much more. With the transfer, in the Age of Faith, of these most sacred of all Christian relics from Constantinople to Paris, a symbolic prestige was transferred both to Paris and to the Capetian dynasty. Louis IX had purchased symbolic prestige that enhanced the legitimacy of the Capetian dynasty and perhaps, as one historian writes, "exalted the throne of France not only in France but throughout Europe." Pope Innocent IV would state: "The Lord has crowned you [Louis] with His Crown of Thorns." And the King of France was one step closer to possessing the divine right of kings.

Now that the relics were in Paris, a chapel was needed to house them and an architect to design it. Blanche of Castile selected Thomas de Cormont, who in 1240 had just completed work on the Rayonnant choir at Amiens. He was given certain parameters in designing the chapel; these emphasized that the relics had once been in Jerusalem and then in the possession of the emperor. The emperor with whom King Louis wanted to be identified was not the one who had pawned the relics, but Charlemagne, the Holy Roman Emperor, who had been sainted, and who was considered the Vicar of Christ and protector of the Catholic Church. Louis IX's father, during his brief reign, had established his descent from Charlemagne on both sides. (Although talent, brains, and a charismatic television personality seem important for success in twenty-first-century America, it was lineage and bloodline that counted in the thirteenth, and the most important bloodline for the legitimacy of a king, since the basis of royal power was now heredity and becoming divine, was direct decent from Charlemagne.) The architecture of the chapel where these relics were to be displayed was to be a reminder of the Capetian dynasty's affiliation with the mighty Charlemagne. Therefore, the architect was instructed to model it after Charlemagne's Palatine Chapel at Aachen, which had, in turn, as we've seen, been modeled after the Holy Sepulchre Church in Jerusalem. The chapel was to provide a symbolic connection with both Charlemagne and Jerusalem. Because of nineteenth-century restorations at Sainte-Chapelle, many of the elements that once echoed Charlemagne's Palatine Chapel and Jerusalem's Holy Sepulchre were eliminated by restorers who, not living in the Age of Faith, did not realize how important religious symbolism in architecture was to the medieval mind.

Four centuries after St. Louis built Sainte-Chapelle, another king, Louis XIV (1643–1715), who overlooked no detail in the creation of his image as the Sun King, would realize the symbolic value of echoing Charlemagne's chapel when he built his royal chapel at Versailles. As interested in absolute political power as in personal religious observance, he built his royal chapel with a central open space, eliminating the floor separating the two levels, so that he, like Charlemagne, could sit on a throne in the high gallery while his servants and the nobility stood in the lower floor looking up at him. And when they did, they would be looking up at their king centered in a circle of light from the rose window behind him. He would be the center of a circle: the perfect geometric form framing the perfect human. This had been Suger's intention when he created the first rose window at Saint-Denis—that jeweled light would be shining on the figure of his king, whose throne was placed directly in front of the window on the upper level of the Basilica of Saint-Denis. While most kings who followed Louis IX to the throne of France built their own versions of Sainte-Chapelle, it was not until Louis XIV in the seventeenth century that a monarch understood the symbolic importance that Suger had known in the twelfth.

Although the relics of the Passion and the symbolism today are gone, we can still see that at Sainte-Chapelle, as at Saint-Denis, walls are filled with stained glass to allow the sun to create the illusion of dazzling jewels on stone floors, and stone becomes delicate tracery. Every time I visit this exquisite chapel, I am overwhelmed by its ethereal, ornate beauty, created by luminous walls of stained-glass in which everything concrete seems to disappear and the mind is allowed to float.

CHAPTER 8

VINCENNES
A Fortress of the Hundred Years War

—

Line 1 Métro to Chateau de Vincennes

BY THE END OF THE REIGN OF ST. LOUIS IN 1270, THE PRES-
tige and power of the French monarchy had never been more secure.
However, sixty-seven years later, after more than three centuries of successfully producing male heirs, the Capetian dynasty came to an end in
1337, and the Hundred Years War began. Although it is generally spoken of as a war between "France" and "England," it wasn't actually a
war between two nation states, but rather a series of wars of succession
to the French throne. It was during one of these wars that Charles V,
King of France, after fleeing the mobs of Paris, built Vincennes.

The Château de Vincennes, seven kilometers east of Notre-Dame,
is the last stop on the Line 1 Métro. If you board the Métro in central
Paris, it will take you about fifteen minutes to travel back to fourteenth-
century medieval France, a century beset by the Black Death, famine,
and the Hundred Years War. As soon as you climb the stairs leading out
of the Château de Vincennes station, you will see, across the boulevard,
the outer wall that surrounds the fortress. In the center of this medieval wall is the Tour du Village, a massive defensive tower, 138 feet high,
through which you enter the area beyond. What you are about to enter
as you pass through the somber archway of the Tour du Village is the
best defensive system of the fourteenth century—the medieval equivalent of our missile defense system—built by a king to protect himself

and his court from the mobs of Paris and from the plague, which had already taken the lives of 80,000 people in Paris.

Upon your arrival at the castle, you cross a metal footbridge that has replaced the medieval wooden drawbridge. This was the first defensive protection for the castle inhabitants who dwelled inside the walls. As soon as you have crossed the bridge, you pass through the Tour du Village, where the governor of the fortress lived during the Middle Ages. Although the tower now has windows, its stone walls in the fourteenth century were pierced only with archères.

As you walk through the passageway cut through the tower, you will see two sets of vertical grooves in the walls. A portcullis—two lattice gratings of heavy iron—once slid in these grooves, so if you had been an unwanted guest, you would have been imprisoned between two sets of gratings. A portcullis was as common to French fourteenth-century defensive structures as a refrigerator is to a twenty-first-century kitchen. Slits for the chains that once raised and lowered the wooden drawbridge can also still be seen, but the drawbridge, a key element of medieval defensive architecture, is gone.

Once you pass through the tower and the outer wall, a fantastic sight—an archetype of medieval fortification, certainly worth a fifteen-minute Métro ride—is waiting. Typical of fortifications built during the Hundred Years War, it is complete with practically every detail of medieval defensive architecture: a moat; an outer wall (enceinte); and a keep, complete with machicolation, or surrounding parapet. Medieval machicolations appear to be decorative but are not so at all. They are projections, supported by corbels, cantilevered out over the walls of fortresses, providing holes for defenders standing on a platform or parapet behind the protection of merlons and crenels (openings between two merlons) to pour hot oil, molten lead, or boiling water on attackers trying to scale the wall. Parapets of this type were first made of wood, but stone came to be used after so many of them caught fire from the fires defenders made to heat the oil, water, and lead—or from an enemy's flaming arrow. The lead roof on top was also a later addition and improvement protecting against the offensive flaming arrows.

I have always found this defensive device, these machicolations, for scalding one's enemy, to be the most architecturally pleasing part of medieval castle construction, giving otherwise bare, grim structures a rather romantic feeling. The moat, also a defensive device, makes Vincennes appear even more attractive today than in the fourteenth century when it was the receptacle of the castle's latrines (*garderobes*). The base of the wall is similar to the bases of Philip Augustus's twelfth-century fortress seen at the Louvre (Chapter Five) and that of the thirteenth-century castle we visited at Angers (Chapter Six), having beneath the waterline a talus (sloping stones added to the wall pyramid-style) to prevent tunneling through the wall. The fortress, or keep, at Vincennes is still protected by a functioning wooden drawbridge which, unlike the drawbridge guarding the outer wall, has not been replaced by a metal footbridge. Since it would have been the weakest point in the fortress's defense, it is protected by a barbican—two little towers on either side.

During one of the restorations, the roadway between the moat and the entrance gate has been straightened. The restorer may have thought the original roadway that existed during the reign of Charles V, which then twisted to the right and to the left, was the result of a drunken engineer and therefore straightened it. However, it had deliberately twisted and turned according to the best defensive engineering of the time, to make it difficult, if not impossible, for an enemy to charge with any momentum or bring up heavy offensive weapons such as catapults, battering rams, or siege towers. Again, at the entrance to the castle, as at the Tour du Village, there is a portcullis, to trap the enemy in a cage before they were able to enter the area beyond the wall. After crossing the drawbridge, you do not go directly into the keep or donjon beyond. There is an open space where the enemy would have been caught in the crossfire of archers shooting from the outer wall and from the keep. The keep itself is as typical of the period as a Levitt house would have been in 1950s America—it is a large rectangle with four adjacent rounded towers. (Keeps built in France during the early Middle Ages were rectangular. Knights, however, traveling through areas bordering the Mediterranean observed how their missiles bounced off the rounded towers, which had been designed by the Romans when they ruled the ancient world. And when the French knights returned home, they either rounded off the corners of their keeps, which had been particularly vulnerable to catapulted stones, or added rounded towers at the corners.)

In order to understand why Charles V built Vincennes, it is necessary to mention the Battle of Poitiers in 1356 and its aftermath. The "Black Prince" (Edward, Prince of Wales) had brought 2,000 men-at-arms and 6,000 archers from England. King John II, who faced him on the field, had acquired the sobriquet Jean le Bon, which I had first poorly translated as "John the Good." However, when reading a French historian of the period, I learned "John le Bon does not mean John the Good," as I had thought, but "Le Bon" means "the trusting, the prodigal, the careless," which he certainly was. John raised money to fight the English from the Estates-General, which was controlled by Étienne Marcel, who was also the mayor of Paris. John arrived at Poitiers with one of the most impressive armies ever raised in France, including "twenty-six dukes and counts, one hundred-forty knights-bannerets, and about fifty thousand soldiers of which a large number were horsemen clothed in steel armour."

King John had positioned his forces in such a way, between the English and their supplies, so that if he merely waited, the English would have starved to death. But according to the ethics of chivalry, which valued and romanticized the heroic, and had contempt for pain, danger, death, and the common soldier, waiting was not chivalrous. So John did not wait. Jean Froissart, the chronicler of the Age of Chivalry, relates that King John attacked, dispatching 11,000 men through a narrow passage that separated the two armies, sending them to their death. Even Froissart, who admired the chivalry of John's actions, admits that this was a tactical blunder.

Before surrendering to the Black Prince, John called his heir, or dauphin—Charles—to his side. He advised him to hurry to Paris to raise money for another army to fight the English and for the ransom that the Black Prince would demand. The ransom that would eventually be paid was 250 million francs, about which another chronicler wrote: "No prince, indeed, had ever before him so nobly flung away the money of the people." He also advised his son to take with him, as advisers, the marshals of Champagne and Normandy. This, like his assault on the English, was a tactical blunder. These two men were not only hated throughout France but considered corrupt and untrustworthy by Étienne Marcel, the man who would have to supply the dauphin with the funds he needed, which brings us to why Vincennes was built. Charles, the dauphin, a weak and sickly eighteen-year-old, returned to Paris as regent, taking the title of "Lieutenant to the King." He called, as he was instructed, a meeting of the Estates-General to raise money. He found the power of Étienne Marcel had considerably increased since he had left for Poitiers. Marcel, previously a leather tanner, had become wealthy "by lending money to the monarchy at high profits." At the time Charles asked him for money, he was not only the mayor of Paris but the leader of the conservative and wealthy bourgeoisie.* Marcel agreed to lend the money if the dauphin would agree to certain conditions, one of which was turning over the two marshals. Charles refused, and as unrest in the city mounted, the young prince sought refuge in the Louvre, the defensive fortress Philip Augustus had built on the edge of the city. Unfortunately for Charles, the Louvre was no longer on the edge of the city. A curious thing had happened during the period Étienne Marcel had become mayor of Paris; he had extended the defensive wall built by Philip Augustus, adding six bastilles, or small fortresses, and increasing Paris by 430 acres. The area by which Paris had been increased was the area between the Louvre and the new wall, so it was no longer possible to secretly escape the city without crossing a large area of Paris. The dauphin, his younger brother, and the two marshals tried to escape. Unfortunately, they did not move secretly enough and were captured by Étienne Marcel, who repeated his demands that the young regent turn over his advisers to the Paris mob. When Charles refused, Marcel ordered one of his men to assassinate the marshal of Champagne, who was standing by the dauphin's side. As the marshal was stabbed to death, his blood spouted all over the clothing of the regent and his brother, traumatizing the two young princes. The mar-

---

* *Bourgeoisie* is a French word referring to the wealthier and more educated members of the Third Estate in France, the three estates being the nobility, the clergy, and commoners. The term *bourgeoisie* came into use with the emergence of the merchant class.

shal of Normandy was killed as he attempted to flee. The bodies of the two men were dragged through the rooms of the Hôtel Saint-Paul while a mob of bourgeois and peasants cheered.

Charles, still covered in blood, somehow managed miraculously to flee Paris. He ultimately roused the nobility to his side, then blockaded and starved Paris into submission. He, like Louis XIV, who in 1651, three hundred years later, would also be forced to flee Paris, would always hate Paris and its people. As soon as Charles was able, he began construction of an impregnable fortress at Vincennes. He transformed the château at Vincennes from a hunting lodge into a base fortified against the people of Paris. It was his grand design to move the court and its administration to Vincennes, creating there a walled city, with grand houses (hôtels) for his courtiers. He even assigned plots of land to his courtiers, on which they were to build their own hôtels. But unlike Versailles, three centuries later, the aristocracy would never live at Vincennes.

The Michelin refers to the château at Vincennes as "this 'medieval Versailles.' " Both Vincennes and Versailles were built by kings who hated Paris. In both cases, their hatred of the city was the result of mob insurrections that had threatened their safety and forced them both to flee for their lives. Those are the main similarities between the two châteaux. However, I should also point out that while the word "castle" or "château" conjures up visions of Versailles, Vaux-le-Vicomte, or Chenonceau in the minds of today's tourist, the castles of the eleventh, twelfth, thirteenth, and even fourteenth centuries were crude affairs that could never have found their way into the grimmest of fairy tales. They were defensive structures, built for safety in a time of war. Once you have been inside a medieval castle of this period, you realize how austere and depressing they really were, and can more readily understand why a crusade to the sunny lands bordering the Mediterranean would be so appealing to knights and kings. The medieval castle's lack of charm is not helped by the fact that most of the tapestries, which provided color and warmth to the cold stone walls, were removed when the last resident left. Only the metal hooks on which they once hung could be seen the last time I was at Vincennes. The Apocalypse Tapestries seen at

Angers were created at the time Vincennes was built. In fact, Charles's court artist drew the cartoons on the back of the fabric of those tapestries that the weavers used. In all probability, similar tapestries would have hung at Vincennes. These tapestries were, in fact, always packed up and removed from the walls when the king left, to be hung on the walls when the king arrived at the next castle on his caravan. Medieval kings were itinerant, traveling from castle to castle within their realm. Even during the early Renaissance, at the time of Francis I, when castles and the Louvre began to be transformed into palaces of luxury, Francis removed tapestries from walls as he caravanned.

Some years later, in 2008, I returned to Vincennes shortly after it had undergone restoration. I had hoped that not only the stone and structure would be restored but that fourteenth-century tapestries, such as those found at Angers, would be hung on the empty hooks so that it would feel less like a prison and more like the fourteenth-century palace where kings once lived. But the hooks remained empty. Nor, I was told by a tour guide who seemed to be angry with me for asking, would tapestries ever be hung on those bare walls. Vincennes, consequently, evokes the grimness of the period in which it was built—a period of plague, hopelessness, and a seemingly endless war.

CHAPTER 9

JOAN OF ARC
1429 and the End of the
Hundred Years War at Orléans

—

TGV from Gare d'Austerlitz to Orléans

WHEN WE VISITED THE FOURTEENTH-CENTURY CASTLE AT Vincennes, the Hundred Years War (1337–1453) was just beginning. Years have passed and it is now 1429, as we join Joan of Arc, also known as the Maid of Orléans because of her miraculous victory in that city that turned the tide for France in this seemingly endless war of succession.

What becomes clear as we travel in Joan's footsteps is that what the people of France in the fifteenth century believed had a truth in the consequences it produced: their faith in the legend replaced despair and bound the fragments of a feudal country into a nation with a messianic patriotism strong enough to finally drive the English out of France. It would be a messianic patriotism that would survive and grow over the centuries, until, in the nineteenth century, it exploded out of France in the person of Napoleon.

It is hard to convey how excited I was when the none-too-brilliant idea came to me of visiting Joan of Arc's miraculous victory at Orléans, a victory that not only changed the direction of the Hundred Years War, but transformed her in the minds of the French from a fanatical virgin into "the chaste warrior sent by God to save France." I called the French Government Tourist Office, hoping they would arrange an English-speaking guide to show me around Orléans, and, miraculously, they arranged guided tours for me beginning on the day I was to arrive in France, even though it was only a week away. Not expecting them to act so promptly, I had planned to spend those three days at a spa in La Baule in Brittany, preparing myself, like an athlete in training, for the wonderful restaurants I intended to visit while researching these day trips through history. But I gallantly canceled my reservations at the spa and headed straight for Orléans.

My plane from New York landed at 6:15 in the morning, and, after dropping off most of my luggage at the apartment I had rented in Paris, I was on a TGV to Orléans by 9:55. In less than an hour, I got off that train, walked across the station platform at the Fleury-les-Aubrais station, and took a five-minute shuttle train to the center of Orléans. Following the instructions on the itinerary e-mailed to me by the Tourist Office, I checked into a hotel they had selected. The hotel was not air-conditioned, and the day was uncomfortably hot. The peeling paint and dirty wallpaper in my room dampened my spirits somewhat and created a rather negative first impression of Orléans, as did the noise from passing trains, which I could hear quite clearly when I opened the window, although that was not as loud, or as frequent, as the buses that I heard while trying to fall asleep that night. The hotel, alas, was a dump, albeit with a charming Art Nouveau façade. As I unpacked, I confess I wanted desperately to get back on the train and go to the luxurious spa at La Baule. When, later that day, I mentioned to my guide that I didn't think I could recommend the hotel they had selected, she said they had chosen it only because it was close to the station. Luckily, hotels are not important in visiting Orléans, because it is a perfect day trip from Paris; with trains leaving the Austerlitz station in Paris for Orléans every hour, it is very easy to get there and back on the same day since the trip is less than an hour. According to both the Michelin and the Gault Millau, Orléans has a very good restaurant—Les Antiquaires—which unfortunately was not one of the restaurants recommended to me during my stay.

I walked over to the tourist office where I was to meet my guide. It was closed. I shook the door. It was definitely locked. I called my contact on my cell phone, left a message on her answering machine—my third since I'd arrived in Orléans—and walked through the city to the banks of the Loire. Expecting an industrial city, I found the architecture of Orléans—except in the area in which my hotel was located—surprisingly beautiful. My route to the river took me along the Rue Royale, which is lined with lovely buildings dating from the sixteenth to the early twentieth centuries. Although the day was very hot, the shade provided by the eighteenth-century arcades that line the street made the walk extremely pleasant.

After reaching the river, I crossed the bridge to the other side, leaving the Old Town of Orléans. The Old Town was where Joan of Arc was brought when she first arrived at Orléans with her troops—on the wrong side of the Loire and the wrong side of the fortress of Tourelles. Although I had read several descriptions of those miraculous ten days during which Joan of Arc broke the siege of Orléans—her miraculous crossing of the river, and her taking of the fortress and the five bastides— I had been unable to visualize what she had done. I hoped I might find some remnants of the fortress that once guarded the bridge and entrance to the city, or of the five bastides she captured, and that this would bring those past events to life. Although the bridge I crossed looked old, it didn't look old enough to have been the one controlled by the fortress of Tourelles in 1429. That bridge, I later learned, had been a hundred yards downstream and no longer exists, nor does the fortress, which the English had taken, thereby severing Orléans' connection with the only area still controlled by the French.

Joan had pleaded with her dauphin for soldiers to break the siege of Orléans and he, considering her claim to have been sent by God to be ridiculous, had given her only a token force of men as a joke, to expose her as a fraud. The dauphin's officers had been instructed to bring her not to Orléans but to the wrong bank of the river to make her appear foolish, since they thought she would have to return to Beaugency, where there was an unguarded bridge across the Loire. The cowardly dauphin had never dreamed that the few men he had given her would ever confront, let alone beat, the English in battle. It was a time when many religious fanatics claimed to have direct communication with God, and when the aristocracy was becoming too sophisticated and cynical to believe in such nonsense. In addition, the dauphin's officers thought that she would not be able to cross the river by boat because the direction the wind usually blew made it impossible to bring boats upriver. When Joan and her forces finally arrived at the crossing, the wind was indeed blowing in the wrong direction. She may have been illiterate, but she wasn't stupid. She angrily confronted the Bastard of Orléans, who had been placed in charge of the French troops at Orléans. (He was another of the dashing Louis of Orléans's bastards—the queen of France had not been Louis's only conquest—and Bastard of Orléans was his title, not a reflection of how I feel about him.) After Joan's victory at Orléans, he would join La Hire as one of her trusted companions-at-arms.

But now she asked him if it were he "that counseled that I should come . . . to this side of the river." And when he confessed it was, she said: "You thought to deceive me and it is yourself above all whom you deceive, for I bring you succour from the King of Heaven. It comes not from love of me but from God himself who, at the request of Saint Louis and Saint Charlemagne has taken pity on the town of Orléans." When he told her that she would have to return to Beaugency to cross the bridge there, she told him and the troops to "wait awhile and all would be well." Then, inexplicably, "as a sign from heaven, the wind changed its direction," and Joan and her men were able to board boats, sail past the English-held fort, land at Orléans, and break the siege. In the mind of the French people, the change in the direction of the wind cemented Joan's identification with the virgin who would save France.

As I walked along the river, I looked for some remnant of the fortress of Tourelles or the bastides on the islands in the Loire, all of which the English had held and Joan had freed during the ten days she was in Orléans. I found none.

While I stood by this river where Joan's heroic battles had taken place, my cell phone rang in the twenty-first century. Madame Baudu from the French Tourist Office had been trying to get in touch with me, and said she would meet me at the cathedral in an hour, which she did.

I took a last look at the islands in the Loire where forts had once stood, and then headed toward the cathedral.

I waited for my guide in front of the cathedral's nineteenth-century western façade, marveling at the huge towers and gigantic statues of Matthew, Mark, Luke, and John. Only the apse remains the same today as it was when Joan prayed here, the rest having been destroyed during either the wars of religion in the seventeenth century or the French Revolution in the eighteenth. Most of the cathedral and the beautiful buildings of Orléans were built between 1589 and 1715, a period of prosperity, when Orléans was the economic center of the Loire Valley.

Before entering the cathedral, my guide led me to a rose window on the southern transept façade that I found intriguing. In the twelfth and thirteenth centuries, a time of deep religious spirituality, a rose window symbolized the "Eye of God." This one, however, was created in the seventeenth century, not a time of spirituality but of political spin, during the reign of the Sun King, whose face is in the center of the window, framed by the flames of the sun. Written below is his motto: NEC PLURI-BUS IMPAR (ABOVE ALL MEN).

My guide, aware that my interest in Orléans centered on Joan of Arc, led me inside to see ten modern stained-glass windows depicting her story.

In the first window, Joan, depicted as a very young girl at Domrémy, is being told by three saints to go to Orléans and lift the siege and then lead Charles to his coronation at Reims. (Charles, afraid to go to Reims for his coronation as French tradition demanded, and having crowned himself at Bourges instead, was contemptuously called the king of Bourges.) When he told her he had already been crowned, Joan pointed out that "Kings of France are made at Reims," that tradition required that he be crowned at Reims with the holy oil supposedly left in the ampoule since the time of Clovis.

The second window shows Joan in a red dress in the small town of Vaucouleurs, where she has come to plead with Robert de Baudricourt, the captain of the royal garrison there, for a horse and escort to accompany her to the dauphin's court in Chinon. De Baudricourt, the man in the green hat, is obviously rich. He is also obviously skeptical. The expression on his face shows he doesn't want to subsidize her mission. In fact, he did not take the seventeen-year-old peasant girl seriously at first. Since many virgins were claiming to be France's savior at the time, when Joan first uttered this claim to Robert de Baudricourt, he treated it with contempt and told his servant to "return her to her father's house." According to legend, or fact, he refused her request twice but she refused to leave Vaucouleurs, where a growing audience of townspeople were becoming mesmerized by what she said. Apparently she was quite persuasive when she said to him: "Have you not heard it said that it has been prophesied that France shall be lost by a woman and restored by a virgin from the Lorraine marches?"

At last he granted her the men and horses. The English would claim that de Baudricourt gave her the horse and escort because she was his "whore as well as of others." But that is not correct. Her virginity, which was repeatedly verified during her short life, was important in the fifteenth century because it was then believed that a virgin could not have dealings with the Devil.

In the third window, Joan is depicted at a reception at Chinon, "miraculously" recognizing the dauphin, who had hidden among 300 of his courtiers. When the dauphin first heard Joan's claim to be the virgin savior, he too thought it nonsense and agreed to see her only so that he could have the malicious fun of exposing the fanatical virgin as a fraud. When Joan of Arc entered the Great Hall at the fortress of Chinon on the evening depicted in the window, she found herself at the end of a long room, 70 feet in length, lit by fifty torches. The cold stone walls were hung with luxurious tapestries. The room itself was filled with noblemen attired in the colorful costumes of the day—their rank indicated by the length of their sleeves.

The dauphin had hidden among the crowd after exchanging his clothes with a nobleman of lesser rank and shorter sleeves. Although another nobleman wore his robes, and Joan had never seen the dauphin, she immediately recognized him, marched straight to him through a room crowded with noblemen. At her trial she said: "When I entered my king's room, I knew him among the others by the counsel of my voice which revealed him to me. I told my King that I wanted to go and make war against the English."[*]

---

[*] Pernoud, p. 46.

When the dauphin demanded proof that she had been sent by God, Joan related an incident that she could have known only by miraculous means.

As the story goes, she said that one night "in the castle of Loches, he [the dauphin] had risen from his bed and, in the privacy of his chamber, prayed on his knees that if he were not the true son of Charles VI, he might be allowed to leave France, seek refuge in Scotland or Spain, and give up the kingdom to the English to survive in peace." She should have stopped there, instead of continuing on to say, "I tell you in the name of Our Lord Christ that you are the true son of the King." Since most people in the royal courts of both England and France, including the dauphin Charles and his mother, believed the dauphin to be a bastard, and not the son of "Mad King Charles,"* Joan of Arc's revelation that he was the true son of the king was heard with a great deal of skepticism— especially by Charles. In fact, it strengthened his belief that she was a fraud. The dauphin had, therefore, good reason not to be convinced that the voices Joan heard were divine. He kept her on the first floor of the Fort du Cadray at Chinon while her virginity was verified and after it was, he sent her off to Poitiers, where she was again interrogated, and her virginity checked once again. Then, and only then, would he grant her a token force to lead to Orléans. Everyone at court believed it was only a question of "when" not "if" Orléans would fall, and the number of soldiers given to Joan were hardly a force considered sufficient to break the siege.

In the fourth window, she is depicted making her entrance into Orléans, and the fifth depicts her victory at the fortress of Tourelles. The next window shows a scene in the very cathedral in which we were standing: Joan is depicted here at Mass at the altar I was looking at, giving thanks for her victory. Joan is then shown in a dress at the coronation of the king at Reims. (She actually refused to wear a dress.)

In the eighth window, Joan is shown at Compiègne, where she was captured by a follower of Jean de Luxembourg, the captain of a Bur-

* Pernoud, p. 53.

gundian company, who imprisoned her in his Castle of Beaurevoir. He kept her there in comfort while he waited for the dauphin, who had now been crowned Charles VII, to ransom her. It was only after she tried to escape, falling into his moat and injuring herself, that he sold her to the English for 10,000 livres of gold.

Joan is then shown bound to the stake at Rouen, a paper cap on her head on which is written, "Heretic, relapsed apostate, idolatress."

In the last window, she is burned at the stake.

From the cathedral, we walked over to the Maison de Jeanne d'Arc, where Joan stayed as the guest of Jacques Boucher, the financial minister for the Duke of Orléans. This charming, timber-framed fifteenth-century house sits in the middle of Place du Général de Gaulle and is surrounded by modern buildings. The houses in the area were all destroyed in 1940 by the Germans, but this one, now oddly out of place, was reconstructed to look exactly as it did when Joan stayed there. During each of her ten days in Orléans, she would climb to the roof, from which there was an excellent view of the English camp.

I highly recommend visiting the second floor of the Maison de Jeanne d'Arc. Although I had been disappointed not to find buildings from the fifteenth century, there are small-scale models on the second floor of what Orléans looked like at the time Joan freed the city. The exhibit is riveting. There is a dramatic sound-and-light presentation in both French and English in which a light moves to each model, illuminating it as a voice narrates the story of how Joan of Arc liberated Orléans. The story of Joan of Arc is so dramatic that I never tire of hearing it, and the narration of these battles captured my full attention. Miniatures of the forts the Maid of Orléans captured, the forts I had hoped to find sitting on islands in the river, are here, enabling me to visualize what Joan actually saw when she arrived and follow her as she freed Orléans.

The exhibition room became dark, and then a light falls on the model of the Porte de Bourgogne, the gate where Joan had entered the city, dressed in full armor on a black horse. For three months, after Joan had arrived at Chinon, the people of Orléans had been hearing rumors that a maid and her troops were coming to break the siege. When she finally did arrive, they greeted her as a saint. They followed her as a savior through the streets, trying to kiss her sword or touch her feet or her horse.

The voice narrating the story has Joan proclaim an ultimatum to the English. In reality, since she was illiterate and could neither read nor write, someone else actually read this ultimatum, which was a letter to the King of England and the Duke of Bedford that Joan had dictated while still in Chinon. However, the words of the ultimatum are hers and, hearing this ultimatum, you have a sense of what the English had to contend with when confronted by this determined "fanatical virgin" who believed so wholeheartedly in herself and her cause that she made others believe in her too. The ultimatum orders the English to leave and "go away into your country, by God. And if so be not done, expect news of the Maid who will come to see you shortly, to your very great injury."

The light moves on to the bastides of the Augustines, which Joan liberated on May 6, as a voice describes the battle and how the fortress of Tourelles was taken by Joan and La Hire.

> The Bastard of Orléans had never expected to actually engage the English and was taken by surprise when his scant forces won this battle. After their victory, he suggested to Joan that they wait until help arrived from the King before trying to take the fortress of Tourelles. She replied, with the same simple self-assurance with which she addressed the English: "You have been at your counsel and I at mine" . . . And then addressing the men who stood at her side: "Rise tomorrow early in the morning and earlier than you did today and do the best you can, be always at my side, for tomorrow . . . blood will flow out of my body above my breast."

She was wounded the next day, just as she had predicted. The following description shows—at least to me—since the fashionable trend in historical writing today concludes that her role in the Hundred Years War was insignificant—how myth and reality played a role in reversing a war that until her arrival at Orléans, the English had all but won.

The English saw the arrow pierce her shoulder, saw her carried away, and, thinking she had been mortally wounded, were relieved to find her human after all. They began fighting with renewed vigor, so much so that the Bastard of Orléans wanted to retreat.

Then Joan returned to the battle. When the English soldiers saw she was still alive, they were then sure she was a witch and began to flee. According to the Bastard of Orléans:

> Then the Maid . . . came back . . . at once seized her standard in hand and placed her self on the parapet of the trench and the moment she was there the English trembled and were terrified. And the King's soldiers regained their courage and began to go up, charging against the boulevard without meeting the least resistence.

After her victory, the lights and narrative continue, leaving Orléans and following Joan's short career, which ended at the stake in Rouen, where we will follow her after leaving Orléans.

My guide then took me to several interesting places in Orléans, including the Musée des Arts, one of the great museums of France, which alone is worth a visit to Orléans, containing paintings and sculptures from the eleventh to the twentieth century. As I was being shown through the Renaissance Hôtel de Ville (City Hall), built a century after Joan's death, I began to feel increasingly guilty about wanting only to see evocations of Joan of Arc while in Orléans.

Then, as I was walking through this marvelous building, dressed in slacks and a white shirt, my hair cut short for the summer, I noticed a sixteenth-century portrait of Joan, sword in hand but in a dress. As I looked at the painting, I realized that I hadn't taken seriously enough the impact of Joan of Arc's mode of dress. I hadn't paid proper attention when I read of "the snickers of the ladies at the Court" of Charles VII when she refused to wear a dress at court. I hadn't taken the charge at her trial for heresy very seriously—the charge that she dressed in "man's clothes" and had "shorn hair"—"of having worn," as the charge put it: "Clothes dissolute, mis-shapen and indecent, against natural decency." The importance of her wearing male clothes was summed up in his memoirs by Pope Pius II (1405–1464). In Rouen he wrote: "She was diligently examined to discover whether she used . . . diabolical aid or whether she erred in any way in her religion. Nothing worthy to be censured was found in her, excepting the male attire which she wore. And that was not judged deserving of the extreme penalty. Taken back to her prison she was threatened with death if she resumed the wearing of man's clothes." Pope Pius added that "her gaolers brought her none but male attire."

I had thought, as Pope Pius probably thought, that the charge was indeed absurd. I had a greater shock when I found out that even though the people of Orléans had celebrated her deliverance of Orléans almost every year since 1433 by having someone portray Joan of Arc entering the city on horseback at the Porte de Bourgogne, the person had been a boy until after World War II, because until the end of that war it was still not considered appropriate for a girl to wear men's clothing.

While looking at this portrait, I also realized I had to stop being angry with Orléans for having been bombed in 1940 and consequently not having any early-fifteenth-century buildings. The town had actually done its best to preserve the memory of her victory, as I would learn when I climbed the stairs to the Centre Jeanne d'Arc, whose fascinating library, given by her biographer Régine Pernoud, is filled with books, magazines, videos, biographies, plays, and poems about Joan of Arc, and, best of all, the transcripts of her trial.

Although I had not found remnants of Joan's past in stone and wood, as I opened drawers and pulled out files in this library, I found as many different Joan of Arcs as there have been centuries since her ashes were thrown into the Seine, since each generation created its own vision of her. The first drawer I opened contained pictures of Joan arranged chronologically, century by century: in armor, wearing a dress, her hair long, her hair short, and, finally, wearing breeches in the twentieth century. Since no one knew what she looked like—the only contemporary sketch of Joan was drawn by a man who had been inspired by her but who had never seen her—the pictures are what people of each age imagined her to be. There are, however, copies of portraits of her cowardly dauphin, whom she revered and led to Reims for his coronation, and who, so jealous of her popularity for having done so, made no effort to ransom her when she was captured or save her from the English, whom he knew would burn her as a witch. These portraits capture the Charles VII that one historian of the Hundred Years War described as being a "weak, knock-kneed, pious little man" having a "miserable physique," with "small grey wandering eyes, his nose thick and bulbous."

Although I was taught in graduate school not to hate historical figures like Charles, I just couldn't forgive him for not ransoming Joan of Arc from the English. Looking at these portraits, I felt I understood why his mother detested him and why his son would lead a rebellion against him. Joan may have revered her dauphin, whom she had crowned king, but he wasn't particularly lovable or reliable. Not only did he make no effort to save Joan of Arc, who was one of two people most important in saving his kingdom for him, but he also repaid the other person, Jacques Coeur, the man who provided the funds for the dauphin's campaigns against the English, by confiscating his properties and sentencing him to life in prison when the war was over so that he would not have to repay the money he owed him. A monarch unrestrained by law, Charles also ordered a member of his court dragged naked from his marriage bed and drowned in a river, and another he ordered clubbed to death after having his hands chopped off.

At the library were also videos of the Joan of Arc celebration dating back to the First World War, and I was able to watch it change over the years. When the festival, the oldest in France, first began in 1433, it was a simple religious procession held on May 8, the date of her victory over the English, but it has since become a ten-day celebration beginning on April 29, the day she entered Orléans, and concluding on May 8, with a Mass celebrating the deliverance of the city from the English at the Cathedral of Orléans.

Several months before the festival begins, a seventeen-year-old girl from Orléans—of impeccable character—is selected to portray Joan of Arc. She is first taken to Domrémy, where Joan of Arc was born, and then to all the places that were important in Joan of Arc's short life. The festival begins with the girl, dressed in armor, and accompanied by townsmen dressed in medieval costumes, crossing the Loire by boat. She is then lifted onto a horse, which, considering the weight of her armor, is no easy affair. She enters the city on horseback at the Porte de Bourgogne, where theatrical scenery makes the entrance to the town appear as it did in 1429. She then leads a procession of townspeople dressed in medieval costume to the Maison Jeanne d'Arc. During the festival, there are reenactments of each of the battles she won on the day she won them; concerts in front of the Hôtel de Ville; a sound-and-light production; fireworks along the Loire; and a medieval fair with jousting contests. Then on May 7, at noon, there is a musical fanfare as the mayor announces the anniversary of the victory. Finally, on May 8, the Mass celebrates her liberation of Orléans.

The festival had been abolished in 1793 during the Reign of Terror because of its religious nature. The "republican" leaders during the Reign of Terror were not only beheading the king, the queen, the aristocracy, about 40,000 people in all, but also beheading statues of kings on church façades, and, aware of the dangers of a politically powerful church, attempting to destroy everything ecclesiastical. In addition to canceling Joan's parade, they destroyed her relics—her hat, her standard, and her sword—and all the statues and crosses that had been erected in her honor.

France was still reeling from the horrors of the Terror when Napoleon Bonaparte, as first consul of France, realized Joan's value as a symbol of liberty and patriotism, a symbol that could help weld the country together. He decreed that the ceremonies celebrating her deliverance of Orléans be reestablished. As an appeal to the fanatical "republicans" of his day, he resurrected Joan of Arc as a patriot and a victim of the reactionary Roman Catholic Church. He issued a decree instructing Orléans to have a ceremony commemorating the deliverance of the city from famine, with songs sung by marchers carrying a replica of the banner that Joan of Arc designed and carried into battle. He also ordered that Joan's statue be commissioned, celebrating "the glory of her exploits etched in our hearts." It was to be a statue celebrating "liberty." (The statue, now in the Place du Martroi, not far from the cathedral, was completed during the reign of his nephew in 1855; the bas-reliefs on the pedestal, done in Italian Renaissance style by Vital Dubay, depict the events in her life.)

After Napoleon discarded his republican guise and crowned himself emperor, Joan remained the symbolic of liberation—liberation from the English. The Maid of Orléans's victory over the English was a perfect symbol for Napoleon, who understood her psychological value. He made her the official symbol of French patriotism, naming her a national heroine. When, in 1815, Napoleon was exiled, Joan of Arc, once the symbol of Napoleon's republican France and then of Napoleon's empire, became the symbol for the Restoration, as reactionary forces emphasized not liberty but her faith and support of the monarchy against the English. Later that century, in the 1890s, during the Dreyfus Affair, both parties claimed that Joan of Arc would have been on their side.

It appears she has the ability to transform herself into a symbol for almost any political group or playwright, into a symbol of nationalism, patriotism, independence, freedom, fascism, republicanism, reaction, liberalism, or feminism.

Maybe the Duke of Bedford was right and she was a witch. At any rate, she was tried as a witch in Rouen, where we go next.

CHAPTER 10

ROUEN
Joan of Arc and Monet

—

Train from Gare Saint-Lazare to Rouen

H AVING VISITED JOAN OF ARC'S VICTORY IN ORLÉANS, I FOL-
lowed her to Rouen where she was burned at the stake. Rouen turned
out to be a delightful surprise, a city filled with fabulous restaurants,
artists creating faience, and a large car-free area of pedestrian streets
lined with eight hundred half-timbered houses built during the Middle
Ages. There is not only a cathedral whose façade Monet painted thirty-
one times, a perfect Rayonnant church, but also a superb Beaux-Arts
museum.* Aside from the plaza where Joan was burned at the stake, the
resulting day trip is sheer delight. I usually don't like places I visit in the
rain or visit without Bob, the sun to warm me and create moving shadows on cold, lifeless stones, and Bob to bring the ancient tales to life
that occurred when those stones were first put in place—and, of course,
for his company over a really good lunch. But the first time I visited
Rouen, I came alone, and in the rain, and I loved it anyway.

That initial trip was a scouting trip—to see if the city could or should
be included as a day trip from Paris. I wanted to learn if it was easy and
pleasant to reach Rouen by train, which it is. The hour-and-six-minute

---

* We found three terrific restaurants in Rouen: Gill on the Quai; Les Nymphéas, near the horrible Place
du Vieux-Marché; and L'Écaille, which wasn't all that far from the station. Although restaurants that are
wonderful in France usually stay wonderful, it is best to check the Michelin and Gault Millau guides to
make sure.

trip from the Saint-Lazare station follows the Seine River from Paris to Rouen, and is incredibly beautiful, especially in the rain. I felt like I was traveling through a sequence of misty Monet landscapes, many of which looked so familiar I felt I had seen them before. And I had—on museum walls. Monet's home at Giverny is a station stop (Vernon) midway between Rouen and Paris, and the route is one on which he and other painters took their easels as they traveled between Paris and the Normandy coast. I wanted to know not only if the trip was pleasant, but also whether the city evoked nineteenth-century Rouen, which Monet had painted, or fifteenth-century Rouen, which burned Joan of Arc at the stake.

The fog was so dense and it was raining so hard the day of this first tour that I couldn't find the cathedral whose façade Monet had painted. I had read André Maurois's description of seeing the three steeples of the cathedral as he emerged from the station in 1928 and expected to see the spires of the cathedral when I left the station, but I didn't. As the rain pounded my umbrella, I didn't know which way to go. As I may have mentioned, I have no sense of direction and needed the spires of the cathedral or a map. I had none of them. It was raining much too hard to open a map, and I saw no spires—unbeknownst to me, between the time Maurois emerged from his station and I emerged from mine, the station had been moved.

While I didn't see the cathedral as I left the station, I did see an enormous, round castellated tower, topped with a pointed cap, called the Donjon Jeanne d'Arc. I sloshed my way toward it, crossing a drawbridge over an overgrown moat, and made my way inside. This thirteenth-century tower was once one of sixty turreted towers of a defensive wall that extended for over five miles around Bouvreuil Castle. It looked vaguely familiar since it was built by Philip Augustus, the same king who had built the castle walls and towers I had seen at the Louvre. Philip Augustus built this fortress in Rouen—the former capital of the English fief of Normandy—after he had stripped King John of England of all his lands in France. King John, you'll recall, was called John Lackland by thirteenth-century Englishmen because he lost Normandy, which English kings had held as a fief from the French king for the previous two centuries. After the outbreak of the Hundred Years War, Henry V of England recaptured Normandy, as well as Rouen, a favorite city of the English kings. It had been back in English possession for ten years when Joan of Arc was brought there in chains. This tower is typical of those built during the thirteenth and fourteenth centuries, with the usual arrow-slit windows, sloping base, three levels, and rounded walls, although its moat was wider and deeper than most others and, to deter attackers, was filled with wolf traps at the time. At first, I thought, because of its name, that this was the tower where Joan had been brought on the evening of December 23, 1430, after she had been captured in Compiègne, and where she was held prisoner for more than four months. This was not the case. That tower, along with fifty-eight others, is gone. The tower I entered was the one in which Joan was brought in manacles and threatened with torture on May 9, 1431. She had been cross-examined for months and, much to the irritation of the English, nothing that she or other witnesses said justified burning her as a witch. The English, not overly concerned with the truth, decided to torture a confession out of her anyway. On that day, she was accompanied by twelve of her judges and two men who specialized in torture. She was threatened with torture if she did not confess to heresy or a relationship with the Devil. Her response to their threats was recorded by witnesses who were there, and what she said more than five hundred years ago in this gloomy, stone tower reveals the futility of using torture to obtain truth: "Truly, though you were to have my limbs torn off and send the soul out of my body, I should not say otherwise; and if I did tell you otherwise, I should always thereafter say that you had made me speak so by force. . . ." Joan's words moved those present so much that she remained unharmed. One of the torturers, Maugier Leparmentier, said that although Joan was "questioned for some time . . . she answered with much prudence so much so that those who were there marveled. Finally we withdrew. I and my companion without having laid hands on her person."

Three days later, the twelve judges decided to vote on whether or not they should torture her—only three of the twelve voted affirmatively. The English were growing impatient. Because of an incident that occurred while Joan was in prison, we know the Earl of Warwick did not want just her death but wanted her burned as a witch. When she became violently ill after eating a piece of fish given to her by the Bishop of Beauvais, the earl became furious and wrote that the king wanted her to recover from that illness because "not for anything in the world would the King have her die a natural death. The King, indeed, held her dear, for he had bought her dear, and would not have her die excepting at the hands of justice, and that she be burnt." I doubt that the King of England, Henry VI, who was only ten years old at the time, cared about Joan's health.

As I left the tower and headed down the Rue de Jeanne d'Arc, I stopped to read a copper plaque on a building next to a wallpaper store that stated that the tower in which Joan had been held prisoner once stood where I was then standing. Looking at the plaque and then looking back at the tower, I began to have some sense of how massive were the walls and towers that once surrounded the castle.

As I continued walking, I found another plaque, this time on the Bishop's Palace, marking the spot where Joan was told that she had been sentenced to be burned at the stake. When she learned that she was to be burned, she cried out, "Ah! I had rather seven times be decapitated than to be thus burned." Death by decapitation, I was surprised to learn, was a privilege reserved for the aristocracy and royal family, and in practical terms it was usually much quicker.

When I read this plaque, I decided to stop wandering aimlessly and head for the spot where Joan's life had ended, so I asked directions and left this charming section of Rouen I had stumbled on by pure chance: a restored medieval neighborhood where narrow, winding streets are filled with half-timbered houses whose slate and tile roofs are steeply sloped and whose gables are supported by oak corbels carved into fantastic animal shapes—an area of bell towers, church steeples, ancient abbeys, and former palaces. I then walked over to the Old Marketplace (Place du Vieux-Marché) with the morbid objective of seeing where Joan of Arc had been burned. When I turned a corner, I entered a square where an old market had once been. It was now filled with every imaginable cheap tourist attraction—a carousel, souvenir shops, fast-food restaurants, an incongruously modern eyesore of a church built in her honor, and an inappropriate aluminum cross marking the spot where she was burned. The square that I had come to see was the only place in Rouen that I would find totally disagreeable. At least in the rain it was fairly empty.

First, I looked for the Church of the Holy Savior, which Joan faced as the flames rose around her. All I saw was a modern church that reminded me of a sunken ship. Then I looked down and found old stones outlining the foundation of where the church had been when Joan, tied to the stake, asked to have a cross. An Englishman heard her request and gave her a little cross he made from a wooden stick. "She put this cross into her bosom, between her flesh and her clothes, and furthermore asked humbly . . . to have the cross from the church . . . before her eyes until death.

As the flames began to rise around her, the "Executioner cried out he was doomed and would never be given God's forgiveness . . . that he greatly feared to be damned for he had burned a holy woman."

This dreadful square, however, did offer one surprise: the Musée de Jeanne d'Arc. The first time I was there, I couldn't find it. When I returned a second time with Bob, he located it, and I understood why I hadn't seen it before. From the outside, it looks like a seedy souvenir shop, not at all like a museum. As soon as he pointed it out, my heart sank once again: I expected our visit to the museum would be a vile experience. While I felt I had to see it and make sure it was as bad as I expected, I saw no reason why Bob had to suffer, but he insisted on coming with me.

We walked through the museum shop, where souvenirs were on sale, purchased two tickets, and descended ancient, winding stone stairs leading to a Romanesque dungeon—and as we descended, we left our century far behind. I had been disappointed that the castle where Joan of Arc had been held prisoner for five months had been destroyed, and that nothing remained of the two places where her trial was held—

that all that was left in Rouen was the single tower where she'd been threatened with torture, which wasn't enough to evoke what Rouen or the castle was like when Joan was brought there. But the museum has a model of that castle and its mighty walls just as it had been when Joan was held prisoner there. The model is complete with the crenellated walls, six gates each protected by barbicans, and the sixty towers, each equipped with nine cannons, including a medieval long-nosed mounted cannon that fired gun-arrows (missiles quickly replaced by lead balls, which were less expensive to make). The model shows that the massive wall surrounded a courtyard in the center of which was a castle very much like Philip Augustus's in the Louvre, and Charles V's at Vincennes. So, having seen the old section of Rouen, where so many buildings from the fifteenth century line the streets, Vincennes, the Donjon of Jeanne d'Arc, and then this model, I was able to picture in my mind the fifteenth-century Rouen of our fifteenth-century heroine.

The museum also contains a replica of the armor she wore, a transcript of her trial, and other documents relating to her trial. But my real surprise was the life-size wax figures arranged in scenes from Joan's life. I usually detest wax museums. I thought the one at fabulous Chenonceau, with its figures of Catherine de Médicis and Diane de Poitiers, trite, the one at Ussé of Sleeping Beauty okay for kids under the age of six, the one at Uzès corny, and the one at La Rochelle to be avoided at all costs. However, for some odd reason I really liked this one, perhaps because my expectations were so low or perhaps because I never tire of hearing the story of Joan of Arc, and it is told quite well here in four languages—French, English, German, and Italian. When you press a button, a life-size scene is illuminated, and a voice is heard in whichever language you select. The displays follow Joan's life, beginning with her journey from Domrémy and ending with her death where she is bound to the stake wearing that paper cap.

In retrospect, although I enjoyed the museum, I am not sure I would suggest going out of your way to visit it. Rather, I would spend my time wandering in the medieval section of Rouen, where the half-timbered houses jut out over narrow winding streets free of cars. There the sounds we hear are ancient sounds, like the chimes of an ancient one-handed clock that marked the hours when Joan was captive in Rouen. Although the medieval wooden belfry that was once there has been replaced by an imposing Renaissance arch spanning the Rue Gros-Horloge, the gilded lead clock is the very same one that chimed in 1429. The clock doesn't have a second hand to tell the minutes, since minutes were not considered important in an agricultural society, but it does display the phases of the moon, which were important then, and personifies the days of the week with Roman gods and goddesses—Diana for Monday, Mars for Tuesday, Mercury for Wednesday, Jupiter for Thursday, Venus for Friday, Saturn for Saturday, and Apollo for Sunday.

I left the Place du Vieux-Marché, taking the Rue Rollon back to the old section of Rouen, and almost immediately found myself at the Renaissance Palais de Justice. It had been built in the fifteenth and sixteenth centuries on the site of an ancient Jewish merchant community and consequently contains in its courtyard one of the city's unsolved mysteries—the burned remains of a Romanesque Jewish building, perhaps the oldest Jewish building in France. It was discovered in 1976, when, during restoration work on the Palais, an earthmoving caterpillar tractor was suddenly swallowed up as the ground collapsed beneath it; no one has since been able to decide what the building beneath the earthmover had originally been, whether it was a synagogue, a residence of a prosperous Jew, or a Hebrew school. It seems to have been built a century before the Abbot Suger built Saint-Denis, when the Jewish community in Rouen was both numerous and prosperous. Columns support Romanesque archways cut into the thick, meticulously cut stones of the building. The bases of each of the columns are decorated with different carvings, the most unusual and enigmatic one being that of two lions lying on their backs and sharing one head. The building appears to have been destroyed by fire about the time Philip Augustus wrested control of Rouen from the English. The Jews had contributed to the prosperity of Rouen from the time of Charlemagne—who felt that Jews, because of "their commercial skills . . . were needed and wanted, perhaps even indispensable"—to the time of Philip Augustus. During those centuries, both English and French kings had protected the Jews, who, according to records, paid exorbitantly high taxes. In 1182, Philip Augustus ended this policy by confiscating their lands, persecuting them, and driving them from both Rouen and Paris.*

Leaving the Palais de Justice, I turned the wrong way along the Rue aux Juifs, and instead of arriving at the Place de la Cathédral, I found myself facing a fabulously ornate Flamboyant Gothic church—Saint-Maclou. Thinking it was the cathedral, I was rather perplexed because it didn't look anything like the paintings I had seen the day before at the Musée d'Orsay. I should have read Victor Hugo's letter to his wife in which he called Rouen "the city of 100 steeples" before I left. As it was, I had no idea the city had so many churches and bell towers. I merely assumed I hadn't studied the paintings of the Rouen Cathedral long enough. Before returning to Rouen the following year, I made my way back through the crowds of people who are always at the Musée d'Orsay, up the stairs to Room 32, which displays four of Monet's thirty-one paintings of Rouen's cathedral. I was determined to engrave Monet's views of the façade in my mind. I hoped that seeing both the paintings and the cathedral façade would help me understand why Monet painted it thirty-one times.

Monet painted the cathedral façade during the winters of 1892 and 1893. During that first winter, he rented a draper's studio above a store at 23 Place de la Cathédral in Rouen, from whose windows he was able to watch the effects of the sun on the stones of the cathedral façade. As the sun began to rise in the early morning, the cathedral portal was cast in a blue silhouette as one of the towers caught the first rays of dawn. Then, as the day progressed, he could see the morning sunlight slowly cascade down the stones of the cathedral until, in the early afternoon, all the shadows were gone and, with the sun full upon it, the tower was bleached almost white. Then he could watch as the stones of the façade glowed red in the setting sun and were slowly enveloped in shadows. His studio was filled with the canvases on which he was working. During the course of each day, as the sun moved across the sky, he moved

---

* In order to visit this building, it is necessary to make an appointment at the Rouen Tourist Bureau prior to your arrival.

from one canvas to another. He did so because, as he wrote in one letter, the painter must "stop work immediately as the light changes in
order to obtain a true impression and not a composite picture." Each
painting was Monet's attempt to capture a single instant, a moment of
his impression of the sunlight on the cathedral façade, "to render my
impression in front of the most fleeting effect." In his letters, he wrote
precisely what he was trying to achieve: "I am seeking 'instantaneity,'
above all, the envelopment, the same light spread over everywhere . . . to
convey what I experience."

He returned to Rouen the next year, but he was unable to rent the
draper's studio where he had worked the year before, and perhaps that
was lucky, because during that first year he was totally unhappy with
his work, writing "I am utterly dejected and dissatisfied with what I
have done. I have aimed too high and only succeeded in spoiling what
is good. I am broken, I can do no more . . . I have had a night filled with
nightmares . . . the cathedral was falling down on me." (I was surprised
to learn that his nightmares, unlike my black and white dreams, were in
pre-Hollywood technicolor, largely in pinks and blues.) But the second
year, while painting in a room at 81 Rue Grand Point, from which he
had a slightly angled view of the façade, his letters are far happier, writing in one "that it seems to me that I will be making progress."

Reading the frustration expressed in Monet's letters, I came to feel
so sorry that he had chosen light and not the façade as his model. Consequently he was unable to stop the sun in its journey across his sky. He
had to wait to capture the effects that he wanted. Unable to see all the
cathedral series in one place, I discovered a most original Web site created by the art department at Columbia University, which has partially
satisfied my curiosity: it has posted copies of twenty-six of the cathedral
paintings so that they look like a sheet of twenty-six stamps on the computer screen. A sun dial placed next to the paintings is designed so you
can stop a digitally moving sun at any point in the sky, and when you
stop the sun, your computer screen is instantly filled with a copy of the
painting that Monet painted at that time of day. What I don't understand is why Monet chose winter months to come to Rouen, since he

expressed such an intense need for a "few more days of sun" to complete his paintings, and Rouen is not known for its sunny winters.

When I returned to Rouen with Bob the following spring, after having intensely scrutinized the paintings in the Musée d'Orsay as well as one at the Musée Marmottan Monet, I still didn't recognize the western façade. The last time I had mistaken another church for the cathedral. This time I didn't see the façade because it was covered with scaffolding.

My trip to the Musée d'Orsay was not altogether necessary because one of Monet's paintings of the cathedral hangs on the wall in Rouen's Musée des Beaux-Arts. One of my great discoveries in traveling through France by train are the country's marvelous and empty provincial art museums—and Rouen's museum is one of my best discoveries. What makes these museums so appealing to me, if not for the museums' directors, who would prefer to have more paying visitors, is that they are filled with great paintings, not with hordes of people. While at the Musée d'Orsay there are always crowds of people on the upper floor, where the Impressionists are exhibited, and each time I was there I was only able to see Monet's paintings of the cathedral briefly before the heads and shoulders of other tourists and tour groups appeared. This was not the case at Rouen's museum. Bob and I were the only people in the room with the cathedral painting for at least thirty minutes, and then only one couple strolled by and left moments later. We were able to view Monet's painting as my professor of art history told me an Impressionist painting should be viewed. We could look at it and then step back away from it—because of where it was hung, we were able to step back and back, almost 90 feet back—without a single person coming between us and the painting. We could watch the painting appear to change from blobs of color into misty shapes and then concrete forms as we stepped back, without any obstructions to our view of this painting or that of any of the others by Monet, Renoir, Sisley, Caravaggio, Vélasquez, Poussin, and Corot.

Having successfully found the cathedral, we went inside to see something created neither in the time of Joan of Arc nor that of Monet, but in the period that followed the end of the Hundred Years War. For years I had wanted to see the tomb that Diane de Poitiers had commissioned for the cathedral when she was a young widow of nineteen, but before I discovered the train, Rouen had always been too long a drive. Diane de Poitiers was the mistress of Henry II, who had built Chenonceau, the most beautiful early-Renaissance castle in the Loire. Having seen Chenonceau, I became fascinated with her story and wanted to see this tomb—she was not only the mistress to a king many years her junior, but a brilliant patron of the arts, and this was the very first project that she commissioned. What was remarkable about the tomb she had created for her husband, Louis de Brézé, is the sculptor she selected to execute the work. When looking for the perfect sculptor to create her husband's memorial, she had the perfect taste and the self-confidence at nineteen to choose a sixteen-year-old boy—Jean Goujon. He would turn out to be "one of the greatest French sculptors of the Renaissance." Diane de Poitiers instructed him to carve her husband both as a naked corpse on a sarcophagus of black marble and as a knight on horseback, and then thinking of her own immortality, also had herself carved on the sarcophagus—kneeling at the head of her husband.

ALTHOUGH THIS CATHEDRAL existed when Joan of Arc was brought to Rouen, she was never allowed to pray or attend Mass here during her five months in captivity. Perhaps the English treated her so harshly because of her insistence that her saints spoke French and not English. Before the Hundred Years War, language had not been emotionally charged in either country. It became so only with the growth of nationalism, which, some say, began with Joan.

In the period prior to Joan of Arc, during the time of Eleanor of Aquitaine and her son Richard the Lionheart, for example, English rulers in French territories spoke French. In fact, it may come as a surprise to readers of *Ivanhoe* that when Richard the Lionheart was given Aquitaine (southwestern France) by his mother, he spoke only French and was not able to speak a word of English. During the course of the Hundred Years War, and in particular, during the time in which Joan of Arc became identified with the virgin who would save France, the transformation of France and England from feudal countries into nation-states began to take place. And as the transformation occurred, the English vassals whom Henry V of England had installed in Normandy, and their heirs, increasingly spoke English. Many stopped speaking French altogether. The English were at the very least annoyed at Joan's trial when she claimed that her saints spoke to her in French. The following exchange is an example:

Question: How do they speak?

Joan: This voice is beautiful, sweet and humble (low) and it speaks the French language.

Question: Does not Saint Margaret speak the English tongue?

Joan: How should she speak English since she is not on the side of the English?

Even before we left Rouen, I felt we were already leaving medieval France behind. As we made our way to the station, we passed streets named for the different guilds that had moved into the city as the Hundred Years War came to an end.

PART TWO

—

The Renaissance

CITIES AND CASTLES

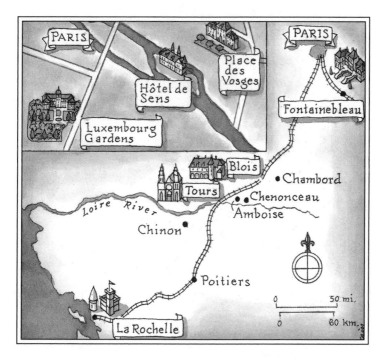

CHAPTER 11

TOURS
The Rebirth of Cities After
the Hundred Years War

TGV from Gare Montparnasse to Tours

*T*OURS IS AN EXCELLENT PLACE TO VISIT THE REBIRTH OF CITIES, which began as the Hundred Years War was ending in the mid-fifteenth century. Unlike Paris, where the Baron von Haussmann bulldozed away most of the city's medieval past, the city of Tours, only one hour from Paris by TGV, possesses a superbly restored medieval district so extensive that it seems to go on forever. And while the city's history spans two thousand years, it is a perfect place to visit the late Middle Ages, the time cities began to flourish again in France.

The trip to Tours by TGV could not be easier. There are sixteen TGVs a day from Paris's Montparnasse station to the Saint-Pierre-des-Corps station just outside Tours. The TGV is met by a shuttle, which drops you off in a station located at the edge of medieval Tours. I spent my first trip worrying whether or not I would make the shuttle, scheduled to leave only two minutes after the TGV arrived. However, the shuttle to Tours was waiting right across the same platform and recognizable by the flood of people leaving the TGV and pouring onto it. On my second trip, I relaxed as Bob and I played our customary game of backgammon, expecting the shuttle would be across the platform. This time it wasn't. It was across the tracks on the next platform, but we just allowed ourselves to be swept along by the stream of people who were rushing for the stairs leading to the tunnel beneath the tracks, and then pouring out on the other side, where the shuttle was waiting. No sooner had Bob and I sat down than the shuttle took off, and two minutes later we were in medieval Tours.

As we left the train, we found ourselves in a nineteenth-century station, which like most French stations built during that century had been built to delight travelers with its glass-and-iron-tented roof above walls inlaid with mosaics of princely castles and whimsical little towns in the Loire Valley—Chinon, Amboise, Blois, Saumur, Azay-le-Rideau—where trains leaving from this station take you. Not only will trains take you to these castles and towns, but there are also tour buses that leave from outside the station both in the morning and in the afternoon to three of my favorite castles—Amboise, Chambord, and Chenonceau.

Tours is a jewel of a city surrounded by a necklace of castles—the castles of kings who lived in the Loire Valley from the time Charles VII fled Paris in 1418 to 1589, when Henry IV finally moved the royal court back to Paris. When I first came to the Loire Valley over twenty years ago, I had visited these castles in the order in which they were built: Charles VII's castles at Chinon and Loches; Charles VIII's (1483–1498) castles at Amboise and Langeais; Louis XII's (1498–1515) castle at Blois; Francis I's (1515–1547) castles at Blois and Chambord; Henry II's (1547–1559) castles at Blois and Chenonceau. As I traveled by car from castle to castle, I felt the flow of centuries as the medieval fortress transformed itself—its arrow-slit windows opening up and becoming mullioned windows that filled the dark, dreary castle with light and air, somber towers becoming whimsical turrets, defensive moats dissolving into landscaped reflecting pools—into the Renaissance palace. These changes took place as the threat of internal war first receded and then disappeared. For the nearly two hundred years the French kings resided in the Loire, Tours was the economic and administrative center of the kingdom, replacing Paris as the royal city. Its merchants satisfied the needs not only of the king, but of his courtiers as well. As the royal realm became increasingly secure, the merchants of Tours became increasingly prosperous.

As soon as we left the station, we saw the fifteenth century rearing up its head in the form of a church steeple not very far away. Walking along the Rue Jules-Simon in the direction of the cathedral spires, we quickly saw remnants of Tours's past from as long ago as the first century, when it was a provincial Roman city. We would, in fact, pass by more than 1,500 years of French history as we made our way from the station to the late-medieval commercial district surrounding the Place Plumereau.

When we turned onto the Rue des Ursulines, we found the remains of an ancient Roman wall standing in the garden of the Archives, built when Tours was called Caesarodunum, or Caesar's Hill, and was a provincial city of the Roman Empire. The wall, draped with vines and decorated with flowers and moss, was quite lovely on a summer day. Walking around the wall, we came across a "poterne"—a secret door— cut into the stones. Our most fascinating discovery, however, was not in the wall, but in the stone pathway adjacent to the base of the wall, where we saw, worn into the stones, ruts made by ancient chariots. Following the wall around, we reached the Rue du Général Meusnier and the remains of an ancient Roman amphitheater whose construction was ordered by the Emperor Augustus. In the first century, Augustus had decreed that Caesarodunum should be one of the fifty miniature Romes that were given to the Roman legionnaires who had fought in Gaul and Egypt. Augustus wanted the legionnaires happy—happy enough to stay far away from Rome, where during the previous century they had caused civil disturbances upon returning from their tours of duty. Caesarodunum was thus built as a miniature Rome, with replicas of all the public buildings found in that city. Fifty thousand tons of stone blocks were ordered for construction of an amphitheater, a theater, a forum, temples, parks, fountains, commercial and residential areas. In the first two centuries A.D., this Roman city extended farther than the suburbs of today—all the way to the station of Saint-Pierre-des-Corps, where I had changed from the TGV to the shuttle. It was a bustling commercial center in those two centuries, connected by the Loire River to the rest of the Roman world.

The ancient stone wall draped with vines and flowers came later, in the third century, when, with German barbarians threatening the safety of this bustling commercial town, the Loire River ceased to be an artery connecting Caesarodunum to the rest of the Roman world of commerce and instead became a threat to its safety. The city began to contract, shedding its Roman rulers and Roman name, and assumed the Celtic name of Turones. Commerce, merchants, and the middle class did not disappear in an instant, any more than a child becomes an adult overnight. The invaders wanted to conquer rather than destroy the civilization that they saw, but they couldn't maintain the complex infrastructure. Since the illiterate barbarian invaders were unable to continue the Roman system of taxation, and the greedy Gallo-Roman merchants were all too happy not to be taxed, everything in the expanded city, from education to sewage, fell into ruin. In the seventh century, Islam closed off the Mediterranean to Europe, the Vikings closed off the Atlantic to trade, and Tours lost the last of its merchants and middle class. The once prosperous town had shrunken by then to the area around the cathedral, which includes the Archbishop's Palace just beyond the Jardin des Archives.

Built on the ruins of a Roman governor's palace, the Archbishop's Palace is today the Musée des Beaux-Arts. In 1792, the French Revolutionary government turned it into a repository for art stripped from churches, abbeys, monasteries, and châteaux in Touraine, including the art at the Château de Richelieu and at Chanteloup. This former palace, once home to Roman governors and Catholic princes of the Church, became a "palace for the people," as labeled by Napoleon, then a consul and pre-twentieth-century public relations genius, who made it one of fourteen provincial Beaux-Arts museums, giving it thirty of the paintings he had looted during his wars. This impressive and uncrowded museum alone makes a visit to Tours worth a trip.

A round tower in the garden of the Musée des Beaux-Arts was once part of the Gallo-Roman ramparts. As you walk around the outside, you will come to the tower and ramparts of Gallo-Roman fortifications and a subterranean passage lined with huge Roman building blocks.

—

JUST BEYOND THE MUSEUM soars the Middle Ages in the form of the Cathedral of Saint-Gatien, which was also built on Roman ruins: the huge, neatly cut stones at the base were laid during the Gallo-Roman period and Gallo-Roman ramparts are attached to the cathedral as well. Like Paris, Chartres, Reims, and Angers, Tours became a cathedral city, a city with an archbishop, whose diocese was based on the old Roman civitas. As the Roman merchant class disappeared, the administration of the city fell increasingly under the influence of the only literate group in town, the clerics connected with the church. It didn't happen all at once. Only gradually did the hierarchy of the Church replace the hierarchy of Rome.

The cathedral, dedicated to St. Gatien, the first bishop of Tours, is the fourth cathedral to be erected on this spot. Its construction began during the regency of Blanche of Castile and the reign of her son St. Louis. Construction continued during the period when the Loire Valley was the center of the French kingdom. Consequently, it contains a succession of styles, from Rayonnant to Flamboyant Gothic, with touches of Renaissance. Particularly beautiful is the Renaissance tomb where the children of Anne of Brittany and Charles VIII sleep peacefully "side by side, the little one with his hands under the ermine marble, the elder with his small hands folded piously . . . guarded by kneeling angels at their heads and feet." The tomb was commissioned in the fifteenth century by Charles VIII, the first French king to have been captivated by the Renaissance, which had already been evolving in Italy while French civilization had come to a halt during the Hundred Years War. The Italian influence is evident here. Seeing this Renaissance tomb juxtaposed to the Gothic tombs accentuates how art had evolved between the two periods, making it easy to understand what art historians mean by the use of the terms "increased naturalism" and "expression of individuality" to describe Renaissance art. You can see at once the individual personalities of the children—lacking in the effigies of medieval tombs—as well as the improved anatomical accuracy and artistry displayed by its sculptor.

Bob and I stopped to look at the stained-glass windows in the choir, which, unlike the windows at the other cathedrals we had visited, were easily seen without binoculars, and better still, provided a description beneath each window—written in both English and French—of what was happening in each pane. While I glanced at a thirteenth-century Tree of Jesse window long enough to compare it with the others we had seen, I found the windows in the Chapel of Saint Francis, which related the story of St. Martin of Tours, more interesting since I was now in Tours.

St. Martin, renowned for establishing monasticism in fourth-century Gaul, was the third Bishop of Tours. His tomb became a major pilgrimage stop on the Pilgrims' Path during the early Middle Ages, supplying Tours with pilgrims' money during its commercially lean years, so that Tours in the tenth and eleventh centuries was the medieval equivalent of a modern tourist town. The story told in the window is meaningful on several levels. Not only does it show why St. Martin's tomb was worthy of a pilgrimage, but also illustrates the transition from the Roman world to the Christian one. In the first window the emperor is giving St. Martin the arms of a Roman legionnaire. (Actually, St. Martin, born in 317, was the son of a Roman military tribune in Hungary, and was converted to Christianity at the age of ten. At fifteen he became a member of the imperial body guard, which was rarely exposed to combat.) In the second panel, St. Martin is at the gates of Amiens, where his regiment was stationed. He has removed his cape and is cutting it in half with his sword so that he can give half of it to a beggar. (According to his hagiographer, it was the middle of a particularly severe winter when St. Martin met this poor man, destitute of clothing, who was "entreating those that passed by to have compassion upon him, but all passed the wretched man without notice, except St. Martin. He had nothing to give but his own cloak, since he had already given away the rest of his garments. He took his sword and divided his cloak into two equal parts, and gave one half to the poor man, while keeping the other half for himself. "Upon this, some of the bystanders laughed, because he was now an unsightly object.") That night, as depicted in one of the panels, Jesus appears to him in a dream wearing the part of the cape he had given to the beggar. In the following panel, St. Martin, after having this vision, is baptized by a bishop. In the sixth panel, the Devil flees at the sight of St. Martin. This panel is interesting for what it doesn't say: St. Martin, before leaving the Roman army, was thrown into prison for a brief time for cowardice, when he proclaimed that his religion prohibited him from fighting: "I will take my stand unarmed before the line of battle tomorrow, and in the name of the Lord Jesus, protected by the sign of the cross, and not by the shield or helmet." This refusal to fight, although interpreted admiringly by St. Martin's hagiographer, was a cause of Roman anger against the Christians in the fourth century. The Christians' refusal to fight resulted in diminished numbers of troops to defend the borders of the empire from the invading Germanic barbarians, who were pouring into Gaul at this time.

The Church of St. Martin, which once contained his remains—the main pilgrimage attraction—was vandalized not by German barbarians, but by the city fathers of Tours, who tore it down to make way for a street. Only two of its towers, now separated—the Tour de Charlemagne and the Tour de l'Horloge—remain to indicate how large it once was.

After leaving the cathedral, we came to the cloister, whose late French Flamboyant Gothic and early-Renaissance architecture is particularly lovely. The royal staircase in the cloister is a smaller version of the magnificent Renaissance staircase Francis I built at his château at Blois. It leads up to an elegant library and vaulted "scriptorium," which is architecturally similar to the Salle des États, also at Blois. The cloister, or La Psalette, as it is called, because its rooms were used for training choirboys rehearsing religious songs, was completed at the end of the fifteenth century and the beginning of the sixteenth.

Leaving the cathedral area, we came to a rather uninteresting royal château. Don't be fooled by the inviting pepper-pot roof and machicolations of the thirteenth-century tower, which are the only reminders that when Charles VII was driven out of Paris he had a residence here. The present occupants, a group of fish collected in an aquarium, have little to tell us about either the monarchy or the rebirth of towns in the fifteenth century.

We turned left on the Rue Colbert and entered what I think is the glorious part of Tours, which culminates with the Place Plumereau, where once feathered hats were made and sold, and which is now a lively square filled with restaurants, bordered by a remarkable array of half-timbered houses. This section was built during a period in which artists and artisans flooded into Tours and the surrounding area, forming large workshops to supply the king and court with the luxuries they demanded. Tours expanded out beyond its medieval walls, once again becoming a densely populated, rich, and powerful town, though not as densely populated as it had been when it was a commercial link in the Roman Empire.

The town's population, which had been decimated first by the Black Death and then by the Hundred Years War, expanded enormously in the late-fifteenth and sixteenth centuries. This was in part due to the policies of King Louis XI, whose twenty-two-year reign was marked by peace and prosperity after more than a hundred years of war. Called the "Spider King" because he "weaved webs of deceit around his enemies," his castle, Plessis-lès-Tours, was even referred to as the "Spider's Web." Philippe de Commynes, his biographer and a trusted companion—one of the few members of the aristocracy allowed to enter Plessis during Louis XI's life—described it in the following way:

> All round the palace of Plessis the king had had erected a fence of stout iron bars and had had imbedded in the wall iron prongs with many points at places such as the opening through which one could enter the defensive ditch. He likewise had erected four towers, all of iron and quite spacious, which gave his archers excellent firing positions—they were really quite wonderful things, and cost more than twenty-thousand francs. Finally, he stationed forty crossbow men, day and night, in the defensive ditch, with orders to fire upon anyone who approached at night, until the hour when the gate was opened in the morning.

Since it didn't sound enticing when it was at its most luxurious, and it is described today as being in ruins, I did not have any desire to visit it and didn't, especially since other castles in the area were described with phrases like "truly royal in its great scale, its grand air," or with adjectives like "majestic" and "harmonious." In addition, Louis XI did not appear at first to be enough of a charismatic figure to hold my interest. With his rickety legs and hooked nose, he was described by historians as being as mean and ugly as both his father, Charles VII, and his son Charles VIII, though I learned he differed from both in that he was highly intelligent, while they were both considered quite stupid. But it was only when I learned that he shared my hatred for his sniveling, dissolute, luxury-loving father that my interest was aroused. Just after returning from Rouen, where Louis XI's father had allowed Joan of Arc to burn at the stake after she saved his kingdom for him, I learned that Louis XI had led or participated in a failed rebellion of nobles against his father at the age of sixteen. As a result, he was exiled to his province of Dauphiné, which he transformed by founding a university at Valence, building roads, protecting Jewish bankers who were instrumental in establishing a sound economy, and creating a unified legal system there (according to Commynes, when he became king, it was his "cherished desire" to establish such a legal system throughout his realm "in order to prevent the tricks and plunderings of lawyers").

A practical but suspicious man, he believed in the efficacy of fear. Averse to war, he raised the largest royal army he could so that no one would be foolish enough to attack him. Historians write that the prosperity and commercial growth of Tours is the result of his policies, and that appears to be true. For example, one of the first things he did after he was securely settled on the throne of France was create a silk industry in Tours to prevent currency from leaving the country. He had initially tried to set it up in Lyon, but was prevented from doing so by Italian silk merchants, so he established it near his château at Plessis le Tours.* He felt the production of silk in France would reduce the country's debt and improve its balance of trade. He also felt that the silk industry could provide work or, as he put it, be one "which all idle people ought to be

---

* It is possible to arrange a tour of the Maison Georges le Manach in Tours, which still produces silk in France, and "is heir to a long tradition of silk weaving in Touraine, dating back to Louis XI," by calling the Tourist Office of Tours.

made to work at," and a third of Tours' population did. The silk industry during his reign employed 40,000 people—800 masters and 6,000
apprentices, plus weavers, dyers, finishers, and merchants. The grand
Hôtel Simon on the Rue de Commerce, built during the reign of Henry
IV, once belonged to one of the great silk manufacturers of Tours.

The innovations he initiated help us understand the commercial
revival that took place in Tours. Historians write that he "realized the
importance of the bourgeoisie," noting that he appointed "men of modest origins," or as Commynes refers to them, "insignificant men" to his
administration, "because they would owe him everything." He ennobled these men from the bourgeoisie, creating a new aristocratic class,
the *noblesse de robe*, men who were dependent upon him for their titles
and therefore far more indebted to the throne than the ancient aristocracy, who were referred to as the *noblesse d'épée*, whose titles and lands
had been granted in exchange for their feudal obligation to provide the
king with knights in times of need. He thus increased his autocratic
power over the towns of France.

I would add that Louis, having taken part in that rebellion of nobles
against his father, had learned that the nobility was never to be trusted.
In fact, members of the nobility were not allowed into his castle at Plessis without first being checked to see if they had hidden a cutlass in their
robes. Also, there may have been another reason. Commynes writes that
Louis wanted the most intelligent men around him. And the reason for
that may be that the most intelligent man at his father's court was not a
nobleman, but Jacques Coeur, France's first merchant prince, who had
created an economic empire centered in Bourges, the town in which
Louis XI was born. Coeur, as financial adviser to his father, replaced
the debased French monetary system with a sound one modeled upon
the system the Médicis had established in Florence. His agents financially aided Louis when he was in exile, helping the young prince to
reorganize his province of Dauphiné. And, perhaps it was the example
provided by Jacques Coeur, who had concluded that manufacturing
silk was far more profitable than importing it and had begun to do so in
Florence, that inspired Louis XI to do the same in Tours.

While the new aristocratic class never tried to emulate the *noblesse*

d'épée in militaristic ways, they did so in material ways. The new aristocracy of Tours built their mansions in the style of the ancient aristocracy's châteaux. They tried to copy the aristocratic style of dress, usually
with less restraint and subtlety. Since they controlled the economic and
political life of Tours, they tried to distance themselves further and further from the rest of the middle class in their community.

For example, if you turn onto Place Foire-le-Roi and stop in the
Jardin de Beaune-Sembleçay, there are the remains of the Hôtel de
Beaune. This once was the home of Jacques Beaune, whose father, Jean
de Beaune, became exceedingly wealthy when he took over Jacques
Coeur's assets in Tours. Once Coeur's clerk, he was able to acquire
these assets after Coeur was arrested and sentenced to life in prison on
unsubstantiated charges of poisoning Agnès Sorel, Charles VII's mistress. Although Coeur confessed to the charges while being tortured,
saying: "I will admit to anything you wish," historians agree that the
charges were false.

Although Jacques Coeur would escape, all debts owed him by
courtiers and the king, money borrowed to finance the war against England as well as luxury items, were cancelled, and his extensive financial
empire throughout France was confiscated.

Couer's former clerk, Jean de Beaune, continued importing luxury
items from the East, as Jacques Coeur had once done, and amassed a
fortune doing so. He set up shops on what is now the Rue de Commerce to sell the items he had imported. He then invested his wealth in
silver at a time when silver coins were being minted in Tours. His son
became a banker and financial adviser to the king.

As you continue along the Rue Colbert, you will pass other mansions
that the members of this patrician class of bankers and merchants built
in Tours. When the Rue de Colbert changes to the Rue de Commerce
you will see the many-storied structures into which artisans and workers were crammed. While they appear charming today, their interiors
were rather short on amenities in the fifteenth and sixteenth centuries.

Before our trip to Tours, I had tried to find a restaurant near the
Place de Plumereau that was recommended by either Michelin or Gault
Millaut and, finding none in the square itself, had made a reservation

at L'Atelier Gourmand on the Rue Étienne-Marcel, a pedestrian-only street one block to the right of the Rue du Grand Marché. Just as Bob and I were arriving, we saw the owner of the restaurant in the street, carrying three loaves of bread and calling "*bon appetit*," to a second-story window across from the restaurant. A few moments later, he placed a plate of navarin d'agneau on a table next to us and a minute or two after that a woman from the apartment across the street sat down at the table. Her meal looked so good I forgot I disliked stewed lamb and ordered it. I did, however, enjoy my gazpacho, which was made without tomatoes and with a heavy hint of mint. After lunch we walked down the Grand Marché, a street lined with so many half-timbered houses with slate roofs and carved oak doorways that I would have believed I was either back in the Middle Ages or on a Hollywood set. Arriving at the Place Plumereau (which literally means "place of feather picking"), we were surrounded everywhere by fifteenth- and sixteenth-century buildings. The square was filled with lively open-air restaurants, tables set with colorful umbrellas, and crowded with people eating and chatting, the air suffused with the aromas of different dishes. It looked so inviting that both of us regretted the two hours spent indoors at the restaurant I had selected, where the food may have been better, but the slow service had consumed far too much of our afternoon. It is here and on the connecting streets where most of the fifteenth- and sixteenth-century middle class of Tours once lived—artists, artisans, proprietors, and workmen who supplied the food and luxuries the nobility demanded. The names of the narrow side streets and squares, lined with their many-storied houses need no explanation if you have a dictionary, such as the Rue des Tanneurs (tanners); Rue des Charpentiers (carpenters); Carroi de Chapeaux (hat makers); Jean Juste (sculptors); Rue Racine and Rue Zola (writers); Rue Lavoisier (scientists). The side streets were also lined with medieval houses and craftsmen's workshops. In fact, the craftsman who made Joan of Arc's armor lived at 41 Rue Colbert.

Great changes had taken place since the twelfth century, when Suger had built his Gothic basilica. Then stonecutters, glaziers, carpenters—all the workmen building cathedrals—had moved from town to town as they completed their work on the cathedrals rising throughout France.

Beginning in the fifteenth century, they had begun to settle down permanently in towns like Tours and Rouen.

We walked out of the Place Plumereau through a covered medieval vaulted passageway, which led to another very small open square. Excavation work was uncovering a first-century Roman building and Gallo-Roman buildings. However, what I find so exciting about Tours is not the remains of a dead Roman city, but the vast number of fifteenth-century shops and buildings that let you experience the revival of cities at that time.

I RETURNED TO Tours on July 26, during the festival of St. Anne, or the festival of garlic and basil—two ingredients that are always found in my kitchen. If you are ever in France on July 26, I heartily advise taking the train to Tours. I never had so much fun sampling the delicious food and wine of the Loire Valley, all of which is set out on an endless number of buffet tables, while other tables and chairs are provided so you can sit and properly enjoy the food. Never was I so glad to have been blessed with an appetite that enabled me to sample it all.

CHAPTER 12

BLOIS
A Sixteenth-Century Renaissance Château

—

Train from Gare d'Austerlitz to Blois

*F*OR YEARS I HAVE VISITED AND LOVED THE FRIENDLY TOWN and early Renaissance château of Blois but had always come by car. At the end of one weekend at the Domaine des Hauts de Loire, a hotel between Amboise and Blois at which we have stayed for over twenty years, I was about to drive back to Paris when I asked its owner, Monsieur Bonigal, about the possibility of returning there by train. He said there was no trouble taking the train back to Paris from Blois, since there were about eighteen trains to and from Paris each day and there was even an Avis rental-car agency right across from the station: acting on this advice, we dropped our car off, and ninety minutes later we were at the Gare d'Austerlitz in Paris. I cannot tell you what a delightful surprise it was to learn that Blois was an easy day trip from Paris by train, because the château at Blois is the ideal castle to see the transformation that took place in sixteenth-century France, when its king, no longer threatened by internal war, modernized his defensive fortress into a palace befitting a king.

A few weeks later, we took the train from Paris to Blois. As we approached the station, we could see the château perched up on its promontory overlooking the Loire River, where it had been ever since the end of the tenth century, when the first count of Blois, Thibault the

Cheat, built the first wooden watchtower there.* He was a descendant of one of the 350 counts appointed by Charlemagne in the ninth century to administer one of the 350 counties into which he had divided up his empire. By the end of the tenth century, this empire had disintegrated into anarchy. With the decline of a central power, ambitious, greedy counts like Thibault and Foulques Nerra, the Count of Anjou (the Black Falcon)—pious but criminally violent men—each wanting an empire of his own, were warring with each other to expand their hereditary domains. And since land was the only source of wealth and power in this moneyless, tradeless time, both men set out to conquer as much as they could of that land we tourists now call the Loire Valley. In this regard, the Black Falcon was the fiercer and more successful of the two, expanding his realm by cold-blooded personal acts (finding one wife barren, he simply dressed her in her best clothes and set fire to her in front of his castle at Angers) and bloody wars. He ultimately overwhelmed the forces of Thibault the Cheat, killing 6,000 of his men in a single battle and wresting control of Chinon from him, thus gaining control of most of the valley. Because of its easily defendable position, Thibault was able to hold on to Blois. In the turbulent centuries that followed the bloody wars of these two men, the need for defensive architecture remained. The square wooden tower on the cliff at Blois, with its curtain wall and ramparts, evolved as medieval defensive architecture improved: successive counts of Blois replaced the square tower with rounded stone towers, walls, battlements, and a moat.

On the way from the station, Bob and I stopped for a few moments at a charming park with an arresting view of the château on the cliff above us. The defensive fortress of feudal lords, centuries in the making, was gone, replaced when a feudal lord became the king, who now had national power and international interests. It was now a Renaissance palace that mysteriously seemed to change its shape as we walked toward it, echoing the different styles of architecture that evolved

---

* The name in French is Thibault le Tricheur, which has been translated as Thibault the Cheat and Tricky Thibault.

between the years 1418 and 1589, when the Kings of France made the Loire Valley the center of their realm.

In fact, as soon as you climb the steps to the château, walk across a large, open plaza filled with the colorful umbrellas of an outdoor café, and enter the courtyard of the château, you will be surrounded by the building's four wings, and each of these wings is different, reflecting the times and personalities of the men who built them, as well as the changes in society taking place at the time they were built.

If you let your eyes move first to the Romanesque Salle des États-Généraux, then to the Flamboyant Gothic wing of Louis XII, then to the early-Renaissance wing of Francis I, and finally to the French Classical wing of Gaston of Orléans, you can literally see the changes taking place artistically, architecturally, and historically over several centuries. There are no moats, drawbridges, portcullises, ramparts, keeps, machinations, crenellations, or arrow-slit windows, as we saw at Angers and Vincennes. The growing need for comfort, for luxury, for facilities to conduct diplomatic functions, and to entertain and impress the nobility and bind them to the court, is expressed in the architectural changes. The feudal function of the nobility as warriors had virtually come to an end as the king grew less dependent upon them to supply arms and money. The nobility functioned now as members of a social hunting party, guests at a banquet (no longer providing food but eating it), or participants in tournaments and games. They amused themselves by jousting, hunting, or attending social and diplomatic functions. For example, the Archduke of Austria, with whom Louis XII, the first king to reside at Blois, was "contesting" various territories, was invited to spend a week here, which he did. This type of diplomacy, revolutionary at the time, consisting of a series of balls, games, tournaments, Masses, and dinners, would become commonplace in the years that followed.

First, note the only vestige of feudal France that remains in the courtyard: a portion of the thirteenth-century Salle des États-Généraux, built by the early counts of Blois on this high promontory overlooking and facing the Loire, where for centuries the knights of Blois watched the

river for the approach of enemy boats. The once impenetrable Romanesque hall remaining from this former time was quite similar in structure
and function to the Romanesque barrel-vaulted Great Hall in Poitiers,
where Eleanor of Aquitaine and her father, William, Count of Poitou
and Duke of Aquitaine, held court and meted out justice to their vassals.
While the Romanesque interior is quite exceptional, the feudal façade
of rubble stone is grim. The hall originally had no windows at all; the
two windows you see were added centuries later. Not only is it architecturally similar, but it was used for similar purposes as well. Just as Eleanor of Aquitaine and her father presided over "the Court of Love" in
Poitiers, where troubadours sang romantic poetry accompanied by the
music of jongleurs in the eleventh and twelfth centuries, here in Blois,
Charles, Duke of Orléans, held court while poets vied with one another
to complete a poem using a first line he had written, reflecting a new
era in which learning was appreciated once again. The hall was also
used when sessions of the Estates-General—a parliament composed of
three estates or classes (the nobility, the clergy, the people), which was
created in 1302 primarily to provide the king with money—were held,
reflecting the appearance of a central government in early-Renaissance
France.

As your eye moves from the feudal hall to the Flamboyant Gothic
architecture of the Louis XII wing, compare the grimness of the older
building with the openness of the newer wing. When a sixteenth-
century nobleman entered the courtyard of this palace, or walked in the
Italian-style gardens, the surroundings were making a statement. The
openness and gracious luxury of the architecture, and the enchantment
of the gardens, implied that this was the residence of a lord who felt
secure from attack and was able to devote himself to his own pleasure
and comfort.

The Louis XII wing at Blois reflects the personality of the king who
built it, possessing more the feel of a modest manor house than the
grandeur of a palace. Louis was the grandson of the dashing Louis of
Orléans, the amorous duke who fathered Joan of Arc's companion the
Bastard of Orléans and had an affair with the Queen of France, causing

concern over the legitimacy of the dauphin, and who also seduced the last countess of Blois. Louis of Orléans talked the pretty young wife out of her virtue and, by pleading poverty, also talked her out of so much money, which she obtained from her cuckolded husband, that the once immensely wealthy count found himself impoverished and forced to sell the château of Blois for 200,000 livres—a sum that Louis of Orléans, because of the countess's generosity, was able to pay. Although Louis of Orléans was murdered shortly thereafter, and consequently never spent any time at his newly acquired château, his son, and wife, Valentina Visconti, the daughter of the Duke of Milan, came to live here. While most marriages during this period were political and economic arrangements, Valentina Visconti, despite all of Louis's affairs, was so in love with him that she died of despair shortly after his death, having carved on the wall of the château words I hope your tour guide will point out to you: "*Rien ne m'est plus, plus ne m'est rien,*" which I have translated into "Nothing means anything to me anymore," the words I would have carved if my love had died.

A little background, some of it gossip, helps us understand larger historical trends. While Louis XII inherited not only Blois, but also his grandfather's title of Duke of Orléans and astounding good looks, he did not inherit his good fortune in love. His uncle King Louis XI (the Spider King) had two daughters: Anne, who was brilliant and clever, and Jeanne, who was crippled and unable to bear children. He forced his handsome, brilliant nephew to marry Jeanne. His motive was political expediency: to prevent his nephew from siring a son, who might threaten the succession of his own son. Events proved his caution to be well founded, since when Louis XI died, leaving Charles a minor under the regency of his older sister, Princess Anne, Louis of Orléans did lead a rebellion of nobles in an attempt to depose her as regent. Anne, however, was shrewd like her father, and Louis spent the next three years in prison. Princess Anne then wisely married her brother Charles—now Charles VIII—to a reluctant Anne of Brittany, so that that rebellious province was brought under royal control. Charles, however, was not clever, not even clever enough to duck his head when entering a low door at his castle at Amboise, where he hit his head and died before he could sire an heir.

When he died, his cousin Louis of Orléans became King Louis XII. Born in Blois, he had spent his childhood there, and now, as King of France, he made it the royal residence. A well-loved king, he reigned so frugally that taxes were actually reduced during the fifteen years (1498–1513) he was in power. When he was accused of living too simply and dressing too shabbily for a king, he replied: "I would much rather they laughed at my meanness than wept at their poverty."

The first thing Louis XII did when he took over the throne was rid himself of the wife he had been forced to marry. His marriage to Princess Jeanne was annulled by the pope but only after she was subjected to a humiliating physical examination in front of twenty-seven witnesses. She was then sent off to a nunnery. (At least he did not burn her alive, as the Black Falcon did when he found *his* wife infertile.) Louis then married Charles VIII's widow, Anne of Brittany, thereby becoming the first monarch of France without threat of internal war from either Brittany—because Brittany was the dowry of his wife—or from the Duke of Orléans—because he *was* the Duke of Orléans. He was therefore the first king unchallenged by internal war.

The next thing he did was level the unneeded medieval walls, ramparts, and keeps that the counts of Blois had been building for centuries, replacing them with the kind of Renaissance gardens he had seen and loved while visiting his grandparents in Milan as a child. After a fire destroyed the Romanesque loge in which he lived as a child, he rebuilt it in the then modern Flamboyant Gothic style, no longer facing the river but the enchanting gardens he had already created, where porcupines, parrots, peacocks, exotic birds, and animals walked freely in the labyrinths created by hedges. Some historians write that Louis cleared away the feudal fortifications to show he was absolute monarch and had no need of them, while others say he merely did so because he liked the openness and luxury of the palaces he had seen while in Italy. But while he tore down the defensive walls and keeps at Blois, where he held court and received foreign ambassadors, he always kept a full garrison of 5,000 soldiers and 1,180 lancers at his castle at Amboise, to which he could quickly retreat in case of danger.* Louis's château at Chambord, also quickly reached, was staffed as well, but not with soldiers—it was kept ready for use as a hunting lodge, hunting being the favorite pastime of the nobility and the king. And since the Loire Valley was where the king and his court liked to hunt, it became, in the sixteenth century, the center of the French kingdom. When Louis went hunting at Chambord, his personal servants at Blois, all 322 of them (a number that increased to 3,000 people and 1,000 horses when his nephew and son-in-law Francis I became king), came as well. The nomadic court became a traveling city as it moved from château to château, bringing with it chests containing hundreds of tapestries to be hung on the walls of Chambord and then brought back to hang on the walls of Blois when he returned. I had always thought the court moved when the stench from the moats, used for sewage and latrines, became too vile; however, my guide insisted that the court moved every three weeks because all the grass in the area had been devoured by the thousand horses in three weeks' time.

Louis's wing possesses a certain unity and harmony of style common in Renaissance architecture, but it is essentially still Gothic, called Flamboyant Gothic because of the decorations, seen at the attic windows and at the entrance to the courtyard, which frames a reproduction of a statue of Louis XII. These decorations are called "flamboyant" because they look like flames. They are lacy, flickering, flaming designs—curving, emerging, and disappearing lines of tracery. The architecture of the Middle Ages permeates the wing in other ways: the slate roof is steeply sloped and high; the continued use of the patterned red and blue brick combined with stone that I find so charming throughout the vicinity of Blois is still used in this wing. It also possesses symbolism common in Gothic art, but the symbolism here is political rather than religious,

---

* The delightful sixteenth-century Renaissance town of Amboise is the stop after Blois, two hours by train from Paris. Both Charles VIII and Francis I spent their childhoods at the château there. Two enormous towers, which make the château unique, were built not for defensive reasons, but so that Anne of Brittany, pregnant with Charles's heir, would have a wide-enough entrance for her carriage to smoothly enter and leave the castle grounds.

expressed in the emblems of royal authority—the fleur-de-lis pattern covering two of the four columns supporting the arched arcade, and the porcupines and ermines, which are the symbols respectively of Louis XII and Anne of Brittany. However, the most important change in the Louis XII wing is the overall concern with comfort rather than defense.

No one would ever accuse Francis I (1515–1547) of living too simply. Although he spent his teenage years living with Louis at Blois, his uncle's frugality left no impression on him. In fact, Francis spent as much on a single piece of fabric—200,000 livres—as Louis of Orléans had paid to purchase Blois. When Francis became king, he inherited a kingdom without debt, but when he died, he left an astounding royal debt of 40 million livres. His extravagance is shown by the wing he built at Blois. The change is dramatic: the manor house has become a palace. There is a monumentality, a brilliance, a feeling of luxury and exquisite taste about Francis's wing that does not exist in Louis's. The increased lavishness is apparent at Blois and overwhelming at nearby Chambord—Francis I never liked Blois. He felt restricted by both the pre-existing buildings and the surrounding town, neither of which corresponded to his taste. He moved to Chambord, which presented a clean canvas for the picture of royal magnificence he intended to paint and, finding Chambord did not fulfill his needs, concentrated his energies on renovating Fontainebleau, where we shall go next.

The first difference you notice when you shift your eyes from Louis's wing to Francis's is that, except for the chimneys, the medieval patterned red and blue brick has been replaced by the carved stone blocks used by the Renaissance architects in Florence. The roof, while still sloped medieval-fashion, is not as steeply sloped as Gothic structures had been. There are no pointed towers. Here you feel the playfulness of the French artist toying with what he has seen in Italy as he tries to embellish, but not totally abandon, his beloved Gothic structure with Renaissance designs. The flaming dormers have turned into scallop shells containing classical statues of ancient Greeks or Romans; the flames have become graceful, carved arabesques making the dormer a reflection of the Flamboyant Gothic dormer of the former period, and the flames rise above a richly decorated cornice of scallop shells. All of the windows of the wing's lower story are framed with pilasters topped with the Corinthian capitals that the Romans once loved so well, and that the French will come to adore. Each of the stories is divided by a double molding, so that pilasters are crossed with the strong horizontal lines that are a feature of Renaissance design. The columns at the entrance are fluted in the style of the ancient world. Niches are filled with classical statues, and windows, while open and airy, are still not symmetrical.

For me, however, the most delightful feature of this loge is the polygonal wedding-cake staircase in the courtyard. The structure and vaulting of this staircase is similar to that of the staircases built in France up to this time, but at Blois the Renaissance designs are carved on wide platforms, which were added at each of the three stories to accommodate guards of honor, who would stand at attention during royal ceremonies.

I am not sure if my fondness for the staircase is derived from its architectural whimsy or from the stories of the murder that took place there, which the tour guides at Blois so marvelously describe in bloodsplattered detail. Actually a double murder, it took place on December 23, 1588, a date my guides referred to as the "Day of the Dagger." In fact, the assassination of the gallant Duke de Guise and his brother, the Cardinal of Lorraine, by Catherine de Médicis's bizarre son Henry III, the transvestite King of France, remains the most famous murder in French history. The first of the murders took place at night when the Duke de Guise was summoned to the king's chambers by messengers. We are told they interrupted the duke's amorous activities with a pretty seventeen-year-old girl. The duke crossed the courtyard and climbed the Francis I staircase, where he was attacked and stabbed by the king's men. The murders are so richly evoked on the guided tours I took that, as I walked through the château's rooms, I could almost smell Henry's perfume and feel his presence, earlobes drooping with dangling jewels, or see him in his gown of pink and silver damask with enormous sleeves embroidered with emeralds and pearls.

Paintings chronicling the murders and their aftermath hang on walls that were once covered with tapestries. There is a portrait of the brave, virile, handsome Duke de Guise, whom the artist has dressed in white to symbolize his virtue. The leader of the Catholic League in the brewing war to rid France of the Huguenots (Protestants), he was the epitome of the chivalric ideal, the noble warrior, the embodiment of all the perfect past of Charlemagne and Roland romanticized by the aristocracy. It was even said that he was a direct descendant of Charlemagne and therefore worthy of the crown. Inside the Francis I wing, there is a painting of the king's men slaying the gallant duke on the staircase; another painting of Madame de Guise, mourning for her two sons—her other son, the Cardinal of Lorraine, was outside the king's chamber when his brother was killed and said before he himself was slain, "I hope that I may not die before I shall hold the head of that tyrant between my knees, and make a crown with the point of a dagger."

The rooms, empty on my early tours of everything but imagination, have now been furnished as they would have been at the time the Valois kings lived there in the sixteenth century, presenting an authentic and entertaining stage set for the events that took place during the reign of Catherine de Médicis's weak and extravagant son. While the French people had accepted Francis's expenditures for a chivalric quest for empire in his Italian wars and for construction of majestic castles, they balked when Henry III, derided by his contemporaries as "an immoral travesty as king," lavished money and jewels on his *mignons* (pretty "boykins," Ronsard called them), and murdered the man who was the embodiment of all the manly sixteenth-century values. The violent homophobic feelings expressed by sixteenth-century Frenchmen toward their transvestite king is understandable, given the king's obligation to sire an heir; the alternative method of succession being not elections but devastating wars. Henry's boast that his heirs would "piss on the graves" of those plotting against him was an empty one, and his failure to produce the heir plunged France once again into civil war— the so called Wars of Religion, which we shall visit at La Rochelle.

As I wrote in my last book, "the nature of the tour you will be taken on as well as the description of the ghosts summoned up from the past can depend a great deal upon your guide." Hopefully your guide will inform you of the fascinating and dramatic events involving the sixteenth-century Valois kings and queens and mistresses who peopled this château and who quite frankly make this tour one of the most interesting in France. On earlier visits, I was told gossipy stories about Francis I; his morose son Henry II; Henry's mistress the beautiful Diane de Poitiers, to whom he gave the crown jewels and beautiful Chenonceau; Henry's Bourgeois Queen, the scheming Catherine de Médicis, and Henry's three weak and sickly sons, who followed him in quick succession.

The stories involving Catherine de Médicis have changed over the years, influenced by the feminist revolution. The guide on my earliest tour emphasized her bourgeois origins, unintentionally expressing in 1974 some of the horror felt in the sixteenth century by Emperor Charles V when he heard that Francis I had married his second son to a woman from the bourgeoisie: "They have besmirched the Valois lilies with a mercantile alliance." It was no small matter at the royal court that Catherine was not of noble blood. Late medieval culture was still an agricultural one, and bloodlines, important today on ranches, were still extremely important at court. Diane de Poitiers had summed up court feeling at the time when she scoffed, "Bah, it is only the shopkeeper's daughter."

On my last tour, when our group reached Catherine de Médicis's study, where 237 carved and painted wooden panels line the walls, my guide, as had my previous ones, opened a number of secret panels by pressing a hidden pedal on the floor. My former guides had been particularly entertaining as they explained how Catherine, the sinister queen, had with Machiavellian cunning hidden poisons behind these panels, and used them, Borgia-style, on people who seemed to die all around her as she schemed her way to thirty years of power. It was poison brought by an Italian cupbearer that killed off Francis's elder son, enabling Catherine's husband Henry to become king. Guides pointed out the mysterious circumstances surrounding the death of the Queen of Navarre, Jeanne d'Albret (Henry IV's mother). Catherine had summoned the fierce Huguenot queen from her small kingdom in the Pyrenees to discuss a political marriage between the Valois princess Marguerite and her son Henry of Navarre. The Huguenot queen was opposed to the marriage and told her son so in a letter in which she stated that while Marguerite was pretty enough, she was overly painted, and that society at Blois was depraved. Her opposition to the marriage ended after receiving a pair of leather gloves from Catherine; she died soon after trying them on. It was rumored that the Florentine leather had been poisoned. Of course, logic tells me these stories probably were apocryphal, for after all, if I were Catherine and skilled in the use of poison, Diane de Poitiers, the mistress whom her husband adored, would not have lived to the age of seventy-one.

In contrast, on my 1990 tour of Blois, a fiery feminist guide was so intent on defending a powerful woman that she spent the entire tour trying to right the historical wrongs of sexual discrimination, not only ennobling Catherine's bloodlines somewhat by elevating her from "shopkeeper queen" to a "descendant of il Magnifico" (the great Florentine patron of the arts), but also ignoring most negative aspects of her reign as regent. The murders were still mentioned but were now committed with noble purpose, as Catherine became the Queen Mother who did what she had to do to save the kingdom for her sons.

When we reached a room connected to Catherine's study, we found a large hole in the center of the room. A prefeminist guide had told my group how Catherine, ignored and detested by her husband, had taken a succession of secret lovers, and then had murdered each one black-widow–style, discreetly disposing of their bodies down this hole. The dramatic content on my last tour received quite a blow when I was told that there were similar holes in most castles throughout France and that its purpose was simply to connect the king's quarters with the guard room on a lower floor so that food could be raised and lowered when the castle was under siege.

The fourth wing of the château is the Gaston of Orléans wing, one of the few existing masterpieces of seventeenth-century classic French architecture, designed by the architectural genius François Mansart. If this prickly perfectionist had had his way, the other three wings would have been leveled so that he could build a palace of "unified and harmonious design." And he would have been allowed to do so if Gaston, Duke of Orléans, younger brother of Louis XIII, had become king. Louis XIII not only secretly plotted to prevent his younger brother

from marrying—he didn't want his brother siring an heir—but also supplied construction funds to divert him from his plots against the crown.
Gaston was, in fact, exiled at Blois, where he was overseeing construction because of previous conspiracies against the king's life. Luckily
for Blois, Louis XIV was born before the demolition crews reached
the charming and whimsical wings built by Louis XII and Francis I,
and Gaston's funds came quickly to a halt. (Mansart was summoned by
the queen and asked to turn his energies toward designing a church—
Val-de-Grâce in Paris—to thank God for the birth of Louis XIV.

On my most recent tour, my guide was far too excited, for my taste,
by the addition of furniture, silk tapestries, traveling chests, ornaments,
and other sixteenth-century furniture that had not been at the château
on my previous visits. I hope these new acquisitions will not divert the
tour guides' attention from the dramatic and quasi-historical events that
took place at the château and encourage them to concentrate instead
on the provenance of material possessions—mentioning Catherine, for
example, only as the possessor of a chest or chair. One of the charming
aspects of touring Blois has always been the stories of murder, infidelity,
sexual aberration, and intrigue. I found these gossipy stories not only
amusing but they helped me feel, as I toured the château at Blois, as
though I were visiting the kings and queens who in the Renaissance had
walked where I now walked.

CHAPTER 13

FRANCIS I and the RENAISSANCE at FONTAINEBLEAU

—

Train from Gare de Lyon to Fontainebleau

FRANCIS I HAD LIVED AT BOTH BLOIS AND AMBOISE. WHEN HE became king in 1528, he announced that he would live in Paris and make the Louvre his primary residence. He didn't. He took one look at the Louvre—then a thirteenth-century fortress—and considered it an unworthy palace for the Caesar he thought he was. He ordered its renovation and moved to Fontainebleau, as we will do now. It is only a forty-five-minute train ride from Paris to Fontainebleau, with trains leaving from the Gare de Lyon every hour. Buses to the château, timed to meet the trains, have been waiting across from the station every time I have come. If you don't like buses, taxis are usually conveniently lined up as well. Or, if like me, you can walk, since the château is less than a mile away.

I am glad that this fabulous château, where, unlike Versailles, there are never oppressive crowds, is so easy and pleasant to reach, because, as a traveler through time, you should return to Fontainebleau many times. For years, every time Bob and I flew into Orly, where the plane from New York once landed, we would rent a car, drive south, and spend our first day visiting the château at Fontainebleau and our first night at L'Aigle Noir.* We would check into the hotel and walk across

---

* We have not stayed or eaten at L'Aigle Noir since it has been modernized, so I do not know if I would still enjoy staying there. The last time we were in Fontainebleau, we enjoyed a very pleasant traditional meal at Croquembouche.

the street to the Farewell Court. Then we would visit Napoleon's rooms or the Galerie François I or just wander around the gardens, stopping at a bench to look at Napoleon's little pavilion in the lake. Each time I return to Fontainebleau, I feel less like a tourist and more like a member of the sixteenth-century royal court as I walk through this rambling château, or amble through the gardens or by the lakes that surround the château.

Although it is not readily apparent, most of Fontainebleau was the creation of Francis I. He razed the old château, built a new one on its foundations, oversaw the planning of its gardens, linked the new château to an old abbey with a long gallery, and then brought Renaissance artists from Italy to decorate that gallery with a new style of art that today is called the "First School of Fontainebleau" (and sometimes "Mannerism"). Nonetheless, Francis's ghost is hard to find at Fontainebleau, except in the Galerie François I, because of Napoleon—even though Napoleon created very little of Fontainebleau. His ghost, and not Francis's, looms over the château and its grounds because so many of the dramatic events of Napoleon's life took place at this château that both he and Francis loved. The Farewell Court, with its glorious staircase, is a perfect example of what I mean. It was created by Francis, but even before we enter the courtyard, we are greeted by Napoleon's golden eagles and Imperial *N*, which he placed upon the pre-existing wrought-iron gate through which you enter the grounds of the château. I can almost see, as I pass through the gate, the ghost of Napoleon open the door of the château and pause before descending the marvelous horseshoe staircase that Francis built, saying farewell to his troops for the last time as he left for his exile on Elba. This, in part, is Bob's fault, because each time we enter the courtyard, Bob, who has read just about everything on Napoleon and who never seems to forget a word he has read, tells me that this is where the Old Guard had once stood weeping, and as we near the steps, he repeats the words Napoleon said: "For twenty years I have constantly accompanied you on the road to honor and glory. . . . Do not regret my fate; . . . Adieu, my friends. Would I could press you all to my heart. Bring me the Eagle that I may embrace it. . . . Adieu, my children; . . . Do not forget me!" Bob does that every time we come to Fontainebleau. He is such a good storyteller that I always forget that this is Francis's courtyard. Instead, I feel the emotionally charged atmosphere as the emperor descends the stairs, embraces and kisses his eagle and his flag, and then gets into one of the carriages waiting to take him to exile, a scene Bob describes so movingly, and so often, that now I start crying almost as soon as I enter the courtyard. I find this ridiculous because I don't even like Napoleon.

After you enter the château, you also have the impression that Napoleon built it, not Francis I, just as you have the impression that Napoleon built Les Invalides and the Place Vendôme in Paris—both of which were actually built by Louis XIV. This is partly because when Napoleon, dissatisfied with being just consul, decided to move from Malmaison, a modest château Josephine had chosen when Napoleon was cloaking himself in republican simplicity, to Fontainebleau, quarters he felt were more suitable for the emperor he intended to be, he found there was not even a chair to sit on. All the furniture, all the beautiful works of art that the Kings of France had lovingly placed in their favorite palace–hunting lodge, had been looted during the Revolution. The château had been stripped of everything that could be carried away. So Napoleon restored Fontainebleau to his taste and filled it with furniture whose design he oversaw.

Napoleon's ghost dominates Fontainebleau in part because its curators, finding that tourists visit Fontainebleau because it is evocative of Napoleon, clutter the courtyard with his imperial eagles, and fill the rooms with Empire furniture. Its rooms reverberate not only with Napoleon's highest hopes, but also with his deepest despair. As you walk through its rooms, you see where he first announced his intention to crown himself emperor; where he told Josephine that they were to be divorced; where he learned that he was, at last, to be a father through his second wife, the Empress Marie-Louise; where, after Waterloo, he learned that his generals had deserted him; where he abdicated; where he said farewell to his faithful Old Guard. In the château's Musée Napoléon, the curators have amassed an incredible collection of Napoleonic memorabilia, oils, and sculptures. The descendants of Napoleon, for some reason, have given their gifts to Fontainebleau rather than to Compiègne or to the the château of Malmaison, which were more his creations. I share the indignation of one art historian, who wrote: "The Musée National du Château de Fontainebleau is dedicated to displaying Empire furnishing. And its collection is incomparable. But is this the proper vocation for a château where the Bonapartes counted for so little?"

There is one similarity between Francis's court and Napoleon's that to a minor extent exists today: when Francis and Napoleon moved to Fontainebleau every autumn, their entire court (15,000 courtiers and 3,000 servants) had to move with them. During both the monarchy and the empire, the inhabitants of the town of Fontainebleau made up for their losses in "off-seasons" (when the court was elsewhere) by charging outrageously high prices for food and lodging when the court was in residence. One of Napoleon's courtiers wrote that "More than one foreigner making an excursion to Fontainebleau thought himself held for ransom by a troop of Bedouins. This aspect of court life is still true for the present-day tourist—off-seasons are definitely less expensive than summer and spring months.

The two men were similar in other ways: both Francis and Napoleon had dreams of empire; both were compared to Alexander, Caesar, and Charlemagne during their lives—and both of them took baths in a room filled with paintings by the greatest masters. However, the most interesting phenomenon to me is why Francis is not only not thought of in those terms today, but hardly thought of at all, except by the tour guides at the many castles he built. In fact, I have found only one decent biography of Francis, while at least one biography of Napoleon seems to be written every year. As hard as I have tried, I haven't been able to get Bob, who remains fascinated by Napoleon, even slightly interested in Francis. I find this strange, since Francis's accomplishments seem to rival those of Louis XIV and Napoleon. He would bring the Italian Renaissance to France by summoning the greatest artists and architects of the age—Leonardo da Vinci, Andrea del Sarto, Francesco Primaticcio, Il Rosso, Niccolò dell'Abate, Giacomo Vignola, Sabastiano Serlio, and Benvenuto Cellini—to Amboise and Fontainebleau. The books that filled Francis's library would form the basis for the Bibliothèque Nationale. For a time, he championed the humanists in France, founding the humanist Collège de France when the Sorbonne refused to include either Humanist studies or courses in Greek and Hebrew, preferring instead to burn the humanist writers as heretics. He would, in fact, be the greatest patron of the arts that France had thus far known, not only in painting but in literature as well. He would build the fabulous wing at Blois, create a majestic castle at Chambord out of a swamp, tear down to its base and rebuild the castle of Saint-Germain-en-Laye, set the style of the Hôtel de Ville in Paris, and turn Fontainebleau from a dilapidated hunting lodge housing monks into a palace fit for kings.

Since Francis did not intend to rebuild Fontainebleau but merely to alter it a bit, the architecture is rambling and charming, topped with the steeply pitched French Gothic roofs and chimneys that I love, rather than the flattened, symmetrical, classical buildings built during the reign of Louis XIV. As much as possible, he used the pre-existing thick medieval walls of the hunting lodge that had been built around an oval courtyard, with a square keep, similar to the one seen at Vincennes. He altered its appearance by adding dormer windows and a monumental entrance—the Porte Dorée—and then, finding the château too small to accommodate the writers, artists, and members of the aristocracy who came to live increasingly at court, he added more wings. The first thing he did was to link his royal apartments in the new château to an old abbey with a long gallery. This became the heart connecting all the wings of the castle. Every treasure that Francis found was brought to Fontainebleau, which he loved and considered his home. When he traveled, besides taking his courtiers and servants, he also took chests filled with tapestries that mirrored the frescoes his Italian artists painted on the walls at Fontainebleau. He would hang those tapestries on the walls of every castle to which he traveled to help him feel at home.

During his reign, every aspect of the castle's interior—from the ornate art on the walls to the luxurious fabrics of the courtier's costumes—was designed to delight, titillate, and amuse the court. However, the purpose of the somewhat pretentious splendor and magnificence of Francis's court was really to proclaim to the world that he was not only a king equal to other contemporary kings, but one superior to them all.

When I walk through Fontainebleau, I try to imagine the palace as it was during his reign, that the people I meet in the halls are not the drab polyester-and-denim-clad tourists from my time, but instead sixteenth-century courtiers, dressed in the dazzling costumes described by François Rabelais, a frequent guest of Francis:

> [The men were dressed] in breeches of velvet, of the same color with their stockings. . . . Their doublet was of gold, cloth of silver, gold tissue or velvet. . . . Their girdles were of silk. . . . Everyone had a gallant sword by his side, the hilt and handle whereof were gilt, and the scabbard of velvet . . . with a band of gold, and pure goldsmith's work. Their caps or bonnets were of black velvet, adorned with jewels and buttons of gold. Upon that they wore a white plume . . . parted by so many rows of gold spangles, at the end whereof hung dangling in more sparkling resplendency fair rubies, emeralds, and diamonds.

And that was just the men! The women were even more splendidly attired, in a colorful array of silk gowns lined with rich fur, embroidered with pearls and jewels.

Appearance, not military prowess, was important in the sixteenth-century court of Francis. Your status in society was measured by the luxury and magnificence in dress that you displayed and no longer by the number of soldiers you commanded. And appearance was important not only in France, but in England as well. The best example of this was the meeting of Francis, King of France, age twenty-six, with Henry VIII, King of England, age twenty-nine, near Calais in 1520, to arrange an alliance against the Holy Roman Emperor Charles V, age twenty. The two young kings, not finding any of the nearby castles regal enough for their pretensions, set up a camp near Calais with four hundred huge pavilions—Francis's tent was 60 feet high and covered with a cloth made of gold threads and decorated with three royal-blue velvet horizontal stripes embroidered with golden lilies, while his queen's tent was of silver and decorated with gems. Henry, not to be outdone, had a prefabricated castle brought from England, in front of which he installed a fountain with a statue of Bacchus pouring wine—really good wine. Not only was the camp, which became known as the "Field of the Cloth of Gold," ostentatiously lavish, it was said by the historian Desmond Seward that some courtiers from both countries spent so much money on their clothes that they "came to the Field of the Cloth of Gold wearing their manors on their backs."

We are able to get a glimpse of Francis's lavish tastes, his peculiar sixteenth-century sense of humor, and the sensuous nature of the court over which he presided if we take the time to enjoy the Francis I Gallery at Fontainebleau, which remains pretty much as it once was during his reign.

Both the problem with and the fascination of this gallery is that the art on view there is court art, aristocratic art, which means it was designed to delight sixteenth-century courtiers familiar with its gossip. While the paintings were executed by great masters of the Italian Renaissance, the frescoes are filled with innuendoes that titillated the perverse and jaded tastes of Francis's courtiers. Visiting it today, without at least an audio-guide, a live guide, or a tour book, is like listening to gossip about people you don't know. When I brought a friend to see this gallery, she refused to consider an audio-guide and then raced through it so fast I could hardly keep up with her. The long gallery looked familiar to her, like so many other galleries she had seen in French aristocratic châteaux, for the simple reason that once the gallery at Fontainebleau was created, the "long gallery" became an integral component of practically every aristocratic château built thereafter. But the gallery was not meant to be just a passageway to somewhere else. It was, as British art historian and disgraced Soviet spy Anthony Blunt writes, "a place to pause," a "beautiful suspension in time," where the art was placed "to be read panel by panel."

The art was executed by the Italian Renaissance painters Il Rosso and Francesco Primaticcio, who introduced Mannerism in France. Being accustomed to my century's cold glass-and-stainless-steel simplicity, I initially found the gallery overly ornate and gilded, filled with stucco figures who didn't seem to know their place and protruded outside the frames of frescoes. But the more I learned about the gallery, the more I became fascinated and at home not only with its opulence but with the exuberance of the animated mix of painting and stucco.

The themes and allegories in this long gallery were supplied by Francis to glorify his reign and tell of his successes and misfortunes. And while the audio-guide helps quite a bit in understanding how the Greek and Roman mythological figures in both the frescoes and stucco sculptures relate to the life of Francis, I truly wished Francis himself had left a tape explaining these frescoes.* After the decorations were completed, Francis held the key (literally and figuratively) to the gallery, which was kept locked and only opened so he could show special guests. He would ask them to supply interpretations to the frescoes, which seemed to be scenes from ancient mythology but were, in fact, allusions to his life. Francis's brilliant older sister, Marguerite of Navarre, herself an accomplished writer and patron of French humanists, wrote him: "Your buildings are like a dead body without you. Looking at the buildings, without hearing your intentions for it, is like reading Hebrew."

Once I learned that the twelve frescoes were puzzles, arranged in pairs, that each of the six frescoes on the right of the gallery provide clues to the meaning of each of the six facing them on the left, that the stucco sculptures surrounding and protruding upon the frescoes also supply clues to hidden meanings to the stories in the frescoes, I found it marvelous fun, as indeed, I believe, Francis intended. You can't look at his portrait—he looks like a mischievous satyr—without knowing he intended wicked fun as well as his own glorification. A sixteenth-century description of one of Francis's dinner parties with La Petite Bande (his inner clique of courtiers) provides us tourists an insight into his particular brand of humor and helps us appreciate the frescoes in the gallery.

What a dinner! . . . Hardly were we seated when each of us was served with wine from a silver cup ingeniously designed with a

---

* Bob's subject—Lyndon Johnson—had left a tape; on bus tours of the LBJ Ranch in the Texas Hill Country, there is Johnson's distinctive twang telling you about the ranch's history.

series of revolting amorous scenes. With each drought each lady swallowed, these engravings became increasingly open to the view of all so that the beholders regarded with keen interest and mirth the lady engaged in drinking her wine. If she blushed at what the ebbing wine revealed, the courtiers laughed at her for her innocence; if she did not, they laughed at her for being too knowing.

The frescoes are revealing, telling us quite a bit about Francis I's life, his ambitions and his failures. We can see his dreams in the first four frescoes. They idealize and glorify him as the perfect, godlike ruler, bringing unity and wisdom to his state. In these frescoes, his birth and accomplishments are compared to those of both Caesar and Alexander the Great.

The Unity of the State fresco idealizes Francis, who is portrayed as a Roman emperor holding a pomegranate, which was the age-old symbol of unity because it contained many seeds in one fruit; and *The Royal Elephant*, which faces it, an ancient symbol of royalty, conquest, and wisdom, alludes to Francis's royalty and wisdom.

An explanation of *The Sacrifice*, although not the most interesting fresco, shows precisely how the puzzle works. We know that the fresco is about Francis because above it there is a gold salamander, the symbol Louise of Savoy chose for her son Francis when he was ten in recognition of the fact that a salamander could not be touched by fire and was therefore considered the symbol of power. We know it is a sacrifice because of the stucco priest and priestess on the right, who are sacrificing an animal. We know it is a festive "sacrifice" and can furthermore surmise that the festivities are a birthday celebration because of the children's masks in the fresco. The woman holding a baby is therefore most likely Louise holding Francis. The *F*, which I once assumed referred to King Francis, refers in this painting not to him, but rather to St. Francis of Paola, after whom Francis was named. Both Louise and Louis XII prayed to him for an heir, and he was canonized when Louise had her wish granted.

The fresco entitled *Ignorance Banished*, is directly across from *The*

Sacrifice. The theme is Francis, who will bring enlightenment to his realm. He is depicted as a Roman emperor, carrying a sword in one hand and a book under the other arm as he enters the Temple of Jupiter. Above the fresco, the salamander (or Francis) is in a stucco temple and protrudes upon the fresco below to make the point that Francis possesses the attributes of Jupiter, the Roman god who was the guardian of law, defender of truth, protector of justice and virtue. In the fresco's foreground are rather unpleasant-looking people, symbolizing the citizens of Francis's realm, who are blindfolded, indicating that they are ignorant. On either side are satyrs, one male and one female, symbolizing the vices to which those who are ignorant must yield. Below the fresco are symbols of deceit, worldliness, and fraud.

While Francis may have wanted the fresco to show that he, a godlike ruler, was bringing enlightenment to the world, that is not precisely what Il Rosso painted. It was one of the first frescoes painted by the Italians at Fontainebleau. While by the end of Francis's reign Italian artists were calling Fontainebleau the "new Rome," that was not their feeling when they first arrived in France. Benvenuto Cellini, the renowned goldsmith of the Italian Renaissance, expressed the early Italian attitude when he wrote that the "French are very uncouth people." The Italian ambassador to Francis's court at Fontainebleau expressed similar contempt for the French king when he wrote: "He rises at eleven o'clock, hears Mass, dines, spends two or three hours with his mother, then goes whoring or hunting, and finally wanders here and there throughout the night, so one can never have an audience with him by day." Seen in this light, scholars have suggested that Il Rosso, a Florentine, while grateful for Francis's patronage, was, in the fresco, expressing contempt for the French as a whole, and it has been interpreted "as depicting Francis, as an enlightened King ruling over a nation of barbarians," entering into the Temple of Jupiter, where he "asks the Gods to remove the blindfolds from his subjects' eyes," whereas Francis thought of himself as Caesar, or even Jupiter (since there is a salamander in the stucco temple above the fresco), bringing enlightenment not just to the French, but to the entire world.

The book under Francis's arm has been interpreted as an allusion to the humanist Collège de France, which Francis created because of his problems with the Sorbonne in Paris. Mired in the strict Catholicism of the Middle Ages, the Sorbonne considered the classical teachings of the Italian Renaissance blasphemous. While a century earlier it had supplied the English with the theological arguments justifying the burning of Joan of Arc, it was now supplying the French Parliament with the theological arguments for burning humanists, most of whom could be found either at Fontainebleau or at the court of Francis's beloved sister Marguerite of Navarre. The Sorbonne not only banned a book written by Marguerite, *Mirror of the Sinful Soul*, but also demanded the arrest of Francis's favorite poet, Clément Marot, who was guilty of eating lard during Lent.

The next frescoes refer to events in Francis's life: his greatest successes and his worst defeats. In *The Education of Achilles*—an allegory praising Francis's education—Chiron the Centaur, who was famed for his wisdom, is educating Achilles in the art of fencing, swimming, lance throwing, hunting, and making music. The chained giants on either side of the fresco suggest that a lack of education means slavery. Although there are other interpretations of this fresco, I decided that it refers to the period in Francis's life when Louis XII, realizing that he would not sire a son, brought his nephew Francis, who was next in line for the throne of France, to his château at Blois to be educated with other young men of the aristocracy. The old king (then in his fifties) felt Francis too frivolous and extravagant, and hoped he could prepare him to be a sensible king. It was then that Francis met and married Louis's daughter, Claude of France, who bore him two sons.

The Battle of the Centaurs refers to Francis's greatest victory, when, during the first year of his reign, he conquered the duchy of Milan at Marignano and thought it was just the beginning of the fulfillment of his dreams of empire. After winning this battle, he wrote his mother: "There has not been seen so fierce and cruel a battle these last 2,000 years," and the letter she wrote back to her son, addressed him as "my Caesar, my Alexander." From the time Francis was a boy at Amboise, his mother and his sister Marguerite doted upon him and called him their "Caesar," their "Alexander," their "Charlemagne." Francis liked the comparisons, and soon after his return to France he could be seen carrying a favorite book of his, *Commentaires de la Guerre Gallique*, by François Demoulins, which was an imagined conversation between Julius Caesar and himself in which they discuss their past victories.

I find *The Shipwreck*, or *The Revenge of Nauplius*, the most interesting of all the frescoes. It alludes to the worst defeat of Francis's life, at Pavia in 1525, which resulted in his imprisonment in Madrid. The myth in the fresco relates how Nauplius, a Greek wanting to avenge the death of his son, who had been killed by Ulysses, lit a beacon on the rocks to lure the ships of the Greeks who were returning from the siege of Troy. Their ships were wrecked upon the rocks.

This fresco is frankly only interesting if you know the court gossip and dramatic events to which it alludes. Nauplius represents the traitor and former constable of France, Charles de Bourbon. He had been one of Francis's most loyal knights. He had accompanied him to the Field of the Cloth of Gold, and had fought with him at Marignano. The trouble between the two men was caused by Francis's mother, Louise, who fell in love with Bourbon. When his wife died, Louise proposed through a mutual friend. Bourbon was furious at the suggestion. He responded: "You are counseling me, to whom the best woman in the entire kingdom of France belonged, to marry the worst woman in the world. I will not do it, not even for all Christendom."

"Those words will cost him dear," Louise vowed. And they did. She took possession of all the lands that Bourbon had expected to inherit through his wife—a substantial portion of France. Bourbon, furious at both the Queen Mother and her son, signed a secret agreement with the Holy Roman Emperor Charles V, Francis's lifelong enemy. The emperor promised him Burgundy in exchange for betraying his king, which he did at Pavia. As a result of that betrayal, Francis was taken prisoner by Charles V.

Jailed in the tower of the Alcázar in Madrid in a single room, Francis was denied all forms of exercise. Accustomed to hunting each day, he nearly died during his two years of captivity. His defiance and refusal to either marry the emperor's sister—who had fallen in love with him—

or cede Burgundy to the emperor captured the hearts and minds of Europe. In France and Italy, he was compared to Charlemagne and Roland; in England to Richard the Lionheart; the romantic Spaniards, who hated their cold Austrian king, idealized the chivalrous young king and compared him to Amadis of Gaul, the Spanish hero of a medieval romance of chivalry.

The next fresco refers to the part of Francis's life that lost him the hearts of his contemporaries, and, to some extent, my admiration. It is entitled *The Fire at Catania*. The myth alludes to Francis's two sons, Henry, age seven, and Francis, the dauphin, age eight, coming to Madrid, where Francis was dying in his prison cell, and remaining in his place as hostages, so that Francis could return to France. In the myth, two boys save their parents from a fire caused by the eruption of Mount Etna. In 1526, Marguerite worked out the Treaty of Madrid, with Charles V, and Francis swore on the Bible that he would abide by it, agreeing to have his two young sons remain as the emperor's hostages in Madrid until the treaty's terms were fulfilled. He also agreed to marry the emperor's sister, saying, none too chivalrously, "On the faith of a gentleman, I'd marry Charles' mule, if necessary, to be again in France."

And while he did marry her when he returned to France, he broke all the other terms of the treaty, and thus by breaking his oath (instead of dying nobly in prison), violated the canons of chivalry. One of the treaty's terms was to restore all lands and titles to Charles de Bourbon, and also to give him Burgundy. Instead, Francis had Bourbon tried and found guilty of rebellion, and he confiscated his remaining lands. Other measures taken against him were considered almost worse than death in medieval society: he was prohibited from using the name Bourbon and from displaying his heraldic arms; most humiliating of all, the door of his house in Paris was painted yellow, the color of Judas in medieval French art.

Francis reneged also on the surrender of Flanders and Artois and on the abandonment of his claims to Milan and Naples. He declared that the Treaty of Madrid had been signed under duress and was therefore not valid. He insisted that he had not been treated as captive kings and members of the aristocracy had been in the past—mentioning that they had been allowed to hunt and attend court festivities—and used that excuse as justification for his breaching the terms of the treaty.

Charles V vented his anger on Francis's sons—about whom Francis seemed to have totally forgotten for three years—placing the young hostages in a dark, barred cell in the tower at the Alcázar, furnished only with straw mats. Their French servants were taken away from them and condemned to a life of slavery in Spanish galleys. By the time the princes returned to France, they were more fluent in Spanish than in French. The dauphin, little Francis, quickly regained his French accent upon his return and was soon amusing the court with his witty verse. Francis I could never forgive his younger son, Henry, the future Henry II, for speaking French with a Spanish accent. According to his biographer, it was important to Francis for a courtier to be "as nimble with his tongue as with his sword." When Henry was sixteen, Francis assigned the beautiful widow Diane de Poitiers to teach his sullen son Henry how to behave like a French gentleman. Henry fell desperately in love with her and although she was ten years older than the young prince, she remained his mistress until his death. *The Death of Adonis* fresco alludes to the death of the dauphin, Francis, whom the king dearly loved. While the painting is actually quite moving without any allusions to secret meanings, I can't resist relating a bit of the gossip you would have known if you had been around in the sixteenth century. In the fresco, there is a grotesque woman embracing a fox, who is thought to be Catherine de Médicis because of a statement made at court by the Countess de La Rochefoucauld at the time: "The Italian woman has the look of the Spartan boy with the devouring fox beneath his cloak." Courtiers referred to Catherine as "la parvenue" because of her inferior bloodlines—she was only the pope's niece and the great-granddaughter of Lorenzo de'Medici. When the pope first proposed a marriage between his niece and the dauphin, Francis had said that he would rather see the dauphin burn before marrying him to a merchant's daughter. But Francis wanted her immense dowry, so he married Catherine to Henry, the son he didn't like, the son he didn't expect to sit upon the throne of France. Catherine is in this fresco because unproven rumors current at the time linked her with the dauphin's death. Although the rumors were unproven, the frescoes are more concerned with court innuendo than with fact.

The following is a combination of fact and rumor. Francis was playing tennis on a very hot day, and had become overheated and was handed a glass of ice water—any American tourist in France knows how the French feel about ice water—and was handed it, moreover, by a Florentine count. When Francis died a week later, it was rumored that the Florentine Catherine had played a part in poisoning the dauphin to clear the way for Henry, who was next in line to be king. Unfortunately for the count, a book on arsenic was found among his possessions, resulting in his unpleasant death—he was torn to pieces at Lyons when his limbs were attached to four horses running in different directions, after which the crowd played soccer with his head. Despite the rumors that have swirled about Catherine ever since, Francis does not seem to have blamed her, and in fact the rumors may have been just the result of the courtiers' hostility toward her mercantile bloodlines or contempt for her plump figure. You have only to look at the elongated, suggestive ladies of Fontainebleau sculpted in stucco relief or see Cellini's *Nymph of Fontainebleau** to be aware that Henry's mistress, lanky, leggy, aristocratic Diane, who was Cellini's model and who rode the hounds and bathed every day, rather than Henry's obese and smelly wife, was the ideal woman of this period. Eleanor—the emperor's sister, whom Francis I had married to win his freedom, with her short stocky legs, and her knees "red from praying," was merely ignored by Francis and by his arrogant court, where "not a man was found to blush for his sins" and where "ribaldry was mistaken for wit."

Leaving the gallery, we enter the bedroom of the king's mistress, Madame d'Étampes (which was altered somewhat by Louis XV into the staircase that you see). Nonetheless, the western wall above the staircase still retains the bedroom's elegant, erotic, suggestive frescoes and stucco nymphs by Primaticcio. Being careful not to fall down the stairs as you look up, you can see Francis's ideal of feminine beauty. Three of

---

* Now in the Louvre.

the frescoes refer to Francis's love life. *The Marriage of Alexander and Roxana*, where Roxana is stepping into Alexander's bed, is so erotic and so suggestive that you wonder why anyone in Hollywood feels the need to be any more sexually explicit. These painted nudes, with their milky-white skin, and the stucco nymphs with their elongated bodies and exquisite Greek faces, were, according to art historian Anthony Blunt, "calculated to arouse desire" and "invite erotic fantasies."

As implied by its name, this was the bedroom of the Duchess of Étampes, the former Anne d'Heilly, who entered Francis's life the moment he set foot in France after his captivity in 1526. She accompanied Francis's mother, Louise, to Bayonne, where the Queen Mother was to welcome her son. Francis's mother and sister decided that the long-legged, blond-haired, blue-eyed maid-in-waiting was the perfect person to help Francis forget his two years of celibacy in a Spanish prison. She did more than merely welcome Francis, she giggled her way into his bed before they left Bayonne, and remained his official—but not only—mistress until he died. Since the official mistress of the king had to be a noblewoman, Francis went to the trouble of marrying her to Jean de Brosse, Duke of Étampes, whom he made Governor of Brittany and then sent far from court. Anne appears to have been as brilliant and as venomous as the Queen Mother herself, taking most of her sarcasm out on Diane de Poitiers, whom she considered the greatest threat to her official position of king's mistress, attacking her whenever possible by pointing out her advancing years (Diane was thirty-two while Anne was eighteen). Tensions between the two women increased when Cellini, searching for the perfect model for his *Nymph of Fontainebleau*, passed over Anne and chose Diane instead. (What were once considered "witty" barbs have either lost something in my translation or I have lost my sense of humor. For example, she said, and the court thought it witty: "Did you chance to know that I was born on the very day that Madame la Sénéchale [Diane] was married?" She also composed rhymes calling her "the wrinkled one."

Francis started work on what is now the ballroom, but it was completed during the reign of his son Henry II. The frescoes painted by Primaticcio, allegories of the hunt, are devoted to Diane. Her symbol, the crescent moon, is intertwined with Henry's monogram. After Henry died, some said that it is not a crescent moon but a *C* for Catherine de Médicis, but I don't believe this. In some cases, Catherine did have an artist take the loop and extend it to look more like a *C*. However, if you travel to Anet, the palace Henry built for Diane, and where Diane retired after Henry died, her crescent moon, intertwined with Henry's *H*, looks identical to the *C* intertwined with Henry's monogram at Fontainebleau. On the other hand, the nudes in the Salle de Bal certainly are plumper and more like Catherine and me than the nudes in the Galerie François I. When Henry became king, art turned away from Mannerism, reflecting Diane's more classical taste.

During the ten years of his reign, Henry, Diane, and Catherine spent quite a bit of time together in Paris, as we shall do now. If you exit through the gates through which Napoleon departed, cross the street, and then walk slightly to the right, a bus will come and take you back in time to meet a train departing for Paris.

CHAPTER 14

HENRY IV in PARIS

—

Line 1 and Line 7 Métro

*T*HERE IS SOMETHING SO EXCITING ABOUT PARIS ONCE HENRY IV arrives. Almost immediately, he began to bring peace and prosperity to a city that had been ravaged by thirty years of war. It was as though the moment he dismounted his medieval steed in Paris, he exchanged the reins of his warhorse for those invisible reins we call the forces of history, turned them in the direction of urban transformation, and reshaped a city torn by war and neglect. For Henry, Paris was the unhealthy heart of the ailing nation he sought to cure.

His reign, which began in 1589, followed the regency of Catherine de Médicis and the reigns of her three foppish sons, a thirty-year period of nine civil wars called collectively the Wars of Religion. (I say Catherine de Médicis's three sons because her husband, Henry II, who valued the manly ideals of chivalry above all, was disgusted by them—one of them, who was to become King Henry III, was a pedophile and transvestite— and wanted nothing to do with them. Once, after taking a look at them, he asked the stalwart Henry of Navarre, the future Henry IV to be his son, and when he refused, he asked him to become his son-in-law by marrying his daughter Marguerite of Valois. Henry of Navarre, as a descendant of St. Louis, was next in line to be king, but there was a problem with fanatically Catholic Paris accepting this particular Henry. Although baptized a Catholic at the insistence of his father, he had been brought up a Calvinist by his mother, and, at the time he became king, he was the leader of the Huguenot forces fighting the Catholic League.

I will not go into the consequent fanaticism of the Huguenots—which resulted in the destruction of untold priceless works of religious art—or the fanaticism of the Catholics—which led to the deaths of tens of thousands of Frenchmen—or how valiant a leader Henry IV was in battle. I will wait instead for historians to make up their minds whether these nine wars were religious wars or political wars—wars in which the feudal aristocracy sought to regain the power and independence it had been gradually losing as power became increasingly centralized in the person of the king. But whether they were religious or political, or both, they destroyed rather than produced monuments we could visit today, so I will skip instead directly to Henry IV's statement, which he either made or should have made, that Paris is "worth a Mass," and which he was said to have made at the Hôtel de Sens.

Hôtel de Sens
Line 7 Métro to Pont-Marie

Henry's marriage in 1572 to Marguerite de Valois, or Margot, as she was called, ended in divorce in 1599. After their divorce, Margot was given the Hôtel de Sens, once the medieval residence of the archbishop of Sens, where she surrounded herself with poets, philosophers, and lovers. By the time Margot moved there, the brick and stone building had been remodeled in the Flamboyant Gothic style, architecture similar to Louis XII's château that we visited in Blois.

For many years, I walked past the Hôtel de Sens as I made my way from my apartment on the Left Bank across the Seine, past the seventeenth-century buildings on the Île Saint-Louis, to the Place des Vosges or to the Hôtel Carnavalet, the Museum of the History of Paris. I loved walking past its lovely medieval garden, always a mosaic of seasonal colors, set against the backdrop of the asymmetrical medieval building topped with the pepperpot turrets, mullioned windows, and dormers decorated with finials and curving leaves of stone. Sometimes I would walk around to the front and peek through the large pointed-arched entrance into its courtyard, imagining that the smaller arched doors in the courtyard led to a romantic past rather than a modern library. At first, I thought it sad that this lonely medieval survivor of Baron von Haussmann's ax was squashed between ugly modern buildings until I saw a model of medieval Paris at the Hôtel Carnavalet—and saw that the Hôtel de Sens had been squashed in between ugly medieval buildings.

The pepperpot turrets and lovely garden and romantic courtyard lost their charm for me when I learned how Margot ended her last love affair here. In a fit of jealous rage, the twenty-year-old Count of Vermond, one of Margot's lovers, murdered a carpenter's son when he learned the young workman was hammering more than nails. Margot, in an equally violent rage, ordered the count's head cut off in the *romantic* courtyard into which I used to peek, while she watched from one of the lovely dormer windows, screaming: "Kill him! Kill him! Here, take my garters and strangle the wretch with them." My guess is that the carpenter's son was a better lover than the count. After this episode, Margot moved to another residence, and once I began picturing the courtyard with the count's severed head rolling in puddles of blood, I began taking another route to the Place des Vosges, along the Rue des Jardins Saint-Paul, where the western side of the street is guarded by the remains of Philip Augustus's wall.

The Place des Vosges
Line 1 Métro to St. Paul

After Henry IV annulled his marriage to Margot in 1599, he married the wealthy but supercilious Marie de Médicis, who provided him with both an heir and a substantial, much-needed dowry. Henry was a practical man. While his many mistresses and amorous intrigues have endeared him to the French, they respected and loved him for never allowing Marie de Médicis to get her hands on the royal treasury while he lived, and for the one love affair in which he was quite faithful: his love affair with Paris. In fact, the next twelve years, until he was assassinated by a fanatical Catholic, were the most peaceful and most productive years Paris had enjoyed. Shortly after his arrival in Paris, Henry met with the city provost, who reported, "His majesty announced his intention to spend his years in this city and . . . to make this city beautiful, splendid and full of all the conveniences and ornaments that he possibly can . . . in his words, he wishes to make this city an entire world and a miracle on earth." And Henry did just that.

When the religious wars were finally over, Henry and his frugal Huguenot adviser, Sully, sat down to look over the nation's finances. They found the treasury not only empty, but 3 million livres in debt. Henry also found, as Louis XI had a century before, that the French people were sending a great deal of money—approximately 6 million livres a year—to Italy for silk. "The King, seeing this . . . thought it best to introduce the manufacture into France" and "gave instruction for the planting of a large number of white mulberry trees." He thought the manufacture of silk would provide employment for his subjects, while ending the drain on French finances. While it didn't work out the way he planned, it did result in the creation of the Place des Vosges—the first major urban renewal project in Paris.

His idea, which he announced in 1603, was simple: ban silk imports and manufacture silk in France. There were a few minor difficulties with this plan. France had few if any white mulberry trees—silkworms will only eat mulberry leaves—fewer silkworms, and no one who knew how to make or manufacture silk. But problems such as these are easily overcome when you are the King of France.

Henry gathered together five wealthy merchants and *persuaded* them to finance the silk industry. Immediately 600,000 mulberry trees and silkworms were ordered. Groves of mulberry trees could soon be seen in the Tuileries Gardens. The English ambassador, Sir George Carew, commented at the time that Henry "hath caused most of the gentlemen . . . of his realm to plant mulberry trees in their grounds for the nourishing of silk-worms and told me he hoped to make his realm the staple for the silk that should be worn in all these northern parts of Europe."

Then, since Paris possessed no artisans who knew how to make silk, Henry proposed to build appealing living and working quarters to attract the Italian artisans who did know. This wonderful place would become the Place des Vosges. He issued the following edict:

> Having resolved for the convenience and ornament of our good city of Paris to make a large square built on four sides which would help establish the silkworms and lodge the workers that we want to attract to our realm . . . and at the same time, the residents of our city, who are very crowded in their houses . . . could stroll and (use) as well on days of celebration . . . I have resolved . . . to commit to this end of the site presently called the horse market, previously the parc des Tournelles and which we wish henceforth to be called the Place Royale.

To finance this immense project, Henry did something that would be the equivalent today of giving five real estate investors land along Fifth Avenue in New York or along the Champs-Élysées in Paris. Henry had no money, but the crown owned most of the site where the Hôtel des Tournelles and adjacent park had been, in the then fashionable district known now as the Marais. In the seventeenth century, anybody who was anybody in the court of France had his pied-à-terre—or *hôtel particulier*—there. (The term *hôtel particulier* refers to the home of an aristocrat—as opposed to a residence of a wealthy commoner.) For example, already living in the neighborhood in what is currently the Musée Carnavalet were Marie de Médicis's treasurer; Diane de Poitiers's legitimized daughter, Diane of France, who resided at the Hôtel Lamoignon; Marie de Guise, who lived at the Hôtel de Soubise (now the National Archives and the Museum of French History); Anne de Montmorency's children at the Hôtel d'Albret; and the Bishop of Orléans on the Rue de Sévigné. These homes would be freestanding, possessing an entrance court and a garden.

———

MOST OF THE LAND that is now the Place des Vosges had become vacant, in 1559, forty years before, when, during a three-day tournament celebrating the marriage of one of Henry II's daughters, the king himself had been killed. On each day of the tournament, Henry II rode his horse between two rows of a hundred armed knights as he entered the arena in the courtyard of the Hôtel des Tournelles. He wore a helmet crowned with black and white plumes, the colors of his mistress Diane de Poitiers, and before the tilting event each day, he met with his opponent in front of Diane and they tipped their helmets to her. On the third day of the tournament, Henry was struck by his opponent's lance, which pierced his visor and embedded itself in his left eye. Henry was taken to the Hôtel des Tournelles, and Diane went to the Church of Saint-Paul (on the Rue Saint-Antoine) to pray for her lover, upon whom her position at court depended. When she returned to the *hôtel*, the royal guards, on the order of Queen Catherine de Médicis, refused to allow her to enter—and Diane therefore knew that Henry had died. After his death, Catherine leveled the palace surrounding the courtyard where Henry was killed.

During the intervening years, the land became a horse market and public dump. Henry IV now gave this land to the five entrepreneurs who at his strong suggestion had invested in the silk industry. The grant came of course with strings attached. They had to build according to Henry IV's designs, which mandated uniform façades of brick and stone, slate roofs, and arcades, which would protect the silk.

Today, when you enter the Place des Vosges, you therefore see that one of the thirty-six buildings surrounding it—the King's Pavilion—is higher than the others and the only one with ornamentation and without shops opening on the gallery—because a shop beneath his pavilion would have been beneath Henry's dignity. He felt that if he lived there himself, the development would be more attractive to the Italian silk manufacturers. Behind the uniform façades, the builders could do as they pleased as long as they provided "mansions and habitations" for the wealthy Italian artisans who knew how to make silk.

Not all the land was owned by the crown. The land on the west side of the project was privately owned and presented the only obstacle to Henry's project. When the owner proved reluctant to part with it, Henry informed Sully of his wish that the owner be "compelled to sell."

As happened with the land that the Baron von Haussmann in the nineteenth century or Robert Moses in the twentieth wanted for their projects in Paris and New York, the owner gave way, only faster.

PLACE ROYALE WAS the name Henry gave the square in 1604. It was changed to the Place des Vosges in 1798, when Napoleon I, as first consul, finding the treasury as bare as Henry had, tried to motivate the departments of France to pay their taxes quickly. The Department of Vosges was the first to pay in full, and Napoleon honored that section of France with the new name.

Almost as soon as the Place des Vosges was built, the developers realized they could make more money by renting the thirty-six pavilions (nine per side) to the aristocracy, rather than giving it to Italian crafts-men, so after Henry IV was assassinated, the aristocracy moved in.

If you have been to Paris and have never visited the Place des Vosges, it will be like discovering another novel by your favorite author when you thought you had read them all. It had been part of our Sunday ritual for Bob and I to have lunch there in the afternoon. The Line 1 Métro takes you to the Saint-Paul stop. You walk east on the Rue Saint-Antoine, a rather dirty but bustling street dating from the time Paris was part of Rome, past the Saint-Paul church at which Diane prayed for Henry's recovery, until you arrive, across the street, at a cream-colored stone mansion: the Hôtel de Sully, which is where the Hôtel des Tournelles had been before Catherine de Médicis leveled it. From this moment, the day becomes sheer magic. After you pass through the hôtel's entrance, a classical archway in the middle of the façade, you find yourself in a marvelous Renaissance courtyard where in all likelihood, if it is Sunday, a single violinist will be playing classical music while people read on stone benches beneath opulent friezes and sculptures. I particularly like the statues of Autumn and Winter in their niches, which you will see if you turn and look up after entering the courtyard. Although named after Sully, Henry IV's closest adviser, it was built for an inept gambler, who sold it to Sully after Henry was assassinated. The architecture is a perfect example of the classical style popular during the time of Henry's son Louis XIII. For the most part, it follows classical strictures, but it still retains the steep roofs, high dormers, and niched reliefs made popular by Diane de Poitiers's favorite sculptor, Jean Goujon.

After you leave the courtyard and enter the Place des Vosges itself, aside from a statue of Louis XIII in the middle of the park and people dressed anachronistically in twenty-first-century clothes, you are back in Henry IV's Paris. You are in a lovely park surrounded by symmetrical buildings of uniform and elegant proportions on all four sides. The uniformity of materials, black-slate pitched roof, textured red brick, and cream-colored stone—the same as those used by Louis XII at Blois—add to a feeling of serenity and peace. The arcaded gallery, a common feature of the towns of Henry's southwest and suggested by Henry to protect the bolts of precious silk from the rain while they were being carried to and from wagons, adds to the feeling of protection and security.

It is amazing how little the Place des Vosges has changed since it was built. Once, while I was in Paris by myself for a few days, I stayed at the luxurious Pavillon de la Reine (once the Queen's Pavilion), which faces the Pavilion du Roi, and visited the square during the week. On Sundays, when Bob and I usually come, the Place des Vosges is filled with tourists eating at cafés, listening to different groups of musicians—you can usually walk around the square under the arcades until you find both a restaurant and a musical group that fits your taste. (There is even a three-star restaurant near the entrance to Sully courtyard whose prices, displayed on a menu by the door, took my appetite away.)

Awakening early on a Monday morning while I was staying at Le Pavillon de la Reine, I walked out into the square and was overwhelmed by its serene elegance and beauty in the morning silence. The early-morning sun highlighted the results of recent restoration. Different sections had been restored by different stone or brick workers. It had been difficult in Henry IV's day to find workers skilled in making and laying brick, but it is obvious that finding them today is even far more challenging. Brickmaking seems to be a totally lost art. While the old bricks are rough and reflect the sun and shadows, giving those sections a seventeenth-century liveliness, the modern bricks are smooth and lacking in texture and depth, but somehow the difference only made me appreciate the beauty and workmanship of the original.

Despite Henry IV's efforts, Paris never became a center for the manufacture of silk, while Lyon, only two hours from Paris by TGV, did. If you make the trip to Lyon's Old Town, in a restored Renaissance hilltop district you can walk through a network of vaulted passages (traboules) created in the sixteenth and seventeenth centuries by silk merchants to protect the delicate fabric. The wealth they acquired is visible today in the mansions and *hôtels* that line the narrow cobblestone streets.

THE PLACE DES VOSGES was not the only public-works project Henry IV built. He was "passionate about building. When he won money playing real tennis he tended to say, 'that will be for my masons.' " He also built the Pont Neuf, one of the first bridges to cross the Seine without the shops and houses that usually lined the medieval bridges of Paris. On one of our first trips to Paris, we crossed the Pont Neuf to the Île-de-la-Cité. Bob and I discovered the Place Dauphine, a lopsided square sheltered from the bustle of the quays. It seemed a miraculous place. One minute we were in the midst of a crowd of noisy tourists, the next we were cloistered in a peaceful triangular square lined with restaurants. Bob and I chose the Restaurant Chez Paul, whose crowded tables were in the sun, where we enjoyed a lovely lunch as we watched old men play boules on the grassy mall.

When Henry arrived in Paris, the Île-de-la-Cité was even more crowded than it is today. The shops of booksellers, money changers, goldsmiths, and jewelers overflowed the island and lined not only the quays on both sides of the river, but the bridges as well. People came to Notre-Dame, to the courts, to the banking offices, to the palace of the king, to the Parlement of Paris—the body responsible for endorsing the king's edicts. The Île-de-la-Cité was also where the president of the Parlement, Achille de Harlay, had his home. Harlay had been one of Henry's faithful soldiers during the wars of religion as well as a supporter of his edicts in the Parlement.

As I have mentioned, Henry was a practical man with a paternal feeling for his subjects. It was Henry who wanted all the workingmen in his realm to have a chicken in their pot each Sunday. Nowhere are both his traits so aptly expressed in stone than they are at the Place Dauphine. When the Pont Neuf was completed, Henry found that he had added with its construction approximately three new acres on the western tip of the island near the Pont Neuf. In March 1607, Henry IV gave this land and the designs for the square to Harlay, who was in turn required to build the Place Dauphine. When Henry noticed three months later that no progress had been made, he added a new condition—that Harlay had to complete the project within three years. Henry added: "If he does not want to do it, find someone else who will undertake it, and tell him that he will profit from the land."

Unlike the Place des Vosges, which was planned to house silk manufacturers and ended up housing the aristocracy, the Place Dauphine actually ended up providing housing, as planned, for the middle class.

This visionary king's plans for still more projects were cut short by his death. After surviving twenty-three attempts on his life, mostly by Jesuits, Henry IV was killed on May 14, 1610, at 4 P.M., when his carriage came to a halt on the Rue de La Ferronnerie during a traffic jam. A crazed red-haired Catholic fanatic, François Ravaillac, who believed he had been summoned by God to kill the Calvinist king, jumped into Henry's stalled carriage and stabbed him three times with a kitchen knife. When Sully heard the news, he rushed to the Louvre, where Henry's body had been taken, only to be refused entry by armed guards, on order of the queen. He hurried to the Arsenal (Bastille), where he was governor and knew he would be safe.

Harlay, a man with a keen political understanding, called a meeting of the Paris Parlement and encouraged the body to invest Marie de Médicis with the powers of regent. Henry had crowned Marie queen only the day before. The Parlement tried and tortured Ravaillac. Even when Harlay threatened to burn his parents alive in his presence, he maintained that he had acted alone.

If the people were, as Henry once said, "an animal which lets itself be led by the noses, especially Parisians," the people of Paris were, when they heard of Henry's death, a crazed animal overwhelmed with grief for their beloved leader. There was no talk of Ravaillac being too incompetent to stand trial due to insanity, as there would be today. After being tortured by the Parlement of Paris, he was brought to the Place de Grève, in front of the Hôtel de Ville, the palace of the people, which Henry had completed only the year before, and where a statue of Henry IV had been placed "above the main entrance signifying the city's allegiance to the King."

The red-haired assassin was then dragged by the grieving populace to the scaffold, where every device of inflicting pain was brought to bear: red-hot pincers pierced his flesh and then molten lead, burning sulphur, and boiling oil and resin were poured on his open wounds. Then he was torn limb from limb as his arms and legs were attached to four horses that pulled in four different directions. It took an hour and a half for him to die, at which point the people of Paris crowded around the body, beating it with clubs and hacking it apart with knives and swords, and then pulling the body parts through the city. According to one historian, a woman in the crowd ate his flesh.

Of course, assassination theories followed his death. Margot, who had remained Henry's good friend after their divorce, told Marie de Médicis that she had information implicating the Duke of Épernon, who had been in the carriage with Ravaillac when Henry was killed. Marie was notably uninterested.

LUXEMBOURG PALACE AND GARDENS
RER Line B to Luxembourg Gardens

At Henry's death, Marie de Médicis became regent and in control of France and its treasury. Frugality, projects for the people, and reliance on the bourgeosie to finance them came to an end in seventeenth-century Paris, and projects for Marie began. Her capriciousness, self-indulgence, mediocre intelligence, and reliance on Italian dandies and astrologers, I have to admit, resulted, however, in one of my favorite places in Paris—the Luxembourg Gardens and Palace. Its gardens are where Bob and I play tennis, and where Bob jogs along gravel paths lined with statues of the queens of France.

Soon after Henry's death, Marie purchased the *hôtel* of Francis of Luxembourg in an area of Paris where a colony of her fellow Italians from Florence had settled. Finding that the property was not large enough to duplicate the gardens, grottoes, and allées of the Pitti Palace in Florence, where she had spent her childhood, she began adding adjacent plots. Only the owners of land belonging to a Carthusian monastery, given to them by St. Louis, refused to sell. That tract was added after the Revolution. In order to duplicate the Pitti Palace exactly, Marie de Médicis asked her family to send the original plans, which she gave to her architect, Salomon de Brosse. He ignored the plans, designing a traditional French quadrilateral château. He did keep a few details of the Pitti Palace, such as the double pilasters, rusticated arches, and the open court, which is a total surprise once you are inside.

For years I had wanted to see the inside of Marie's palace, but because it is now used by the Senate of France, it is open only on the first Sunday of the month and our Sundays in Paris have become somewhat of an inviolable ritual. We always have breakfast at the one sunny café on Place Contrescarpe at the top of the Rue Mouffetard, then shop for fruit, cheese, and paté as we walk down the Rue Mouffetard, followed by dancing and singing with French shoppers who gather at a plaza at the bottom of the hill. There, song sheets are given out and music is played by a long-faced gentleman who looks as though he stepped out of the Toulouse-Lautrec print of the Moulin Rouge. Then, sometimes stopping at the Roman Arena on our way, we walk to the Place des Vosges for lunch.

Luckily, because Bob was writing a book about the United States Senate during the time Lyndon Johnson was its leader, we were given a special weekday tour of the French Senate. I could not believe how lavish, how sumptuous, the interior is. You enter a large courtyard surrounded on four sides by loges; the main entrance is topped by a lantern dome of gilded lead placed above two sets of Doric columns. The inte-

rior decorations—inlaid and parquet floors, blue-and-gold painted paneling, frescoes everywhere, a profusion of ornaments, elaborate coffered
and painted ceilings—really makes one want to overlook the pejorative
aspects of a spendthrift nobility who built places like this by taxing a
starving populace, especially when one looks at the drab modern architecture of today. A staircase now replaces a gallery where Marie hung
twenty-four paintings of herself by Rubens, depicting her with perhaps
more curves and intelligence than she actually possessed, and with certainly less vulgarity than suggested by Sully's memoirs. These paintings
can now be seen at any time in the Louvre in the Galerie Médicis, Gallery 18.

Now you can come to the Luxembourg Gardens to listen to concerts, have lunch, play tennis, jog, or read a book by the reflecting pool
surrounded by statues of the queens of France, or find shade in the
summer near the Médici Fountain, which was inspired by a grotto in
the Boboli Gardens. The little pool that extends from the grotto and
makes it one of my favorite spots to read was added, as was the bas-
relief depicting Leda and the Swan, when, in the nineteenth century,
the Baron von Haussmann ran a road through the original site and the
grotto was moved closer to the palace.

During the five years of Marie de Médicis's regency, she enriched
her favorites with gifts and more than doubled taxes, partly to pay for
them. Conditions became so bad that Catholics and Huguenots banded
together against the crown. In 1617, Louis XIII, with his close friend and
adviser Charles d'Albert de Luynes, murdered Marie's Italian dandy,
Concino Concini, and had his wife, Leonora, burned as a witch in the
Place de Grève. Louis then imprisoned his mother in his castle at Blois,
from which she escaped, being lowered from the château by ropes with
the help of—hmmmm—the Duke of Épernon, that very same man who
had been in the carriage with Henry IV when he was killed.

CHAPTER 15

THE SIEGE of LA ROCHELLE
and the
END of the REFORMATION in FRANCE

—

TGV from Gare Montparnasse to La Rochelle

WHEN I SET THE PARAMETERS FOR THIS BOOK, I LAID DOWN A rule that I would not include any place that took more than ninety minutes to reach by train. But then I fell in love, and when you fall in love, all rules are broken, and it was love at first sight when I arrived in La Rochelle. I just love walking around the city's picture-book harbor guarded by two ancient and enormous fortress towers. I love climbing its Lantern Tower, perhaps the oldest lighthouse in France. I love walking under its medieval arcades or along its fifteenth-and-sixteenth-century streets. I love swimming off the public beach in town. I love eating at its fabulous restaurants. I love taking boat rides from the harbor to Île de Ré, Île d'Oléron, and Fort Boyard, or just hopping on one of the frequent water buses so I can see the harbor from the sea and pretend I am sailing into the seventeenth-century city of La Rochelle, which is precisely what it still looks like from the bow of any boat. In fact, I had such a wonderful two days the first time I was there that I had to return. And when I did, I liked it even more than I had the first time. The truth is, I just love La Rochelle.

It is more than ninety minutes from Paris: it is ninety minutes on the TGV to Poitiers, and then another fifty-five minutes on the same train, but no longer traveling at high speed, to La Rochelle.

But while it is a long train ride away, La Rochelle is, relatively speaking, closer to Paris today than it was in 1627, when it took D'Artagnan and the Musketeers nine days to march there from Paris to take part in the Siege of La Rochelle. But unlike the Musketeers, you are there not to blockade the city and starve its citizens into submission, but to have a fabulous lunch, which you can do if you leave the Montparnasse station at 8 A.M., as we did. While you can go and return in one day, that would be a mistake. Then you couldn't have both lunch at André, a restaurant near the medieval towers that have guarded the harbor for centuries, where the fish is so fresh you can watch fishermen carry your lunch from a boat to its kitchen to be grilled while you enjoy a drink at your table on the dock, and also have dinner at Richard et Christopher Coutanceau, a two-star restaurant, with large picture windows overlooking the harbor where on a pleasant evening you can watch the puffs of clouds float across a Fragonard sky, as a distant lighthouse in the harbor slowly slips into a darkening sea and sky till it becomes only a blinking red light in a sea of black, while you savor your homard breton à la coque.

On our first trip, I thought the food at Coutanceau so memorable that before we returned I made reservations for both nights we were going to be there. On that return trip, though, we needed a place for lunch—I knew better now than to waste any of my appetite on the train, so after dropping our bags off at the hotel, we headed directly for the docks in search of a restaurant. Having brought neither my Gault Millaut nor my Michelin, which I usually consult in selecting restaurants, I walked along the docks looking at the tables of different restaurants and the dishes on them and chose André, where the tables were carefully set with tablecloths and napkins, and where a delicious aroma emanated from a bowl of mussels swimming in a light cream sauce, which I then ordered for my first course. After tasting this glorious dish, I asked, with my not-so-glorious French accent, for the recipe. I knew my accent hadn't improved over the past twenty years when the waiter responded to my request for the recipe with a statement that of course the mussels were fresh: "The restaurant has its own mussel farm and the mussels arrive fresh each day, as does all the fish."

On my first trip to La Rochelle, I reserved a room with a view of the sea at the Hôtel Les Brises, which the Michelin had awarded a red rocking horse—a symbol that over the years I found indicated a pleasant hotel. As our taxi pulled up to our hotel, my heart sank: I saw a stark, modern rectangular block. I had forgotten that Michelin reviewers are fond of modern French architecture. Our room was a small, low-ceilinged square, one wall being a glass sliding door leading to a terrace with a view of the port. I was beside myself with grief because I had chosen a charmless modern hotel without a swimming pool, apparently situated on the border of a giant mile-wide mud flat, whose mucky width was punctuated by a line of large blocks of stone. Our room, however, was clean and functional, and I could see the guard towers of the old port from the terrace.

The management, which could not have been nicer, arranged for a taxi to take us to the center of the old town, less than three kilometers away. We spent a wonderful afternoon there, and, after a fabulous dinner at Richard Coutanceau, we walked back to the hotel through a park bordering the edge of the mud flat. The next morning, the French tide, about which I had totally forgotten, had covered the mucky expanse of mud with water, and when I opened my eyes, all I saw from my bed were sailboats floating on a beautiful sky-blue sea.

Suddenly, this charmless modern hotel had transformed itself into a favorite hotel, to which I returned on my second trip. At night, when the towers of La Rochelle are lit, the stones of old La Rochelle turn to gold, and the view from the terrace is magical. We never again took a taxi to town because as we fell more and more in love with La Rochelle, we fell increasingly in love with walking along the sea toward the medieval towers guarding it. Magically, the walk from the hotel seemed shorter each time we took it. There is a Relais et Château hotel in the center of the town, but I so loved seeing sailboats either float outside my window when I awoke, or, later in the day, race toward the shore before the rapidly receding tide, that I managed to do without a terry-cloth robe and found I was quite able to turn down my own bed (although I would not have minded a maid leaving an evening chocolate on my pillow).

Our first trip to La Rochelle was on the Wednesday before the July 14 weekend (Bastille Day), the French national holiday. When we awoke, we not only saw sailboats, but heard the ominous sounds of drums and electronic guitars tuning up (or at least I hoped they were merely tuning up) for the day's festivities. As we walked toward town, we found a large portion of the park blocked off for a rock concert being held that night. Since it was a Wednesday, in addition to the rock concert, it was market day. The guidebook I was using at the time suggested coming to La Rochelle on a Wednesday in order to see the lively market. I would have preferred coming on Thursday, so that I could have avoided the crowds of the lively market. This national holiday is also the day when a great many French families begin their six-week summer vacation, so while there wasn't a single English-speaking tourist in town, it was very crowded with French.

As we were walking along the edge of the harbor in the center of the Old Town, we came to a canal similar to, but smaller than, one we had seen that the Romans had built to connect Narbonne to the Mediterranean. This canal had been built by Eleanor of Aquitaine, who, in the twelfth century, after inheriting the entire southwest of France when her father died, had ordered a nearby marsh to be cleared, a harbor constructed, and this canal dug to her nearby château, so that boats carrying the silks she had ordered from the Orient could bring them directly to her. That marsh became La Rochelle (or Rupella, as it was then called). Since La Rochelle was located in part of the area she inherited, under medieval law the city first became a part of the royal realm of France when she married the French King Louis VII, in 1137, and then became part of the royal realm of England when she divorced Louis and married Henry II of England in 1152. The city's allegiance continued to switch back and forth between the two countries during the Middle Ages, a time when national identity was not a prism through which anyone looked. By the thirteenth century, La Rochelle had become a rich and prosperous mercantile center. By the time of the Wars of Religion in the sixteenth century, it had become the richest city in France. It was also the capital of the Huguenot rebellion; during those wars, its citizens paid almost the entire cost of Henry of Navarre's battles against the Catholic League.

Nine years after Henry of Navarre became King Henry IV, he converted to Catholicism, and, hoping to stop his subjects from killing one another, he passed the Edict of Nantes in 1598, which gave Protestants freedom of worship in places where their faith had already been established. This act was criticized by the Catholics for being too lenient and by the Huguenots for not being lenient enough. The citizens of La Rochelle—the Rochellais—who had paid for his wars, were angry with Henry for both his conversion and his stipulation that while they were allowed to practice their Calvinist religion in their city, they also had to allow Catholics to practice theirs. In any event, for a brief period of time—twelve years—until a Catholic fanatic assassinated Henry, La Rochelle became an even richer mercantile center, increasing foreign trade, especially with England, and providing a safe haven for Calvinists and dissidents from France, Germany, and Spain.

La Rochelle was not only rich, it was independent—although not as independent as the seventeenth-century mercantile city-states of Italy. Over the years, ever since Eleanor of Aquitaine had ordered that the marsh be turned into a harbor, each time La Rochelle switched its allegiance from France to England to France, the town was granted, as an incentive to do so, greater rights and independence, until during the reign of Louis XIII it alone stood between the king and absolutism. By 1621, La Rochelle seemed impregnable.

Its city walls (Chemin du Rempart), whose remnants you can see as you walk about the town, protected it from attack by land. The entrance to the port was defended by two mighty fourteenth-century towers that flanked the narrow entrance to the harbor and protected the city from attack from the sea. Today they still face each other: La Tour Saint-Nicolas, with its rectangular walls and crenellated keep, the symbol of the independence, military power, and richness of the city; and La Tour de la Chaîne, a rounded tower, built ten years later. Each night a chain was pulled between the two towers to close the port. A century later, a lighthouse was built: La Tour de la Lanterne, 70 meters high, on a rounded base topped with a Gothic spire. Then, in 1627, the impossible happened. The city that seemed impossible to take was taken.

There are numerous explanations as to why the siege of La Rochelle took place. If you look at it through the lens of historical perspective, as I did as a graduate student, it was "a feudal rebellion against central authority that was put down" as France evolved from realm to nation. Seen through the biographer's eyes, it was just part of Cardinal Richelieu's "genuine attempts to forge a single national culture." Seen through the economist's eyes, it was to advance the economic interests of Richelieu, who had formed a trading company (Compagnie des Cent-Associés—Company of 100 Associates) that was in competition with the entrepreneurs of La Rochelle.

But if you see the siege through the eyes of the people who lived at the time, through their memoirs and letters, you find there are enough intrigues and plot twists to fill a dozen novels. In fact, Alexander Dumas did fill *The Three Musketeers* with many of the plots and intrigues that I found in the memoirs written at the time. Since D'Artagnan, who did exist, and the Musketeers, who were the king's personal bodyguards, did take part in both the actual and the novel's Siege of La Rochelle, I made sure to have read Part One of *The Three Musketeers* before boarding the TGV so that on the train I could read Dumas's description of the siege, which is in Part Two. Dumas's account, which makes the trip to La Rochelle more interesting, is similar to the memoirs except that D'Artagnan lives on in the novel but, alas, was killed at the siege.

But two questions my history books and Dumas do not answer is why the Rochellais chose to starve to death rather than surrender, and why Louis XIII, not a particularly cruel man, allowed such cruelty to take place? Did Louis XIII give Richelieu a free hand because the town was a threat to his absolutism or because of his hatred of the Duke of Buckingham, with whom he believed his queen was having an affair?

Louis's hatred of Buckingham originated a few years before the siege and is ensnared in a plot far more twisted than the one that appears in *The Three Musketeers*. If, in fact, the actual events sound sometimes like pranks we would have hatched in high school or college, we should remember that although the people involved may have been kings and queens, dukes and duchesses, they were mostly of college age or younger when these events took place.

Louis XIII had problems that need psychiatric rather than historical analysis, so I may be just a bit out of my league here. Since after he became king at the age of nine, his mother, not wanting him to inter-fere with *her* regency, began beating him every day in order to keep him submissive, it is not too surprising that he grew up to be a stuttering hypochondriac fearful of women. He was married to Anne of Austria at the age of fourteen, and while he loved Anne in his own unique way, he really didn't want to sleep with her. One of his doctors explained that he needed to be beaten to be aroused. The man who would become his closest adviser, Charles d'Albert de Luynes, realizing the need to con-summate the marriage as well as the need to produce an heir, actually carried the fourteen-year-old king screaming to the bed of his young wife.

Richelieu, also aware of Louis's aversion to sex, and of the neces-sity of producing an heir to the throne, was trying to marry off Louis's younger brother Gaston, as year by year the possibility of Louis and Anne producing a dauphin became less likely. Louis, while perhaps not sexually unfaithful to Anne, did have favorites, most notably a man, the insolent nineteen-year-old Marquis of Cinq-Mars, who was involved in a plot to murder Richelieu and in another self-aggrandizing but treasonous plot with Spain. He was eventually tried by a judge, who ordered both Cinq-Mars's head and the crenellated towers of his Loire castle—the symbol of a feudal lord's power and authority—to be lopped off. Louis's relationship with Cinq-Mars leads one to speculate that his aversion to sex with Anne may have had another explanation.

Luynes's wife, Marie de Rohan, (who, after Luynes's death in 1621, would become the Duchess of Chevreuse), was Queen Anne's clos-est friend from the time she was fifteen and the queen fourteen, and they would remain close friends all their lives. From the time Marie de Rohan was a young, seductive girl with red-blond hair and deep, dark blue eyes until the time she died at the age of seventy-nine, she was involved in one intrigue after another, including plots to overthrow both Louis XIII and, when she was in her seventies, his son Louis XIV. She was truly one of history's great troublemakers. I, however, find her one of the most intriguing women I have ever come across. She appears to have enchanted every male who came in contact with her, including her biographer, who excuses her actions by writing that since she was a woman, the weapons she used in her youth were her sex appeal and wit, weapons with which she was amply endowed. When they were gone, when she was old and no longer beautiful, she picked up a sword and led the charge against the royal forces at Orléans during the Fronde— the aristocratic rebellion at the beginning of Louis XIV's reign.

La Rochefoucauld, France's most famous writer of maxims, was not kindly disposed toward her when she was old, sarcastically noting that she "is an ancient fortress, now completely in ruins—the citadel had been destroyed by many sieges. They say it often surrenders unconditionally."

When Marie was twenty-three, she fell in love with Lord Holland, a close friend of the Duke of Buckingham, when the two young Englishmen came to the French court. According to La Rochefoucauld, Count Holland was "one of the handsomest men in the world." He won Marie's love and persuaded her that her friend Queen Anne, who was not having much fun in bed, should have a love affair similar to their own, with the Duke of Buckingham. They plotted to have the Duke of Buckingham seduce the queen.

Buckingham, while as handsome and charming in real life as he is in *The Three Musketeers*, seems to have been a bit more foppish than the character in the novel. For example, in the first three days after his arrival in Paris in 1623, he was said to have worn twenty-seven different sets of clothes, one of which was a white velvet ensemble covered in diamonds and "loosely-sewn pearls" that dropped off as he walked. It was common knowledge that he had gained entry to Queen Anne's bedroom at this time, (the king and queen's "bedroom" included a large sitting area into which an inner circle of courtiers were admitted) and that Louis XIII, after he was informed of this, could be continually heard muttering, "Please God, adultery shall never enter into my house."

Two years later, in 1625, Buckingham invented a pretext to see Queen Anne while she was in Amiens, and this time gained entrance into Anne's bedchamber, where we are told that "he threw himself to his knees and made the violence of his passion obvious." He was also reported to have kissed her as they walked in a garden. Although the pair were not reported to have been alone together in the bedroom, their meeting became a widely known scandal. When Louis learned of the meeting, he flew into a fit of jealous rage and banned Buckingham from ever entering France again. Buckingham vowed to return, one way or another. He landed on the Île de Ré, off La Rochelle, where the Rochellais supplied him and his men with food. The French army, which was besieging the city from the land, bombarded his camp, forcing him to return to England, where he began amassing a fleet of 150 warships upon which the Rochellais were depending to break the siege before he was assassinated by a religious fanatic very much like the one who assassinates him in *The Three Musketeers*. Louis was convinced that Anne had been unfaithful to him and perhaps suspected that she was involved in one of the plots to assassinate him, as well as being involved in plots with her brother the King of Spain. On his deathbed, he said, "I may have to forgive her but I don't have to believe her."

Marie and perhaps Queen Anne were also involved in a tangled plot to assassinate Richelieu, which would become known as the Chalais Conspiracy of 1626. The exact nature of the plot is blurred by a cowardly confession by Gaston, the king's younger brother, who, fearing decapitation, not only confessed the conspiracy to assassinate Richelieu, but expanded it to include the assassination—rather than death by natural causes—of Louis XIII by Marie, Queen Anne, the Count of Chalais, and others. Marie's plan was to disrupt Richelieu's arrangements for the marriage between Gaston and the heiress Mademoiselle de Bourbon. Marie convinced Anne, who was still childless, that if Gaston married, his children would inherit the throne, and she would be sent back to Spain. She persuaded the queen to tell Gaston that Louis was sickly, and that if he should die, she would marry him (Gaston) if he were not already married. Marie then convinced the Count of Chalais, the king's master of the wardrobe, who would literally lose his head over her he was so wildly in love, to carry messages from the queen to Gaston at his château in Blois. When Chalais returned, Marie drove him insanely jealous by telling him Richelieu was in love with her, and he agreed to carry out her plans to assassinate the cardinal. Not only Chalais, Marie, and Gaston, but also the illegitimate sons of Henry IV, the Duke of Rohan and the Prince of Soubise, were involved in the conspiracy to murder the cardinal.

But because the cardinal had spies everywhere, the plot failed. Gaston was summoned from his château at Blois to court, where he was questioned and confessed to anything Richelieu suggested. The Count of Chalais was arrested and imprisoned in a dungeon where he was questioned repeatedly about his role in the conspiracy. However, the passionate count's ardor was at first undiminished, as seen in the letters that he wrote from his cell to Marie. Calling her his "goddess," he would write in one, "If those beautiful eyes that I adore regard this letter, I augur well for my fortune, and if the contrary happens, I no longer desire my liberty, because in it I shall find my punishment." Richelieu, who had intercepted the lovesick count's letters, and knew that Marie had not replied to any of them, convinced Chalais that Marie was occupied with other love affairs, and then Chalais denounced her as "the life and soul of the conspiracy."

He was tried, found guilty, and sentenced to death by beheading. Chalais was grateful. He had expected to be drawn and quartered. However, his gratitude was premature. Unfortunately for Chalais, the executioner was not an expert at his job and the decapitation took him thirty-one strokes. Gaston, however, escaped the gallows by marrying Mademoiselle de Bourbon, as Richelieu had wished, and denouncing both the queen and Marie. Marie escaped imprisonment this time—there would be a second time—by accepting exile to the estates in Lorraine of her second husband, the Duke of Chevreuse. Immediately upon her arrival there, she convinced her husband to ally himself—and his knights—with those of England and of her Huguenot relatives Rohan and Soubise, who were planning to save La Rochelle from Richelieu. Their plan consisted of having the English fleet, commanded by Buckingham, arrive at the Île de Ré, where it would join forces with the Huguenots at La Rochelle, then the last remaining Huguenot stronghold.

After defeating the Huguenot forces, the king and Richelieu discussed what to do with the queen and her friend. They were in total agreement that Marie was "the root of all evil" and the cause of leading Queen Anne astray. Marie was exiled to Tours and the queen was forbidden to correspond with her. In fact, just about everyone was forbidden to correspond with her. Anne, hearing rumors that Richelieu was not satisfied with merely exiling Marie to Tours but was planning to imprison her, arranged that Marie be sent a prayer book bound in green if it was safe for her to stay in Tours or one bound in red if Richelieu had decided to arrest her. When Marie received a red prayer book, she dressed herself as a man in a black cloak and doublet, mounted a black horse, and rode south toward the Spanish border with her jewels and two servants attending her. Hearing of her flight, Richelieu sent men to arrest her before she crossed the border. When she arrived at a southern town near La Rochefoucauld's château, she was without papers and money, her horse exhausted, its saddle covered with blood from a sword wound she had received in a duel along the way. In desperation, she wrote La Rochefoucauld, whom she knew was also forbidden to correspond with her, the following letter: "Sir, I am a French gentleman who asks your aid to preserve his liberty, perhaps his life. I have fought an unhappy duel and have killed a nobleman of distinction. This forces me to leave France in haste, as I am pursued. I believe you to be generous enough to serve me without knowing me. I need a carriage and a valet to attend me."

La Rochefoucauld sent her what she wished, and when he was later questioned by Richelieu, admitted he "had a suspicion of who the stranger was, though he was not absolutely certain." (Consequently, he would be arrested upon his return to Paris and placed in the Bastille for a brief period.) As soon as Marie crossed the border into Spain, she was met by an escort sent by Queen Anne's brother, the king of Spain, who treated her royally until she was able to return to France.

During the time Marie, her husband, her relatives, and her lover's friend (the Duke of Buckingham) were still trying to raise an army to save La Rochelle by land and sea, the Rochellais saw the French army build Fort Louis and fifteen other bastions to surround their city. They saw the arrival of 30,000 well-paid soldiers, so well paid that some Huguenots were among them, and they gave up all hope of supplies reaching them by land. Provisions dwindled and food became scarce. The minutes of the meetings of the mayor and city aldermen at the Hôtel de Ville record their regret at having supplied Buckingham with their stores of food when he had occupied Île de Ré the year before. At first, they had not been worried about supplies reaching them by sea, since they expected Buckingham's fleet to arrive with food and ammunition, but as the months passed and food became even scarcer, the mayor and alderman debated whether they should surrender or let the city starve to death.

As you read the minutes of these meetings held in 1627, you begin to understand why they decided not to surrender. The St. Bartholomew's Day Massacre was discussed by the town leaders as though it had happened not fifty-five years before, but the day before. They recalled how, in the events of the massacre, not only Henry's Huguenot followers were slaughtered as they slept, but also Huguenots all over France. A large number of Huguenots who survived the slaughter had fled to the safety of La Rochelle, where they stunned the citizens there with exaggerated details of the massacre. The terrified Rochellais reacted to the news of the slaughter by pulling down the Catholic churches in their city and using the stones to build walls to protect themselves from the attack by Catholic forces that would, in fact, commence and fail the following year, 1573.

The number of Huguenots killed by royal forces during the St. Bartholomew's Day Massacre was probably about 10,000 in all. However, survivors of the massacre arriving in La Rochelle reported that the number was an astounding 100,000, a number that was published in a Protestant pamphlet and circulated throughout the city, and it was the 100,000 number that the people of La Rochelle believed to be true in 1572. Now, in 1627, they still believed it, and they believed that they, like Henry's soldiers sleeping in the Louvre, would all be slaughtered by the king's soldiers if they surrendered.

The Rochellais had felt secure, protected from attack by the wall they had built around their city and by the two huge towers guarding the entrance to the port. You can still see both the wall and the towers today. However, they had not taken into account the evil genius of Richelieu, who decided not to attack the city, but rather devised an ingenious method of starving its citizens by preventing supplies from entering. The Rochellais were first curious and then horrified as they realized what Richelieu had planned. They watched in horror as stones, from fifty-three French ships, were thrown overboard to create a long, broad barrier three kilometers outside the entrance to the harbor, completely cutting it off from the sea. Keeping just outside the range of La Rochelle's guns, they built what became known as "Richelieu's Dike" (*digue*), an idea thought up by the king's naval architect, Clément Métezeau, and a mason, Jean Thiriot. After the stones were laid across the harbor, tree trunks, sharpened so that they could pierce the bow and sink any ship trying to enter La Rochelle, were embedded in the stones. In the Musée de Beaux-Arts in La Rochelle, there is a painting, *Richelieu sur la Digue de La Rochelle à La Rochelle*, by Henri Motte, which shows what the dike looked like in 1628.

As soon as I saw the painting, I realized with a start what I had seen the first night I arrived in La Rochelle from the window of my hotel. Those large, peculiar-looking blocks of stones crossing the mud flat were actually the remains of Richelieu's dike. My hotel, Les Brises, had been built at the edge of the harbor where Richelieu had built his dike. Today, at low tide, when the harbor is a huge expanse of mud, you can still see those remains. At low tide in 1627, before the huge pointed spikes designed to pierce the bows of ships were put in place, Richelieu entertained foreign dignitaries and ladies of the French court on those stones. Starving citizens of La Rochelle could see Richelieu's guests promenading across their harbor.

La Rochelle, which could not be taken, was starved to death. Its ships could not leave, and the British ships could not enter to deliver supplies. The city was sealed like an Egyptian tomb. By October 26, 1628, 28,000 of its 33,000 citizens had already died of starvation, and hundreds more were dying each day. No one had the strength to bury them. The Duchess of Rohan, Marie's aunt, who had remained in the city to await the arrival of her husband's forces from Languedoc, chose to boil her leather chair and try to eat it rather than surrender. Other Rochellais boiled their shoes—after the oxen, horses, donkeys, dogs, cats, and even the rats were eaten.

A meeting was held that October day at the Hôtel de Ville. When, at an earlier meeting, surrender had been suggested, the Mayor Jean

Guiton had angrily pounded the table with his sword, saying, "Yonder poniard shall serve to pierce the heart of whoever dares to speak of surrender."

He had convinced the aldermen and peers that their fate would be that of the Huguenots sleeping at the Louvre on St. Barthlomew's Day if they surrendered. He convinced the members of the council then and at subsequent meetings that it was better to die free and independent. But on October 26, when he rose to speak, he fainted from hunger.

Buckingham had already been assassinated when an English fleet of 110 warships finally arrived at La Rochelle. The citizens who were still strong enough to come to the harbor saw that fleet, their last hope, enter the harbor but not dare to bring their ships too near the partially submerged pointed spikes. Twice they saw the ships attempt to blow up the dike and fail. Once the English found their cannons useless, they simply returned to England. When the Rochellais saw the ships turn and leave, they saw their last hope leave, and on November 1, 1628, after a siege of twenty-four months, the 5,000 citizens who were still alive sued for peace.

OPPOSITE THE HÔTEL DE VILLE, in the center of La Rochelle, there is a square with a marvelous statue of Jean Guiton. Before he was elected mayor of La Rochelle, he had been admiral of the La Rochelle fleet, and had once defeated the French navy in a battle in which he was outnumbered two to one. In a later battle, he would not be so lucky, but he was elected mayor anyway. The statue is as Guiton was: proud and defiant, hand on the sword with which he had hit the conference table. On the ground around the statue, in the stones of the square, are mosaics representing the fifteen French forts that surrounded La Rochelle during the siege.

One afternoon, Bob and I walked from the port to the center of the old town and had coffee at an expensive café—Le Café de la Poste. From our table, we could see the statue and the Hôtel de Ville, where Guiton had for months kept the aldermen from surrendering, where he had reminded them of how the crown had treated Huguenots on

St. Bartholomew's Day. The Hôtel de Ville was built during the reign of Henry IV—that brief period of peace in France. Its lavishness and opulence is indicative of the wealth of La Rochelle at the height of this mercantile city's commercial power. It looks like a little fortress. Its towers, the symbol of the city's feudal rights and independence, were still standing when we arrived. Usually, towers are the symbol of the power and independence of the landed aristocracy, but at La Rochelle the towers were a symbol of the city's independence. Although the Hôtel de Ville appears to be a fortress with machicolations and crenellations, the appearance is merely symbolic. The walls are too low to defend itself against attack. The inner courtyard is a splendid example of Flamboyant Gothic architecture. There are four statues in alcoves, symbolizing the virtues esteemed by the city: Temperance, mixing water into the wine; Strength, dressed in a lion's skin and carrying a broken column; Justice with a scroll of laws in one hand and a scepter (now missing) in the other. Wisdom was a nineteenth-century addition. There is a plaque on the outer wall of the building to another mayor of La Rochelle, Léonce Vieljeux, 1865–1944. There are many stories about this fiery old mayor I would like to believe. It is said that during the occupation of La Rochelle during the Second World War, he pretended to be a dithering old man by day but was the leader of a massive resistance by night. He refused the German demand to hang a Gestapo flag on the façade of the Hôtel de Ville or to allow propaganda posters anywhere in the city. When asked for a list of the Jews living in La Rochelle—and this is a story I want to believe but don't—he replied that there were no Jews, only Huguenots, living in La Rochelle. Then, to ensure their safety, he altered church records to provide each Jewish family of La Rochelle with a Huguenot ancestry dating back for centuries. He was deported during the Second World War and shot by the Germans at the age of seventy-nine. The fierce tradition of resistance and nonconformity had clearly been handed down through the centuries.

As we made our way back to the harbor, we noticed a sign saying FORT BOYARD, SON ET LUMINERE, (COMMENTARY IN ENGLISH). We went in to find out when the show took place—and found out there were so few visitors that it took place whenever anyone bought a ticket. The show consisted of a large model of Fort Boyard, which Napoleon I built in 1804 at the widest part of the harbor, 5,000 meters across, to prevent ships from sailing into the harbor. When construction began, artillery had a range of only 1,000 meters. By the time construction was completed, the increased range of artillery made the fort obsolete. It was nicknamed "Fort Useless" and subsequently used as a prison. The little show was actually quite enjoyable. The walls of the model opened up so that the interior was exposed and an audiotape described each section of the fort: the kitchen, the officer's quarters, etc. If you see it before taking the boat to Fort Boyard, the visit there will be more interesting. In fact, the only place I advise not visiting in La Rochelle is the wax museum—the Musée Grévin. And, if you are like me, you might opt for the shorter, rather than the more extended boat rides to the neighboring islands, or just take the ferry or water bus—but you shouldn't come to La Rochelle without seeing the harbor from the sea.

PART THREE

—

The Age of Louis XIV

SEVENTEENTH-CENTURY FRANCE

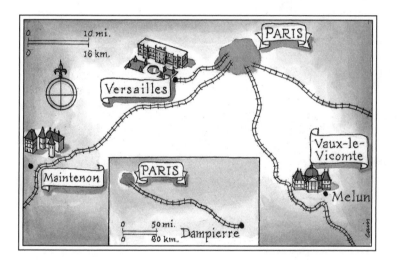

CHAPTER 16

MAGICAL VAUX-LE-VICOMTE

—

RER Line D to Melun

WHILE TRAVELING TO VAUX-LE-VICOMTE, ONLY THIRTY-TWO kilometers from Paris, is not quite as simple as taking the train to Chartres, Versailles, Chantilly, or nearby Fontainebleau, it is well worth the trouble. From the Gare de Lyon in Paris, it is only twenty-eight minutes to Melun by train (Grandes Lignes), and trains run about every hour. You can also take RER Line D, which will take forty-eight minutes. The station is an unpleasant (six-kilometer) walk to the château, so I suggest taking a taxi, which you can call from the station. Bob and I expected to take a bus to the château, as a popular travel guidebook had suggested, but when I walked over to the rows of buses in a parking lot adjacent to the station, and asked one of the drivers which bus went to Vaux-le-Vicomte, he laughed—I think he had heard the question before—and said I would have to wait till Saturday, the only day it ran.

Since it was only Wednesday, I called a taxi by pressing the call button on a taxi phone box outside the station. Miraculously, unlike the result of pushing similar buttons on boxes in Paris, a taxi arrived in a few minutes. We arranged for the driver to return in three hours to take us back to the station. If you are well organized, and if you know which train you will be taking, I suggest having your concierge arrange for a taxi to meet your train, take you to the château, and return in two or three hours to take you back to the station. But that is not necessary.

As I have written before, there may be more beautiful places than

Vaux, but I haven't seen them. Seen from the garden, this domed Baroque palace seems to float upon a great square reflecting pool. And walking inside the château is like walking inside a many-faceted jewel. Its rooms are elaborately ornamented in a Baroque style that evolved from the Mannerist decorations we saw at the Francis I Gallery at Fontainebleau: a harmonious combination of stucco, gilding, and painting. Walking in the gardens, you feel, as André Le Nôtre, the creator of the gardens, had hoped you would feel, that you are walking in a garden intended for gods—in Elysium.

Since my previous book was published, there has been a wonderful addition to the gardens at Vaux—golf carts—which Bob and I really enjoy. Because the gardens are so huge, we rented one and were able to zip around Le Nôtre's gardens, moving swiftly down the central allée, past parterres with intricate swirling designs laid out like elegantly woven Oriental carpets, past carefully pruned shrubs, looking more like statues than bushes, detouring to side allées on gravel paths when we encountered steps. The gardens, as is the case with all Le Nôtre's landscapes, were designed to enhance the view of the palace and to harmonize with it. The central allée leads from the center of the château terrace into the distance to a hill crowned by a huge statue of the Farnese Hercules,* the Greek hero who could not be defeated, a hero with whom the creator of this château, Nicolas Fouquet, mistakenly identified himself. In the past, it had taken me over an hour to walk to the statue, and an hour back, but with the golf cart I could visit the statue and still have enough time and energy to tour the château.

However, I don't think zipping around the gardens in a golf cart is what Le Nôtre had in mind when he designed the garden at Vaux. He had wanted to create a garden that evoked the pagan paradise ancient Greeks had once envisioned, the Elysian Fields, which only those favored by the gods could enter. In order to help you feel as though you were walking in Elysium, he filled the garden with statues of mythological Greek gods.

---

* Today, the Farnese Hercules is one of many copies of the original Greek statue, which was actually in Fouquet's garden.

At the time Le Nôtre was creating the garden at Vaux, he and the rest of the French seventeenth-century intellectual world were trying to absorb the revelation that the earth and man were not the center of the universe, that it was only an illusion that the universe revolved around the earth.* Le Nôtre and his fellow artists responded with a growing distrust of nature and of the senses combined with a corresponding reliance on reason and geometry.

As a result, Le Nôtre's gardens became more formal than those of his father, relying on the use of geometric patterns, perspective, and illusion, rather than on flowers whose color and smell appeal to the senses. Instead, graceful crystal plumes of water spout from a multitude of elaborate fountains. The gardens should be seen when they are in operation (on alternate Saturdays, from 3 P.M. to 6 P.M., when the buses run) and are best seen looking back at the château from the Farnese Hercules, which stands in the center of a long, broad, sweeping vista bordered by forests on both sides.

Nicolas Fouquet, Vaux's creator, was a slim, handsome, charming, dark-haired man with flashing eyes framed by long dark lashes. Courtiers noted that he had a smile women found as irresistible as the jewels he lavished upon them. He dressed in the rich costume of a magistrate, with a little cap, a broad collar, and a dark robe, over which he threw a cape of Genoa velvet embroidered with flowers. Although he had been a sickly child, he became a man of boundless nervous energy and intelligence, of superb taste, possessing an uncanny ability to recognize and inspire great talent—both young and old.

Fouquet came to power in 1653 after the Fronde riots, in which the Paris mobs, members of Parlement, and the aristocracy united to drive Cardinal Mazarin, ten-year-old Louis XIV, and his mother, Anne of Austria, out of Paris. Fouquet, as *procureur-général* (attorney general), was faced with the decision of siding with the cardinal or with the Frondeurs. At the time, the Frondeurs seemed invincible, and it seemed unlikely that the cardinal would ever return to power, yet Fouquet took

---

* Although Copernicus had theorized that the earth revolved around the sun in the sixteenth century, his theories were not confirmed or accepted until the invention of the telescope in the seventeenth century.

a gamble and sided with the cardinal, worked at winning supporters for Mazarin among the bourgeoisie, protecting his financial interests and property. He also kept the king and his mother, who had retreated to his château at Saint-Germain-en-Laye, abreast of conditions in Paris. When Mazarin returned to power in 1653, he rewarded Fouquet by making him, along with another man—Marquis Abel Servien—superintendent of finances. He recommended Fouquet to the young king by saying that "if they could get women and building out of his head, great things might be done with him."As the protégé of Mazarin, he developed the art of embezzlement—which he learned, at Mazarin's feet—to new heights, amassing by his tutor's methods one of the great fortunes of France. As superintendent of finances, he paid the government's bills partly by borrowing upon his own credit, but in the process tangled up the public purse with his own. While he was successful in keeping the royal armies armed and provisioned and the royal coffers filled, he was even more successful in fraudulently filling his own. It should be added, however, that whenever Mazarin needed money, he asked Fouquet, not Servien, to dip into public funds for it. "In 1656, when Mazarin needed money to pay the army, Fouquet raised 300,000 livres in four days from his family and friends, sending the silver in wagonloads to Mazarin at La Fère." Fouquet copied one of Mazarin's techniques of hiding funds he embezzled by becoming a tax-farmer under a false name and then lending money to the state at high interest.

Fouquet's main talent, however, was not embezzling money, but putting it to use. Gifted with a connoisseur's eye, he gathered together the greatest artists of the day to create Vaux and oversaw every detail of their work. He was one of the greatest patrons of the arts in France, the essence of the Renaissance man. While he reminded me of Lorenzo de'Medici in Renaissance Florence, he thought of himself as a seventeenth-century Maecenas, that ancient Roman patron of the arts, who, like himself, was both an adviser to a great ruler (in Maecenas's case to the Emperor Augustus) and the most renowned literary patron of his day. (Among Maecenas's protégés were both Horace and Virgil.) All Nicolas Fouquet's love for the arts, as well as 16 million livres, was poured into Vaux-le-Vicomte. He also used his money beneficently to provide artists and writers with pensions and rooms in his château. He took the trouble of sending patés and cheeses daily, as well as a yearly pension of 1,600 livres, to the invalid novelist, poet, and satirist Paul Scarron, whose wife, Françoise d'Aubigné, later became Madame de Maintenon, the last wife of Louis XIV. He loved to argue in Latin with Jesuit philosophers, discuss the latest scientific and philosophic ideas with the greatest minds of seventeenth-century France, and gather around his table the greatest artists and most talented authors, a place where the food, served on gold plates, was cooked by Vatel, the greatest of chefs.

Some artists, like Le Nôtre, he discovered when they were young, and some, like Pierre Corneille, when they were old and out of fashion—and that endeared Fouquet to me. Corneille apparently had his faults. He was not a scintillating conversationalist or a desirable addition to Fouquet's dinner table. According to the biting comment of one hostess, "He should be listened to through the mouth of an actor." He was also not a particularly good judge of the talent of others, advising Racine to give up writing, since "he had no talent for the stage." When Fouquet took him under his wing, the playwright was impoverished, depressed—determined never to write again. Recognizing Corneille's greatness, Fouquet gave him a pension, praise, and an idea for a new play. And he kept encouraging him until he began writing again.

Artists and writers adored Fouquet and in turn he adored and supported them. From 1654 on, he gave the absent-minded poet La Fontaine 1,000 livres a year on condition that every three months he give him a new poem. Books were dedicated to him, and he appeared as a character in Mademoiselle de Scudéry's novel *Clélie*, in which he is described as a "man who makes nothing but what is great, and whose mind by its vast range cannot conceive little designs."

When Fouquet bought Vaux, it was a small domain containing only a tiny fortress and three little villages. The first thing he did was raze them. The second was to plant a forest where the villages had been. In the seventeenth century, a forest signified more than trees to a man intent on rising above his station. Just as the feudal tower was a symbol of feudal authority, the forest was a symbol of a feudal lord's rights, a place where he could hunt and cut down trees for firewood, while the peasantry was forbidden to do so. And Fouquet, whose family motto was "How high shall I not climb?" was very intent upon rising above his station. He therefore instructed Le Nôtre to design a park so that it seemed to be carved out of the forest.

To build Vaux, he brought together a team of relatively unknown young men whose work had caught his keen eye. He had watched the architect Louis Le Vau transform an old château at Le Raincy into an elegant residence and hired him after visiting the Hôtel Lambert on the Île Saint-Louis, which he also designed. In creating Vaux-le-Vicomte, Le Vau, who was known not to pay attention to detail but was "thinking always of a general effect," worked closely with Fouquet, who paid attention to everything. Fouquet chose Charles Le Brun to oversee the painting and decoration; and Girardon, Guérin, Lespagnandelle, and Poissant for sculpture. Le Brun had a talent for organizing a team of artists, suggesting to Fouquet that Le Nôtre join the team to design the gardens at Vaux, and Fouquet agreed. Le Brun and Le Nôtre had become friends while apprentices in the workshop of Simon Vouet and would work together throughout their lives. Fouquet gave Le Brun the opportunity to deploy his full artistic talents in the decoration of his château, and Le Brun would never again paint as sensuously and movingly as he did at Vaux. Art historians generally agree that his work at Versailles lacks the vitality it has here. The allegorical paintings in the various rooms of the château are by his own brush, and he provided the designs for the garden sculptures and for the decorative sculptures in the château. Le Brun would become, under Louis XIV, the director of the French Academy of Painting and Sculpture and arbiter of French artistic style for thirty years.

Eighteen thousand men worked on building Vaux and its gardens. When the château was finished, Fouquet filled its library with 38,544 manuscripts, many of them very rare, that he intended to read "in his old age when he would no longer read a welcome in ladies' eyes." Ancient Greek marble statues, two Egyptian mausoleums, seventeenth-century busts of Socrates and Seneca, tables of porphyry, rare mosaics, a copy of the Talmud, several old copies of the Bible, and other rare treasures filled the château's rooms.

Fouquet commissioned and oversaw every detail of the château's construction. As you walk through the halls at Vaux, you can see Fouquet's handwritten changes on Le Nôtre's framed landscape designs.

The Room of the Muses, where Molière's plays were performed for Fouquet, is filled with sensuous vitality, eight muses luxuriously reclining in pairs at the corners of the ceiling. Clio, the muse of history, with Prudence and Fidelity at her side, occupies the center and holds a key, symbolizing the fact that the past is the key to the future. Thalia, the muse of comedy, draped in blue velvet, a garland of red flowers flowing from her hair, holds a smiling mask in her hand, while above her an eagle holds a banner with Fouquet's motto, *QUO NON ASCENDUM* (HOW HIGH SHALL I NOT CLIMB?) in his beak. Euterpe, the muse of music, is playing the flute; Terpsichore, the muse of dance, is holding a lyre; Calliope, the muse of oratory, is holding a book; and Urania, the muse of astronomy, holds a compass and a globe. Nyx, the goddess of night, dressed in a film of black, is drawn through the clouds by two black horses. The carvings seem to burst out of the Baroque frames created to hold them. The subjects are mythological in an idealized, rational, classical landscape. There is a similarity between the Baroque art at Vaux, which combines painting with stucco sculpture in full relief, and the Mannerist art at Fontainebleau in the Francis I Gallery, but Le Brun has refrained from using the devices of illusion and foreshortening that Primaticcio and Il Rosso had. There is also a major difference between viewing the creations of Le Brun at Vaux and seeing those at Versailles. At Vaux you can view them calmly and at your leisure, while at Versailles I had to hold on to a railing—with both hands—in order to avoid being carried away by a riptide of tourists.

The huge, domed grand salon, far more Roman and imperial than the rest of the château, remains unfinished to this day. In 1661, Louis XIV's mistress described the mosaic floor as "a rich carpet embellished with birds, butterflies, arabesques, fruits and flowers." As you look up, you find an empty sky, where Le Brun was to have created symbolic paintings depicting Fouquet's accomplishments, but after its owner's arrest in 1661, Vaux was frozen in time.

On August 17, 1661, Fouquet invited Louis XIV and the French court to a grand party at Vaux-le-Vicomte. Fouquet's building of a grand châ-teau at Vaux was not unusual, nor was inviting the king. (Louis XIV had been to Vaux at least two times before the party. Both Richelieu and Mazarin had built sumptuous châteaux while they had been min-isters to the king. René de Longueil had built Maisons-Laffitte (also an interesting and easy day trip) while superintendent of finances, and had often entertained Louis when the king hunted in the forests of Saint-Germain-en-Laye. And Jean-Baptiste Colbert, of course, built Sceaux. But this party went beyond most others.

Historians note that the party was equaled by only one or two celebrations over the entire history of France. Meals were served on solid-gold plates. Men who liked to gamble found purses filled with gold when they awoke in the morning, while women were given rare perfumes. There were ballets, concerts, and a play—*Les Fâcheux*—written by Molière for the occasion and performed by moonlight. Molière, dressed in everyday clothes, greeted the assembled courtiers opposite the cascade, saying he had no actors and no time to prepare the entertainment that was expected, unless some unforeseen help was forthcoming. A shell thereupon opened to reveal a Naiad, and actors dressed as statues came to life. *Les Fâcheux* satirized the king's court-iers as syncophantic bores (*fâcheux*) while praising the king himself. La Fontaine's "Song of Vaux" also flattered the king with the lines:

All fight at Vaux to please the king
Music, the water, the sun, the stars

Athénaïs de Montespan, the king's mistress, exclaimed when she saw the château,

It was not the well-appointed residence of a minister . . . it was a veritable fairy palace. All in this brilliant dwelling was stamped with the mark of opulence and of exquisite taste in art.

When the king walked from the château to the canal, he did so through crystal walls of water, spouting from two hundred jets of water.

A seventeenth-century visitor to Vaux commented, "The air was filled with the sounds of a thousand fountains falling into marvelously fashioned basins, as if it were the throne of Neptune."

Most guidebooks will tell you that Fouquet's downfall was the result of that party he gave at Vaux, to which the king and his entire court were invited. But while Louis accepted the invitation, he had already decided to arrest Fouquet and he had, in fact, begun subtly to move against him by undermining the sources of his power.

Louis's suspicions—and Fouquet's downfall—began not in August when the party was given, but in March, when Mazarin, knowing he was about to die, warned the twenty-two-year-old king about Fouquet's financial manipulations. He also recommended another young minister, Colbert, to the king, as a safeguard or spy against Fouquet.

After Mazarin's death, Colbert saw his chance to become superintendent of finance, and plotted Fouquet's downfall. He found 6 million livres Mazarin had hidden at the Château Vincennes and shrewdly turned the money over to Louis. From that moment, Louis trusted him implicitly. "To keep an eye on Fouquet, I associated with him Colbert . . . a man in whom I had all possible confidence for I knew his intelligence and application and honesty," Louis would write in his memoirs.

He appointed Colbert as Fouquet's "assistant," which meant that every afternoon Fouquet went over accounts with Louis, and every evening Colbert would show Louis how Fouquet had falsified those accounts.

While Fouquet didn't offer to defend himself against the intrigues at first, he did purchase an island and fortress—Belle-Île off the coast of Brittany—for a sum of 1.3 million livres. In 1658, he began repairing the existing ramparts to create a fortress there. At the same time, he continued building the merchant marine fleet there, which his father had begun under the auspices of Richelieu, but also began purchasing warships from Holland. While his friends claimed at his trial that he was creating a fleet to attract "all the trade of the North, and render a great service to the King," Colbert contended that he was creating a fleet to oppose the king. Aware of his precarious position, he had a secret tunnel dug from his house in Nantes to the Loire, where a boat waited to take him to Belle-Île, if necessary.

But Louis XIV, while certain Fouquet was guilty of embezzlement, did not feel he was in a position to arrest his popular and powerful financial minister. His popularity extended from the Parlement, where his position as *procureur-général* protected him from investigation, to the coterie of artists he lavishly subsidized, to, most important, Louis's own mother, Anne of Austria, whom Fouquet had often supplied with funds and who was very fond of him.

The Queen Mother's fondness for Fouquet, however, was about to be undermined—by her old friend Marie, now the Duchess of Chevreuse.* When, on June 27, 1661, the Queen Mother visited the then impoverished duchess at her château in Dampierre, Colbert was there. His daughter was about to marry the duchess's son, bringing with her a large dowry. During the course of the marriage negotiations, Colbert and the duchess had become allies. The two of them told Anne how Fouquet was threatening the power of the king by extending his power, by buying the support of members of Parlement, and by promoting his friends and relatives by means of public money. They told her about the armed vessels he had purchased from Holland and suggested treasonous motives for the fleet and his purchase of the fortress at Belle-Île. By the time the Queen Mother completed her visit to her friend's château at Dampierre, her mind was so poisoned she was ready to accept Fouquet's arrest.

Learning from spies of Colbert's success in turning the Queen Mother against him, Fouquet tried to persuade Louis's young mistress, Louise de la Vallière, to intercede with the king on his behalf—using a technique that had proven successful with other women. His mistake was that he didn't understand that Louise, unlike Louis's other mistresses, really loved the king and could not be swayed by gifts or money.

He offered her 20,000 pistoles if she would speak highly of him to the king. According to one of Louis XIV's biographers, Vincent Cro-

---

* The intrigues in which the Duchess of Chevreuse involved the Queen Mother with the Duke of Buckingham are described in the chapter on La Rochelle.

nin, Louise replied, "With scorn in her voice," that "not for a quarter of a million pistoles would she commit such an indiscretion," and she complained to Louis that Fouquet had insulted her.

Until Fouquet made the mistake of approaching the king's mistress, Louis XIV, aware of Fouquet's political and financial abilities, had been willing to forgive him if he would admit to his past mistakes. Even after learning of Fouquet's financial discrepancies, Louis did not want to replace him, but rather, appreciating his talents, would have preferred to reform him. In his memoirs he wrote: "It may be a cause of astonishment, that I was willing to employ him at a time when I was aware of his peculations, but I knew that he was intelligent and thoroughly acquainted with all the most intimate affairs of State, and this made me think, provided he would confess his past faults and promise to correct them, he might render me good service."

After Fouquet approached Louise, his fate was sealed. In the intrigues that followed, Fouquet underestimated the young king. Although Louis XIV had told Fouquet at Mazarin's death that he would be his own chief minister ("*Il est temps que je les gouverne moi-même*"), Fouquet, knowing Louis's passion for women, hunting, and the ballet, had not taken him seriously. Fouquet seems not to have taken the measure of the man with whom he was dealing, while Louis understood Fouquet all too well. Now the king tricked him into selling the position of procureur general, which had protected him from investigation. Hinting that he would appoint Fouquet to Mazarin's old post as head of government, if only a conflict of interest between his parliamentary position and his potential position as minister could be resolved, he persuaded Fouquet to sell his parliamentary position to Achille de Harlay. (When he learned that Fouquet had decided to sell, Louis informed Colbert, "He is digging his own grave.")

While Louis XIV was attending the party at Vaux-le-Vicomte, Colbert was in Paris making arrangements for Fouquet's arrest.

And finally there was the incident of the forest. The king liked the view from the balcony of his apartment at Vaux—except for one large, rather barren-looking clearing. He mentioned this to his host, and when Louis awoke the next morning and stepped out on the balcony, the clearing was completely filled with full-grown trees.

Recounts Athénaïs: "Fouquet, with airy presumption, expected thanks and praise. This, however, was what he had to hear. 'I am shocked at such expense!' " However, some years later, when he mentioned to his host while staying at the Château de Petit-Bourg that trees blocked his view from the royal suite, and the host had the trees removed while he slept, the king did not complain.

Louis was so infuriated that he wanted to arrest Fouquet on the spot. His mother, however, persuaded him that this would be unseemly behavior for a guest. So he waited for eighteen days. During this time, he outsmarted Fouquet once again by creating a pretext for going to Nantes and requesting that Fouquet accompany him there. It was only in Nantes that Fouquet realized that it was the king's purpose to close off Belle-Île to him—which he did. Then, as Fouquet left the royal presence, D'Artagnan, the most trusted of the royal musketeers, arrested him, while a co-conspirator of Colbert watched, making sure that the minister could not escape to the safety of his island. He was held prisoner first at Angers, then Saumur, Amboise, Vincennes, and finally in furnished apartments at the Arsenal in Paris, where he was held during the three-year trial. La Fontaine, who tried to see him during this time, laments that his patron, who so loved beauty, was unable to see the beauty of the Loire Valley while captive, since Fouquet's windows were boarded up.

During the three years he was prisoner, all the artists he had supported, with one exception, Molière, supported him.

While most of the judges were in favor of merely exiling Fouquet from France, the king intervened and increased the sentence from exile to life imprisonment. Fouquet, who loved beauty and women, would spend the rest of his life under heavy guard in a cold, damp dungeon in the Pignerol fortress located in the Alps. His harsh treatment is thought to have been the inspiration for Dumas's *Man in the Iron Mask*.

Colbert, who considered even this harsh treatment too kind, would have been happier with his death. Madame de Sévigné was convinced that it was Fouquet's "cold and vengeful" archenemy, Colbert, who was responsible for the harshness of the sentence: "It is not from on high that vengeance so low and cruel as this originates . . . not from the heart of the master. Vengeance is being done in his name, profaning it," his most faithful supporter wrote.

WHEN TWENTY-TWO-YEAR-OLD LOUIS XIV saw Vaux-le-Vicomte, he saw a château and gardens far more beautiful, more spectacular, more impressive than any of the young king's own palaces. But while Louis would arrest and imprison Nicolas Fouquet eighteen days after his last visit to Fouquet's château, he had no hard feelings toward the team of artists Fouquet had assembled to design, build, and decorate Vaux and its fabulous gardens. After the king arrested Fouquet, he brought the team, and most of the exotic trees that Fouquet had planted at Vaux, to Versailles, where we will go next, to turn his simple hunting lodge there into a great palace. And while Louis would build a more impressive château than Vaux, he did not create a more beautiful one.

CHAPTER 17

VERSAILLES

—

RER Line C to Versailles Rive Gauche

O N OUR FIRST TRIP TO FRANCE IN 1974, BOB AND I DID WHAT most American tourists do—we visited Versailles. Eleven years later, in 1985, we returned. Both visits exhausted my supply of superlatives. I was simply overwhelmed by its grandeur and opulence. Versailles made me feel I had traveled back in time to the glorious age of Louis XIV, when Paris and the Île-de-France were the center of the Western world. So when I conceived the idea of traveling chronologically through history, I felt that Versailles and its gardens were the perfect prism through which to visit this golden age. Its art, architecture, and landscape designs, devoted to the glorification of Louis XIV, made it the perfect place to experience the height of absolutism in seventeenth-century France.

It was 1991, only six years later, when I tried traveling to Versailles by RER from Paris. The trip began well enough. The ride from the Saint-Michel Métro-RER station, where I boarded the train, was only thirty-five minutes, and the ten-minute walk from the station to the palace was actually quite pleasant. But when I arrived at the lot just outside the gates of the palace, I found it filled—not with cars, but with a phalanx of tour buses. And when I passed through the gates and entered the immense courtyard in front of the palace—a courtyard far larger than that at Fontainebleau, where Napoleon had said farewell to his troops—I found it teeming with people waiting to enter the famous State Apartments. They were standing in a line that snaked past the gate where I stood, curved around Bernini's equestrian statue of Louis XIV in the center, and extended across the entire breadth of the enormous court-yard. I didn't try to enter the palace—I dislike lines and crowds, as I have suggested earlier. I repeatedly took the train to Versailles, trying different times of the day and different seasons of the year, hoping to find a window when the crowds at the palace and grounds were small enough for me once again to enjoy its beauty and grandeur. But each time I came, the buses and crowds had preceded me.

Then, on another trip to France, in August 1999, as Bob and I were walking along the Boulevard-Saint-Germain in Paris, I saw a sign out-side a FNAC store (a Paris retail chain that sells everything from televi-sion sets to tickets to cultural and sporting events) advertising the Fêtes de la Nuit at Versailles. We went in and learned that the Fêtes were a series of outdoor water musicals, performed at the Basin of Neptune in the gardens at Versailles. We purchased two reserved seats for a bal-let the following Saturday night, entitled *Dreams and Nightmares*—the dreams and nightmares of Louis XIV.

We arrived in the town of Versailles early enough to walk around the palace gardens and to have dinner before the show. I had made reserva-tions at Le Potager du Roy, on the Rue du Maréchal-Joffe, which I had been told was a favorite local restaurant. I found it much friendlier and considerably less expensive than the elegant one-star restaurant Les Trois Marches, where we had eaten before. We had a marvelous din-ner. The only flaw was the restaurant's air-conditioning, which stopped working during our meal, but our discomfort was nothing compared to that of the chef who, dripping with sweat, kept sticking his head out of the kitchen for air.

Before dinner, we walked in the palace gardens, designed by André Le Nôtre, who had designed the gardens at Vaux-le-Vicomte. Gardens in seventeenth-century France, I should emphasize, were not thought of in the same way we think of gardens in America today: they were con-sidered a major art form on a par with painting and architecture and, like painting and architecture, meant to serve "the highest policies of the state"—which, in the case of Louis XIV, was the king's glorification.

The thematic changes that had taken place in the design of these gardens at Versailles, which Le Nôtre planned only a few years after he designed the gardens at Vaux-le-Vicomte, reflect the changes that were taking place in society during that very brief period—in particular, the growth of absolutism under Louis XIV.

Le Nôtre's father, who oversaw Louis XIII's gardens, had been the first landscape designer to emphasize the importance of harmony between a château and its gardens. His son would become famous for his use of this concept. At Versailles the gardens were planned philosophically and geometrically as "an abstract representation of the cosmos." Le Nôtre had Louis XIV personify Apollo, the Sun God, around whom the world was revolving. This brilliant idea did not originate with Le Nôtre, but with Charles Perrault, the author of *Cinderella* and *Sleeping Beauty*, who was living at Versailles at the time.

As Bob and I walked down the central allée from the palace, down the horseshoe steps, we came to the Basin of Latona, where Louis XIV as the Sun King was first expressed. This glorious fountain has tiers of golden frogs circling a woman clutching two small children. And just as at Fontainebleau, where mythology was used to tell the story of Francis I, mythological tales were employed throughout Versailles to remind the courtiers of the greatness of Louis XIV. The myth being told at the Latona fountain was one with which all the courtiers at Versailles were familiar: Latona, Zeus's first wife, is fleeing with her children, Apollo and Artemis (Diana), from the wrath of Hera, Zeus's jealous second wife. Hera sent shepherds to stir up mud in a pond, thereby preventing Latona from drinking. Latona had Zeus turn the shepherds into frogs doomed to swim forever in muddy waters.

The courtiers were aware that Latona represented Anne of Austria, Louis XIV's mother, and the myth is used symbolically to represent Anne's flight from Paris with her two young children—Louis XIV and his younger brother—during the Fronde. The frogs who surround the pool represent the Frondeurs, or Parisians. The frogs, however, were not spouting water the night we were there, nor do they usually spout water. In fact, none of the ninety-nine fountains of Versailles were spouting that night. During the time of Louis XIV, the fountains were turned on only as he approached and then turned off after he passed because Versailles never had enough water to supply its fountains, which is the reason Louis began construction of an aqueduct to bring water from the Eure River—eighty kilometers away—which we shall visit next at Maintenon.

We then walked over to the Basin of Apollo. Dark green hedges form a great horseshoe at one end, and arcs of Grecian urns and Grecian statues, framed by the hedges, circle the fountain of the Sun God. Apollo, in his chariot drawn by four horses, is rising from the fountain, about to bring light to the earth. In the seventeenth century, the courtiers knew it was really Louis XIV, the Sun King, depicted as Apollo, who was symbolically enlightening the world. If the courtiers didn't make the connection at this fountain, they certainly would have by the time they entered the Salon of Apollo, in the palace—where Louis XIV sat on his throne under a ceiling painted by Le Brun, of Apollo in his sun chariot. If they still didn't make the comparison, Louis's rising in the morning—Le Grand Lever—and his retiring each night—Le Grand Coucher—were lavish rituals, attended by select courtiers. It was as though it were the rising and the setting of the sun.

Of course, for people to identify Louis XIV with Apollo, for him to be thought of as the Sun King, there had to be some element of truth in the comparison. It would have been ridiculous to think of Louis XIV's rabbit of a father as a "Sun King," but Louis XIV had brought to heel once powerful and independent feudal lords, who came to Versailles and exchanged honor (and chivalry) for the "honor" of waiting on him. These courtiers were, in effect, in orbit about him. The nobility, the only people who were thought to matter in the seventeenth century, were either at the great social events taking place at Versailles or in social exile. And during the early years of his reign (1643–1715), when the arts and sciences flourished in France, before he turned to religion and wars, it did seem as though he were enlightening the world and that Versailles was its center.

While it may have been Perrault who first conceived the idea of portraying Louis XIV as Apollo, and Le Nôtre who used the theme throughout the gardens at Versailles, it was Le Brun who employed the idea throughout Versailles and then throughout France. When I visited Orléans, for example, I had been shown a rose window Louis XIV had given to the cathedral there. The original medieval rose window, representing the eye of God, had been destroyed, and its replacement contained the theme Le Brun favored: the Sun King's face, his hair depicted as the flames of the sun.

Le Brun was in a position to ensure that the idea was executed not only by himself but by artists throughout France. After seeing Le Brun's work at Vaux-le-Vicomte, Louis XIV recognized his artistic talents and his organizational talents. He first made him director of decorations at Versailles and then director of the French Academy of Arts in 1661. Louis XIV was quite candid about what he considered the function of the Academy. He told its members: "I entrust to you the most precious thing on earth—my fame." During the twenty years Le Brun was director—some say dictator—of the Academy, this "fame" was well protected as Le Brun decided what was art and what was not.[*] He did away with the pre-existing loose system of apprenticeship, in which young artists studied under established artists, and turned the Academy into a bureaucratic organization totally under his control, and hence, under the control of the monarchy. From 1661 to 1681, the twenty years of Le Brun's control, the function of art was the glorification of Louis XIV and his image. It was Le Brun who knew what to do with Perrault's concept of Louis XIV as the Sun King, how to use it. He used it repeatedly at Versailles and repeatedly throughout France, until Louis XIV became synonymous with the mythical god, until the symbol took on a reality of its own—until Louis XIV became the Sun King.

After dinner we walked over to the Basin of Neptune, where the water musical was being held. As we walked, we were joined by more and more people, until the thin stream of people became a river that widened as we walked. There must have been over a thousand people pouring through the gates, but it didn't matter how enormous the crowd became because our seats were reserved and there was room, as

---

[*] I may present a more negative view of Le Brun than is called for since my view of him has been colored by a statement he made to women: "Inspire but do not write."

there is room in the gardens, for all the people who visit Versailles. As I watched, I could almost believe I was back in the seventeenth century and watching a spectacle presented by the Sun King, a spectacle that one mustn't miss because it was like no other spectacle I have ever seen. It was like celebrating the Fourth of July, New Year's Eve, and the *Lion King* all rolled into one unimaginable extravaganza. I was awed. It was an outdoor ballet in ten acts, performed in front of incredible explosions of fireworks and fountain displays, more than even Fouquet had arranged in 1661 at his great fête at Vaux. Actors and dancers dressed in lavish costumes were joined by horses prancing on an outdoor stage. Behind them crystal plumes of water spouted from the fountain and tumbled into dancing waters. The water was painted by colored lights, creating the stage set for the fantasies and illusions in the life of the Sun King. The entire summer evening had been as close to perfect as an evening could be. It was magical. It was what is supposed to happen when you are on a vacation.

The next week, however, I made the terrible mistake of visiting Versailles during an August day. My two trips to Versailles could be called, like the title of the show we had just enjoyed, *Dreams and Nightmares*, in this case the dreams and nightmares of Ina Caro.

The commuter train from Paris to Versailles was easy to take, perhaps too easy. The walk from the station was only ten minutes and pleasant, but when I arrived, the buses had beaten me. The parking lot was filled with them and it was only 10:10 A.M. The line was long, but it had not yet become serpentine. I got on the end, and as I waited to buy my ticket, it snaked even longer.

Then a loudspeaker announced, first in French and then in English, that a guided tour of the Petit Appartement was being given, and tickets were available at Gate B.

I left for Gate B, hoping other people in the line would remain where they were. They did. There were only a few people in line at Gate B, and I quickly got my ticket and was told that a tour in English would be given at ten forty-five and I should go to Gate D. At ten forty-five, a woman opened the door, looked at my ticket, and let me in. My group was small, and as we walked through the private apartments of the last

Kings of France, a well-informed guide entertained us with details of its occupants. The rooms were plush, but they were not the Hall of Mirrors (Galerie des Glaces) or the other palatial public rooms that I associated with Versailles. I was visiting the rooms where Louis XIV went after he had his public *coucher*, the rooms in which he enjoyed the company of mistresses like Louise de La Vallière, Madame de Montespan, and Madame de Maintenon, the rooms in which Louis XV enjoyed the company of Madame de Pompadour, the rooms in which Marie-Antoinette and Louis XVI had actually lived. We visited the bedroom, study, and drawing room decorated by Mignard, which had been given to Madame de Pompadour when she came to live at Versailles, the "*petits cabinets*," a "string of small rooms" where Louis XV felt at home and enjoyed private suppers. It was a pleasant tour.

Then, like a gambler who makes one bet too many, I made a mistake. My ticket entitled me to go to the State Apartments after the tour. As we were going through the private rooms, a door had swung open for an instant revealing the Hall of Mirrors jammed with people, jammed like a subway car at rush hour or on the way to a baseball game. It was a swarm of people, more people than I had ever seen in a single room. So I should have known better. But when my tour was over, I went.

I passed a man renting audio-guides and rented one. All the guards were so accommodating, everyone was as nice as could be, and then I entered Hell. I was determined to see the rooms that I had visited twenty years before and had marveled at. I entered each room, fought my way through the crowd of people to the rope that separated the priceless furniture and art from the tourists, and then turned on my tape-player. I had been warned by the woman who had taken us through the private apartments to ignore the guides supplied by tour buses, because they were filled with misinformation. Nonetheless, I had to listen to them since they drowned out the voice in my ear. I held my ground, refusing to move out of the way for these guides and their groups, no matter how much they glared at me. I was determined to listen to my audio-cassette and see the room at the same time.

I had wanted to see the king's bedchamber, since I believed that this room evoked Louis's political genius. It was there he broke the spirit of the aristocracy. Nobles who once were independent and powerful in their own isolated castles were brought to Versailles, where they spent their lives elegantly dressed and meticulously performing meaningless court rituals, including helping the king get dressed and undressed. It was in his bedchamber, facing the rising sun, that a hundred courtiers were given the honor of attending the morning ritual of Grand Lever and another hundred the evening ritual of Grand Coucher. The person who was given the candlestick to hold while the king undressed was, one countess wrote at the time, granted a "much-envied mark of distinction." Now, when these descendants of fighting knights donned *their* armor, they were probably heading off not to battle but to one of the innumerable costume parties that made the immense palace glitter in the evenings.

I had also wanted to return to the Hall of Mirrors, where busts of Roman emperors in porphyry and marble and antique statues of Greek gods stood under a vaulted ceiling painted by Le Brun. Crystal and silver chandeliers and gilt and crystal candelabra are reflected in seventeen arched mirrors. In my mind, the arcade of seventeen arched mirrors had, over the years since I had last visited this magnificent hall, come to be a reflection of more than the seventeen arched windows, more than the chandeliers and candelabra or the splendor of Le Grand Siècle. I felt the hall was a reflection of France's socioeconomic foundation hidden beneath the gilt. Louis XIV and Colbert were as concerned with their country's balance of trade in the seventeenth century as we are today. For example, the mirrors at Versailles were manufactured in France. Before Louis XIV, fine mirrors had been imported from Italy, because no one in France knew how to make them properly, but Louis and his minister Colbert were determined to make France economically self-sufficient. They could not, however, simply begin to manufacture mirrors. Since Venice made the finest glass in the world, Venetian artisans were enticed to France by extravagant salaries and perquisites to teach the art. Then Venetian foremen were recruited to set up a factory in Paris. (Economic competition in the seventeenth century was not taken lightly, and, in fact, two of the best mirror artisans smuggled out of Venice to France were poisoned by Italian secret agents before they were able to teach French apprentices Venetian secrets.) As soon as the industry was in place, the tariff on imported mirrors was doubled. By the end of Louis's reign, the finest mirrors in the world were made in France, and Voltaire could write: "The fine mirrors made in our own factories, which now decorate our houses, cost far less than did the little ones which used to be imported from Venice." Louis and Colbert did the same for many French industries, encouraging high quality by awarding prizes to the French master craftsmen who produced the finest-quality products (or "master pieces"). "We have beautiful and ornamental materials which are both cheaper and better than those brought from abroad," Voltaire wrote.

Colbert desired not only to limit imports but to increase exports. Versailles was designed to glorify Louis XIV, but also to be a showcase displaying to ambassadors and foreign visitors French products of such excellent quality and taste that when they returned home they would purchase the French products for their residences and sing their praises. Foreign dignitaries attending state functions held at night in the Hall of Mirrors could hardly help but be impressed by the mirrors reflecting the glow of four thousand candles—and by the silver furniture, the Savonnerie carpets, the Gobelin tapestries, the vases, the laces, and the marble from Languedoc used throughout the palace.

If you look up at the ceiling painted by Le Brun, it glorifies Louis's victories in a war with Holland, the country most competitive with France; when normal means of commercial competition proved inadequate, Louis and Colbert went to war. Louis said the Dutch "absorb nearly all the profits of trade in all parts of the world and leave only a very small portion to the other nations." When in 1672 the Dutch placed an embargo on French wine and brandy, Louis declared war on them.

I may have seen the Hall of Mirrors on this visit—or I may not. The visit was a blur. When I left the palace, I was exhausted. Making my way back to the RER, I realized I still had the earpiece of the audio-guide stuck to my left ear and a cassette hanging over my shoulder, and had to trudge back to the palace to retrieve the credit card I had left as security. My day had been comparable to shopping at a department store during the Christmas season.

Back at my apartment, I dreaded taking my next trip, which was to Maintenon, the home of Louis XIV's last wife. I decided I had to go the next day. My trip to Versailles had been equivalent to doing a belly flop off a high diving board, and I knew the longer I waited to tour again, the harder it would become. In retrospect, my advice is to definitely go to Versailles, definitely attend a performance of the Fêtes de la Nuit or any of the Grandes Eaux Musicales des Versailles (water musicals), and most certainly visit the gardens and the Trianons, but if there is a long, serpentine line in the courtyard, avoid the palace, and never, never go in August.

CHAPTER 18

THE SECRET CASTLE
of MAINTENON

—

Train from Gare Montparnasse to Maintenon

*I*RAVELED TO MAINTENON THE DAY AFTER MY DEBACLE AT Versailles, to see whether traveling there by train would be a pleasant day. Bob, after listening to me complain about my trip to Versailles, insisted on coming with me to hold my hand. Some years before, we had driven to the Château of Maintenon, which is in the center of a small town with the same name, and he remembered not only a magical castle but a pleasant restaurant in the square outside the château's gates. I myself thought Maintenon would be a lovely way to visit the last period of Louis XIV's life: the time when the Sun King met and married the Widow Scarron, who, as his morganatic wife—meaning she was not recognized as queen, and any children of their union would be ineligible to inherit the crown—brought a dismal cloud to cover what should have been the glorious sunset of his reign.

We took the 10:25 train from Montparnasse, and arrived at the station called "Maintenon" at 11:17. When we walked outside, we found a large parking lot but no town and no taxis. I called the three numbers I had found in the *Pages Jaunes*. There had been four, but I had mistakenly thought three numbers was sufficient and did not copy down the number of the fourth—Allo Taxi Leprince (06 09 21 08 07)—which turned out to be the only company that would have responded to my call and sent a cab to meet the train. Since the three numbers I had written down were busy, I asked a rather harried-looking woman at the ticket window, who was busy doing nothing, if there were any taxis to take me to the château. Not bothering to look up, she waved at me to go away. When I repeated my question, she said, "*Non.*" I walked outside again and looked for a sign pointing to the château or the town. All over France there are marvelous directional signs, but there were no signs in the parking lot outside this station or any signs when I walked down to the lonely-looking road beyond the station parking lot or, for that matter, any signs of life. I reluctantly returned to the station and asked the unpleasant woman at the ticket window how far it was to the château. She waved me away again, but I persisted until she mumbled, "*Centre ville.*" Realizing this was all the information I was going to get from her—my interviewing skills had never been as persevering as Bob's—I left. There were, as there invariably are, two directions on that lonely unmarked road that ran past the station: the one to the left, which I selected, and the one to the right—which in fact led to "centre ville" and the château.

It was Bob's fault. He should have remembered that whenever we are lost he asks me which way we should go, and then goes in the opposite direction, and is invariably correct. We began a walk that I prayed wouldn't be like my unsuccessful trek from the Ècouen station to the Château d'Écouen, or similar in any way to my recent experience at Versailles. Although we were walking in the wrong direction, there was a lovely surprise at the bottom of a hill. The road ran beneath part of a marvelous ruin of the aqueduct built by Vauban during the reign of Louis XIV. Now covered by vines, wildflowers, and missing stones, so that spaces of sky appeared between its arches, it was a glorious ruin. We both decided that if we never reached the château, which I felt was a distinct possibility, the view of this aqueduct was worth the forty-minute train trip. This ancient aqueduct, which I could see marching across a manicured modern golf course, was intended to bring water from the River Eure to the gardens of Versailles. I was reminded of the Roman Emperor Augustus, who had given the city of Nîmes as a reward to the legions for defeating Cleopatra. The emperor had his engineers divert a river around a mountain in Lanquedoc to bring water to Nîmes so that his soldiers would have as many fountains in their new city as there were in Rome. Louis XIV had engineers design an aqueduct to fill his 1,400 fountains at Versailles, so that the fountains and "the waterfalls should cease neither day nor night." The difference between the Sun King and Caesar Augustus was that Louis did not have an endless supply of slave labor to build his aqueduct, but had to pay 10,000 stonecutters and 20,000 soldiers to build his.

In 1684, Louis XIV and the members of the Academy of Sciences, who had worked on the plans, came to watch 30,000 workers begin construction of the aqueduct. Periodically over the next four years, the king would come to Maintenon to oversee the work and visit his illegitimate children who were living there. During this time, he poured money not only into the aqueduct, but into renovating the château. Epidemics broke out among the workers, and piles of corpses were carried off in carts, but the work continued. Then, in 1688, the work came to a halt, as the soldiers, already weakened by sickness, were transferred to fight in the War of the League of Augsburg.

That war, which Louis thought would be over quickly, lasted ten years and drained the royal treasury. Louis would have to sell his gold plates. The silver furniture that once sparkled in the light of four thousand candles in the Hall of Mirrors at Versailles would be melted down to pay for these wars, and there would never be money enough to finish the aqueduct. Although the plan originally included building three series of arches to carry the water from the River Eure to Versailles, only one aqueduct would be built. Consequently, the fountains at Versailles are seldom turned on. It was the inadequate water supply that caused most of the objections to Versailles at the time.

I knew we couldn't be too far from the château, since I had read that the aqueduct could be seen through an arch in the courtyard, that the "vista is closed by the astonishing aqueduct of heroic, indeed, Roman proportions." Geneviève de Noailles, who owned the château some years later, felt that the ruin had a grandeur belonging to Louis XIV.

Having been reminded again that I have no sense of direction, I stopped as soon as I saw a woman—at a gardening establishment, complete with waterfalls and weeping willows—to ask if I was walking toward the town and château. "There is one road and you are walking the wrong way on it," she said—but she said it graciously and, unlike the bureaucrat at the station, took as much time as necessary to tell us how to reach the château. It took us about six minutes to walk back

to the station and another fifteen to reach the charming town of Maintenon. Just as we were entering the town, Bob noticed a sign saying TAXI
24 HEURES. I copied the number down and, later, when we were ready
to leave for the station, I called Allo Taxi, which responded quickly—
almost before I had time to turn off my cell phone.

The town, with a population around 4,000, is small and delightful. The time of our arrival, however, was not perfect: it was noon, the
very moment the château closed for the two-hour lunch. We found a
table at Le Saint-Denis, the restaurant across from the château where
we had had a pleasant meal years before. That experience was not to
be repeated. It was the only restaurant open on Mondays, so I advise
coming to Maintenon between Wednesday and Saturday, when the
town's other restaurants, Le Bistrot d'Adeline and Le Petit Marche,
are open.

I love French castles—not the dreary, walled, and moated medieval
fortresses with huge defensive towers at each corner, but the early-
Renaissance castles whose architects waved their fifteenth-century
wands over forbidding walls to make them disappear. They changed
the barren space that once separated walls from moats into gardens
designed to look like the tapestries hanging on the castle walls, then
transformed smelly moats into reflecting pools. They reduced the huge,
grim towers in size until they became whimsical crenellated turrets. At
the Château of Maintenon, pepperpot turrets are playfully reflected in
the artificial lake that surrounds it.

It is not typical of the classical châteaux built during the reign of
Louis XIV, but a throwback, like its owner, Madame de Maintenon, the
Sun King's last wife, to an earlier time. And while it is similar in design
to the fairy-tale Château d'Ussé in the Loire Valley, which inspired
Charles Perrault to write *Sleeping Beauty*, its owner was not a young
and beautiful princess but something of a witch. Most of the château at
Maintenon had been built two centuries before for Francis I's finance
minister. When Madame de Maintenon became its owner, however, she
added one wing, and Louis XIV sent his landscape designer, Le Nôtre,
to create the wide canals around the castle, so that it seemed to float
on water. Like all country homes bought by the new aristocracy, Francis's minister kept one square thirteenth-century tower to show that the

castle wasn't new, but then leveled the rest of the fortress and rebuilt it to meet fifteenth-century standards of comfort and beauty. In fact, this thirteenth-century tower was also kept by Madame de Maintenon when she renovated the castle in the seventeenth century. The whimsical turret tops were added in the nineteenth.

Louis XIV gave Madame de Maintenon, who was born Françoise d'Aubigné, the money to buy this castle in 1674.* Before she became its owner, she had been known as the Widow Scarron. With the purchase of the land and castle came the new title. She was, at this time, neither "Royal Mistress" nor wife. Her ambition was to be queen despite the fact that she was born a commoner. While her father was of noble descent, and a Huguenot comrade-in-arms of Henry IV, he was also a counterfeiter and in prison for participating in one of Marie de Rohan's conspiracies to overthrow Louis XIII. Her mother, however, was a commoner, the daughter of the governor of the Prison of Niort, where her father resided at the time of her birth. When Françoise was seventeen, she married writer Paul Scarron, and at twenty-five she became the impoverished Widow Scarron. While she was married to Scarron, she had turned her home into a salon, which was attended by the great writers and artists of the day. Madame de Sévigné wrote of her: "Mme Scarron, before her days of grandeur, was frequently of the company, and has lost none of the charm which made the salon of her poet-husband so attractive during his later years. She has an amiable and marvelously just mind. . . . It is pleasant to hear her talk. These conversations often lead us very far, from morality to morality, sometimes Christian, sometimes political."

It was at her salon that she met and became friends with Athénaïs de Montespan, the king's mistress. When Louis XIV first met Madame Scarron, he didn't like her or her friends, including Madame de Sévigné, with whom she dined "every evening," as well as Madame de Lafayette. Both of these friends had antagonized him by openly defending his former superintendent of finances, Nicolas Fouquet, at his trial.

---

* In addition to the funds he gave her for the education of his bastards, he gave her 100,000 pounds when he heard the property had come on the market.

When Athénaïs de Montespan became pregnant for the first time, it was necessary to find a "discreet" and "trustworthy" governess who would keep the child a secret, since Athénaïs was married at the time to the Count of Montespan, who was legally the father of any children that she and Louis would have. According to Saint-Simon, "Mme Scarron's respect, wit, pleasantness and desire to please delighted Madame de Montespan," but Louis didn't want this widow, who always dressed in black and seemed always to be preaching, to be the secret governess of his bastards.

When the Widow Scarron was first asked by Athénaïs to be the governess, she refused, saying piously that she was loath to be a party to an adulterous liaison. She finally agreed, after consulting her confessor, who told her she had to take the position if the king asked her. She insisted that the king *personally* ask her. Athénaïs de Montespan had her way and the king did so, reluctantly.

A house was purchased for her at 25 Boulevard Montparnasse, just outside of Paris* in which she would keep the child. Madame de Sévigné, who took her home after dinner one evening, was suspicious of Madame Scarron's altered circumstances—she had until recently been quite poor and living at the Convent of Val-de-Grace: "We found it pleasant to take Madame Scarron back at midnight all the way to the end of the Faubourg Saint Germain, almost at Vaugirard, in the country; a lovely, great mansion where no one enters. There is a garden, lovely, fine apartments; she has a carriage, servants and horses. She is dressed modestly and magnificently, like a woman who spends her life with people of quality. . . ."

Secrecy was important. Madame Scarron went to great lengths to ensure that no one was allowed to enter this house and see what was inside, and Athénaïs, for her part, designed a dress to hide her condition. When Athénaïs went into labor at Saint-Germain-en-Laye,† a messenger was sent to Madame Scarron, who came to the castle in a carriage

* The House is now 23-25 Boulevard du Montparnasse and 132 Rue de Vaugirard. It was rebuilt in 1712 for the Prince of Condé.

† Before moving to Versailles, the king and court resided at the castle at Saint-Germain-en-Laye, which now houses an archaeological museum and is a twenty-minute RER trip from Paris.

and waited outside for the child to be born. It was then smuggled out of the castle and handed to her in the waiting carriage.

Athénaïs proved prolific. The courtiers came to recognize the dress that she had designed. Nine times the Widow Scarron whisked away her children. During this time, the king and the widow talked more and more. She convinced the king that he must reconcile himself with the Church and mend his ways. After the fifth child, Athénaïs started to become concerned at the length of these conversations. Madame de Montespan enjoyed her position as Royal Mistress and the power it gave her. She had, in fact, poisoned at least one young woman whom she thought might attract the king and threaten that position, but she had, at first, been oblivious to her friend's attractions and ambitions. First, Athénaïs tried to marry her off to a duke, but Madame de Maintenon refused. Athénaïs next suggested to the king that she be made an abbess, but when offered, the widow again declined. Then the king came up with another idea, one antithetical to his mistress's intent. He decided to reward the Widow Scarron for her "discretion and care" by providing her with a place large enough for the growing number of children. She was instructed to seek an estate easily reached from Saint-Germain-en-Laye so that she would not be far from court. When she first saw the "meadows all around and a river flowing through the moats" at Maintenon, she exclaimed: "This is where I want to spend my final days." The two women would continually quarrel over the children: Madame de Maintenon complaining to her confessor and to the king "that whatever rules she made for the children were immediately reversed by their mother." Nonetheless, the two women continued to be friends, and Athénaïs de Montespan came to spend more and more time at Maintenon, as did the king. Louis sent Le Nôtre to improve the gardens, and workmen to improve the château.

When two o'clock finally came, Bob and I walked into the courtyard of the château. We turned the corner and saw the moat and the aqueduct in the distance. I thought it was one of the most beautiful sights I had ever seen. Entering the château, we passed under a relief of St. Michael killing his dragon. We walked up the staircase to the first floor, where there is a portrait and eighteenth-century prints of Madame de Maintenon. Looking at her portrait, I could see why she was not well liked at court. She was referred to as the "old lady," the "ugly lady," the "sow," and the "she-monkey." The king referred to her as "Your sturdiness." Saint-Simon said of her: the poverty "in which she had lived so long had narrowed her mind and debased her heart and feelings," while Sainte-Beuve comes closer to the reason she was so disliked: "There is not a single moment of abandon in the entire life of Madame de Maintenon." The Duchess of Orléans, the king's sister-in-law, who was a close and perceptive observer of people, had watched Madame de Maintenon displace Athénaïs de Montespan as the king's mistress. I should mention that the duchess really didn't like Madame de Maintenon, whom she called the "old pruneface" and "sorceress" and blamed for removing all the fun at Versailles as well as for the persecutions of the Huguenots. The Duchesse of Orléans would write:

> Goody Scarron . . . told the King that his affliction was sent him by Heaven, as a punishment for the sins he had committed with Montespan. She was eloquent . . . and by degrees the King became accustomed to her, and thought she would effect his salvation.
>
> It was her habit to ridicule everybody, under the pretext of diverting the King . . . she filled the King with a bad opinion of the whole Court, solely that he might have no desire for any other company than that of herself and her creatures.

The duchess, in fact, blamed Madame de Maintenon for the king's revocation of the Edict of Nantes, his ill-conceived wars, and all troubles that befell his reign during the years she was his main adviser.

The room I like best in the château was Louis XIV's bedroom, with its portraits of four of his predecessors—Louis XII, Francis I, Henry IV and Louis XIII—above each of the doors and a copy of Rigaud's portrait of Louis XIV dressed for his coronation. As I looked at this portrait it seemed to me as though he were about to take part in a ballet rather than a coronation. I remembered how Fouquet, knowing how much the young king liked to dance, had misjudged him. I wondered once again if the king had been honest in his memoirs when he wrote he would have forgiven his financial minister if he had only confessed. But whether or not he would have forgiven him when he was a young king, I knew, with Madame de Maintenon's portrait fresh in my mind, Fouquet would never have lasted after she wheedled her way into the king's heart.

Indeed, she did wheedle her way into the king's heart by showing love and concern for his children. She was forty-five when Louis first became interested in her. When he saw the loving care she gave the children, he commented, "Madame de Maintenon knows how to love. There would be great pleasure in being loved by her."

Sometimes the worst possible thing is to get what you ask for. Madame de Maintenon wanted to be Louis XIV's wife and queen. After becoming his confidante, she gradually convinced the king to get rid of Athénaïs de Montespan. She had raised Madame de Montespan's son the Duc du Maine, who loved his governess and not his mother. According to the Duchess of Orléans, the Duc du Maine persuaded his mother to retire from court for a short time in order that the king might recall her. Being fond of her son, and believing him to be honest in the advice he gave her, she went to Paris and wrote to the king that she would never come back. The Duc du Maine immediately sent off all her packages after her without her knowledge; he even had her furniture thrown out of the window, so that she could not come back to Versailles.

Then Louis XIV asked Madame de Maintenon to be his mistress. She refused, because, she said, to do so would be sinful, even with a king. Instead, she told him to live on better terms with Marie-Thérèse who, upon hearing this, was grateful to Madame de Maintenon.

Two years after the queen died in Madame de Maintenon's arms, she and Louis XIV were secretly married. He would, however, because of her birth and her former marriage to a burlesque poet—which he thought would open him up to ridicule—never make her queen or announce their marriage publicly. While she had wanted to be queen, she was not totally happy being Louis's wife. Her marriage to Paul Scarron—who was paralyzed from the neck down when she married him at the age of seventeen, saying: "I prefer to marry him than go to a convent"—had been a marriage in name only. Being essentially frigid by nature, this had suited her just fine. Now, in 1686, she was married to Louis XIV, who, as the Duchess of Orléans puts it, "was always fond of sex." At the age of seventy, Louis XIV made love to Madame de Maintenon twice a day, much to her annoyance. At seventy-eight, she consulted her priest to find out if it was necessary to accommodate her husband; the priest informed her it was her duty as a wife to do so.

IT SEEMS A SHAME to leave the age of Louis XIV at Maintenon. This castle, reminiscent of the Middle Ages, simply does not evoke an age of epic dramas, of biting wit and satire, of literary salons, of heroic and dramatic art of the Age of Louis XIV. One could imagine meeting Madame de Sévigné, Corneille, Racine, La Rochfoucauld, or Molière at Vaux-le-Vicomte. One could expect to see the classical paintings of Nicolas Poussin or the heroic art of Charles Le Brun on the walls at Vaux or at Versailles, but not here. Maintenon today is a charming place to visit, but I, like the eighteenth-century courtiers, sensing the narrow-minded piety with which Madame de Maintenon clouded the reign of the Sun King, was happy to return to Paris.

PART FOUR

—

The Coming of the French Revolution

PARIS IN THE EIGHTEENTH CENTURY

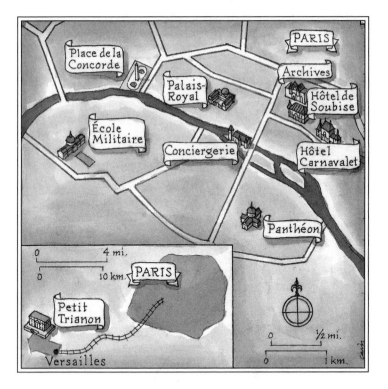

CHAPTER 19

PARISIAN SIGHTS

—

Introduction

WE HAVE BEEN TRAVELING THROUGH THE HISTORY OF FRANCE for seven centuries, taking the train from Paris to places throughout France whose architecture and historic significance evoked a particular era. We have traveled to these sites chronologically, traveling from one century to the next, visiting places in the order they were built, beginning our journey through time with a fortress and cathedral built in the eleventh century and continuing architecturally through the ages up through the seventeenth century, so that we would have a sense of traveling through time.

Our travels were made easy by Emperor Napoleon III and Baron von Haussmann, who, wanting to make Paris the center of Europe, laid the foundation for the most marvelous system of trains. Consequently, we have been able to travel from the heart of modern Paris to the hearts of ancient cities like Laon, Chartres, Reims, Angers, Tours, Rouen, and La Rochelle, trips I found to be sheer magic since not only had the cores of these cities remained unchanged for centuries, as the modern city expanded outward, but also because the trains whisked me through the sprawling, modern, faceless suburbs and deposited me in the ancient past.

But now, as we reach the eighteenth century, there is going to be a change. Although for seven centuries we have traveled mostly outside Paris, the eighteenth century is different. We are not going to leave Paris.

Instead, we will take the Métro and the RER, the suburban railroad, which can be boarded at a number of Métro stations within the city. Not only is it possible to visit the eighteenth century without leaving Paris, but to understand this volatile century it is far better *not* to leave. This is because after the death of Louis XIV in 1715, the center of France, so long at Saint-Germain-en-Laye and Versailles, moved back to Paris. During the years that followed the Sun King's death, the city was revitalized as Louis XV and his mistress, Madame de Pompadour, built the Panthéon, the École Militaire, and the Place de la Concorde, while the aristocracy and bourgeoisie built or restored their Parisian palaces and homes. Staying in Paris, we can more easily understand how the French monarchy, seven hundred years in evolving from an elected-first-among-equals whose domain was limited to the Île-de-France into an absolute monarch ruling all of France, self-destructed in the short space of eighty-nine years into the chaos of revolution.

Remaining in Paris also has the advantage of letting us see the century as it evolved by visiting many places rather than one. Unlike previous centuries—when change seemed to travel on the back of a snail and a single castle like Angers, frozen in time, could evoke a hundred years, cultural, military, and economic change is speeded up in the eighteenth century as France evolved quickly from the absolutism of Louis XIV to revolution. In Paris we can practically see the architecture change along Métro stops, from the rigid and monumental classicism of Louis XIV to the sensuous Rococo curves of Louis XV, as the iron fist of absolutism lost its grip during the reigns of the two weak kings who succeeded him.

Staying in Paris lets us see the century from the view of different segments of society: through the eyes of the king, his mistress, his aristocracy, and his subjects, whose stories taking place over the course of eighty-nine years help us to understand how the monarchy and aristocracy self-destructed.

We can, for example, see this decline through the eyes of the Duke of Orléans by taking the Line 1 Métro to the Palais-Royal stop, which lets us off at the duke's palace. When Louis XIV finally died in 1715, after outliving his son and his grandson, he left his nephew the Duke of Orléans as regent for his five-year-old great-grandson, and the first thing the duke did was move the court and government from Versailles to the Palais-Royal, his palace in Paris. Paris thus once again became the real capital of France. This regent was not like Blanche of Castile, Catherine de Médicis, or Anne of Austria—previous regents who were mothers of young kings and consequently fiercely determined to preserve the monarchy for their sons. The Duke of Orléans was a man next in line to be king.

I knew the eighteenth century had to be visited in Paris the moment I stepped out on the terrace of the Palais-Royal and saw the sloping roofs of the Louvre—then the king's palace—just a heartbeat away. While I could see that the Palais-Royal was grand, I could also see it was not nearly as grand as the king's palace, which the Duke of Orléans had to see every time he stepped out on his terrace. As I stood on that terrace, I thought how, after Louis XIV died early in the century, the regent held nightly dinner parties at which he and his guests discussed the English constitutional monarchy as a preferable alternative to absolutism in France. I understood why he allowed his guests to openly express their growing dissatisfaction with the doctrine of the divine right of kings, and why, by the end of the century, the Palais-Royal had become the center of revolutionary activity. It became clear why the regent's heir, also called the Duke of Orléans, cast the deciding vote to send his cousin—Louis XVI—to the guillotine.

We can also see the eighteenth century through the eyes of the growing intelligentsia, the men of the Enlightenment, men who believed their age was enlightened by reason, by walking a few blocks to the nearby Hôtel Canavalet. Once the home of Madame de Sévigné but now a museum of the history of Paris, it contains more than thirty eighteenth-century rooms salvaged from *hôtel particuliers* in Paris. They have been restored and furnished so that you can see the very salons where, at the beginning of the century, literary, philosophical, and political ideas were at first merely discussed, but then during the course of the century became centers for activists and revolutionaries. Invitations to these salons were not based on bloodlines, but on talent and the ability to converse well, since the Age of Enlightenment was also called the age of conversation. Men such as Montesquieu (*The*

Spirit of Laws), Diderot (*Encyclopédie*), Voltaire ("Essay on the Customs and the Spirit of the Nations"), and Jean-Jacques Rousseau (*The Social Contract*) would meet in these rooms to freely discuss political ideas, which, over the course of the century, became the basis of both the French and the American revolutions.

We can see the eighteenth century through the eyes of the aristocracy by getting back on the Line 1 Métro and taking it to the Saint-Paul station, because it is only a short walk from that station to the Hôtel de Soubise in the Marais, where the aristocracy, upon leaving Versailles, built or restored their palaces and where guests with the proper bloodlines, men and women who still assumed that the ideals of chivalry were axiomatic, would, oblivious to the growing discontent around them, enjoy musical evenings in a sensuous Rococo interior with decorations and murals indicative of their lax morality.

We can also see the century through the edifices built by the king and his mistress: the École Militaire, which was Madame de Pompadour's pet project; the Panthéon, whose transformation from a religious shrine to an atheistic temple helps us understand both the lethargy and the amorality of Louis XV on the one hand, and also how his subjects' reverence for the monarchy turned into contempt; the Place de la Concorde, where sipping tea at the Hôtel Crillon, built by Louis XV to house government offices, enables us to understand Talleyrand's words: "No one who did not live before 1789 knows the sweetness of life"; and the Petite Trianon at Versailles (the refuge of Marie-Antoinette), whose stories help us to understand the demise of the monarchy from within. If, unlike me, you have a sadistic side and enjoy tours dwelling on bloody and gory details, such as rats nibbling at prisoners' toes, you should take the guided tour of the Conciergerie, where the aristocracy and Marie-Antoinette waited to be taken off to the guillotine.

PALAIS-ROYAL
Line 1 or Line 7 Métro to Palais-Royal

The perfect place to begin our visit to the eighteenth century is the Palais-Royal, located directly across from what is now the Louvre—the eighteenth-century palace of the king. If we take either the Line 1 or Line 7 Métro to the station Palais-Royal, we will be just steps away from the arcaded courtyard and garden of the Palais, where Louis XIV played with his little brother, the future Duke of Orléans, and where the duke's descendant, another Duke of Orléans, plotted, 145 years later, to send another king, his cousin, to the guillotine.

When you enter the courtyard, the first thing you see are striped, modern sculptures that Bob really likes. I find them jarring and would have preferred the restorers of the garden to re-create the miniature fort, complete with its outer walls and bastions, from which little Louis XIV fired his toy cannon, loaded with blanks, which nonetheless almost set the palace on fire. Walking beyond an arcade that separates the garden in two, you will see a classical garden lined with rows of trees that have been pruned so that they look like hedges on sticks, which I think is more in keeping with the age we are visiting.

The buildings enclosing the gardens have been mostly restored to the way they were in the eighteenth century. It is an architecture that was a reaction to the classical formality and absolutism of Louis XIV. If you want to see exactly what I mean, walk across the Rue de Rivoli and then left to the eastern façade of the Louvre, where you can see the finest example of Louis's classical style.

On the left, as you enter the courtyard of the Palais-Royal, are the Comédie-Française and the Théâtre du Palais-Royal, where, before Madame de Maintenon cast her religious spell on Louis XIV, causing him to ban the theater and the opera, Parisians laughed at the greed, hypocrisy, and vanity of Molière's characters in plays such as *Tartuffe* and *Le Misanthrope*. After Louis XIV's death, the theater would once again be the most popular form of entertainment.

The palais was originally built by Cardinal Richelieu. Wanting to have a residence near his king, he used part of the wealth Louis XIII had given him (as minister his income was 3 million livres a year) to buy up parcels of land near the Louvre and then leveled medieval ramparts and built a luxurious but comfortable palace and lavish gardens. When he died in 1642, he bequeathed, perhaps out of gratitude, the "Palais Cardinal" to his king. When Louis XIII died one year later, Anne of Austria, his queen, became regent for Louis XIV and almost immediately moved from the Louvre, which at that time had all the amenities of a fortress, to the cardinal's more comfortable palace, complete with a gold-fitted bathroom. The Palais Cardinal, or Hôtel de Richelieu, as it was alternately called, then became known as the Palais-Royal. The classical gardens were redesigned to accommodate a very young king who loved to play at being a soldier, a pastime he unfortunately never outgrew. Nothing remains of the gardens Richelieu created but a beautiful circular pond where the soothing sound of its fountain creates a peaceful place to read, while the only remnant of the palace from Anne's time can be seen at 8 Rue de Valois.

The royal family was not able to enjoy the comforts of this palace for very long. During the Fronde (1648–1653)—the rebellion against the crown—Anne and her two young sons were forced to flee the vulnerable Palais-Royal in the middle of the night, to the safety of the fortress at Saint-Germain-en-Laye. When Louis XIV was able to return to Paris, he returned, remembering this humiliation, to the more secure Louvre, while the Palais-Royal eventually became the property and private domain of his younger brother—the Duke of Orléans—who had Le Nôtre redesign the gardens in 1674.

Louis XIV was king for seventy-two years, from 1643 to 1715, and most of his reign was glorious. In fact, when the seventeenth century was on the verge of becoming the eighteenth, the great debate taking place in the salons of Paris and the court at Versailles was whether the age of Louis XIV "equaled or surpassed the centuries of Pericles and Augustus," the golden ages of Greece and Rome, and it did seem that the Grand Siècle was indeed superior to any time that had come before it. But by the time Louis XIV finally died, his unnecessary wars had brought France to the verge of bankruptcy.

After the Duke of Orléans became regent for the five-year-old Louis XV, the Palais-Royal became, as Versailles had been, not only the center of government, but also the center of entertainment. The duke was back among the gambling casinos and theaters that he loved. Moral restraint was ended as masked balls were held under the glowing light of paper lanterns; the theater again became the Parisians' most popular form of entertainment. The Comédie-Française and the Palais-Royal Theater were reopened, and the opera found a home in the Palais-Royal's grand salon.

We are told that the period was marked by moral laxity and that the "Palais-Royal became notorious for the regent's debauchery." However, the regent, although referred to as a "paragon of promiscuity," seems to have been far better than memoirs would have us believe. For example, the rumors that he, as next in line as heir to the throne (the Duke of Orléans was always next in line as heir to the throne and throughout the centuries had always been the biggest threat to the monarchy) after becoming regent, tried to poison Louis XV, seem to be untrue. Although he ended each night with a drunken orgy, he also ended religious persecution and the disastrous religious wars of Louis XIV. I commiserate with his attempt to set straight the financial crisis that Louis XIV's wars had created. In his admiration for all things English, he created the Bank of France in Mazarin's palace across from the Louvre, and in 1717 placed in charge of it a Scotsman, John Law, with instructions to model it on the Bank of England. The paper money issued by the Bank of France—the first paper money issued in France—became virtually worthless. Its shares, sold by John Law, became inflated, resulting in a bubble that burst—meaning that in one day shares lost almost 90 percent of their value.

At the regent's candlelit dinner parties, which he held in the Palais-Royal most nights, both host and guests left in a drunken stupor. According to the Duke of Saint-Simon, these parties, or salons, do not sound terribly convivial. The regent had "the odious habit of setting people at each other's throats, so as to have nothing to fear from their attachments, and to learn by allowing them to speak against one another."

The discussions at these dinner parties, as at the other salons throughout Paris, no longer compared the monarchy with the golden ages of Greece and Rome. Instead, they expressed a growing dissatisfaction with France's absolute monarchy and a growing respect for the English constitutional monarchy. Although the regent failed to actually do so, he said he wanted to make the government of France more like that of England, which he praised "because they had no system of sending people into exile and no *lettres-de-cachet* and because their king can forbid no one anything except the entrée to his own palace, and can keep no one in prison without a trial." Upon becoming regent, he had ordered hundreds of prisoners released from the Bastille who had been imprisoned there by secret *lettres-de-cachet* accusing them of religious nonconformity. (Those democratic feelings did not, however, prevent the regent from imprisoning Voltaire, a frequent dinner guest at the Palais-Royal, in the Bastille, for eleven months in 1716 for what he considered an insult.) He was certainly not successful in abolishing *lettres-de-cachet*. They were still being delivered by the king's musketeers long after the regency ended and Louis XV became king. When I came across a *lettre-de-cachet* written by Louis XV in 1770 to the Duke of Choiseul, one of his ministers, I was reminded of a really bad Western movie in which the hero is told to get out of town by noon. The duke had been unable to hide his feeling toward Madame du Barry, who was rumored to have "slept her way from brothel to the throne"— and who, after the death of Madame de Pompadour, became the king's official mistress—and expressed his contempt for, as he put it, her "Bacchanalian entertainments in which the King delighted." The king sent the following *lettre-de-cachet*, either at Madame du Barry's prodding if we believe her memoir, or because the duke was about to involve Louis XV in yet another unnecessary war he didn't want. "Cousin," he began, "the little satisfaction your services have given me obliges me to banish you to Chanteloup, where you must go within twenty-four hours. I would have sent you to a place much more remote were it not for the particular regard I have for the Duchesse de Choiseul [a frequent visitor to Louis XV's bed] whose health and welfare are of great interest to me. . . ."

In another letter, he ordered the Abbé Bernis "to go to one of your abbeys, whichever you choose, in twice twenty-four hours from now. . . ."

Not only did Louis XV (1715–1774) continue to issue these letters of banishment and exile, but he once—on January 22, 1771—issued them to every member of Parlement. Only peasants were paying taxes, and Louis had hoped to resolve the state's financial problems by expanding the tax base to include other groups of French society—including all members of Parlement. When the legislators rejected his plan, he responded by having his musketeers deliver *lettres-de-cachet* exiling every member of Parlement—to Pontoise, the most boring place he could imagine.

The regent's palace burned down in 1763, and again in 1781, and was rebuilt during the reign of Louis XVI and Marie-Antoinette by the grandson of the regent, also the Duke of Orléans, who called himself Philip Égalité. He was a man of "amiable but despicable character" who upon inheriting the property, bought up more land around the palace as an investment, enclosed the gardens with arcades, and topped the ground-floor shops with apartments, which were built and leased, some say, to pay off his enormous gambling debts, although he had inherited an immense fortune.

At one end of the courtyard is the gloriously romantic restaurant Le Grand Véfour, where Napoleon dined with Josephine (and where I would love to dine each night if we were fabulously wealthy).* Today the restaurant's sensuous eighteenth-century decor has been perfectly restored to the time when it was called the Café Chartres (after Philip Égalité, since he was the Duke of Chartres as well as the Duke of Orléans). It is hard to imagine what the courtyard was like in the years just before the Revolution, since now, when you leave Le Grand Véfour after dinner, the gardens are empty and the shops in the arcades closed,

---

* I would actually love to alternate between Le Grand Véfour and Taillevent, my favorite restaurant in France. When the Michelin took away one star in 2007—the reviewer must not have had their lobster bisque with chestnuts—I thought it was the Michelin that ought to be improved, not Taillevent. Its owner graciously accepted his loss, not with suicide, as some restaurateurs have done in the past, but with the marvelous statement "We will try to do better."

and the courtyard is filled with an eerie silence. In the late eighteenth century, it was a bustling place both night and day, filled with numerous coffeehouses, casinos, brothels, wig and lace makers, puppeteers, acrobats, guitarists singing bawdy songs, orators standing on café chairs screaming out the news of the day or revolutionary ideas to enthusiastic crowds. It was in one of these shops that during the Reign of Terror, a Norman noblewoman, Charlotte Corday, purchased the kitchen knife with which she stabbed the Jacobin journalist Marat on July 13, 1793, as he was taking a bath.

The Palais-Royal was the "private domain" of the Duke of Orléans, where the king's police were not allowed to enter. In fact, it was the only place in France where people were free to criticize, slander, and mock the king and queen, if Philip Egalité allowed it, which he did. He was responsible for the insidious rumor that spread through eighteenth-century Paris—and through history as well—that when Marie-Antoinette heard the peasants were starving, she said, "Let them eat cake if they could not afford bread." Although the statement had been made by a Queen of France, it was not Marie-Antoinette, but rather Marie-Thérèse, Louis XIV's queen, who uttered those words. Philip Égalité not only allowed and encouraged café orators to rant against the king, and oversaw the printing of news sheets slandering the queen, but, in his desire to be king, cast the deciding vote that sent Louis XVI to the guillotine. Even those who backed replacing Louis XVI with Philip Égalité held the duke in low regard and only backed him reluctantly. Count Honoré Mirabeau, a statesman and writer, who desired a constitutional monarchy and who was one of his supporters, wrote that "depending on him is like building on mud. But he is admired by the mob, he loathes the King, he loathes the Queen even more, and if he needs courage we'll give him some."

There are only two days a year—the third weekend in September, a weekend called Journées du Patrimoine—on which the sumptuous interior of the Palais-Royal is open to the public so that you can see, as I saw, and as the Duke of Orléans once saw, from the long terrace on one side of his palace, another palace, so near and yet so far, a palace not only much grander than his, but one that would *be* his, if only his cousin the king would die.

Hôtel Carnavalet
Line 1 Métro to Station Saint-Paul

After leaving the Palais-Royal, I heartily suggest getting back on the Line 1 Métro and taking it to the Saint-Paul station. After leaving the station, if you cross the Boulevard Saint-Antoine and walk a few blocks along the Rue de Sévigné to the Rue des Francs Bourgeois, you will find the Hôtel Carnavalet, now a delightful museum of the history of Paris. Originally built during the Renaissance (1548–60), it acquired its name from its second owner, Françoise Kernevenoy, whose husband was nicknamed "Carnavalet." A century later, the great architect François Mansart added a wing, and in 1677 it was rented by Madame de Sévigné, whose letters describing the world of Louis XIV have charmed readers for centuries. When Madame de Sévigné moved there in October of 1677, she ebulliently exclaimed,"Thank God, we have the Hôtel Carnavalet, we must get along without parquet floors and the little fireplaces that are so fashionable nowadays, but at least we'll have a handsome courtyard and a beautiful garden, all in a fine part of town."

Today there are two courtyards. One leads to the museum, but be sure to enter the other one—on the Rue de Sévigné—first. If you do, you will be seeing what Madame de Sévigné saw when she entered her home and "beautiful garden." When you look up, you will notice beneath the balustrade the marvelous Renaissance bas-relief carvings personifying the Four Seasons (carved by Diane de Poitiers's favorite sculptor, Jean Goujon) that decorate the façade. However, it was when I looked down and saw the garden beds that I had a delightful surprise. Whoever designed them had a quirky sense of humor, which I believe Sévigné would have appreciated. The flowers and shrubs form punctuation marks, reminding today's visitors that this was once the home of the world's most elegant letter writer.

Madame de Sévigné occupied the first floor (our second floor), reserving the ground floor for her daughter, to whom most of her 1,500 letters were written. Her friends who visited her here included Madame de Lafayette, Madame de Maintenon, the fabulist Jean de La Fontaine, the playwright Pierre Corneille, and the Duke of La Rochefoucauld. They might have spent the evening discussing the trial of Fouquet, whom she adored, or listening to a reading by Molière of his *Femmes Savantes*, or by Corneille of his *Pulchérie*. The dining room where they ate was destroyed during the Revolution. However, Room 21, the Sévigné Gallery, on the ground floor, contains some remnants from her past: the desk at which she wrote her letters, and which she brought with her from her home in Brittany, as well as portraits of her and her daughter.

Some historians call her dinner parties salons, but the great Parisian salons of the eighteenth century were more formalized than Madame de Sévigné's evenings. But the museum also contains rooms—the very rooms—in which the great eighteenth-century salons were held. There are no less than thirty of them here. I could not help but wonder if these exquisite settings—with inlaid cabinets, lightly colored wall panels, paneling carved with trees whose leaves are shields or helmets or musical instruments, glittering chandeliers, damasks, embroideries, and brocades—provided an atmosphere that inspired and elevated the conversations that took place. I wondered as I walked through these rooms if we today provide our intellectuals too drab a setting to raise their thoughts.

These thirty rooms are where the eighteenth century salons— evenings devoted to conversation—would have been held during the time of Louis XV and XVI. As you walk through the rooms, you will see the portraits and busts of the great men of the Enlightenment, men who believed their age, unlike the Dark Ages that preceded them, was enlightened by reason and science, men such as Voltaire, Helvétius, Diderot, Montesquieu, and Rousseau, who lived at this time and argued in these salons of Paris. It was an age skeptical of tradition and confident that powers of human reason would lead to "civilization's advance and progress." Just as our age is the age of contact sports, the eighteenth century was the age of conversation, of "free and unfettered discussion upon every subject in heaven or on earth." To talk well was then considered the highest attribute that any person could possess. It was the one art at which all endeavored to excel. Jean-Jacques Rousseau would write: "One learns much more from authors' conversations than from their books, and the authors themselves are not the source from which one learns the most. It is the spirit of social gatherings that . . . pushes one's vision as far as it can go."

These salons were arenas in which ideas were contested and refereed by women who were said to have "sharpened their wits as they lost their beauty," so that they could become "the intellectual companions to men." These women competed with one another for witty guests and literary celebrities as professional football team owners today compete for players. They guided the conversations and kept them pleasant and could "make or unmake many a career." One of the most influential hostesses (Madame de Tencin) bitterly commented that another hostess (Madame Geoffrin) came to her salon "to see what she can collect out of my inventory" (her inventory being her celebrities).

The guest lists of the more influential salons were based on ability and talent, and allowed members of the bourgeoisie to enter, and with them their democratic values and the ideas of the Enlightenment: ideas that accepted as axiomatic that reason would lead to progress. At these salons, authors and artists were brought "into direct relation with distinguished patrons, especially foreigners, and thus contributed greatly to the spread of French art and letters." Once invited to a salon, a guest could return each week, so the hostess selected her guests with care. The ability to converse well was important to success and acceptance, and the only sins the hostesses could not pardon were stupidity, awkwardness, and sentimentality.

Some nineteenth-century intellectuals were unaware of the salon's immense influence on the comtemporary political and social world. Marcel Proust, for example, "insisted that politics was scrupulously avoided." Talleyrand, that ultimate pragmatist of a politican, whose power miraculously survived the French Revolution, Napoleon, and the Restoration that followed, was not so naive. When Talleyrand was asked why he spent so much time in these salons instead of discussing politics, he replied: "But women are politics."

Madame Tencin held small intellectual gatherings of friends and political reformers, and was said to have had a formidable ability to direct the conversations so that the political and philosophical ideas of the day were discussed. As a young woman, she had been placed in a nunnery, for which the horrified Abbé Fleuret, the first object of her decidedly unnunlike attentions, found her ill suited. Abbé Fleuret, we are told subsequently, helped her make her way to Paris, where her youthful behavior was considered scandalous even in a morally lax century. The more I read about her, the more fascinating she became. As an older woman, she transformed her youthful powers of seduction into an easy charm that allowed conversation in her salon to flow easily.

The novelist and playwright Jean-François Marmontel, one of her frequent guests, marveled at her finesse and suppleness, writing: "what activity were concealed beneath this naive air, the appearance of calm and leisure!"*

It was at Madame de Tencin's salon that the philosopher Helvetius attacked the theories of Rousseau, stating that men are motivated only by self-interest. Voltaire, who had met John Locke while exiled in London, brought back to the salon Locke's attack on the divine right of kings, which he discussed with Montesquieu. It was at Madame de Tencin's that Monstesquieu honed his political ideas on the file of Voltaire's satire, and said he was inspired to write *De l'Esprit des Lois*, which discusses separation and balance of powers in government, ideas so important to the U.S. Constitution. It was here that Montesquieu with characteristic seriousness and Voltaire with amusing irony openly discussed and questioned the concept of absolutism—the basis of royal power in France—while Diderot attacked the Catholic Church and clergy as well as the divine right of kings. The liberal ideas of the time were compiled in Diderot's seventeen-volume *Encyclopédie*, which was banned by the king in 1758 but nonetheless secretly printed.

---

* Jean-François Marmontel was a dramatist, novelist, and contributor to Diderot's *Encyclopédie*.

Hôtel de Soubise
(Archives Nationales)
*Line 1 Métro to Saint-Paul or Line 11 Métro
to Rambuteau*

After leaving the Hôtel Carnavalet, you have only to walk a few blocks along the Rue des Francs-Bourgeois to the Hôtel de Soubise, where the eighteenth-century aristocracy met, gossiped, and listened to music. These aristocratic gatherings were also called salons, although the qualities sought in the guest list were totally different from those in the salons held by women such as Madame de Tencin. Members of the bourgeoisie, no matter how talented or witty, were not invited. Here invitations were based on birth, not intelligence. What was deemed important was that guests had family trees with roots firmly planted in feudal times, that their manners were impeccable, and that they were properly attired. The ideas of the Enlightenment had barely touched this class.

This was the aristocracy descended from knights, who centuries before had received their huge estates in exchange for military service to the king, and, with those estates, their place in society above all other classes. Their ideas of chivalry—honor, glory, Platonic love, and gentle-manly behavior—which they accepted without question, dated from this early period, and had been, like the aristocracy itself, anachronistic for centuries, since at least the time of Joan of Arc, when the paid army came into being. This "code of chivalry" had by the eighteenth century degenerated into little more than a code of gentlemanly behavior. Of all the more modern trends, only materialism and moral laxity, both anti-thetical to the twelfth-century code of chivalry but characteristic of the eighteenth century, permeated the Rococo walls of salons such as those held here at the Hôtel de Soubise.

I have to admit I never would have paid any attention to the Hôtel de Soubise, located at 60 Rue des Francs-Bourgeois, if it hadn't been for the delicious eighteenth-century court gossip I found in memoirs about its owner, the Princess of Soubise (Anne de Rohan-Chabot). These memoirs describe how squabbling between the pious Madame de

Maintenon and Louis XIV's official mistress, Athénaïs de Montespan, gave the Princess of Soubise the opening she wanted to seduce Louis XIV, who weary of their bickering, was in need of distraction. This the voluptuous princess generously provided, and he subsequently provided her with funds for the purchase and construction of the palace at 60 Rue des Francs-Bourgeois.

Although Bob and I had been to exhibitions at the Hôtel de Soubise when it was the French National Archives, I never paid much attention to the building in which the exhibitions were being held—or indeed even noticed the carvings and murals that decorated the rooms—until I learned of the method by which its construction was financed. It was only then that I noticed the erotic Rococo interior decorations, the curved lines, arabesques, and exquisite ornamentation that once provided appropriate surroundings for the Princess of Soubise, after whose family it was named. The activities of the Princess of Soubise give us insight into the lavish expenditures of the aristocracy at this time as well as their morals, which are summed up not only in the princess's adulterous affair with the king, but also in the fatherly advice given about this time by the Duke of Coigny to his daughter: "Remember that in this country vice is immaterial, but ridicule is fatal."

The Hôtel de Soubise was one of many palatial homes (*hôtel particuliers*) constructed around a courtyard built in Paris at the beginning of the century. The aristocracy began returning from Versailles about this time, because Versailles had ceased being fun after Louis XIV secretly married the fanatically religious Madame de Maintenon. This migration accelerated after Louis XIV's death in 1715, when the Duke of Orléans, as regent, moved from Versailles to the Palais-Royal. When the aristocracy returned, they began building or remodeling their homes in the Marais, which you can see today, an area of the city that had once been a marsh (*marais*), but which had become an increasingly fashionable area after Henry IV created the Place des Vosges (Place Royale) in the seventeenth century.

The eighteenth century was a time when aristocrats were open to ridicule if they appeared impoverished and unable to modernize their ancient accommodations—and ridicule, as the Duke of Coigny pointed out, was the kiss of social death. As is the case with the Hôtel de Soubise, when the nobility remodeled, they left a remnant from the past, so that all who entered would know that their family's lineage dated back to feudal times, and that the present owner had proper bloodlines; that is to say he was descended from a nobleman of the sword (*noblesse d'épée*) and not one of the insignificant, newly ennobled bureaucrats (*noblesse de robe*), like Colbert, whom the aristocrats of the blood began to drive from political power after the death of Louis XIV.

The Princess de Soubise was considered a ravishing beauty, with red hair and a milky complexion—physical assets she employed to achieve her ends. The Duke of Saint-Simon wrote of the princess that "she had lived for her beauty; her ambitions and the uses to which she could put both. I do not believe that she had many other thoughts or was ever ready to entertain more serious considerations."

When I saw her portrait, one of which hangs in Versailles, and another at the Hôtel de Soubise, I was terribly disappointed. She was no Diane de Poitiers, Marie de Rohan, or Madame de Pompadour, women whose appearance fit my concept of a royal seductress. She was rather a little plump, a little smug, with a weak mouth. The portrait was so poorly lit that I couldn't tell the color of her small eyes, but unlike those of the other three women, I felt they seemed arrogant rather than intelligent. I learned from memoirs that the Princess de Soubise was always dieting, but not for the same reasons I diet, to keep as slim as is possible for a person with my appetite, but "to preserve the brilliance and freshness of her complexion." Slim boyish figures were not in vogue during the reign of Louis XIV.

In 1673, the princess became a "*dame du palais*" (a title given to a lady-in-waiting to the queen who could trace her lineage centuries back to a time before the bourgeoisie was ennobled), but four years later she realized that she and her husband were financially destitute. By coincidence, this was the same year that the bickering between Madame de Maintenon and Athénaïs was at its height. While her "beauty" didn't appeal to me, it certainly appealed to Louis XIV, who became totally infatuated with her. It certainly wasn't her intellect or wit that attracted him, of which everyone agrees she was notably lacking. The timing was

fortuitous for the Princess de Soubise, since the voluptuous, witty Athénaïs, instead of being witty that year and devoting herself to creating the
fêtes, which the king liked, was trying various intrigues to rid herself of
Madame de Maintenon, who simultaneously was trying to rid herself
of Athénaïs by lecturing the king on morality, pointing out the hellish (literally) consequences of his adulterous affair with his mistress. As these
two former friends squabbled and intrigued over the king, Louis XIV
noticed the new *dame du palais.* "In no time the King fell in love with
her," the Duke of Saint-Simon would write. "Everything has its season,
and Mme. de Montespan [Athénaïs] was beginning to bore him."

One biographer of the Sun King describes the Princess of Soubise
as being deeply in love with her husband, and attributes a semi-noble
motivation for her sending her impoverished husband off to tend to his
estates so that she could arrange an affair with the king. Speaking as a
woman, I don't believe that for a moment. The Duke de Saint-Simon
writes: "By the infamous connivance of her husband, [she] prostituted
herself to the king and secured all sorts of advantages for that husband,
for herself, and for her children." The princess's affair with the king
seems indicative of both the growing materialism and the increasingly
lax attitude toward fidelity in marriage that was prevalent at the time,
especially among the aristocracy. While I can't know for sure if her aim
was purely materialistic, she was quite successful. As soon as she sent
her husband away from court, telling him that his estates far from Versailles needed supervision, she put on a pair of emerald earrings ("des-
titution" among the aristocracy did not have quite the same meaning as
it did among the peasants in France), a pre-arranged signal to the king
that the coast was clear.

For a short period, there wasn't anything the king could deny her.
Everyone at court was well aware of what was going on in a private
room, at the far end of a larger public room, overlooking the courtyard
at Saint-Germain-en-Laye. It was here that many not-very-discreet but
very prolonged meetings took place. Her husband obligingly stayed
away from court, never revealing to anyone that he knew what was going
on between his wife and the king. The result of their liaison was the
future Cardinal of Rohan. Surely, the Prince of Soubise had to notice

the new addition to his family when he returned from the tour of his estates, as well as the new, comforting additions to his bank accounts. Not only were their debts paid off, but they had enough money to buy and remodel the marvelous Hôtel de Soubise—as well as to construct another palace for the princess's illegitimate child by the king.* The Hôtel de Rohan, which was given to this child, can be seen around the corner at 87 Rue Vieille-du-Temple (Louis XIV's illegitimate children were always well taken care of).† Over the entrance to the former stable at the Hôtel de Rohan is a wonderful Rococo relief of *The Horses of Apollo*, hinting that the Cardinal of Rohan's real father was not the Prince of Soubise but the Sun King.

The princess may have seemed beautiful to Louis XIV, but once she lost her front tooth, the king lost interest in her, although he continued to "favor" her and her child. Wit and conversation had never been her main attraction—in fact, the king had always found her boring—but once she lost the tooth, he found it impossible to understand anything she said.

In 1700, the Prince of Soubise, formerly financially embarrassed, would henceforth be referred to as possessing incredible wealth. He purchased a fifteenth-century Renaissance hôtel owned by the Guise family. In 1704 he instructed his architect (Pierre-Alexis Delamair) to renovate the hôtel, preserving, as much as possible, the existing medieval and Renaissance structures. Unfortunately, Delamair did not think the work of the Renaissance artist Primaticcio, which had adorned the walls of the former palace, worth retaining. He did keep the Salle des Gardes, or guardroom, where the former owners, the Guise family, had planned the St. Bartholomew's Day Massacre in 1572, and if you

---

* His palace in Strasbourg is now the marvelous Musée des Beaux-Arts, which, with the new TVG line, is a delightful and highly recommended day trip.

† For example, Louis XIV made his illegitimate son by his mistress Athénaïs de Montespan the Duke of Maine. Although you can still see the fabulous gardens of his estate at Sceaux—well worth the twenty-minute trip on the RER—the palace has been destroyed. His wife's dinner parties at the Hôtel Biron (now the Rodin Museum), designed by Gabriel, were notorious for their lavishness. One memoir notes that Voltaire and his mistress, Madame Chatelet, after making their rounds of salons, arrived there once at midnight. Unfortunately, the sensuous Rococo decorations were removed after the Revolution, when it was turned into a Catholic School.

walk around the hôtel to the Rue des Archives, you will find a pair of
fourteenth-century corbeled turrets that the Guises probably instructed
their architect to retain when they oversaw their renovations in the sixteenth century.

With its neoclassical exterior and Rococo interior, the palace is
typical of structures built at the beginning of the eighteenth century,
during the last years of Louis XIV. Although I had visited exhibitions
here several times before, this time I was concentrating on visiting an
eighteenth-century palace. When I entered the horseshoe courtyard,
or cour d'honneur, I was a bit taken aback that I had never noticed
how magnificent it was; it was as grand as any French palace or Italian palazzo that I might have swooned over if I had been touring the
countryside. On each side of the courtyard stood paired columns, creating open colonnades leading to a monumental entrance. The entrance
is derivative of the classical Greek temple, composed of two stories of
paired columns, but separated by arched French windows and topped
by a pediment upon which statues personifying the four seasons are
lounging. Wings to the left and to the right of this entrance are decorated with statues personifying the four elements (fire, earth, air, and
water), carved by Guillaume Coustou and Pierre Bourdy.

This was a palace obviously constructed with total disregard for
expense. After I entered, determined to ignore the twentieth-century
exhibits, I headed straight for the rooms I knew preserved the sumptuous interior Rococo decorations completed during the reign of
Louis XV, the rooms of the Princess of Soubise and her son. Here you
can understand what is meant by artists freeing themselves from the
restraints imposed by the Sun King and his director—or dictator—Le
Brun. The art that can still be seen—especially in the oval salon, where
musical evenings were attended by other members of the aristocracy—
is bedroom art, playful, sensuous, frivolous, filled with curves, lovely
colors, and themes of love rather than formal and grandiose themes. It
is an art of the aristocracy, who had come to, or perhaps always did, live
for their own pleasure, and that possesses the same "ephemeral, floating quality" of court life at the time, rather than heroic art glorifying the
king. The themes and myths are no longer of war and glory but deal

with love and seduction. The myths painted on the walls are not the epic battles of Apollo or Mars but the affairs of Psyche and Venus. As you walk through these rooms, you will see *Venus at Her Toilet* by Carle Van Loo and *Venus at her Bath* by François Boucher. The sensuousness is particularly appropriate for the residence of the Princess of Soubise. I find the white and gold oval salon with its four arched French doors and four matching arched mirrors quite luxurious. Above the doors and mirrors are eight sensuous paintings by Charles Natoire depicting the myth of Cupid and Psyche, as interpreted by the fabulist La Fontaine. The ceiling in the room is the blue sky, decorated with open-work branches of gold.

Although I have read that the paintings are not as fine as the sensuous paintings by Boucher in the white and gold bedchamber of the princess, I think the oval room is simply glorious. So did Prince Charles de Soubise, Maréchal of France, who after inheriting the palace in the mid-eighteenth century, oversaw the interior decorations. Being a fine amateur musician, he regularly held musical salons in this room, where invitations were extended to other aristocrats, people with proper lineage or bloodlines. Describing one musical evening at the Hôtel de Soubise, the Duke of Croy wrote "that, outside the court, nothing so splendid has been seen for twenty years. . . . Room after room and the . . . great staircase . . . was ablaze with lights. A host of the very best people, the service, and the magnificence of everything reflected the greatest credit on the Prince.

Some exceptions were made to the aristocratic guest list for the duke's musical evenings. Thomas Jefferson, although a plebeian, was invited, and so was Madame de Pompadour, but only after she became Louis XV's official mistress. Born Jeanne-Antoinette Poisson—a name that was the subject of contemporary snide remarks, since *poisson* means "fish"—Madame de Pompadour was the first official mistress of a king not to have come from the nobility. Her accession to the position of official mistress was "a total revolution in the manners and morals of the Court" since until that time, the official mistress had always been "a lady of quality," and by the eighteenth-century definition, Madame de Pompadour was certainly not. She was a product of the eighteenth-century salon. Voltaire was her friend and admirer before she became his patron. He said she was "a bourgeoise, the flower of finance, witty, elegant, graced with many gifts and talents, but with a manner of feeling that lacked the grandeur and coldness of aristocratic ambition." One historian viewing her portrait by Boucher and amazed by her beauty, asked: "Was she one of nature's masterpieces—or just one of Boucher's?"

The Prince of Soubise, unfortunately, became famous neither for his musical evenings nor for his musical ability, but for his military skill, of which he had none. When he went off to war in 1757, he handed his cocker spaniel for safekeeping to Madame de Pompadour, who had personally selected him to be the general facing Frederick the Great of Prussia at Rossbach. He was to suffer a humiliating defeat in which the Prussians came into possession of a great deal of land that was formerly French. While the crushing defeat by the Prussians doesn't appear to be totally Soubise's fault, he took the blame for both the defeat and the loss of French possessions and became the satiric brunt of jokes and caricatures at Versailles in songs such as the following:

> *I've lost my army—wherever can it be—*
> *oh! thank goodness! I see it coming towards me—*
> *horrors! It's the enemy.*
> *The Hôtel de Soubise was to let, they said,*
> *the Prince having gone to the École Militaire.*
> *It would cost him nothing now to build a new house,*
> *he could do it with the stones that would be thrown at him.*

That winter, Madame de Pompadour insisted that Soubise come to Versailles and did her very best to console him. When the prince mentioned his defeat one evening at supper, Madame de Pompadour told him "not to talk shop."

ÉCOLE MILITAIRE
Line 8 Métro to École Militaire

The École Militaire, mentioned in the verse which suggests that the Prince of Soubise should have attended this military school before going off to war, is located at 1 Place Joffre, at the far end of the Champ de Mars. While it is a fine example of the work of Madame de Pompadour's favorite architect, Jacques-Ange Gabriel, who succeeded Le Brun as director of the French Academy of Arts, I would not go out of my way to see it. However, if you decide to visit the Eiffel Tower and find the crowds there too overwhelming, you can take a short walk to the other end of the Champs de Mars and walk around the deserted perimeter of the military school designed by this great neoclassical architect.[*]

If you walk along Avenue de Lowendal, you will have a wonderful view of this imposing building, which looks much the same as it did when Napoleon arrived as a young cadet in 1784. To me, the central portion of this neoclassical building, resting beneath a typically French square-based dome, looks like a Greek temple, complete with a Greek-style pediment and four giant Corinthian columns. Two low colonnaded wings on either side of the central building relieve an otherwise severe façade. If you are lucky, you will see through the fence, as Bob and I did, elegant cadets exercising their equally elegant horses in the parade ground.

This military school was the pet project of Madame de Pompadour. From the time she became Louis XV's official mistress, she began looking for a project similar to Madame de Maintenon's (a school for daughters of impoverished noblemen at Saint-Cyr), by which Madame de Pompadour hoped, as she wrote, to "immortalize the King, make his nobility happy, and inform posterity of my attachment to the State and to H.M." So when Madame de Pompadour's mentor, Joseph Paris-

---

[*] I have nothing against the Eiffel Tower. I think it is spectacular when viewed in the evening while having dinner at the nearby Au Bon Accueil or when crossing a bridge after dark to the Île Saint-Louis but not when viewed from a line of tourists waiting below.

Duverney, a very close friend of her mother, a man who had grown quite wealthy supplying the Louis XV's armies, proposed a military academy where the sons of impoverished noblemen "and sons of officers killed and wounded in battle might be trained to become officers," she immediately suggested the idea to the king, who agreed.

The project was initially financed by a tax on gambling. When the tax proved insufficient, Duverney supplied the difference. It was Duverney who had introduced Madame de Pompadour to the king in 1745—and who was said to have supplied Louis XV with far more than military supplies. The handsome young king, whom even the most circumspect of historians describe as "indolent and selfish," was, in fact, too indolent even to obtain his own mistresses. When his queen, the Polish princess Marie Leszczinska, whom her father, Stanislaw, called one of the two "dullest queens in Europe" (the other being his wife), decided that after two sons and eight daughters she had fulfilled her duty, Louis XV instructed servants to bring women to him. After Madame de Pompadour, his mistress for several years, became tired of having sex with the king, she found whores in the town of Versailles for him to sleep with.

Before Jeanne-Antoinette Poisson was given the Marquisate of Pompadour in Limousin (purchased for her with money lent by Duverney) and became the Marquise of Pompadour, Louis XV had her instructed on the rules of court etiquette and ritual—rules that had been evolving since the time of Henry III and that were meticulously observed during the reigns of Louis XIV and Louis XV—so that this bourgeois woman, of disreputable lineage, wouldn't embarrass him at court in Versailles. Only when her instruction was completed was she allowed out of bed and presented at court.

THE PANTHÉON
RER Line B to Luxembourg or Line 10 Métro
to Maubert-Mutualité

The Pantheon in Rome is a temple dedicated to the gods. I think one of the reasons I love France so much is that its people chose to dedicate *their* Panthéon to their great writers and other great men.

While the Station Maubert-Mutualité, on Line 10, is the closest Métro stop, it does involve walking up a rather steep hill to reach the Panthéon, but there are several outdoor cafés, where, if necessary, and I have always found it necessary, you can rest while enjoying a cup of coffee along the way. If you lose your way, just take the street that appears most vertical and it will lead you there. If you take RER Line B, you can avoid the hill, but you will have to walk several extra blocks.

Since Bob and I love to take books and read by the elegant reflecting pool in the nearby Luxembourg Gardens, we frequently walked from our apartment on the Quai de la Tournelle, through the student quarters, past the Panthéon, to the majestic gardens just beyond. As a consequence, the Panthéon, like so many unbelievably beautiful buildings and squares in Paris, has become so familiar a part of our walk that it is pretty much ignored by us—at least during the day. At night, however, as we eat our Berthillon ice cream, which we seem to do most evenings after dinner, at le Flore en Île, a café on the Île Saint-Louis near our apartment, we can see its white dome illuminated against the black sky, crowning a hill between the Sorbonne and the Luxembourg Gardens. It looks so spectacular at night that I always try to get a table by the window because I never get tired of looking at it. I am sure that anyone seeing it during the day for the first time would be overwhelmed by its beauty, as was French architect A. F. Peyre, who in 1806 wrote that "there is such harmony in every part of the interior and the relative proportions are so well designed that it would be impossible to add or subtract anything without destroying its charm and all the enjoyment procured by this ingenious design."

The Marquis of Marigny, Madame de Pompadour's brother, who was made Louis XV's superintendent of buildings at her request, selected Jacques-Germain Soufflot rather than Gabriel, his sister's favorite architect, to design what was originally to be a church, since Gabriel, a secularist, was not anxious to design a church. "The principal objective of Soufflot," according to Maximilien Brebion at the Royal Academy of Architecture, was "to incorporate the lightness of the Gothic style with the purity and magnificence of Greek architecture at its best."

The history of the construction of the Panthéon is not only fasci-

nating but a window that allows us to peek into the turbulent relationship between Church and State in the eighteenth century. If you take a
guided tour of the Panthéon, you will probably be told—incorrectly—
that the construction of this imposing building resulted from an incident
in Metz, where Louis XV, a very religious man, nearly died after hero-
ically fighting in the War of the Austrian Succession. Consequently, you
will be told, he made a pilgrimage to the Church of Sainte-Geneviève,
Paris's shrine to its patron saint, to thank God for his salvation. Finding
the shrine in as much need of salvation as he had been, he promised the
abbot there to make the needed repairs.

That was not, however, precisely what happened. Louis XV was, as
I have mentioned, lazy and indolent rather than heroic. He preferred
his activities to be in bed and not on a battlefield. In 1744, during the
Austrian War of Succession, however, when the French appeared to be
losing, Madame de Tencin, the politically powerful hostess of the most
influential salon in Paris, devised a plan to have Louis's mistress at that
time, Madame de Châteauroux, persuade him to lead the French forces
against the Austrians at Flanders. In a letter to a friend at court, she
wrote: "Not, between ourselves, that he is fit to command a company of
grenadiers; but his presence would do much; the people love their King
from habit; they will be enchanted to see him take this step—to which
he will have been incited. His troops will do their duty better; and the
generals will not dare openly to neglect theirs any longer."

Madame de Châteauroux, the former Marie-Anne de Nesle, whose
curves and charm had already succeeded in procuring a duchy from the
king that brought her an income of 85,000 francs a year, was happy to
play a role in French politics, and convinced Louis to get out of bed and
seek "glory" by going to war, which he reluctantly did. He left for battle,
accompanied by his mistress and her two sisters, whom he dropped
off in Metz. He continued on to the nearby army camp, where, after a
few days he became bored with army life and returned to his mistress
in Metz. He became seriously ill on August 8, 1744, and by August 12,
everyone had given up hope for his recovery. His mistress and her two
sisters were blamed for bringing the wrath of God upon their handsome king. An overly enthusiastic clergyman refused to administer last

rites until the dying king ordered his mistress's departure from Metz and from his life, which he did, out of fear of eternal damnation. The three women were almost killed during their carriage ride back to Paris by the mourning populace, who blamed them for their king's illness. Soon after their departure, a doctor finally arrived, and the king miraculously recovered. A Parisian poet gave Louis the name *le Bien Aimé* (Well-loved), which he was at that time since his people believed he had risked his life in battle for them. When news arrived in Paris that he was on the mend, all of Paris went wild with joy, one man kissing the horse of the courier who brought the news of his recovery. Louis was welcomed back to the city as a hero. Drawing back the curtain of his carriage window and peering out in astonishment at the cheering crowds, he asked, "What have I done to deserve this?"

Ten years passed between the time Louis returned from Metz and the time orders were given to construct Sainte-Genevieve. Madame de Châteauroux had been replaced by Madame de Pompadour, and the sobriquet *le Bien Aimé*, although still applied to Louis XV, was used derisively. The construction of Sainte-Geneviève seems to have been more an attempt by the king to restore his popularity by civic improvement than the fulfillment of a pious promise.

The project had all the right public-relations connotations—if we can apply modern concepts to the eighteenth century. St. Genevieve, to whom the church was dedicated, was a peasant who rallied the people of Paris in 451 to defend themselves—by praying—from Attila the Hun, who was marching their way, and she became the city's patron when Attila's forces turned before reaching Paris. A church honoring her and containing her relics had been built by Clovis, who an inaccurate legend states was converted to Christianity by St. Genevieve. (Clovis was converted to Christianity by St. Remi, Bishop of Reims, as you may recall from our trip to Reims, and was the first French king to ally himself with the Catholic Church. Louis is a derivative of his name.)

Louis XV's indolence resulted in an unfortunately rather long construction time. By the time the last stone was finally put in place in 1790, not only had Louis XV died, but the Revolution was well under way. The timing for its opening was therefore rather poor, since the

Revolution was violently anti-Catholic. St. Genevieve's relics, which had attracted pilgrims from the fifth century to the seventeenth, were at that moment joining other religious relics in being thrown into the Seine. The Marquis of Villette, at whose home* Voltaire was a frequent guest, made a novel suggestion of how to put this marvelous structure to use: "In the tradition of the Greeks and Romans, from whom we have received the maxims of liberty . . . let us have the courage not to dedicate this temple to a saint. Let it become the Pantheon of France! Let us install statues of our great men and lay their ashes to rest in its underground recesses."

The idea was accepted a year later, and the first body to be interred was Villette's friend Voltaire. On July 11, Voltaire's sarcophagus was transported to the Panthéon in a Roman chariot of "imperial proportions," on which, in addition to Voltaire's witticisms, were inscribed the words of Brutus: "Oh gods, give us death rather than slavery." The procession was led by a full orchestra, a calvary troop, workers who had dismantled the Bastille carrying balls and chains found in the prison, four actors carrying a golden statue of Voltaire, and a golden casket containing ninety-two volumes of Voltaire's writings. Considering the anti-Catholic nature of the procession, I thought it rather amusing that the cortege made its way to the Panthéon "in a series of 'stations' . . . stopping at the sites of Voltairean Triumphs," just as the religious processions of the past stopped at the stations of saints.

The remains of Mirabeau, the nobleman who tried and failed to create a constitutional monarchy, were also brought to the Panthéon in 1791, but the era was a time of violently changing ideologies in France, and when, two years later, Mirabeau's ideas of constitutional monarchy fell into disgrace, his remains were unceremoniously removed from the Panthéon. Marat's head (the rest of him was safely buried in Lyon) suffered the same fate of being interred and disinterred. The ephemeral nature of heroic status became apparent during the Reign of Terror, as numerous former heroes fell out of favor with the ruling party and had their interred remains removed; a rule was therefore instituted requiring

---

* This is the château where the last scene in *The Da Vinci Code* takes place.

that "patheonizations" could take place only after ten years had passed since "the death of the 'great man' in question."

The change from church to pantheon resulted in a number of alterations to the structure, including the removal of religious friezes, which were replaced with wonderful political friezes and the unfortunate elimination of forty-two windows in Soufflot's original design to successfully create an atmosphere more appropriate to a mausoleum for the "Dead Heroes of France." Consequently, the building, although a spectacular sight in the evening when viewed from the Le Flor en Île, no longer incorporates "the lightness of the Gothic style with the purity and magnificence of Greek architecture at its best," as it once did. The airy building with sunlight streaming in through open arches and windows that I saw in eighteenth- century paintings is now rather cold and forbidding.

During the nineteenth century, when the government in France changed from republic to empire, and then monarchy, and back to empire, the function of the Panthéon changed as well, twice becoming a church, until finally, after the funeral of Victor Hugo in 1885, it was consecrated permanently as a place where, as it is carved in large letters under the pediment at the entrance: A GRATEFUL FATHERLAND THANKS ITS GREAT MEN.

PLACE DE LA CONCORDE
Line 1, Line 8, or Line 12 Métro to Place de la Concorde

I am eternally grateful to Louis XV and Madame de Pompadour for the Place de la Concorde, or as it was briefly called, Place Louis XV. Facing what may be the most majestic octagonal square in the world, designed by Jacques-Ange Gabriel, is the Hôtel de Crillon, originally the home of the dukes of Crillon, which provided Bob and me with more afternoons of sheer pleasure than I could ever count. After an afternoon of walking around Paris, there was nothing more pleasant than sitting in the hotel's lavishly marbled salon, sipping tea while listening to the soothing music of a harp. As we rested on an elegant settee, nibbling tiny, ridiculously expensive sandwiches, I knew a place like this could only have been built at a time when there was a total disregard for cost, and I could understand at last the full meaning of Talleyrand's words "No one who did not live before 1789 knows the sweetness of life." (Unfortunately, in 2006, the management of the Crillon decided it no longer could afford a harpist, and I have decided that without a harpist, I could no longer afford, or wanted their tea. I sincerely hope they change their minds.)

Next to the Hôtel de Crillon, across the Rue Royale, is a building with an identical exterior, which is now the Naval Ministry. I was able to see the interior during the September weekend called Journées du Patrimoine, the one weekend each year when the public is allowed to enter its lavish Rococo interior, and was stunned by the working conditions the French government provides its naval bureaucracy. Originally used by Louis XV to store his royal furniture, many rooms, such as the Grand Gallery, still contain the furniture of the crown. While looking at furniture usually bores me, that was not the case with the furniture and paneling of these opulent rooms. The Grand Gallery, for example, is exquisite. Each piece of furniture, as well as each of the carvings on the walls, doors, and ceiling, is a work of art that delights the eye. Everything in the room has so obviously been made by artists and master craftsmen (who I have since learned, achieved the highest standard of work because their work would be confiscated if a piece of furniture or carved paneling didn't meet the required standard. Before a craftsman was allowed to create a piece of furniture, he was required by the guild to spend six years learning from a master craftsman how to do so. At the end of that six years, he showed his competence by producing a "master piece."

These standards, however, came to an end with the Revolution.

The planning of the Place de la Concorde began in 1748, when the aldermen of Paris, overjoyed at Louis XV's recovery at Metz, asked their beloved king for permission to commission a statue in his honor and for him to find an appropriate place to put it. Once the king assented, they quickly commissioned Edmé Bouchardon,[*] then con-

---

[*] You can see a fountain he created on the Rue de Grenelle.

sidered Paris's finest neoclassical sculptor. He worked for nine years on the statue but died shortly before it was completed. As he was dying in 1762, the statue already cast but not the pedestal, whose design included four female statues symbolizing Force, Prudence, Justice, and Peace, he contacted his lifelong rival, Jean-Baptiste Pigalle, and asked him to complete the work.

The planning of the square by the king also began in 1748, with the submission of plans by sixty architects and the subsequent selection of Gabriel to design it. For years, almost every guest at Versailles was shown Gabriel's plans for the elegant square bordered on one of the eight sides by two classical buildings (now the Crillon and Naval Ministry) with long colonnaded façades, and on another side by a dry moat and balustrade. Louis XV selected a site between the river, the Louvre, and the Champs Élysées.* Since it was the first square (if an octagon can be called a square) in Paris that was not enclosed on all sides, some art historians contend that Gabriel had been influenced by the naturalism of Rousseau when he "opened the square to the spectacle of nature" by leaving three sides open so as not to block off views of the Seine, the Tuileries Gardens, and the Champs-Élysées. That may be true, but it is just as likely that given Louis XV's lack of interest in anything other than sex and gardening, he probably just couldn't make up his mind what to put on the other sides to enclose it.

Years passed—fifteen of them—before the site was selected and made ready to receive the statue. During that time, Louis's father-in-law, Stanislaw, constantly lost patience with the king for his indolence and for his taking so long to select the plans, let alone start construction. At one time, he told his son-in-law that he had conceived of the idea of Place Stanislas in Nancy "in bed one night and by the next afternoon had twenty thousand workmen engaged on it."†

Stanislaw, who had been given Nancy when his daughter married the king, built his square there in three years, between 1752 and 1755.

---

* The crown owned most of this land, but the heirs of John Law owned a small part of the site.

† Nancy and Strasbourg have become wonderful day trips since the TGV was extended. The fabulous eighteenth-century Place Stanislas in Nancy and the Palais de Rohan in Strasbourg should be included on your trip through history.

It is a sublimely elegant square that perfectly captures a brief moment in history when France, in the process of losing her colonies and military power, had reached the height of her world influence in manners and art. The three-hour trip from Paris's Est station to Nancy has been reduced by half, but even that may be too long to justify traveling there to see the eighteenth century, since the Place de la Concorde, evoking approximately the same period, is so easily reached by the Métro.

Call it "being out of touch with the public" or a lack of public relations sense, but Louis XV chose the end of the disastrous Seven Years War in 1763, at which time France ceded to Great Britain most of its empire in North America as well as Senegal, the Grande Antilles, and India, to celebrate the opening of the "Place Louis XV." (Madame de Pompadour is blamed for the disastrous war, since she persuaded Louis to ally France with Austria, previously France's enemy.)

Gabriel's two marvelous buildings, now the Hôtel de Crillon and the Marine Ministry, survived the Revolution. The equestrian statue of Louis XV did not. It has been replaced by an obelisk. The statue had been commissioned by the Paris alderman to honor their "brave" king. But by the time the king completed the square, the affection Parisians had once had for him had totally disappeared. The pride they once had in his official mistress, that "one of their own should rise so high and occupy a place hitherto reserved for the nobility" was replaced with "pitiless hatred," as the king became more and more despised.

Even getting the statue to the square had turned out to be a fiasco when the cart carrying it repeatedly became stuck in mud. The Parisian crowds jeered: "They'll never get him past the Hôtel Pompadour" (now the Élysée Palace). Louis XV had purchased the hôtel for Madame de Pompadour in 1753, at which time she infuriated the Parisians when she tried to appropriate part of the adjoining Champs-Élysées for use as a vegetable garden. When the crowds saw the four female figures on the pedestal of the statue, they began to chant the names of each of the king's four mistresses: Vintimille, Mailly, Châteauroux, and Pompadour.

However, the *Gazette de France* reported that after the statue was put in place in the center of Place Louis XV, fireworks, "a sham battle on the Seine and the dancing in the streets, with free wine and meat, were enthusiastically attended." Two days later, a placard saying HERE, AS AT VERSAILLES, WITHOUT HEART AND WITHOUT COURAGE was attached to the statue.*

Before Place Louis XV became Place de la Concorde, it became La Place de la Revolution. On August 10, 1793, the statue of Louis XV was removed from its pedestal and replaced with François-Frédéric Lemot's statue of Liberty. The new statue was soon joined by the guillotine. And under the eyes of liberty, the heads of Louis XVI and Marie-Antoinette, Philip Égalité, Madame du Barry, Robespierre, Danton, and 1,341 other members of the *ancien régime* fell into baskets on the Place de la Concorde.

Royal and aristocratic blood have long since been washed away and replaced by lighting that bathes the monuments of the square in a warm, even light each night. The City of Paris has been experimenting with lighting its monuments and buildings since the fourteenth century, when Philip V "ordered candles to be lit in three sites every night." The city no longer uses candles or spotlights but by 2006 was spending $260,000 each night using concepts of lighting developed by François Jousse, who studied methods used by theatrical lighting experts and urban architects. While that seems an extravagant electric bill, I think the expense is well worth it.

We once rented an apartment nearby on the Avenue Gabriel, and I found it sheer delight to come home each evening after dinner and see the Place de la Concorde with its statues and fountains lit. After we lost that apartment, I once made Bob reserve a room at the Crillon for one night, although we couldn't really afford it, just so I could walk out after dinner and see the square. When I was told that Stanislas Square in Nancy, with its five palaces, was the most magnificent and grandiose square in France, I persuaded Bob to take the three-hour train ride to Nancy and spend the weekend there. We did indeed find it incredibly elegant, but it wasn't as beautiful or as elegant as the Place de la Concorde. I don't think anything compares with walking out of the Crillon,

---

* I was not sure if I correctly translated the last word in this eighteenth-century quote—*entrailles*. I translated it as "courage," but it could be "guts."

and seeing the fountains, the obelisk, the nineteenth-century statues representing cities of France (Strasbourg, Lille, Rouen, Brest, Nantes, Bordeaux, Marseille, and Lyon).

The wonder of the experience is magnified because the scene is not enclosed, and not confined to the Place de la Concorde. The open vistas make it for me the heart of the Paris I love and one of the true wonders of the world. From the Place de la Concorde, your eyes can wander down the entire length of the Champs-Élysées to the Étoile and see the Arc de Triomphe bathed in light, or turn to the north and see the Madeleine, or east to the Tuileries and the Louvre. But it is looking south that I find most thrilling, across the bridge, across the Seine, to the Assemblée Nationale, to the gold-domed Invalides beyond, and then, to the right, the Eiffel Tower, which sparkles every evening hour for ten minutes like a giant diamond clock pinned on the black velvet night.

CHAPTER 20

The PETIT TRIANON of
MADAME DE POMPADOUR and MARIE-ANTOINETTE

—

RER Line C from Invalides to
Versailles–Rive Gauche

THE WORK OF JACQUES-ANGE GABRIEL, MADAME DE POMPADOUR'S favorite architect, was influenced by recent archaeological discoveries of Greek temples, and marked the end of the sumptuous Rococo style and the beginning of a style noted for its noble simplicity and classical proportions. Gabriel designed the Petit Trianon at Versailles, which is considered his finest work, although I personally prefer the Place de la Concorde. The Petit Trianon, completed in 1768, evokes not only the world of a king's mistress, Madame de Pompadour, but also that of Queen Marie-Antoinette.

One of the problems of getting to Versailles is that it is much too easy. If you decide, as most people who come to France do, to make the trip there* and then find yourself as discouraged as I have been with the crowds at the fabulous palace itself, you might want to spend your time visiting this perfect eighteenth-century neoclassical gem. If you walk to the rear of the palace, you will find a tiny train that will transport you through the gardens to the Petit Trianon. If the lines for the train are

---

* Take RER Line C from the Invalides station to Versailles–Rive Gauche; SNCF rail from either the Gare Montparnasse to Versailles-Chantiers or from Gare Saint-Lazare to Versailles–Rive Droite. The trip from Paris to Versailles takes between twenty and thirty-five minutes.

too long, it is a very pleasant one-mile walk. I know this because the last time I went to Versailles with Bob, we were confronted with a seemingly endless line of tourists that neither of us had any desire to join. I suggested a walk in the gardens so the trip wouldn't be a total waste. We then began a very enjoyable walk through the gardens, which were large enough to accommodate Louis's entire court then, and can handle any number of visitors today without overcrowding. When we came to the beginning of the Grand Canal, we took a path angling off to the right and soon arrived at what had once been the village of Trianon, before Louis XIV added the area to his garden. We didn't bother visiting the Grand Trianon—first called the "Porcelain Trianon," where Louis XIV and his mistress Madame de Montespan spent amorous afternoons, and which became the "Marble Trianon" after Louis's secret marriage to the pious Madame de Maintenon, who replaced the porcelain with marble when the palace was overrun with lizards.

The Petit Trianon was created at the request of Louis XV's mistress Madame de Pompadour, whom Will Durant describes as "one of the most remarkable women in history, dowered with such beauty and grace as blinded most men to her sins, and yet with such powers of mind that for a brilliant decade she governed France, protected Voltaire, saved Diderot's *Encyclopédie,* and led the *philosophes* to claim her as one of their own." Practically every contemporary memoir comments on the exquisite taste with which she remodeled each of the seventeen estates, including the Élysée Palace, which Louis XV gave her. While most of these palaces were destroyed during the Revolution or are now closed to the public, her elegant taste and style can still be seen at the Petit Trianon.

She and her brother (whom Louis XV made Marquis of Marigny and superintendent of buildings at her request) oversaw Gabriel's construction of this tiny pavilion. Its purpose was to provide Louis with a private place near his botanical garden. It was apparently difficult to interest Louis in anything, but he did like scientific gardening, and Madame de Pompadour, who disliked sex, was always trying to find other ways to amuse him. To this end, she produced 122 plays in which she played the leading role, had a hothouse built for his plants, and constructed this tiny palace near his garden. She requested that fleet commanders of the

Royal Navy bring back exotic plants from France's colonial empire—an empire whose loss is blamed by some historians on her lack of diplomatic skills. She created a kitchen garden, the Potager du Roy (also the name of the delightful restaurant at which we had eaten in Versailles) where her king, who she knew loved eating strawberries while sipping champagne, could watch France's first strawberries grow.

The Petit Trianon was designed with large French doors that opened onto a porch overlooking the king's garden. Mascarons above the doors were carved to represent the seasons, while carved groups of happy children and vases filled with flowers decorate the balustrade on the roof. Each of the four façades is slightly different, but the design of the tiny palace is considered totally elegant and harmonious. Inside, a charming frieze of ducks, pigeons, swans, and chickens circles beneath the ceiling of the main salon, seemingly supported by Corinthian pilasters now painted white and gold.

Madame de Pompadour died in 1764, four years before the Petit Trianon was finished, and the interior evokes not the king's mistress, but the taste and style of the young Queen of France—Marie-Antoinette. Louis XVI gave what he called a "pretty cube of stone" to his young wife when he became king. And she loved her gift. The Petit Trianon's small size is indicative of Marie-Antoinette's desire for a simple and more intimate atmosphere than she found at the Palace of Versailles.

Marie-Antoinette arrived in France from Vienna in 1770 at the age of fifteen and was only nineteen when she became queen. Although she was said to be intelligent, her mother, the Austrian Empress Maria Theresa, had totally neglected her education. She "had no taste for serious reading" when she arrived in France during its most literate century. While she refurnished the tiny palace with outlandish luxury, including blue leather-bound books, the books were for decoration and never read. Although she would be accused of building a "pleasure house" plastered in "gold and diamonds," the Petit Trianon was her personal retreat where she hung portraits in her bedroom of her father and a favorite aunt, both painted in religious attire.

Marie-Antoinette replaced the scientific garden of Louis XV with an English garden. She had the straight paths, as well as the classical and geometric designs of Le Nôtre changed into curves around her toy palace. She added grottoes and created lakes fed by winding streams. She had rustic thatched-roof cottages built around the lake, and called the area the Queen's Hamlet. She wanted the Petit Trianon to appear to be in the countryside and not at Versailles, which she hated. Before any work was started on the gardens, fourteen models—complete with trees and grass—were made for her before she was satisfied with the design. One guide states that she wanted the area to "express the Rousseauistic feeling of the return to nature." Marie-Antoinette was said to have read Rousseau, and perhaps this was its actual purpose. Unfortunate rumors were spread by the Duke of Orléans throughout Paris that the queen dressed herself as an "Arcadian milkmaid," tending cows and goats "bedecked with ribbons," but in actuality, the area was run by a farmer, who sent the produce raised at Trianon to the palace kitchens.

Marie-Antoinette loved playing billiards, cards, and backgammon at the Petit Trianon, which she filled with delicate tables. She covered the windows with festooned drapes. She was a child and enjoyed playing childish games, like blind man's bluff, on the lawn. The tiny palace was a small, intimate place, where she did away with the ceremony created during former reigns, which she detested and found "tedious in the extreme." It was only here she felt she could be herself. But its intimacy, the very reason she liked it, was detrimental to the monarchy. It could accommodate only a few members of court. Louis XIV had brought the unruly aristocracy, who in every century had been too willing to revolt against the king, to Versailles and had tamed them by giving them meaningless tasks and rituals to perform there. He had filled their evenings with lavish entertainments that made Versailles the social center of France. During his reign it was social death and boredom to be exiled from Versailles. During the reign of Louis XV, the rituals established by Louis XIV were continued, but he also created private rooms at the palace where he enjoyed a second secret life with his mistresses and favorites. (These rooms can be seen on a guided tour without standing in line, but they lack the magnificence of the State Rooms that draw the crushing crowds.)

As court ritual during the regency of Louis XV became less important in the eyes of the monarchy, the aristocracy felt less and less reason to remain at Versailles, and those who had not returned to Paris during the regency returned to their country estates during the reigns of Louis XV and XVI. By the time of Louis XVI, some noblemen began to avoid it. Since the king and queen saw "persons furnished with proper introductions" only on Sundays, and then for just "a few minutes," the aristocracy soon decided "that it was a waste of time to make a long journey simply to be received ungraciously . . . they preferred to stay at home."

According to Talleyrand, Marie-Antoinette created her most vicious enemy—the Duke of Orléans—by not inviting him to the little dinners she held at the Petit Trianon. According to Talleyrand's memoirs:

> The Duke of Orléans saw himself each day farther removed from that familiar society of which the queen had given the first example to the court of France, and of which Little Trianon was the ordinary rendezvous. . . . At the gates of this charming retreat, the queen felt that she could lay aside the chains of her grandeur. Queen at Versailles . . . at Trianon, she wished to be there only the most amiable of women and to know only the sweetness of intimacy. Seeing that no one had absolutely a right to the favour of being admitted to these little excursions, it was only the more desirable, and the more calculated to excite the desire of being invited. The Duke of Orléans could not conceal his envy, even under the cloak of indifference. At one of these fetes, he planned with some ladies of the court as little in favour as he was, the means of mingling with the people admitted to look at the illuminations; and, having thus penetrated into the garden, he avenged himself, for not having been invited, by such loud jeering and noisy gaiety that the queen was informed of it, and keenly hurt. These little fits of animosity had so irritated the Duke of Orléans that it was not difficult to lead him on to more serious measures of opposition.

In a roundabout way, the exclusivity of the parties held at the Petit Trianon led to one of the most damaging incidents in Marie-Antoinette's life, an incident that was publicized and distorted in newsletters edited by the Duke of Orléans and his presses at the Palais-Royal.

Cardinal Louis de Rohan, the illegitimate son of the Princess of Soubise and Louis XIV, dreamed of being first minister to the king, as Richelieu had been. His first diplomatic experience was a disaster, when, as ambassador to Vienna, his behavior as a "womanizing fop" resulted in the Empress Maria Theresa's request that he be recalled immediately. When he returned to France, he infuriated the queen by appearing uninvited at one of her private little parties at the Petit Trianon. In his attempt to get back in favor with the king and queen, he became embroiled in what has become known as the Diamond Necklace Affair in the 1780s. The necklace, which Simon Schama calls a "dinosaur of rococo jewelry" had been made at Louis XV's request for Madame du Barry, who became royal mistress when Madame de Pompadour died, but the king died before it was purchased. The jeweler who had laid out the money for it but who had not been paid, tried to sell it to Marie-Antoinette, whom he knew loved diamonds. She refused, however, either because she found Madame du Barry's taste overly ornate and the necklace vulgar or because she had taken to heart her mother's reprimand after her recent purchases of a diamond necklace (369,000 livres), chandelier earrings (30,000 livres), and a diamond bracelet (250,000 livres). The Empress of Austria, hearing of those purchases, had written her daughter: "A Queen can only degrade herself by such impossible behavior and degrades herself even more by this sort of heedless extravagance, especially in difficult times. I know only too well what expensive tastes you have. . . . I hope I shall not live to see the disaster which is all too likely to occur."

When Marie Antoinette refused to purchase Madame du Barry's necklace, the jeweler publicly threatened suicide. Then two swindlers, a Madame de Motte-Valois and her husband, hearing about the necklace, devised an elaborate plan to steal the diamonds, which almost succeeded. They convinced the credulous Cardinal Rohan that the queen really wanted the necklace but did not want the king to know she was buying it, and that the cardinal could make his way back into her good graces by secretly arranging for her to buy it. The cardinal, after making arrangements with the jeweler to pay for the necklace in installments, which the cardinal thought the jeweler would receive secretly from the queen, took the necklace and handed it over to the swindlers, expecting they would deliver it to the queen. Instead, they sold it, diamond by diamond. The details of this delicious but involved plot, which can be found in all biographies of Marie-Antoinette, as well as in Simon Schama's book *Citizens*, and which should have been part of the plotless, boring movie *Marie Antoinette*, include a fake royal authorization for the purchase of the necklace and a cloak-and-dagger meeting in the gardens at Versailles, where, in order to convince the cardinal that the queen would secretly pay for the necklace, a blond milliner impersonating Marie-Antoinette and dressed in the queen's favorite white muslin gown, met the cardinal in the dead of night—so he couldn't see her face—and signaled him by pressing a red rose into his hand and saying, "You know what this means." Since the jeweler did not receive the payments for the necklace promised by Cardinal Rohan, he complained to the queen.

Marie-Antoinette, unaware of the role played by the two swindlers, thought the cardinal had stolen the necklace and had him arrested for the theft. The ensuing trial proved the innocence of both the queen and the cardinal and the guilt of Madame de Motte-Valois and her husband. The swindlers were caught and Madame de Motte-Valois was branded (not on her arm, as thieves were usually branded, but on her breast, by accident, as she twisted to get free). The true story of the diamond necklace, however, never reached the public. The Duke of Orléans, still smarting from social snubs, spread rumors, which were printed in "news sheets" at the Palais-Royal, which the public trusted more than the official, censored newspapers. The public was told that Marie-Antoinette was "a spendthrift and vindictive slut who would stop at nothing to satisfy her appetites." The arrest of the cardinal was twisted into a story in which the cardinal, a simpleton, had rejected the advances of a lascivious queen, who had purchased the extravagant diamond necklace at a time when peasants of France were starving.

After the trial ended, it was rumored that she had decorated the walls of the Petit Trianon with diamonds.

—

ON OCTOBER 5, 1789, Marie-Antoinette and Louis XVI were forced by an angry mob to leave Versailles. Accompanied by the entire court and the National Constituent Assembly, they were led to the Tuileries Palace—which no longer exists. On August 1, 1793, Marie-Antoinette was taken to the Conciergerie, where we will go next.

CHAPTER 21

THE CONCIERGERIE

—

Line 4 Métro to La Cité

URING THE FIRST TWENTY YEARS OR SO OF MY VISITS TO
Paris, I had avoided visiting the Conciergerie on the Île-de-la-Cité.
Since I had gone to great trouble to find medieval buildings in Paris,
and even more trouble to visit similar buildings all over France—
such as the barrel-vaulted Salle des États-Généraux at the Château of
Blois, where a French medieval parliament intermittently met, and the
eleventh-century Great Hall in Poitiers, where Eleanor of Aquitaine's
grandfather, William the Troubadour, meted out justice to his vassals—
it was a bit peculiar that I didn't want to see the interior of the medieval
structure where the Capetian kings of France held court for more than
four hundred years.

It certainly looks inviting enough. Seen from the Right Bank, or
from a *bateau mouche*, the four ancient turrets, topped by conical roofs,
create a romantic, picturesque silhouette on the Île-de-la-Cité. But I
never had the faintest interest in going inside. The oldest tower, which
is fatter than the others, and has a crenellated walkway below its slated,
restored roof, dates from the time of St. Louis. Perhaps the problem was
my knowledge that this romantic-looking tower was where people in
the thirteenth century were tortured until they confessed or talked. It
was given the name of Bonbec Tower by someone with a decidedly dark
sense of humor, since "bon bec" means gift of gab.

As I arrived at the end of the eighteenth century, however, I had to face the fact that, despite my abhorrence of war of any kind, I clearly could not, on my journey through French history, ignore the French Revolution. I therefore decided to take a guided tour of the Conciergerie and learn if its interior evoked that horrible interlude when so much of what I would have loved to have seen was destroyed.

Approaching the Conciergerie from the Right Bank, on the Boulevard du Palais, I was confronted with a fourteenth-century rectangular tower whose façade is adorned with a magnificent Renaissance clock, the first public clock in Paris. Below two angels holding up Henry III and Catherine de Médicis's coat of arms is written THIS WILL GIVE A THIRD CROWN TO HE WHO HAS ALREADY BEEN GIVEN TWO, which means that God will give a crown in heaven to King Henry III (Catherine de Médicis's transvestite son), who was King of Poland before becoming King of France in 1574. On either side of the clock are the allegorical figures of Law and Justice—the Conciergerie was the court of law at the time the clock was placed there in 1585, while beneath Law and Justice is written THIS MACHINE, WHICH DIVIDED THE HOURS INTO TWICE SIX, EXHORTS US TO OBSERVE JUSTICE AND TO SERVE THE LAW.

The Salle des Gardes, which has survived from the thirteenth century when the concierge, or royal governor in charge of the palace, resided here, is the largest surviving medieval hall in France. This immense vaulted Gothic hall was where the Capetian kings for centuries meted out medieval justice during the day and food at night, when it was turned into a banquet hall that accommodated as many as 1,000 guests. It is, once again, used as a catering hall, rented for galas whose guests are hopefully unaware of its macabre past as they enjoy their dinner. A chill went through me the first time I entered this "vast antechamber of death," as it was known when it was used to cram together prisoners about to be guillotined during the Reign of Terror. Count Beugnot, imprisoned here in 1793, wrote, "I know nothing so cruel as to wake up in a prison cell, in a place where the most horrible dream is less horrible than reality." By the time I returned, years later, the addition of audiovisual displays and wax-museum rooms produced a numbing effect of a totally different kind.

While I usually find French tours entertaining, my first tour of the

Conciergerie was not one of those times. In fact, I was not quite sure whether it was a plus or a minus to understand what my guide was saying. (Tours are given in English, but not as often as in French.) It is, however, no longer necessary to have a guide, since the Conciergerie is filled with audiovisual displays, including a film in both English and French, that take you through the French Revolution as you walk through its rooms. While I didn't find any of my visits to the Conciergerie what I would call enjoyable, I wish I had taken them before my first college European history course so that the twists and turns of the French Revolution that made my eyes glaze over would have been easier for me to understand and perhaps more interesting. I have always had a lot of trouble staying awake when reading about war and destruction.

The guide on my first tour tended toward the gory. He dwelled upon as many bloody details as he could muster, including a vivid description of rats nibbling at the feet of decapitated prisoners, which I thought was totally unnecessary since the decapitated prisoners were no longer at the Conciergerie.

Our guide went to some length explaining that decapitation was really a humane form of punishment—how quick, how painless, it was. He told us that only six to eight seconds elapsed from the time the prisoner left the wagon and his head fell into a basket. Competitions were held between executioners to see who could do it the quickest, one executioner holding the astounding record of 186 in one day. So many people were killed that bodies weren't buried, just placed in heaps.

He explained it was considered a privilege to be decapitated, a punishment reserved for the nobility, since no hands touched the victim. Although reading vividly detailed descriptions of Joan of Arc being burned at the stake and of Henry IV's assassin being drawn and quartered had made me aware that decapitation was indeed preferable to other forms of medieval executions, my guide failed to convince me of the humanitarian virtues of the guillotine. I am afraid he lost his argument with me completely when he offered our group a step-by-step description of the process: of a person first placing his head on the block, then having it chopped off, and then being able to look back at its body since the head was still living for a brief time after decapitation.

Our guide further weakened his argument when he pointed out that the guillotine wasn't always effective on the first try, giving an example of how a blade became stuck twice in one gentleman's neck before he finally died. The executioners then grabbed the bloody head by its hair and held it up for the crowd to see, since the mob's view might have been blocked by the two hundred or so guards who surrounded the prisoners.

As he led us through the Conciergerie, he brought us to a room he said was where Marie-Antoinette was brought in August 1793, dressed in black and accompanied only by her little pug dog. Like our tour group, she would have passed the sixty cells, each crammed with 15 to 20 prisoners, before she reached this tiny prison cell. This may or may not have been the cell in which she actually stayed from August until her execution on October 16. That room was 12 feet by 12 feet and half below the ground, and since it was near the Seine, moisture formed on the bare stone walls. The queen was provided with a bed, a table, two cane armchairs, and a washbowl. A screen provided her with the only privacy from the two guards, who watched her day and night and regularly brought her white flowers. (All of this need not be imagined since it has been re-created wax-museum–style.) Until the concierge's wife brought her two books, neither of which may have been on her list of favorite books, *Captain Cook's Travels* and *A History of Famous Shipwrecks*, her only distractions from boredom were her dog, the back-gammon or card game played by the guards outside her cell, and the two meals she was brought each day. A woman also came each day to do her hair, which, although she was only thirty-six, had overnight turned completely white. She has been described as spending her months in this cell, just sitting in her chair twisting her watch. At night she could lay awake listening to the public clock chime the hours, or the sobs of other prisoners. An attempt was made to free the queen, which Dumas has romanticized in *Le Chevalier de la Maison-Rouge*, which is almost as exciting reading as *The Three Musketeers* but far too depressing to be as popular. There was no way Dumas could alter the queen's fate, but the book does re-create the atmosphere of the Revolution, although not as well as Dickens's *Tale of Two Cities*.

While the Conciergerie is an excellent place to imagine the monarchy dissolving into a caldron of chaos during the Revolution, I'm not sure that either the Revolution or the Terror are places to visit while on vacation. Bob certainly didn't think it was. Although he had accompanied me on practically all of my trips, he refused to come on the Conciergerie tour, saying he would rather go back to our apartment on the Quai de la Tournelle and read a novel.

From a tourist's point of view, my point of view, the Revolution is the missing heads of statues once lining the façades of Notre-Dame de Paris and Reims, burned reliquaries and broken shards of glass that once were stained-glass windows. It is the looted castles of the aristocracy and their missing furniture, and all the things we can no longer see. The Conciergerie is informative, but too depressing to waste a day of one's vacation. Like all war, it is watching humanity step backward in time. By the time I left the Conciergerie, I had had quite enough of the ideologue's interpretation of "Equalité, Fraternité, Liberté" and the guillotine, and was quite ready for Napoleon, as were the French, after their seven years of Revolution.

PART FIVE

The Empire and Restoration

THE BOURGEOIS CENTURY

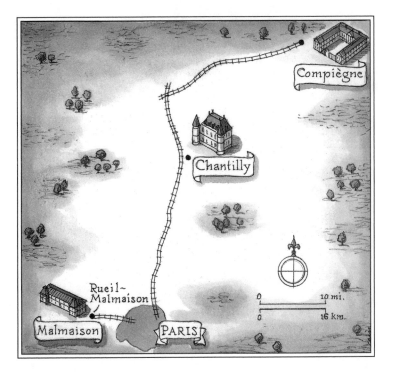

CHAPTER 22

NAPOLEON as CONSUL at MALMAISON

—

RER Line A1 to Rueil-Malmaison

Malmaison is the country estate where Napoleon and Josephine lived during the Consulate, when they were young and in love, while Fontainebleau and Compiègne are two of the palaces where Napoleon lived after he crowned himself emperor. When I first visited Malmaison, I felt it evoked the republican façade Napoleon created to gain and retain his position as first consul, while the palaces of Fontainebleau and Compiègne evoke the Napoleon that Napoleon really wanted to be—the emperor. The Consulate was the remarkable period (1799–1804) following the Revolution in which the young Napoleon not only brought to an end the horrors of the Reign of Terror and the incompetence and corruption of the Directory, but also passed the Code Napoléon, which guaranteed every French citizen an education, equality before the law, and freedom of religion, as well as opening all careers to talent and transforming palaces, including the Louvre, into museums for the people. Though it may have been Napoleon's most glorious period, it was not so glorious with respect to his accommodations.

During the Consulate, Napoleon would travel to his country estate at Malmaison at the end of each ten-day week in Paris (during the Revolution the seven-day week had been changed to a ten-day week called the *decadi*) and spend three or four days there. Tourists can visit this brief period in French history at Malmaison, where rooms are almost as they were then, though some furniture and decorations from the period when he was emperor have been added. At Malmaison, I can visualize the daily life of a very young and human Napoleon, while at the dazzling palaces of Fontainebleau and Compiègne I can see only the image Napoleon wanted people to see. At Malmaison you can almost see Napoleon and Josephine walking hand in hand in the garden, or visualize Napoleon cheating at childish games and cards.

I should warn you, however, that when I have spent an inordinate amount of time trying to find an easy way of reaching a place by train, I am tempted to exaggerate its glories. Malmaison may be such a place. While Bob and I have thoroughly enjoyed *some* of our visits to both châteaux at Malmaison—the one in which Napoleon and Josephine lived, and the nearby Château de Bois-Préau, which Josephine added to the property after Napoleon divorced her, and which is now a historically fascinating Napoleonic museum—and while I feel that a visit here provides a revealing insight into Napoleon's personality, that there is something quite wonderful about its intimacy, I believe the glorious palaces of Fontainebleau and Compiègne are where Napoleon would have wanted you to visit his life. Napoleon left the Consulate as quickly as possible to become emperor, quickly reviving, as he left, "the etiquette of the old monarchy." When I learned that Josephine had purchased Malmaison for her lover, Captain Hippolyte Charles, while Napoleon was off campaigning in Egypt, and that when Napoleon learned Josephine had purchased it for 400,000 francs, he passed a law "forbidding married women from buying property without their husband's consent," I decided to leave the Consulate and Malmaison as quickly as he did, and visit his empire at Compiègne.

CHAPTER 23

NAPOLEON at COMPIÈGNE

—

Train from Gare du Nord to Compiègne

*L*OUIS XIV SAID COMPIÈGNE MADE HIM FEEL LIKE A PEASANT and Versailles like a king, but personally, my trip to the château at Versailles made me feel like a sardine, while my trip to Compiègne, from beginning to end, made me feel like a pampered time traveler speeding through the centuries.

There are very good reasons why I like Compiègne and the Sun King did not. First, it is so easy to reach by train. The main-line train trip from the Gare de Nord is only forty minutes and leaves you quite close to the château. Second, and I'm sure most important, the château you visit today is not the dreary, comfortless fourteenth-century fortress where Louis XIV and his mother stayed during the summer hunting season, and which he so disliked. That château, built by Charles V, is gone. It was replaced, in the eighteenth century, by the Sun King's great-grandson Louis XV, who fell in love with Compiègne's game-filled forests when he was eighteen, and, as soon as he became king, ordered his architect, Jacques-Ange Gabriel, to make the 1,300-room hunting lodge more comfortable for him and Madame de Pompadour.

Gabriel, who designed the Place de la Concorde, the École Militaire, the Musée Rodin, and the Petit Trianon at Versailles, died before Compiègne's renovation and reconstruction was completed. It was not Gabriel's fault that the renovation took thirty-seven years—from 1751 to 1788—to complete. Since Louis XV did not want to be disturbed by construction while he was hunting there, Gabriel had to remove the medieval fortress and erect a modern one on its foundations while the king was not in residence, and Louis XV, accompanied of course by his vast entourage, was in residence—sometimes for months at a stretch— no fewer than thirty-three times. Eventually, a few years before Louis XVI lost his head, a restrained neoclassical château was completed on the foundations of Charles V's medieval fortress, which, in turn had been built on foundations of a ninth-century castle. Napoleon would be the ultimate beneficiary of Louis XV's expenditures, Madame de Pompadour's good taste, and Gabriel's design.

The best view of the château is from the garden, where you can step back and admire its beauty. So many American government buildings have copied this neoclassical style that its design has become almost a cliché, and it is hard to appreciate just how lovely and harmonious it is and how splendid it must have seemed when first built. By an ingenious device, Gabriel kept the castle a uniform height throughout, even though he added an additional floor on the garden side. The result is a château as grand as Versailles, and an interior as luxurious and sumptuous as any palace in France.

None of the luxurious furniture chosen for the king and his mistress made it through the Revolution. The Jacobins, in need of money, held month-long auctions, during which all the furniture and art objects were sold. That, however, does not affect today's tourist, since Napoleon I, finding the château empty, had neoclassical architects Percier and Fontaine refurnish and restore it more luxuriously than Louis XV and Madame de Pompadour once had. Believing Compiègne to be his most impressive and palatial castle, Napoleon chose it to receive Marie-Louise, the Austrian archduchess he married after his divorce from Josephine. She would bring Napoleon about as much luck as her great aunt Marie-Antoinette had brought Louis XVI.

Preparations to receive his new bride began well in advance of their betrothal. In fact, they began in September 1807, long before he had either divorced Josephine or even selected the princess he would marry. Renovations commenced roughly the moment Marie Waleska, the Polish countess with whom he was having an affair, informed Napoleon that he was not sterile. Upon learning he could found a dynasty, he simultaneously began preparations to divorce Josephine and to marry some young royal princess. The gardens were planted in 1807. Napoleon's gardener, Louis Berthault, because of problems with the terrain, tried to combine the symmetry of the formal French garden with the natural look of the English garden, but Napoleon did not like the result. As he walked in the gardens at Compiègne in 1809, he told Berthault that his landscaping evoked his "conceptual indecisiveness" and ordered him to create a completely natural-looking garden leading to the forest.

After defeating Austria, Napoleon spent time at Schönbrunn, the imperial palace outside Vienna, where he traveled back and forth on a road shaded by arched boughs of ancient trees. Whether it was to make his new bride feel more at home, or because he simply found the arched trees impressive, he ordered his gardener to create a similar arched pathway leading from the château terrace at Compiègne to the forest. When I stood on the terrace looking toward the forest of Compiègne, I could see the Allée Napoléon, which dramatically appears to extend forever as it makes its way from the château through the forest to the horizon and beyond. It is quite an impressive vista, as I am sure Napoleon intended.

Napoleon not only wanted to impress his new bride; he wanted her to be comfortable as well. Since they would be spending the hot summer months at Compiègne, he told his gardener to plant trees to shade the rooms Marie-Louise would occupy. His thoughtfulness also included ordering the construction of three pavilions along a covered path from the château to the forest, so that when Marie-Louise walked there she would have a place to rest if she became tired. One of these delightful pavilions still exists and can be seen in the garden today.

While Napoleon was considerate of Marie-Louise's comfort and happiness, making sure her dog and her parrot (who called her by her name) arrived safely in France, he was not particularly considerate of his courtiers. In fact, imperial life at Compiègne, for everyone other than Napoleon, seems to have been a bore. Waiting for the guide to conduct us through the castle is nothing compared to what courtiers had to endure as they waited for Napoleon and his bride to arrive on March 15,

1810. According to the Prince of Clary, who was visiting Compiègne on that day, a reception and sumptuous banquet that had been prepared to greet the new empress did not take place, since Napoleon, who was as impatient in love as he was in dining, not only raced out to meet her on the road before she ever got to the castle, but, ignoring the lavish reception that had been prepared to welcome them, whisked her quickly past the waiting courtiers and "in true Corsican style bedded her" as soon as they arrived at Compiègne. According to the Prince of Clary:

> When they finally arrived, they were preceded by marshals, generals, equerries, chamberlains, pages. . . . When the empress arrived, she jumped quite nimbly from her coach, promptly embraced the whole family, and mounted the staircase on Napoleon's arm. . . . Everyone thought her very well looking, very tall, much better than they expected. As she has the advantage of Him by half a head, she did look quite striking. We lined up on each side, and the family disappeared into the private apartments. . . . After that we cooled our heels, and heaven knows it was tedious! it was, I think half-past twelve or one in the morning when our ladies were informed they might go to bed, and they did not have to be told twice.

DINNER WITH THE new empress would prove to be almost as tedious as it had been waiting for her arrival. Unlike Josephine, she was totally lacking in wit and charm. One dinner companion complained that her single contribution to their conversation was to ask, "And how many children do you have, Madame?"

During the Empire, just as during the reigns of the last Bourbon kings, Napoleon had his *grand* and *petit lever* and *coucher*, attended by courtiers specially selected for the honor. And, just as during the monarchy, the main amusement for the guests at Compiègne was a day spent hunting. However, there was a difference between hunting with the lethargic Louis XV and hunting with the hyperactive Napoleon. It was not only sex and eating, but also hunting, that was done quickly. The Prince of Clary, describing a hunt in which he participated, tells us that "the Emperor is off like a flash" and "takes a fresh horse" so that "one has no chance of keeping up" and once the stag is killed, the party returns to Compiègne "at full gallop."

On our last visit to Compiègne, Bob and I took the tour of the castle, and I suggest that you do the same so you can see the rooms in which Napoleon and Marie-Louise lived and entertained, as well as those in which the emperor's nephew Louis Napoleon would live forty-eight years later during the Second Empire (1852–1870). A guided tour is the only way you can see these rooms and should be taken even if only the French-speaking tour fits into your schedule. (You will be given a printed English translation of the tour guide's description.) The guide's jokes are not included, so you do feel a little left out when all the French tourists start laughing. After my French improved enough so that I could understand spoken French—which took more years than I care to admit—I learned that the jokes were not particularly funny and that I had not missed all that much.

Our tour of Compiègne could not have been more pleasant. I asked the guide to speak slowly as I couldn't understand her high-speed French, and she was very accommodating, pausing to repeat in English little items like "this is a chair for pregnant women" or showing me how the top of Napoleon's desk slid away so that he could slide his papers back into a secret drawer no one knew was there. It was quite ingenious. I would love such a desk, just to hide the mess I make. Bob has no need of such a device since his desk is always neat.

The castle, she explained, had belonged to the Kings of France since the time of the Merovingians (the dynasty of Frankish kings who ruled the area from the fifth to the seventh centuries), who had always spent their summers hunting in Compiègne's 35,000-acre forest, after which they decamped to Fontainebleau for an autumn of hunting at the 62,000-acre forest there. The River Oise, which runs through the town and connects with the Seine, made travel easy between Compiègne and either Paris or the sea. Consequently, practically all the people we have encountered on our journey through France's history—from seventh-century King Dagobert (the first king to be buried at Saint-Denis) to Napoleon—stayed here.

The foundations of this castle date back to the time Charlemagne divided his empire among his three grandsons in 840. Charles the Bald—the grandson who received the western part of the empire, which of course is now France—disappointed at not having received Charlemagne's capital city of Aix-la Chapelle (Aachen), duplicated Charlemagne's castle and cathedral there at Compiègne. In the fourteenth century, Charles V built a modern fortress and church on those foundations: these buildings were larger than, but otherwise similar to, the castle and chapel we visited at Vincennes, the castle that Louis XIV detested.

After Napoleon was sent into exile, the kings of the Restoration loved Compiègne because its 1,300 rooms could accommodate 500 guests, making it a great place for royal house parties. (Guest quarters included a bedroom and at least one outer room for the guest's servants.)

Louis Napoleon, referred to disparagingly as the Bourgeois Emperor, liking Compiègne more than any of his other châteaux, made it the center of the Second Empire, and consequently it has become the place French curators of the regional museums send most of the furniture and art created between the years 1852 and 1870. The result is the Museum of the Second Empire. The last time I visited Compiègne, it was necessary to call, or have the concierge at your hotel call, a day in advance, to arrange to visit the museum.

Although Compiègne could accommodate 500 guests, Napoleon III found the château inadequate for as many guests as he wanted to invite, so he instructed his architect, Eugène Viollet-le-Duc, to renovate nearby Pierrefonds, a medieval fortress that had been built by the dashing Louis d'Orléans, whom we met at Blois in the fourteenth century. Pierrefonds was a total ruin when Napoleon I bought it for 3,000 francs. Viollet-le-Duc did not so much restore as re-create the ruins into a fairy-tale Gothic castle—into what nineteenth-century Romantics wanted a medieval castle to be. Pierrefonds looks fantastic from the road, but once I was inside, I felt as though I were walking through a Walt Disney set rather than a medieval fortress. I think I may have become overly annoyed at the restorer when, walking down a hall in the castle, I came across an alcove in which a shrine had been erected, such as one might expect a pagan to erect to worship his gods, but which Viollet-le-Duc had built in honor of himself, so that tourists or visitors to the castle would be reminded that it was he, Viollet-le-Duc, who was the creator of this place.

The bus to Pierrefonds leaves regularly from the Compiègne railroad station—but I am not recommending you take it unless you are accompanied by a small, bored child, who will probably love the fairy-tale castle.

THE SECOND REASON I like Compiègne so much more than the Sun King did is the Musée de la Figurine Historique, an unusual museum that I thought was almost worth the trip all by itself. Louis XIV could not have seen this because it did not exist until 1948, and even if he *had* seen it, he would not have liked it, because most of the 30,000 little hand-painted figurines that fill the museum are participating in historical events that took place during Napoleon's reign and not his. The Sun King liked everything to revolve around himself.

There are dioramas from many scattered historical periods. For example, there is one in which the little figurines are reenacting Joan of Arc's capture at Compiègne. However, the museum is primarily about the glory of Napoleon and his victorious battles.

The tiny figurines reenact Napoleon reviewing his troops, and engaging in his most famous battles, and they make this museum a treasure for those who, like Bob, are fascinated by Napoleon. The scenes are peopled with little soldiers meticulously and authentically dressed in their nineteenth-century uniforms, arranged in historically accurate positions as they fight at Marengo, Austerlitz, and Borodino, and lose at Waterloo, and solemnly march in the funeral cortege of December 15, 1840, when Napoleon's remains were returned from St. Helena.

That return was one of the dramatic events in the history of France. King Louis-Philippe (1830–1848), courting the Bonapartists, sent his son and Napoleon's few living marshals and ministers to St. Helena to escort the great emperor's remains back to Paris. When the men opened the coffin, they began to weep when they saw the emperor they knew and loved remarkably preserved, even though nineteen years had passed since he had died. (His coffin had been lined with tinplate, mahogany, two layers of lead, and finally with ebony.) After resealing the old coffin, they placed it inside a new red porphyry sarcophagus.

After reaching France, the massive coffin was placed on top of an elegant barge that had Napoleon's legendary golden eagle as its prow, the sides adorned with garlands of flowers, banners, tripods burning incense, and a platform that had been made to appear like an ancient temple. Snow was falling as the barge then made its way up the Seine, where, despite the cold, enormous crowds lined the banks of the river to pay their last respects to the great hero of their nation. Standing among the mass of people were veterans of Napoleon's faithful Old Guard dressed in their old uniforms, now threadbare and embellished only by the medals they had won. Four miles north of Paris, the barge docked, and the sarcophagus was transferred to a funeral coach drawn by twelve white horses. The diorama at Compiègne captures the pageantry of the moment after the procession of soldiers, sailors, and dignitaries accompanying Napoleon's coffin has passed through the Arc de Triomphe, on its way down the Champs-Élysées to its final resting place in the Hôtel des Invalides.* Tricolor flags extend from the rear of a gold-leafed coach, topped by the sarcophagus resting on a magnificent green granite platform, draped with purple velvet and emblazoned with golden Ns. On horseback at the four corners of the coach ride the last of the great marshals who won so many victories under Napoleon: Las Cases, Bertrand, Gourgaud, and Marchand. It was thrilling for me to see this funeral cortege with Bob, who knows the story of Napoleon so well, and, as we stood before the diorama, was able to repeat for me the words old men in the crowd cried out as the emperor's coffin passed: "Vive la Grand Armée," just as, when we visited Fontainebleau, he was

---

* Anyone interested in Napoleon should visit his tomb at the Hôtel des Invalides in Paris.

able to recite Napoleon's farewell speech to his troops. It was the next-best thing to having been there.

The diorama I found most fascinating was not spectacular but rather a simple campfire scene. Napoleon, wrapped in his cloak, warms himself by the fire. Napoleon "could not endure the smallest degree of cold; had fires lighted in July, and wondered why others did not suffer like himself from the first breaths of a north wind." Standing guard, bare-chested, is Roustam, Napoleon's Marmeluke, who, after being captured in Egypt, became the emperor's loyal orderly.

Bob, on the other hand, was drawn to the diorama depicting the Battle of Waterloo, which occupies the center of this tiny museum. It is huge. All the allied and French forces are in their actual positions. Wellington's headquarters are to the northwest in the direction of Brussels, Blücher and his Prussian troops to the northeast, and Napoleon and his forces are positioned to cut a swath between them. There are many explanations—including heavy rain and Napoleon's state of health—why such a master strategist did not take advantage of this position and was ultimately surrounded and lost the battle. (For those possessing a fanatical interest in the Battle of Waterloo, I suggest a book entitled *Waterloo* edited by Lord Chalfont, which presents an hour-by-hour account of the battle from the French, English, and German perspectives. For those who like computer games, there is even a PBS interactive battle simulator in which you can pretend to be either Napoleon or Wellington, depending on your preference.) After seeing this diorama, I decided to visit the Waterloo battlefield myself, although it had not crossed my mind before.

My interest in this museum may have been piqued by a little shop on the Quai de la Tournelle near the apartment that we rented for many years. We often stopped as we were walking past to look at the legion of wonderful figurines in the window. During the first years of our stay, we would enter the shop and watch the elderly father, and then, years later, his daughter, painstakingly paint each one with loving care, making sure all the details of the uniforms or gowns were absolutely correct. Although I don't like collecting anything but memories and books, I wouldn't mind having a shelf of these figurines in my living room with Napoleon saying farewell to his Old Guard at Fontainebleau.

Compiègne's late-Gothic-style Hôtel de Ville, in which the museum is located, considered to be the most beautiful town hall in France,* had already been built when Louis XIV came there. He would have seen the clock tower, with the English, Burgundian, and German soldiers, each holding a mallet, dressed in fifteenth-century uniforms worn at the time of Louis XII and Francis I. When Viollet-le-Duc restored the town hall in the nineteenth century, he replaced these soldiers with "picantins"— fifteenth-century Swiss soldiers. Although there are terrific restaurants in town, I wasted some of my appetite on an ice-cream cone in the square while I watched the three Swiss soldiers swing their mallets and ring the bells, which they do every fifteen minutes. It probably bothered Louis XIV that it was not his statue but one of Louis XII—similar to the statue at Blois—in the cental niche. The king is flanked by Joan of Arc and Charles Vll.

In the middle of the square stands a large statue of Joan of Arc. I have read that there is an equestrian statue of the Maid of Orléans marking the spot in Compiègne where she was captured in 1430, but I couldn't find it.

THERE ARE TWO exceptional restaurants in Compiègne: La Part des Anges and Rive Gauche; and two terrific bistros: Le Bistrot des Arts and Le Palais Gourmand, with its beautiful Art Nouveau decorations. It is fitting that there are so many lovely places to eat while visiting Napoleon and his nephew at Compiègne, since it was during the time of Napoleon I that eating in restaurants became fashionable in France. This happened because so many aristocrats had lost either their heads or their fortunes during the Revolution. Consequently, talented chefs lost their employers and began opening restaurants and writing cookbooks to support themselves after Napoleon restored stability to France. Although Napoleon didn't want to waste more than twenty

---

* Personally, I think the city hall in Nancy is more beautiful.

minutes on dinner, one of the most popular books during the Empire—
an eight-volume guide to the proper etiquette of eating entitled
Almanach des Gourmands—recommended five hours as the proper
length of time for that meal. When I learned this, I felt the author may
have been responsible for the insufferable length of meals at some of the
finer restaurants in France today. One of the longest meals I have ever
experienced, which may have been close to five hours, was at Le Grenier
à Sel in Nancy, because we ordered the tasting menu. It began with foie
gras in a paper-thin chocolate crust. I never would have ordered this
dish—which I ate and, to my surprise, loved—but we had read that the
creations by the restaurant's young chef were alone worth the train ride
to Nancy, so we made the mistake of ordering the tasting menu. While
each dish was a marvelous taste treat, the time between courses was
so excruciatingly long—I think everything must have been cooked to
order—that by the third hour of our meal Bob and I had nothing left
to say to each other and just wanted to leave, although we were aware
that there were quite a few courses to come (as was our waiter, who
was determined to serve them all and serve them at the same unhurried
pace). I noticed that the French couple sitting at the next table, who
had begun their tasting menu chatting happily away at the same time
we had, were, as the hours passed, also sitting at their table in somber
silence. While I highly recommend Le Grenier à Sel, I advise against
ordering the tasting menu if you are a couple traveling alone, together,
for over a month.

Not only was the length of time to be spent over a meal a topic of discussion during the early years of the Empire; some of the more heated
discussions—no longer were the intelligentsia arguing over the separation of Church and State, the rights of man, or political equality under
the law—were over the proper hour to have one's main meal.* Between
the beginning of the Consulate (1799) to the end of the Empire (1815),
the hour was set progressively later in the day. During the old regime,
it had been customary to sit down to lunch at about two in the after-

---

* It is interesting to note that as the Roman Republic evolved into the Roman Empire, food became
increasingly lavish and important.

noon, the time when I start to get really hungry. At the beginning of the Empire, those who valued good manners dined at four o'clock. By 1807, publisher Louis Prudhomme would write: "The earliest one should dine is six o'clock, if one wants to be different from the bourgeoisie." I guess I am very bourgeois since I think there is nothing more glorious than a long lunch about one, while Bob must be quite aristocratic since he seems to most enjoy eating a second supper at eleven or twelve at night. My appetite, being quite egalitarian, allows me to enjoy eating at any time, since I would never let him eat alone.

MOST PEOPLE WHO come to Compiègne are unaware that there is a castle and a figurine museum there, or that there are truly fine restaurants. They come only to visit the Armistice Clearing, where, on November 11, 1918, the armistice ending the First World War was signed in a wagon-lit (railroad car). While I am less interested in the vicissitudes of war, even I can understand why Bob finds the Armistice Clearing museum so dramatic. So, on one of our trips, when we arrived at Compiègne, I asked a taxi driver waiting outside the station how much he would charge to take us to the Armistice Clearing and wait. I actually pointed to the words Armistice Clearing in my guidebook since *Clairière de l'Armistice* is not within my realm of pronunciation: no matter how hard I try, my tongue will not make the effort to produce *Clairière* with anything approaching the French pronunciation of that word. He said 100 francs. It actually turned out to cost 130 francs, or about $28, because Bob found the museum so fascinating I couldn't get him to leave.

A duplicate of the dining car or wagon-lit in which the 1918 Armistice was signed stands in the clearing, and there is also a little museum. Railway tracks lead up to it. Although the town of Senlis was at first discussed as a possible site for the signing ceremony, it was dismissed because of the townspeople's violent hostility to the Germans, who had shot the mayor and innocent hostages during the war. It was decided that a secret site had to be chosen. It was kept so secret that even the Germans didn't know where they were going. They arrived well after dark in a small town in France, where a single railroad car that had once been used by Napoleon III was waiting, draped in green satin with the emperor's monogram and a crown. As they boarded the train, "The station was lit by torches. On the platform a smart company of riflemen presented arms in a fairyland setting. . . . Their train left for an unknown destination. The night was pitch black, and the carriage windows had been screened."

"On November 8, at 7 A.M., the train stopped. The occupants wondered where. Through the windows which had now been uncovered," they saw, in the words of their commandant, "nothing but a marshy coppice, grey weather, a sky covered with low lying rain-clouds."

"A few yards away stood another train wrapped in mist. A gendarme disclosed the secret: they were in the forest of Compiègne."

The ground in the forest glade was so marshy that Marshal Foch's train and "that of the Germans had to be connected by a duckboard which was used to go from one car to the other." The tracks that brought the two cars to the forest had been intended for a spur of the railway to carry heavy artillery that was no longer needed.

One of the first orders Hitler gave after defeating the French in 1940 was to have the railroad car in which the armistice was signed brought to Germany. There is a famous film clip that supposedly shows Hitler doing a jig when the car arrived in Germany. I learned on my first visit to this museum that Hitler had stamped his foot only once; a French photographer doctored the film, replaying the stomp, forward and backward, several times, so that it appeared that Hitler was doing a jig.

Although the actual wagon-lit was destroyed by Allied bombing, the car in the glade was manufactured at the same time, and is an exact duplicate of it. Also, everything that had once been in the original car when the Armistice was signed had been safely stored by the French and is now in the dining car at the glade so you can see the exact setting of this great event in French history.

The museum contains slides and pictures from the First World War that are truly extraordinary. We stood in front of little viewers—similar to those I had peered into as a child in penny arcades on the boardwalk at Asbury Park, New Jersey—where you turn a handle to see fabulous still pictures taken during the First World War that appear to move, of soldiers in foxholes, of horse-drawn wagons. I believe Bob could have spent the entire day looking at those pictures.

But for me the most moving moment of our visit was first seeing a memorial to freedom erected by the French between the two world wars—a sculpture of a slain bird—as we drove into the Armistice Clearing, and then seeing a photograph in the museum of that memorial covered with a huge swastika flag after the Germans conquered France. To understand the horrors of war, the Armistice Clearing in the Forest Glade of Compiègne is a must, as are the nearby Normandy Beaches and cemeteries.

CHAPTER 24

The RESTORATION (1815–1848)
at CHANTILLY

—

Train from Gare du Nord to Chantilly

C HANTILLY IS, I BELIEVE, ONE OF THE THREE MOST BEAUTIFUL châteaux in France, the other two being sixteenth-century Chenonceau and seventeenth-century Vaux-le-Vicomte. Of these three fairy-tale castles, Chantilly is the easiest to reach from Paris but the hardest for an American to understand.*

The trip to Chantilly is so easy. You can take either a main-line train or the D Line of the RER. The main-line train leaves from the Gare du Nord, the same station from which you took the train to Compiègne. Reservations are not necessary. If you go by RER, take the D train in the direction of Creil or Orry-La-Ville. You can leave from either the Gare du Nord or the Chatelet–Les Halles RER station. The escalator trip down, down, down to the RER platform at the Gare du Nord seems almost as long as the thirty-minute trip to Chantilly. Both the RER and the main-line train arrive at the same station, where taxis have always been waiting to take me to the château. On most of my trips, however,

---

* Chenonceau is the most difficult of the three to reach by train, requiring a TVG to Tours, then a shuttle to the main station in Tours, where you can either join a tour group that regularly leaves from the station, rent a car, or transfer to a local train. King Henry II gave this château to his mistress Diane de Poitiers, who oversaw its creation as I described in *The Road from the Past: Traveling Through History in France.* If you want to join a tour group leaving from the station in Tours, you should make arrangements ahead of time with the tourist office there.

I preferred walking along a tree-shaded path near a road bordering a forest where the powerful noblemen who once owned Chantilly hunted with their guests. The walk took me a little less than a half hour when I wore heels, and considerably less time when I wore sneakers. Once, after touring the castle and its grounds, I decided I wanted to return to the station by taxi, and I simply walked to the gatehouse at the bottom of the hill on which the château is located and asked the guard to call me a cab. One can also ask for a cab to come at a specified time.

One trip to Chantilly—for centuries the ancestral home of the princes of Condé, the title given to the descendants of the Bourbon royal line*— was so grand it made me feel a bit aristocratic. The owner of an American TV cable network whom Bob had met at a New York cocktail party had rented Chantilly for a gala she was throwing for potential advertisers and invited Bob and me to attend. We were picked up in a long black limousine, and forty minutes and fifty-two kilometers later, we were at Chantilly. Our arrival was heralded by the sound of hunting horns while liveried footmen dressed in gold-trimmed red cutaway jackets helped us from our car and escorted us into the château, making me feel as though I were being ushered into one of the duke's lavish dinner parties during the Restoration, a time when, according to Balzac, "the splendors and pleasures of the table . . . were brought to high perfection." After most of the guests had arrived, a public relations person connected with Chantilly asked if anyone in the group would like a tour of the museum's art collection, which is, after the Louvre, considered the finest in France. It contains some of the finest work of the world's greatest artists. For example, it has three Raphaels, including *The Three Graces*, which may be the most beautiful Italian Renaissance painting I have ever seen. The library at Chantilly possesses not only 13,000 volumes, but *the* most priceless volumes. The collection includes the first French translations of Latin authors, 200 illuminated medieval manuscripts, 700 books from before 1501, and 2,500 from the sixteenth century. Our guide turned the pages—we were not allowed to touch them—of the

---

* The Prince of Condé, also Duke of Bourbon, was the first prince of the blood, or heir presumptive, until the Duke of Orléans and his line became the first prince of the blood or heir presumptive.

fifteenth-century illuminated manuscript *Très Riches Heures du Duc de Berry*, illustrating that duke's day-by-day aristocratic life in minute-by-minute detail. The Clouet Gallery has the world's largest collection of drawings—400 portraits of the kings and courtiers—by the official royal portrait painters (Clouet and his son) during the sixteenth century.

I felt like I was visiting old friends as I walked through the room looking at sketches, drawings, and portraits of kings, queens, courtiers, and mistresses whose castles I had visited and whose memoirs I had read on my travels through the history of France. While I saw 90 portraits (including those of Anne de Montmorency, the Duke of Guise, Francis I and his queen, Claude of France) that are on display in the gallery, I didn't learn the full extent of the collection until I received a letter from the American Friends of Chantilly asking for a contribution for the restoration of the remaining 310.

When the guests were asked if anyone wanted a tour of the castle, we quickly said "yes," and just as quickly our host and the other guests, who preferred attending a cocktail party, said "no." Luckily, giving a tour to only two people didn't deter the museum's PR person, and we were given a tour that both of us will long remember. Although Chantilly had never been particularly crowded when I had visited it, I confess I loved being alone with Bob in these treasure-filled rooms as our guide turned pages of medieval manuscripts usually imprisoned in glass cases—as they should be—and brought out originals where only copies had been on display.

Nothing in this collection is ever allowed to leave the château and travel to other museums, nor are the paintings even allowed to leave the positions on the wall where the last owner of Chantilly, Henry of Orléans, the Duke of Aumale, hung them, so that they are now arranged just as they had been by him, rather than by period or style. Trying to look on the bright side of the restrictions that were part of the deed of gift, the brochure writers point out that this arrangement allows the modern tourist to see how collectors hung their art in the nineteenth century; however, I found it somewhat discombobulating, since it transfers emphasis from the paintings to the collector (which was probably the intention of Aumale when he drafted the deed of gift creating the Condé

Museum; he is responsible not only for restoring the castle at Chantilly but also for restoring *to* the castle paintings and other works of art that had belonged to the princes of Condé for centuries but had been removed during the looting that took place during the French Revolution. Art collecting was made easy for this duke when he inherited Chantilly during the Restoration. His father, Louis-Philippe, was King of France (a descendant of the Orléans royal line), and Aumale was able to have paintings, manuscripts, and works of art returned to him, even items that had been placed in the Louvre, thereby demonstrating the advantages for an art collector who is also the son of the ruling monarch.

I have made many trips to Chantilly, more than to most places, not only because this fairy-tale château, surrounded by reflecting lakes of still water, is so very beautiful: Aumale described it as being "like a swan asleep on the water"—but also because, at first, being very American, I found it quite impossible to understand. On one of my visits, I walked away from the château toward the park below, turning now and then to look at it, and each time I turned, the castle seemed more beautiful. As I sat by the reflecting pond that had been transformed from a moat, the castle seemed to float. I sat there for some time and reflected on all of my previous tours of this château and realized why I hadn't understood exactly what I was visiting. I had wanted Chantilly to accommodate me by being frozen in time and evoking a specific period of French history: either the early Renaissance of the sixteenth century or the Restoration of the nineteenth, which followed Napoleon's exile to Elba. Chantilly refused. It was simultaneously medieval and classical and evoked a continuum of time rather than a precise period. Moreover, it did not reflect the economic conditions—the Industrial Revolution—taking place in France during the time it was being restored.

Although, during the course of our journey through the history of France, we have visited a number of castles, they have been, with one exception, the castles of kings: thirteenth-century Angers; fourteenth-century Vincennes; late-fifteenth- and early-sixteenth-century Blois, sixteenth-century Fontainebleau; seventeenth-century Versailles, and late-eighteenth- and early-nineteenth-century Compiègne. The one exception was seventeenth-century Vaux-le-Vicomte, which was built not by a king, but by a king's finance minister. Each of these castles had one thing in common: their architecture and stories evoked the socio-economic characteristics of the period in which they were built, a specific period. Chantilly, however, is two connected châteaux, one having been built in the sixteenth century and the other in the nineteenth century, and both refuse to evoke a specific point in time. It is, as Aumale desired it to be, a castle that evokes the entire history of his ancient aristocratic family through many centuries. This is a family who received the land on which the castle was built in the distant past, in exchange for military service to the king, at a time when armies were not paid in cash but in land. The creation of an aristocracy—the *noblesse d'épée*, or nobility of the sword—was the result of this feudal arrangement. The land they were given, and the castles on it, were inherited, century after century—passed on intact from eldest son to eldest son and never a daughter—according to the laws of primogeniture.

Consequently, Chantilly evokes a fluctuating relationship, taking place over many centuries, between one of the oldest and most powerful noble families of France and the monarchy, a relationship in which Louis XIV temporarily brought the aristocracy to its knees at Versailles in the seventeenth century, and to which the aristocracy, personified by the House of Orléans, responded by bringing the monarchy to its knees at the guillotine in the eighteenth century.

I realized as I was sitting by the lake that my problem in understanding the château was that at the time the Duke of Aumale was restoring and rebuilding Chantilly so that it would "reflect the personality of the duke and his ancestors," my grandparents were sailing steerage-class to America to start a new life, deliberately leaving their past and even their names behind in Europe, and that I, as their descendant, did not understand the significance or value that lineage, bloodlines, family trees, and ancestors possessed for Aumale, who inherited the title and lands associated with Chantilly. I did wonder, however, whether if I, like Aumale, had been descended from the Kings of France through both my father and my mother, I would still think of my blood only in terms of good and bad cholesterol.

On the other hand, if I, like Aumale, traced my descent from the

House of Orléans, and the Bourbon princes of Condé, I am not quite sure how proud I would be of these ancestors. The history of this noble family includes one member who was beheaded for treason, another who had his lands temporarily confiscated for treason, and another, Philip Égalité, the duke's great-grandfather, who voted to have his cousin the king guillotined. I can understand why, in 1852, a law was passed, forbidding anyone from the House of Orléans to own property in France. I notice that while the last owner of this château was Henry of Orléans, and that while the *H* and *O*, his monogram, is carved in stone along with the Condé coat of arms at Chantilly, there does not seem to be much emphasis in the brochures of Chantilly on the fact that he was the direct descendant of Philip Égalité, and there is no mention of the 1852 law at all. While the title Duke of Aumale dates back to William the Conqueror, the duke, along with his entire family, who bore that title, lost his head during the French Revolution, and King Louis-Philippe bestowed the title on his own son. The last owner of Chantilly is referred to more frequently as the Duke of Aumale than as Henry of Orléans. Nor do the brochures emphasize the fact that Chantilly was given to the state as a donation only after the duke was threatened with confiscation.

THE CHÂTEAU OF CHANTILLY that I was visiting came into existence when, after the Battle of Waterloo, the aristocracy sailed back to France as Napoleon was sailing for Elba. Upon their return, King Louis XVIII restored their confiscated lands and castles and what remained of their possessions. Aumale inherited Chantilly from his uncle, the last Prince of Condé, whose son and heir, the Duke of Enghien, had been executed by Napoleon. Aumale's father, Louis-Philippe, a descendant of Louis XIV's brother, and grandson of Philip Égalité, would be King of France from 1830 until 1848, at which time he was forced to flee to England.

The first time I visited Chantilly, I had just finished reading a biography of the mighty sixteenth-century warrior Anne de Montmorency, Francis I's boyhood friend and comrade-in-arms in so many battles.

I had read that Montmorency had rebuilt a Renaissance castle there about the same time that Diane de Poitiers had rebuilt Chenonceau in the Loire Valley. I had hoped, as I mapped out my train tour through history, that Chantilly would provide a stop at a typical sixteenth-century château owned by an aristocrat—that it would evoke the home of a mighty nobleman of the sword who had inherited land granted to his ancestor by a king in the twelfth century in exchange for military service. I was unaware that Chantilly was almost totally reconstructed after the French Revolution.

The Petit Château of Chantilly of today rests on foundations that were laid by ancestors perhaps in the eleventh and certainly by the four-teenth century. In the sixteenth century, Anne de Montmorency tore down and replaced his father's medieval fortress with an early Renais-sance château but kept the foundations of his father's château. And although the feudal towers—the symbols of feudal independence—had been removed, Montmorency instructed his architect to incorporate whimsical ones into the design of his sixteenth-century château, just as Diane de Poitiers had done at Chenonceau.

As soon as you arrive at the courtyard in front of the château, you are greeted by a statue of Montmorency, seated on his huge medieval warhorse. He was a mighty defender of the faith and the monarchy, not only under Francis I but also under Francis's son Henry II. Under Henry, Montmorency, not the king, controlled the government and was responsible for merciless measures against the Protestants, or heretics. For a while, he continued as counselor to Catherine de Médicis and her sons. The more you learn about the details of his life, the easier it is to understand why members of the aristocracy and princes of the blood were guillotined. He was the cruelest, most heartless brute I have ever read about, and one of the hardest to kill. He is said to be the model for Monsieur le Marquis in Dickens's *Tale of Two Cities*, the aristocrat whose coach kills a child of a lower class and is concerned only with his own inconvenience and delay.

Montmorency was notorious for his cruelty against his prisoners. Compared to an "enraged wild bull," he ordered his men after one battle to "go hang that man there, run this one through with a pike or shoot him, at once . . . or cut those scoundrels in pieces. . . . Burn that village, set fire to everything for a quarter of a mile." On October 18, 1538, he entered the town of Guyenne with 9,000 men, arrested, hung, decapitated, and burned the rebels, or sent them to the galleys. His cruelty was long remembered in Guyenne. "Twenty-five years later, at the age of seventy-five, still an indomitable warrior, while engaged in hand-to-hand combat with a Protestant heretic, his head was smashed, his face slashed by his opponent's sword five times, his spine broken by an arquebus (a heavy forerunner of the musket), and yet he fought on (and, before dying, broke his opponent's jaw)."

He was one of several sons of France's mighty barons whom Louis XII had brought to Blois to be educated with Francis I (then the dauphin). When Francis became king at twenty-one, he and Montmorency set off to conquer Italy, and the two young men fought side by side at Marignano and celebrated together the young king's conquest of Milan, a victory that made Francis falsely believe he would soon conquer the world. While Montmorency had considerable political power during the reigns of both Francis I, who made him constable of France, and Henry II, he lost a power struggle with the Guises during the short reign of Francis II in the mid-sixteenth century and was driven from court.

Chantilly was the favorite of Montmorency's 130 castles, and once out of power, he was able to divert his almost unimaginable energy from torture and government to the construction of the first beautiful Renaissance château there. Tearing down his father's medieval fortress, Montmorency hired the architect Jean Bullant and instructed him to create a château at Chantilly on a tiny island south of the main castle that would incorporate the Renaissance architecture he had seen on his campaigns in Italy. He also amassed an impressive library, which was in part returned when the Duke of Aumale inherited Chantilly. The Petit Château is all that remains from the sixteenth century.

Although not readily apparent, Chantilly today is two châteaux: the Petit Château, which dates from the time of Anne de Montmorency, and the Grand Château, which Aumale restored and rebuilt on the triangular base of the ancient château destroyed during the Revolution.

Aumale, wanting to preserve a concrete connection of continuity with the past, made certain that fourteenth-century foundations were preserved when he reconstructed his château in the nineteenth century. Instructions were given that the modern château should "reflect the personality of the duke and his ancestors, and to make of Chantilly a monument to the glory of French culture."

Both Anne de Montmorency and the Duke of Aumale owned the château at Écouen as well as Chantilly. When turning his possessions over to the Institute of France, Aumale stipulated that he would have the right to live at Chantilly during his lifetime. Before concluding the arrangements, he removed everything he valued from Écouen and moved it to Chantilly. Montmorency's stained-glass "grisaille" windows, telling the love story of Psyche and Cupid—now in the Psyche Gallery at Chantilly—were once at Écouen and are a rare example of nonreligious stained glass of this period. The painting of ten of Montmorency's twelve children—five boys on one side of the chapel and five boys on the other—was also removed from Écouen. A fresco of Montmorency's pregnant wife accounts for their eleventh child. The inlaid wood, also from Écouen, is particularly beautiful, containing nine different types of wood. (Not knowing, when I visited Écouen, that Aumale had removed so much of the decorations there, I had thought the bare walls and sparsely furnished château reflected the personality of Montmorency—the cold-hearted man who had tortured so many people to death.)

The Mausoleum, created in 1648, at the end of the chapel's nave, holds Montmorency's heart and those of his descendants. This remarkable sculpture is by Jean Goujon, whom Diane de Poitiers discovered when he was a young boy and who later became the most famous sculptor of his time. It consists of a pelican, the symbol of eternity in the Renaissance, at the foot of a group of statues: Justice; Religion (who is holding a sacred heart in one hand and the Church in the other); Minerva, with an eagle of war; Cupid holding a heart in his hand; and Piety.

When I asked my guide how the hearts made it through the Revolution, knowing that relics of this type were destroyed by vehemently anti-Catholic revolutionaries, I was told that reliquaries had indeed been removed from the chapel and dumped in a ditch when the castle was sacked but that a local innkeeper had found the precious box that contained the hearts and hid it until the Restoration.

In the Clouet Gallery you will come across sixteenth-century paintings of the royal family under whom Montmorency served. There is a portrait of Francis I as a young man of twenty-one, when he and Montmorency set out to conquer the world, and another when he was old and sick, after his return from captivity in Spain, where both he and Montmorency had been held prisoners after their defeat at Pavia. There are portraits of Francis's brilliant sister Marguerite of Navarre, who entertained her brother with her writings and who, with Montmorency's assistance, arranged for Francis's release from prison in Spain; Claude of France, Francis's queen; Henry II, his son, whom Montmorency served and for whom he governed France; and Francis II, who married a member of the Guise family and drove Montmorency from court.

While there is an Orléans Gallery, displaying portraits of the Orléans family, it was during my guided tour of the Gallery of Battles that I first began to understand the nature of Chantilly and the fluctuating relationship between the owners of this castle and the monarchy. The paintings in this room depict the battles fought in the seventeenth century by the Prince of Condé, who was given the title "Grand Condé" (Great Condé) because of his victory at Rocroi, in which he saved Paris from the Spanish. While the paintings show a man who inherited the military prowess of his ancestor Montmorency, Dumas paints a different picture of him when he includes the Prince of Condé as a character in his novel *The Vicomte de Bragelonne*, emphasizing the cruelty that he also inherited from Montmorency. Dumas writes that he was a member of "a pitiless race without mercy even for genius." As you look around this room, you can decide for yourself whether Dumas was correct in his description of the Grande Condé as having "that clear and keen look which distinguishes birds of prey of the noble species . . . with rather an eagle's beak than a human nose. . . . Now, on account of his rank, everybody at the court respected M. Le Prince, and many, seeing only the man, carried their respect as far as terror."

The Grand Condé (1621–1686), who considered himself the king's equal, lived at the same time as Louis XIV (1638–1715), employed the same landscape designer, Le Nôtre, to design his gardens, and had France's greatest chef, Vatel, oversee his kitchen.* In a preview of the lavish entertainments the Sun King would hold later at Versailles, the Grand Condé hosted sumptuous banquets and great fireworks displays at Chantilly.

In the Gallery of Battles, there is a painting depicting his victory at Rocroi, where he fought on the side of the monarchy, and there is also a painting entitled *The Repentance* by Michel Corneille. While other paintings in the room depict famous victories of the Grand Condé when he fought on the side of Louis XIV, *The Repentance*, our guide explained, is comprehensible only if you know that not all the Grand Condé's victories were in support of the king, but that he instigated a rebellion by aristocrats against the throne—the Fronde, the rebellion that drove Anne of Austria fleeing in the middle of the night from the Palais-Royal with young Louis XIV and his brother. In this painting, the Grand Condé, dressed in Roman armor, is holding back Fame, while the Muse of History, Clio, is seated on Chronos, the personification of Time, tearing out pages from the book of history in which Clio had unwisely recorded Condé's shameful victories. It was not Condé who commissioned this painting, but his descendant who was anxious to be in the good graces of an aging Louis XIV.

One of the portraits in this château is of the unfortunate last Duke of Enghien, whom Napoleon executed in 1804, and who, rather than his cousin, Aumale, would have otherwise inherited Chantilly. I am sorry I saw this painting because I had a picture of the Duke of Enghien, created by memoirs written by people who either loved him or hated Napoleon, as a "young, handsome, and chivalrous" hero who died so gallantly in the moat at Vincennes that the soldiers who shot him refused to take his possessions even though they were entitled to them. Instead, this painting depicts an insipid child with long curly hair.

There is not only a castle at Chantilly, but an indoor tennis court

---

* Vatel had been Fouquet's chef but was hired by the Prince of Condé when Fouquet was imprisoned.

(Jeu de Paume). I find it amusing that it survived the Revolution because it was a perfect place for dancing, which was a popular pastime during the period in which about 40,000 aristocrats lost their heads. There is also a small park in which Louis-Henry, Prince of Condé in the eighteenth century, directed his landscape designer to create a gigantic board game on the lawn, so guests at his parties could amuse themselves by pretending to be board pieces. It is apparent that Louis-Henry was quite a character. He made between 20 million and 40 million livres during the financial bubble created by John Law during the reign of Louis XV. While others in France were asked to return their excess profits when the bubble burst, no one dared ask the powerful Prince of Condé to return his. He used the money to create one of the most popular attractions at Chantilly—the stables—called a masterpiece of eighteenth-century architecture. The stables were another frivolous fancy of Louis-Henry, who hired the architect Jean Aubert to construct a temple to the glory of the horse and hunting in which no expense was to be spared.

While visiting the palace, try to walk over to these ridiculously luxurious stables, or "Grandes Écuries," which now contain the Living Horse Museum and where, if you are lucky or plan ahead, you will be treated to a show of prancing Lipizzaner horses. It wasn't just that Louis-Henry was passionate about hunting; he also believed in reincarnation and expected to return as a horse and "wanted to assure his future comfort." The result was the creation of the world's only palace for horses where all the sculpted decorations celebrate the horse and the hunt.

My Favorite Emperor
and Me

—

W E HAVE ARRIVED AT THE END OF OUR JOURNEY THROUGH eight centuries of French history, which began in the twelfth century at the Royal Abbey of Saint-Denis on the outskirts of Paris. We have traveled century by century, beginning with places built earliest in time, traveling chronologically by train from Paris each day to places whose architecture and art evoked the age we were visiting. Since architecture has evolved over time, we could feel the flow of years as we traveled, instead of a blur of kings or a confusion of ages. Learning about the period in which the sites were built and about the lives of the people who built them, we could understand why fortresses, castles, cathedrals, or palaces were built the way they were and no other: why, for example, moats were built around medieval fortresses when times were insecure, and then transformed into reflecting pools during the Renaissance, when there was order in the realm.

During the years in which Bob and I were traveling through France's history, the French government substantially extended the places we could reach by TGV, making the map of France an even more sumptuous smorgasbord of places we could reach easily from Paris. For more than ten years we have been able to stay in Paris, never having to pack or unpack, while taking day trips by train to wonderful places throughout France.

Our journey through time ends in nineteenth-century Paris, a city much of whose previous two-thousand-year history was wiped away when the Baron von Haussmann, under the direction of Napoleon III, transformed it from a medieval tangle of muddy cobblestoned streets filled with sewage into a modern city of radiating boulevards, built wide enough to prevent the erection of barricades, a pastime that had become quite popular with revolutionary eighteenth- and nineteenth-century Parisians. In a period of extreme authoritarianism, Haussmann was able to condemn and replace dark, twisting medieval streets with straight boulevards. He was able to dictate that these new boulevards be lined with uniform six- and seven-story limestone buildings, with ceiling-high windows opening onto balconies supported by either caryatids or fluted pilasters, that the height of these buildings could not exceed 65.6 feet, that their roofs had to slope at 45 degrees, and that wrought-iron balconies had to be placed at the same height as those of the neighboring buildings.

The poor who had once lived in the medieval high-density slums were driven to the outskirts of Paris, which have not been subjected to urban renewal and where the poor remain today.

Louis Napoleon was elected president in 1848, and then, a few years later, in 1852, was overwhelmingly approved as emperor—Napoleon III. That the memory of his uncle Napoleon Bonaparte played a role in electing him president and giving him his consequent mandate as emperor (many of the more than 5 million people who voted for him in the presidential election appear to have thought they were voting for his uncle) is a fact accepted by both historians and by Louis. In the hope of attracting an eagle—his uncle's legendary symbol—he placed a slab of bacon on his head during one of his first election campaigns. Louis Napoleon was not the charismatic military hero his uncle was; in fact, he was somewhat ludicrous in that role, but nonetheless he is my hero and not his uncle, because he created the Paris I love and made this book possible. My bourgeois emperor dreamed of making Paris a city of marble as Augustus did for Rome, and he wanted to make Paris, as Rome had been, the center of the world—the center of Europe, really. And just as all roads had once led to Rome, all rail lines led to Paris by the time my emperor was removed from power. My sphinx was not "without a secret," as his countrymen said, implying he was stupid, but was as Queen Victoria noted, a quiet, gentle, simple man, shrewd and "so full of tact" that he was able to stay in power long enough—twenty-two years—to carry out most of his ambitious plans. He hired the Baron von Haussmann to clear the slums of Paris, and in doing so Haussmann transformed the medieval city into a modern nineteenth-century bourgeois city filled with parks and magnificent vistas. Although there were howls of protest as he condemned much of the city, contemporary medieval accounts don't make the old city sound particularly appealing. They describe the streets of Paris as being used not only for transportation but of also being used for sewage and garbage disposal. The subsequent plagues that resulted—in 1832, more than 20,000 Parisians died during a cholera epidemic—were said to have been caused by the polluted water supply that Napoleon III also replaced. In fact, the urban Middle Ages, according to contemporary accounts, doesn't sound very much like a place a modern tourist would want to visit.

Not only were the new wide boulevards lined with marvelous mansions, but they were laid out to link grand public structures, such as the Opéra Garnier with the Palais-Royal, and they also led to a circle of railroad stations that in essence replaced the medieval gates to the modern city and that would connect Paris with the rest of France and Europe. Twenty years after Napoleon III became emperor, all of France would be connected by rail.

Since one of these stations, the Gare d'Orsay, has been converted into a museum, you don't have to imagine, but can now experience, how travelers once dined while they waited for their train to the southwest, by having either lunch or a midafternoon tea at the second-floor frescoed dining room at the Musée d'Orsay. We have often enjoyed breaking up our tour of the museum by having coffee in this glorious space, eating a plate of French cheeses and crusty bread about three in the afternoon, relaxing in comfortable green wicker chairs placed around well-spaced tables, in a room where the walls are decorated with gilt moldings, and exceptional frescoes, and where huge mirrors reflect magnificent chandeliers, giving the illusion that the chandeliers are receding into infinity, the same effect achieved at the royal residences of Versailles and Rambouillet. This was the restaurant in which travelers ate while they waited for their trains to depart, or in which they dined after they arrived. All the Paris railroad stations had such luxurious restaurants. In fact, this restaurant is not even the most sumptuous remnant of the age—that honor goes to Le Train Bleu at the Gare de Lyon. To really feel as though you were back in the nineteenth century, you should have Sunday dinner there. Its opulent turn-of-the-century decorations are simply breathtaking.

It wasn't only the restaurants that were opulent, but the waiting rooms as well. Down the corridor from the restaurant at the Musée d'Orsay is the palatial marble-walled station waiting room, restored to the way it once had been for nineteenth-century travelers, complete with statues and paintings of a quality that would have once adorned palaces of the nobility. This part of the museum has been restored to what it had been when the Musée d'Orsay was the Gare d'Orsay.

The entire museum, now devoted to nineteenth-century art, was originally a hotel and station built as a palace for the middle-class traveler—not what we call the middle class in America, but the upper middle class, the nouveaus riches, the bourgeoisie. Their main desire was to live and be treated as the aristocracy once had been. They built their new mansions along the new boulevards that replaced the Paris slums.

One of these mansions is now the fabulous Jacquemart-André Museum on the Boulevard Haussmann. Once the nineteenth-century palatial home of a banking family who had acquired immense wealth, its owner, Edouard André, purchased land from the state, recently condemned and cleared by Haussmann, to make way for one of the modern boulevards of Paris. He and his wife, Nellie Jacquemart, filled the mansion with Flemish masters, eighteenth-century French masterpieces, and priceless works from the Italian Renaissance. They were so wealthy that on one occasion they outbid the Louvre for a Rembrandt they wanted. It was this class of people who benefited from the new Paris and the Second Empire.

On my last visit, I felt I could not experience nineteenth-century Paris unless I attended an opera or ballet at the place Louis Napoleon had ordered up for his nineteenth-century constituency—where for example, Edouard André and Nellie would have spent the evening—the centerpiece of the Second Empire: the Opéra Garnier. First, we tried to purchase tickets at the ticket agency where I usually buy tickets to events but were told that all the performances during our stay were sold out. Undeterred, I suggested that we go to the Opéra Garnier to see if we could get tickets there. At the box office, Bob asked for tickets to anything during the next few weeks. The woman at the ticket window said: "A few minutes ago I would have said no, but now, unfortunately for you, I can offer you the best of the best—and for this afternoon." The "unfortunately" was because the tickets were outrageously expensive, but Bob bought them nonetheless and the experience of seeing a lavish opera production in the best seats in this opulent theater was well worth it. Since there were a few hours before the performance, we had time to take a tour through the opera house, and were told its intriguing history, which I suggest you do whether or not you see an opera.

The Opéra Garnier is truly a palace of dreams, a colorful neo-Baroque gem sparkling in a gray Paris. That afternoon, as we walked up the wide staircase composed of thirty-three varieties of different-colored marbles, I tried to imagine it filled with women whose voluminous nineteenth-century ball gowns were so wide that they were compared to fully rigged ships. When we entered the theater, I looked at the ceiling designed by Marc Chagall, which was definitely not nineteenth-century neo-Baroque, but somehow worked. Seated in the center of the theater, I looked at the boxes on either side, which were arranged so that the audience could more easily see one another, and tried to imagine them filled with nineteenth-century occupants, the men in formal black and white, the women in gowns of silk threaded with gold metallic strands and crystal beads (or black velvet scrolled on ivory satin in patterns resembling the filigree ironwork designs of the railroad stations that so intrigued nineteenth-century artists like Monet). Our seats were fabulous and Mozart's music was sublime. Sitting there in this glorious palace built in a city filled with palaces, my mind drifted back to the soaring cathedrals, the moated fortresses, and opulent castles I had visited, and I could think of no better way to end my magical journey through time.

Acknowledgments

—

My first and foremost debt is to Robert Caro, my husband and traveling companion on my travels through France, first by car and then by train. When I told him my idea of driving through history in France—originally from the Roman ruins of Provence to the World War II invasion beaches in Normandy—he was skeptical but drove, no matter how far we had to go. Afterwards, he thought it was such a great way to travel that he urged me to write a book about those travels and helped me every step of the way. When we fell in love with Paris and didn't want to leave, I suggested that we take trains from Paris and travel chronologically through the history of France. He was skeptical about using the train to travel back in time but accompanied me on practically all my trips no matter how early the train was scheduled to leave. Without his advice, encouragement, and unwavering faith in me, these books would not have been possible. As his researcher on *The Power Broker*, *The Path to Power*, *Means of Ascent*, and *Master of the Senate*, I learned the importance of visiting places you write about. As my husband and traveling companion, he has turned every one of the trips we have taken together into a totally delightful experience.

I also would like to thank the late Bertram Taylor III, a true gentleman, who generously rented his apartment overlooking Notre-Dame and the Seine to Bob and me whenever we were able to spend two months in Paris. I shall miss him, as will everyone who knew him.

I would like to express my thanks to Robert Weil, my editor at Norton, who has been so supportive and taken such care in editing this book. Because of his unerring literary sense, I think he has improved every page of this book. It has been a pleasure to work with him. I would also like to thank Phil Marino, his most agreeable assistant; Fred Wiemer, my copy editor; André Moraillon and Madame Baudu of the French Tourist Office, reluctant though she was to tell me her first name, and my agent, Martha Kaplan.

SOURCE NOTES

—

CHAPTER 1. *Saint-Denis: The Monarchy and the Gothic Cathedral*

All statements from Suger himself in this chapter are from Abbot Suger of Saint-Denis, *Abbot Suger on the Abbey Church of St.-Denis and Its Art Treasures*, edited, annotated, and translated by Erwin Panofsky, 2nd ed. (Princeton: Princeton University Press, 1948).

All statements on iconography in this book are from Émile Mâle, *Religious Art from the Twelfth to the Eighteenth Century* (Princeton: Princeton University Press, 1982) and *The Gothic Image: Religious Art in France in the Thirteenth Century* (New York: Harper & Row, Torchbooks, 1958).

Statements about St. Bernard are from a lecture by Janetta Rebold Benton, *St. Denis: Gothic Is Born: Royal Abbey of Saint-Denis and the Energetic and Egocentric Abbot Suger* (New York: Metropolitan Museum of Art, n.d.).

Other sources for this chapter are Abbot Suger of Saint-Denis, *The Deeds of Louis the Fat*, trans. with an introduction and notes by Richard Cusimano and John Moorhead (Washington, D.C.: Catholic University of America Press, 1992).

The Chronicle of Saint-Denis dates the conversion of Clovis in the year 496.

Peter Abelard, *The Story of My Misfortunes*, trans. Henry Adams Bellows (New York: Macmillan, 1972).

Vincent Scully, *Architecture: The Natural and the Manmade* (New York: St. Martin's Press, 1991).

Anne Prah-Perochon, "Enormous Compasses." *France Today*, January-February, 1999.

CHAPTER 2. *Laon: Early Gothic*

All statements by Guilbert de Nogent himself are found in Guilbert de Nogent, *The Autobiography of Guilbert, Abbot of Nogent-sous-Coucy*. Medieval Sourcebook, Bk. III, Chap. VIII (n.d.).

Statements on medieval architecture are largely based on Whitney Stoddard, *Art and Architecture in Medieval France: Medieval Architecture, Sculpture, Manuscripts, the Art of the Church Treasuries* (New York: Harper & Row, 1972); Jean Gimpel, *The Cathedral Builders*, trans. Teresa Waugh (New York: Grove Press, 1983); and Andrew Martindale, *Gothic Art* (London: Thames & Hudson, 1967).

Other sources for this chapter are Michel Bur, *Histoire de Laon et du Laonnais* (Toulouse: Privat, 1987); John James, *The Traveler's Key to Medieval France: A*

Guide to the Sacred Architecture of Medieval France (New York: Knopf, 1986); and Martine Plouvier, *Laon: The Upper Town* (Amiens: Images du Patrimonie, 1994).

CHAPTER 3. *Chartres: The High Gothic Cathedral at Chartres*

"The king should not invest bishops": Elizabeth M. Hallam, *Capetian France: 987–1228* (London and New York: Longman, 1980).

"We are like dwarfs": Robert S. Hoyt, *Europe in the Middle Ages* (New York: Harcourt Brace, 1957).

"no great thought": Victor Hugo, *Notre Dame of Paris*, trans. John Sturrock (New York: Penguin, 1978).

Other sources for this chapter are Henry Adams, *Mont-Saint-Michel and Chartres* (New York: Penguin, 1986); Adolf Katzenellenbogen, *Sculptural Programs of Chartres Cathedral: Christ, Mary, Ecclesia* (New York: W. W. Norton, 1959); Andrew Martindale, *Gothic Art* (London: Thames & Hudson, 1967); Malcom B. Miller, *Chartres Cathedral: The Stained Glass and Sculptures* (London: Pitkin Pictorials, 1975); and *Chartres Cathedral* (Hong Kong: Pitkin Pictorials, 1989).

"If I have seen": Letter from Sir Isaac Newton to Robert Hooke, 1675.

CHAPTER 4. *The Coronation Ceremony at the Cathedral of Reims*

All statements made by Gregory of Tours in this chapter are from St. Gregory, Bishop of Tours, *History of the Franks by Gregory Bishop of Tours*, trans. Ernest Brehaut (New York: Columbia University Press, 1916).

The date of Clovis's conversion varies. Some sources put it as late as 506.

Other sources used in this chapter are Hans Jantzen, *High Gothic: The Classic Cathedrals of Chartres, Reims, and Amiens* (Princeton: Princeton University Press, 1957); Jean Diblik, *Reims: Comment Lire une Cathédrale* (Paris: Les Editions d'Art and d'Histoire ARHIS, 1998); Robert Branner, *Gothic Architecture* (London and New York: George Braziller, 1961); and Régine Pernoud, *Joan of Arc: By Herself and Her Witnesses* (Lanham, Md.: Scarborough House, 1994).

CHAPTER 5. *The Louvre: A Late-Twelfth-Century Fortress*

Sources for this chapter are Robert Chazan, *Medieval Jewry in Northern France: A Political and Social History* (Baltimore and London: Johns Hopkins University Press, 1973); Irving A. Agus, *The Heroic Age of Franco-German Jewry: The Jews of Germany and France of the Tenth and Eleventh Centuries* (New York: Yeshiva University Press. 1969); Robert S. Briffault, *The Troubadours*, ed. Lawrence F. Koons (Bloomington: Indiana University Press, 1965); and Mary McAuliffe, "Wall to Wall," *Paris Notes*, March 2001.

CHAPTER 6. *Angers: Blanche of Castile's Early-Thirteenth-Century Fortress*

and

CHAPTER 7. *Sainte-Chapelle in Paris*

"with all possible haste"; "Best speed"; "weal and woe"; and "courage": Régine Pernoud, *Blanche of Castile*, trans. Henry Noel (New York: Coward, McCann & Geoghegan, 1975).

All statements from Joinville himself in these chapters are from Jean, Sire de Joinville, *Life of Saint Louis by John of Joinville*, trans. René Haque (New York: Sheed & Ward, 1955).

"Queen Blanche ought not"; "Crowning at Reims"; "Intolerence for heretics": Marge Wade Labarge, *Saint Louis: The Life of Louis IX of France* (London Eyre & Spottiswoode, 1968).

"Soissons": Maurice Keen, *Chivalry* (New Haven: Yale University Press, 1984).

"It was so cold": *Grandes Chroniques de France*, Vol. VIII (n.d.).

Other sources used in these two chapters are from Jean Richard, *Saint Louis: Crusader King of France* (New York: Cambridge University Press, 1992); Gilles Mauger, *Saint Louis: Le Chant des Béatitudes* (Paris, Letouszey & Ané, 1960).

"it was from that hour": Elizabeth Boyle O'Reilly, *How France Built Her Cathedrals: A Study in the Twelfth and Thirteenth Centuries* (New York and London: Harper Brothers, 1921).

"Welfare of his people": *Congrès Archéologique de France*, Vol. II (1908).

Appraisal of the Apocalypse Tapestries is from Émile Mâle, *Religious Art from the Twelfth to the Eighteenth Century*; and André Lejard, Le Maistre de Sacy, *Les Tapisseries de l'Apocalypse de la Cathédrale d'Angers*. Livre ancien. (Folios in my possession.)

Another source for the Apocalyse Tapestries is René Planchenault, *Tapisseries d'Angers* (Paris: Caisse Nationale des Monuments Historiques et des Sites, n.d.).

CHAPTER 8. *Vincennes: A Fortress of the Hundred Years War*

Statements made by Froissart in this chapter are found in Jean Froissart, *Chroniques*, ed. George T. Diller (Geneva: Droz, 1991).

Other sources for this chapter are Jean Chapelot, *Le Château de Vincennes: Une Résidence Royale au Moyen Age* (Paris: CNRS Editions, 1994); and J. R. Gaborit, *L'Art au Temps des Rois Maudits: Philippe le Bel et ses Fils, 1285-1328* (Paris: Musée du Louvre, 1998).

CHAPTER 9. *Joan of Arc: 1429 and the End of the*
Hundred Years War at Orléans

Unless stated otherwise, all statements from Joan of Arc herself in this chapter and
the next are from Régine Pernoud, *Joan of Arc: By Herself and Her Witnesses*,
trans. Edward Hyams. (Lanham, Md.: Scarborough House Publishers, 1994).
Marina Warner, *Joan of Arc: The Image of Female Heroism* (New York: Knopf, 1981).
Description of the dauphin and battle scenes are from Victoria Sackville-West,
Saint Joan of Arc (Boston: G. K. Hall & Co., 1984).

CHAPTER 10. *Rouen: Joan of Arc and Monet*

"limbs torn off" and "wooden cross": Régine Pernoud, *Joan of Arc: By Herself and
Her Witnesses*.
"seeking 'instantaneity' ": Barbara Ehrlich White, *Impressionists Side by Side: Their
Friendships, Rivalries, and Artistic Exchanges* (New York: Knopf, 1996).
Monet letters cited are from Joachim Pissarro, *Monet's Cathedral: Rouen 1892–1894*
(New York: Knopf, 1990).

CHAPTER 11. *Tours: The Rebirth of Cities After the Hundred Years War*

"side by side": Anthony Blunt, *Art and Architecture in France: 1500–1700* (New
Haven: Yale University Press, 1999).
All statements from St. Martin himself in this chapter are from Sulpicius Severus,
On the Life of Saint Martin, trans. Alexander Roberts, *A Select Library of Nicene
and Post-Nicene Fathers of the Christian Church*, Vol. II (New York, 1894).
Statements made by Commynes in this chapter are from Phillipe Commynes, *The
Universal Spider: The Life of Louis XI of France*, trans. and ed. Paul Kendall
(London: Folio Society, 1973).
Other sources for this chapter are Henri Pirenne, *Medieval Cities: Their Origin and
the Revival of Trade*, trans. Frank D. Halsey (Garden City, N.Y.: Doubleday,
1925).
Pierre Matthieu, *History of Lewis the Eleventh: With the Most Memorable Accidents
Which Happened in Europe During the Two and Twenty Yeares of his Raigne*
[*sic*] (London: George Eld, 1614).

CHAPTER 12. *Blois: A Sixteenth-Century Renaissance Château*

Statements on Renaissance architecture are largely based on Anthony Blunt, *Art
and Architecture in France: 1500–1700*, Pelican History of Art Series (New York:
Penguin, 1988).
Other sources for this chapter are Frederic J. Baumgarten, *France in the Sixteenth
Century* (London: Macmillan Co., 1995); Irene Mahoney, *Madame Catherine*

(New York: Coward, McCann & Geoghegan, 1975); and Philippe Tourault, *Anne de Bretagne* (Paris: Perrin, 1976).

CHAPTER 13. *Francis I and the Renaissance at Fontainebleau*

Interpretations of frescoes and "counted for so little": Jean-Marie Pérouse de Monclos, *Fontainebleau*, trans. Judith Hayward (Paris: Éditions Scala, 1998).

"uncouth people": Benvenuto Cellini, *The Autobiography of Benvenuto Cellini*, trans. George Bull (New York: Penguin Classics, 1956).

"new Rome"; "in breeches"; and "He rises": Desmond Seward, *The First Bourbon: Henry IV, King of France and Navarre* (Boston: Gambit, 1971).

"Court art"; "whoring"; The men were": Desmond Seward, *Prince of the Renaissance: The Golden Life of François I* (New York: Macmillan, 1973).

"What a dinner": Grace Hart Seely, *Diane the Huntress: The Life and Times of Diane de Poitiers* (New York and London: D. Appleton-Century Co., 1936).

Henri Zerner, *The School of Fontainebleau: Etchings and Engravings* (New York: Abrams, 1969).

"More than one foreigner": Louis Constant, *Memoirs of Constant, First Valet de Chambre of the Emperor, on the Private Life of Napoleon, His Family, and his Court*, trans. Elizabeth Gilbert Martin, Vol. II, Chap. V (New York: Century Co., 1907).

All statements from Cellini himself in this book are from Benvenuto Cellini, *The Autobiography of Benvenuto Cellini*, trans. George Bull (New York: Penguin Classics, 1956).

Interpretations of frescoes are found in Jean-Marie Pérouse de Monclos, *Fontainebleau*, trans. Judith Hayward (Paris: Éditions Scala, 1998).

CHAPTER 14. *Henry IV in Paris: The Hôtel de Sens, the Place des Vosges, and the Luxembourg Gardens*

"smell his armpit": Desmond Seward, *The First Bourbon: Henry IV, King of France and Navarre* (Boston: Gambit, 1971).

Quotations regarding the Place de Vosges are found in Court Historian of Louis XIV, *Memoirs of Henri IV: King of France and Navarre* (Paris and Boston: Grolier Society, Connoisseur Edition, No. 15), p. 283.

"The King, seeing this" and "Silk": Hilary Ballon, *The Paris of Henri IV: Architecture and Urbanism* (New York and Cambridge: Architectural History Foundation; MIT Press, 1991). The research in this book was groundbreaking in uncovering Henry IV's plans of using the Place Royale to provide housing for Italian silk makers.

"Red-haired" and "silk factory": Mark Greengrass, *France in the Age of Henry IV: The Struggle for Stability*, 2nd ed. (London and New York: Longman, 1995).

"passionate about building": Jean-Marie Pérouse de Monclos. *Fontainebleau*.

Other sources for this chapter are Irene Mahoney, *Royal Cousin: The Life of Henri*

IV of France (Garden City, N.Y.: Doubleday, 1970); and Staff of the Luxembourg Palace, *Luxembourg Palace* (Paris: Beaux-Arts, 1999).

CHAPTER 15. *The Siege of La Rochelle and the End of the Reformation in France*

All quotations regarding the Siege of La Rochelle are from Émile Racaud, *Le Siège de La Rochelle: Journal Contemporain, 20 Juillet 1627–4 Juillet 1630* (A&T Éditions, 1999–2001). (Translations from this source are by Ina Caro.)

All quotations concerning Marie de Rohan and the Count of Chalais are from H. Noel Williams, *A Fair Conpsirator: Marie de Rohan, Duchesse de Chevreuse* (New York: Scribner, 1913).

Quotations about Richelieu are from Warren Hamilton Lewis, *The Splendid Century* (Garden City, N.Y.: Doubleday, 1957), p. 83; Anthony Levi, *Cardinal Richelieu and the Making of France* (New York: Carroll & Graf, 2000); and Jean-François-Paul de Gondi, Cardinal de Retz, *Memoirs of Cardinal de Retz: Containing All the Great Events During the Minority of Louis XIV and the Admininstration of Cardinal Mazarin*, Connoisseur Edition, No. 15 (Paris and Boston: Grolier Society, n.d.; first printed, 1705).

"The Siege of La Rochelle": Alexander Dumas, *Three Musketeers*. Part 1 (New York: Modern Library, 1999).

The Yad Vashem, an Israeli organization that has a list of "Righteous Gentiles"—non-Jews who saved Jews during the Second World War—does not record the name of Mayor Léonce Vieljeux. At my request they are trying to verify that he told the Germans there were no Jews living in La Rochelle, only Huguenots. Although I do not know if his acts of heroism, and there were many, involved saving Jewish lives, I have included this story because I want it to be true.

Other sources for this chapter are Harold Grimm, *The Reformation Era, 1500–1650* (New York: Macmillan, 1954); J. C. Bonnin, *La Rochelle et Ses Tours* (Rennes: Éditions Ouest-France, 1999); and Michael Prawdin, *Marie de Rohan, Duchesse de Chevreuse* (London: George Allen & Unwin, 1971).

CHAPTER 16. *Magical Vaux-le-Vicomte*

"Great things"; "Mazarin"; "Embezzlement"; "Tax farmer": Anatole France, *Clio and the Château de Vaux-le-Vicomte*, trans. Winifred Stephens (London: John Lane The Bodley Head Limited, 1928).

"By the infamous": Louis de Rouvry, Duc de Saint-Simon, *Memoirs of Louis XIV and the Regency*, Vol. II, trans. Bayle St. John (New York: J. Pott, 1901), p. 375.

All statements from Athénaïs de Montespan herself in this chapter are from Françoise-Athénaïs de Rochechouart de Mortemart, Marquise de Montespan, *Memoirs of Madame la Marquise de Montespan, Written by Herself*, Connoisseur Edition, No. 15, Vols. I and II (Paris and Boston: Grolier Society, n.d.).

All statements from Louis XIV in this chapter are from Louis de Rouvry, Duc de

Saint-Simon. *Historical Memoirs of the Duc de Saint-Simon*, Vol. I (1691–1709), Vol. II (1710–1715), trans. Lucy Norton with an introduction by D. W. Brogan (New York and London: McGraw-Hill, 1967, 1968); and *Secret Memoirs of Louis XIV*, Connoisseur Edition (Paris and Boston: Grolier Society, n.d.).

All statements from the Duchess of Orléans are from Elizabeth-Charlotte of Bavaria (Duchesse d'Orléans), *Secret Court Memoirs of Louis XIV and of the Regency* (Paris and Boston: Grolier Society, n.d.).

All statements by Madame de Sévigné are from Frances Mossiker, *Madame de Sévigné: A Life and Letters* (New York: Knopf, 1983).

All citations from Cronin are from Vincent Cronin, *Louis XIV* (Boston: Houghton Mifflin, 1965).

CHAPTER 17. *Versailles*

Sources for this chapter are Jacques Barzun, *From Dawn to Decadence* (New York: HarperCollins, 2000); Nancy Mitford, *Sun King* (New York: Harper & Row, 1966); Louis de Rouvry, Duc de Saint-Simon, *Memoirs of Louis XIV and the Regency*, Vol. II, trans. Bayle St. John (Akron, Ohio: M. W. Dunne, 1901); and William Howard Adams, *The French Garden, 1500–1800* (New York: Braziller, 1979).

"Moliére": Kenneth Woodbridge, *Princely Gardens: The Origins and Development of the French Formal Style* (New York: Rizzoli, 1986).

CHAPTER 18. *The Secret Castle of Maintenon*

All statements from Madame Sévigné herself in this chapter are from Marie de Rabutin-Chantal, Marquise de Sévigné, *Letters of Madame de Sévigné to Her Daughter and Friends* (London: Routledge, 1937).

"Vista": Marcus Binney, *Country Life: The Châteaux of France* (London: Mitchel Beazley, 1994).

"spend my final days": Nancy Mitford, *The Sun King* (London: Sphere Books Limited, 1966).

"Speak ill of": Elisabeth Charlotte, Duchess d'Orléans, *Court Memoirs of Louis XIV and the Regency*, limited edition of 250 copies, translation of 1807 Strasbourg ed. (Paris and Boston: Grolier Society, n.d.).

Elisabeth Charlotte, Duchess d'Orléans, *A Woman's Life in the Court of the Sun King: Letters of Liselotte von der Pfalz, 1652–1722*, trans. Elborg Forster (Baltimore and London: Johns Hopkins University Press, 1984).

"being loved by her"; "was content": Vincent Cronin, *Louis XIV* (Boston: Houghton Mifflin, 1965).

"Madame Scarron": *Memoirs of Madame la Marquise de Montespan, Written by Herself*, Vol. 11, Connoisseur Edition, No. 15 (Paris and Boston: Grolier Society, n.d.).

CHAPTER 19. *Parisian Sights: Palais-Royal, Hôtel Carnavalet,*
Hôtel de Soubise, École Militaire, the Panthéon,
Place de la Concorde

Description of Palais Royal: Johannes Willms, *Paris, Capital of Europe: From the Revolutions to the Belle Époque* (New York, London: Holmes & Meier, 1997).

"paragon of promiscuity": Will Durant and Ariel Durant, *The Story of Civilization, Part IX: The Age of Voltaire* (New York: Simon & Schuster, 1965).

All statements from Madame de Sévigné in this chapter are from Marie de Rabutin-Chantal, Marquise de Sévigné, *Letters of Madame de Sévigné to Her Daughter and Friends.*

Proust quote is from Steven Kale, *French Salons: High Society and Political Sociability from the Old Regime to the Revolution of 1848* (Baltimore, MD: Johns Hopkins University Press, 2004).

Statement by Marmontel is from Janet Aldis, *Madame Geoffrin: Her Salon and Her Times, 1750–1777* (New York: Putnam, 1905).

"Inventory"; "fit to command": Amelia Gere Mason, *The Women of the French Salons* (New York: Century Co., 1891).

Statement by Rousseau in this chapter is found in Leo Damrosch, *Jean-Jacques Rousseau: Restless Genius* (Boston: Houghton Mifflin, 2005).

"Twenty-four": David Mynders Smythe, *Madame de Pompadour: Mistress of France* (New York: Wilfred Funk, 1953).

"Ephemeral, floating": Pierre Goubert, *The Course of French History* (London and New York: Routledge, 1991).

All statements citing Saint-Simon, and "Odious habit"; "She had lived for her beauty"; "Everything has its season": Louis de Rouvry, duc de Saint-Simon, *Historical Memoirs of the Duke de Saint Simon*, Vols. I and II, ed. and trans. Lucy Norton.

"Lettre-de Cachet": *Secret Court Memoirs of Louis XV and XVI: Taken from the Memoirs of Madame du Hausset, Lady's Maid to Madame de Pompadour, and from the Journal of Princess Lamballe*, Connoisseur Edition, No. 16, Vols. I and II (Paris and Boston: Grolier Society, n.d.).

"Depending on him": Nestah Webster, *The French Revolution: A Study in Democracy* (London: Constable & Co., 1920).

"Vice is immaterial": Adèle d'Osmond, Comtesse de Boigne, *Memoirs of the Countess de Boigne, Vol. I (1781–1814), Vol. II (1815–1819)*, ed. Charles Nicoullaud (New York: Scribner, 1907).

"I've lost my army"; "Voltaire": Nancy Mitford, *Madame de Pompadour* (New York: Harper & Row, 1954).

"Ordered candles": *New York Times*, December 23, 2000.

"Soufflet's objective": Andrew Ayers, *The Architecture of Paris: An Architectural Guide* (London: Edition Axel Menges, 2004).

"Tradition of the Greeks": Marvin Carlson, *Voltaire and the Theatre of the Eighteenth Century* (Westport, Conn.: Greenwood Press, 1998).

"Immortalize the King": Evelyne Lever, *Madame de Pompadour: A Life* (New York: Farrar, Straus & Giroux, 2002), p. 144.

CHAPTER 20. *The Petit Trianon of Madame de Pompadour and Marie-Antoinette*

All statements by Talleyrand himself in this chapter are from Charles Maurice de Talleyrand-Périgord, Prince de Béné, *Memoirs of the Prince de Talleyrand*, trans. Raphael Ledos de Beaufort (New York: Putnam, 1891).

"Had no taste": *Memoirs of the Court of Marie Antoinette, Queen of France, with Sketches and Anecdotes of Her Private Life*, by Madame Campan, first Lady-in-Waiting to the Queen. Vols. I and II, Connoisseur Edition, No. 15 (Paris and Boston: Grolier Society, n.d.).

"A Queen": Desmond Seward, *Marie Antoinette* (New York: St. Martin's Press, 1981).

CHAPTER 21. *The Conciergerie*

"vast antechamber": Simon Schama, *Citizens: A Chronicle of the French Revolution* (New York: Knopf, 1989).

Other sources for this chapter are Michel Dillange, *The Conciergerie*, trans. Angela Moyon (Paris: Éditions Ouest-France, 1995); Georges Poisson, *Paris au Temps de la Révolution* (Florence: Casa Editrice Bonechi, 1987); and Antonia Fraser, *Marie Antoinette: The Journey* (New York: Doubleday, 2001).

CHAPTER 22. *Napoleon as Consul at Malmaison*

All statements from Napoleon's valet in this chapter are from Louis Constant, *Memoirs of Constant: First Valet de Chambre of the Emperor on the Private Life of Napoleon, His Family, and His Court*, Vols. I, II, and III, trans. Elizabeth Gilbert Martin (New York: Century Co., 1907).

"Now the etiquette of the old monarchy": Laure Junot, Duchess d'Abrantès, *At the the Court of Napoleon: Memoirs of the Duchess d'Abrantès*, introd. by Olivier Bernier (New York: Doubleday, 1989).

"Republican simplicity": Imbert de Saint-Amand, *The Wife of the First Consul*, trans. Thomas Sergeant Perry (New York: Scribner, 1890).

CHAPTER 23. *Napoleon at Compiègne*

All statements by Meneval himself in this chapter are from Baron Claude-François de Meneval, *Napoleon: An Intimate Account of the Years of Supremacy, 1800–1814* (New York: Random House, 1992).

Quotations regarding Armistice of Clearing are from Colonel Codevelle, Curator of the Carrefour de l'Armistice, *Armistice 1918: The Signing of the Armistice in the Forest Glade of Compiègne*, published by the Friends of the Armistice of Compiègne.

"Corsican style": Imbert de Saint-Amand, *The Happy Days of the Empress Marie Louise*, trans. Thomas Sergeant Perry (New York : Scribner, 1898).

Other sources for this chapter are Philip E. Jodidio, *Compiégne* (Paris: Connaissance des Arts, 1991); and J. Christopher Herold, *The Age of Napoleon* (Boston: Houghton Mifflin, 1963).

CHAPTER 24. *The Restoration (1815–1848) at Chantilly*

"enraged wild boar": Desmond Seward, *Prince of the Renaissance*, p. 197.

"Twenty-five years": Francis Decrue, *Anne de Montmorency: Grand Maître et Connétable de France à la Cour, aux Armées et au Conseil du Roi François Ier* (Geneva: Mégariotis Reprints, 1978); and Alexandre Dumas, *The Vicomte de Bragelonne* (Oxford: Oxford University Press, 1995).

Coda: My Favorite Emperor and Me

Napoleon I's wonderful plans for Paris were carried out by his nephew Napoleon III, because he would not borrow money to carry out his plans. He said, "When we have peace then we must busy ourselves in making Paris the most beautiful city in Europe": Maurice Guerini. *Napoleon and Paris: Thirty Years of History*, trans. Margery Weiner (New York: Walker & Co., 1967).

Gérard Fontaine, *Charles Garnier's Opéra: Architecture and Exterior Decor*, trans. Ellie Rea. Paris: Opera National de Paris, 2000.

M. F. Hoffbauer, *Paris à Traverse les Âges* (Paris: Bibliothèque de l'Image, n.d.).

INDEX

—

ABOUT THE AUTHOR

Ina Caro received her master's degree in history, with a concentration in medieval history, after studying at Columbia and Long Island Universities. Shifting her attention to the more recent past, Caro has worked as sole researcher on the award-winning biographies of Robert Moses and Lyndon Johnson by Robert A. Caro, to whom she is married. Never relinquishing her love for medieval France, she and her husband have traveled extensively throughout France by train and car, studying its history at the sites where it occurred. In the spring of 2011, Caro received an honorary doctorate from the Graduate Center at the City University of New York.